When Push Comes to Shove

Real Life on Dead Tour

The Journals of Hollie A. Rose

Copyright Holly A. Rose p/k/a Hollie A. Rose 1988, 1989, 1990, 1991, 1992,
Copyright Holly A. Rose p/k/a Hollie A. Rose 2024
All rights reserved. No part of this book may be reproduced or shared in any format or by any electronic or mechanical means, including information and retrieval systems, without express permission in writing from the publisher or author – which you might get – just freaking ask. Contact the author at HollieRoseBooks@gmail.com for information.
Reviewers may quote short passages.
ISBN 979-8-9916320-0-3 (Paperback edition)
ISBN 979-8-9916320-1-0 (Audiobook edition)
Library of Congress Control Number – 2024920245
Credits and permissions are listed on page 396 and are considered a continuation of this copyright page.
Date of first publication November 2024
Published by Furthur Books Inc. Middlefield, Connecticut
Cover by Furthur Books Inc.   (Bubble Photo, Deb "Sunshine" D'Amato, used by permission.)
Book design Furthur Books Inc.
Formatting by Furthur Books Inc.
Subjects and Themes;
Music, Rock'n'Roll, Subcultures, Grateful Dead, Memoir, Diary, Journal, Deadheads, the 1980s, Friends as Family, Hippies, LSD, Marijuana, THC, Hippie History, Grateful Dead Tour, Drugs, the War on Drugs, Cross-Country Road Trips, Peace, Love, Understanding, Forgiveness, Karma, Life, The Universe, Everything.
Please visit – FlamingoHippie.com

Disclaimer:
Most names, and some identifying information in this book have been changed to protect the guilty, the innocent, the stoned, and the stupid.
If you think you are in this book, I wouldn't point it out to anyone just yet in case you do something unappealing herein.

Dedication
This one's for Kurt

I met Kurt in the summer of 1983 in Berkeley. He had on a T-shirt that said, "Tibetan Puppy Moon Fungus." I loved him right away. Not the 'jump your bones' kind of love, but the kind where it was like we'd been waiting our whole lives to meet.

I was still pretty much a Connecticut based hippie chick (even though I went to 23 shows in my first calendar year!) which meant that after every tour and every New Year's run, I'd go home to Connecticut until the next tour. The freakin' Dead kept playing "Keep Your Day Job" and I treated that like some sort of divine message. <insert eyeroll here>

Kurt became a part of me. He lit up my life and became one of my favorite people on the planet. After every tour, Kurt would say, "Come with us. Don't go back to Connecticut. That's no fun."

I always shined him on. Treated the suggestion as if it was nothing but a joke. As if such a thing wasn't actually possible for the likes of me.

For some reason, giving him a ride to the airport at the end of Spring Tour 1986 (Hartford – a home show for me) sticks in my mind. He practically begged me to park my van in the long term parking and get on the plane with him and his crew. As usual, I laughed. "Thanks Beautiful, it's just not realistic." He tried harder than he'd ever tried before to entice me to leave Connecticut behind and really live free.

When he died, at Chief Hosa Campground during the 1987 Red Rocks Shows, I was thoroughly devastated.

And yet, I did Fall Tour like usual, and then I went home to Connecticut, like usual.

And I flew out for 1987-1988 New Year's, like usual. And I flew home to Connecticut after New Year's, like usual.

And it was zero degrees for a week (or at least that's how it is in my memory) and I hated EVERYTHING.

I was mad at the weather. I was mad at the world because I'd never get to party with Kurt again. I spent a week stomping around the house being a completely miserable bitch.

None of this was fair!

All the things I'd lost!

All of the time I would not get to spend with my beloved Kurt...

And here I was, stuck in Connecticut.

And then.

Almost like an actual lightbulb.

It occurred to me that while it was entirely too late for time spent with Kurt, it was absolutely not too late to grab ahold of time with the many other people I'd come to love through my years on Dead Tour.

Fuck this staying in Connecticut shit! Kurt was right! All this time he was right! I was not stuck here. I can go on tour!

By January 23, 1988 with Kurt's voice in my ear and his sparkly eyes in my heart, I was on a plane back to California, back to my people, back to where I belonged.

Kurt got what he wanted in that respect. He finally got me to go on tour full time.

I love you so much Kurt. I have literally never stopped thinking of you. You changed my life, and I wish I could hug you again.

If you're reading this dedication – know this – this book would never have existed without Kurt.

Contents

xiii	Prologue
	Nothing else shaking so you might just as well
xx	Foreword
xxiii	Flyer
1	Chapter 1 Summer 1988
	The Northwest
9	Chapter 2 Fall Tour 1988
	Landover and Philly
15	Chapter 3 Fall Tour 1988
	New York
19	Chapter 4 Fall 1988
	The Southern Semester
28	Chapter 5 Fall 1988
	JGB Halloween and Tahoe
34	Chapter 6 Fall 1988
	In and Around the Haight
43	Chapter 7 December 1988
	Long Beach through New Year's
53	Chapter 8 Winter 1989
	SF and A New President
60	Chapter 9 Winter 1989
	Super Bowl, the End-of-Fulton-St., Kaisers
70	Chapter 10 Winter 1989
	LA to Connecticut
78	Chapter 11 Winter 1989
	A Quick Trip to San Francisco
85	Chapter 12 March 1989
	Georgia and Alabama
91	Chapter 13 Spring Tour 1989
	Atlanta to Louisville
101	Chapter 14 Spring Tour 1989
	Chicago, Milwaukee, Minneapolis, and Colorado to SF
111	Chapter 15 Spring Tour 1989
	Irvine and Frost
119	Chapter 16 Spring 1989
	Life Between Shows

126	Chapter 17	Summer 1989
	Shoreline and Oregon	
135	Chapter 18	1989
	The Tail-end of Summer Tour	
142	Chapter 19	Summer 1989
	Cal Expo	
147	Chapter 20	Summer 1989
	Greeks, more Greeks, a House, and The Who	
154	Chapter 21	Summer 1989
	A Quick Trip to Connecticut	
160	Chapter 22	Fall 1989
	Shoutin' and Shakin'	
169	Chapter 23	Fall 1989
	House Party and Turkey Day	
177	Chapter 24	December 1989
	Shows and Holidaze	
186	Chapter 25	Winter 1990
	It's Like This...	
195	Chapter 26	Spring Tour 1990
	Landover, Hartford, Canada	
205	Chapter 27	Spring Tour 1990
	Good Cop, Bad Cop – Albany, Atlanta, and N'Awlins	
214	Chapter 28	April/May 1990
	JGB, LA Three Times, Garrett's B-day, and a Dead Car	
223	Chapter 29	June 1990
	Cal Expo and Shoreline	
230	Chapter 30	Summer 1990
	Eugene – DeadFeat	
236	Chapter 31	Summer Tour 1990
	Indy, Chicago, Losing Brent	
245	Chapter 32	Summer 1990
	Reggae on the River, Jerry, Mom & Ed, Movin' Out	
254	Chapter 33	Fall Tour 1990
	Ohio and Philly	
261	Chapter 34	Fall Tour 1990
	NYC	

271	Chapter 35	Europe Tour 1990
		Amsterdam, Stockholm, and Essen
280	Chapter 36	Europe Tour 1990
		Berlin, Frankfurt, Amsterdam Again
286	Chapter 37	Europe Tour 1990
		Hamburg, Paris, London
293	Chapter 38	Fall 1990
		No House, No Buds, No Nothin'
299	Chapter 39	Winter 1991
		House Magic and some Oakland Shows
308	Chapter 40	Spring 1991
		When Shit Hits Fans
314	Chapter 41	Spring Tour 1991
		Landover, Albany, Nassau
325	Chapter 42	Spring Tour 1991
		Atlanta, Orlando
333	Chapter 43	Spring/Summer 1991
		N'Awlins, Cal Expo, Cloverdale, and East Coast DeadFeat
342	Chapter 44	Summer/Fall 1991
		John You're Such an Asshole – Reggae – Avoiding Shows
351	Chapter 45	Fall 1991
		Fare You Well Bill Graham
356	Chapter 46	Winter 1991/1992
		Holidaze, Hitchhikers, Oakland Shows, and A Job (Shudder)
365	Chapter 47	Spring 1992
		Kaiser, Oakland, Albany, New Jersey, Also – Beau's Bad Blood
374	Chapter 48	Summer 1992
		You Shouldn't Say 'Fuck You' to Your Friends
377	Afterword	
		Some things get burned to ashes by fire, and some things get forged
387	Glossary	
395	Acknowledgements	
396	Permissions	

Prologue

Nothing else shaking so you might just as well

In the Land of the Grateful Dead, 1988 was a golden summer for us pot smoking, LSD swinging Tourheads. The cosmos was putting all its dancing skeletons in a row like there'd recently been some sort of harmonic convergence or something. The scene was robust and lush. The band was delivering stellar shows. Everything was vibrating at high frequencies. Everything was possibility and magic. Something was really happening here. Something was really coming together and it glowed in comparison to the American landscape that was not orbiting around the Dead.

Like a wave we were growing, gaining mass and velocity in a cosmic, spiritual way that lent gravity and importance to the lighthearted everyday fun. We were particles in the universe being drawn together to create a new star. We became a spinning, shining sun, created as if an entire solar system needed our light.

I'd been a touring Deadhead since 1983 (reaching my 100th show milestone in July 1988), but I always went home to Connecticut between tours. I'd only been committed to a full-time life on Dead Tour since January 1988. I was seeing new vistas at every turn, and sharing it all with people I loved ferociously. I was now living in a dream land where synchronicity was commonplace, where magic really worked, and where everyday life was vibrant and colorful. My travels afforded me the opportunity to meet locals around the country and it pleases me now to consider how family came to me from those fields of locals. Like hand plucking a bouquet of the most beautiful flowers. How they too were being swept along by this irresistible tie-dyed tide.

I had found my people. Not just Deadheads, but Tourheads. Those of us who, in 1988, let our entire lives revolve around little but the Dead and each other.

Tourheads were a rare breed. We shunned the 9 to 5 conventions of the normal world. Tour was our job, and if you lived on tour, you sold something; tie-dyed clothing, imported textiles, beadwork, stickers, cassette tape covers, food, ice-cold beers, kind buds, mushrooms, LSD, something. You had to sell something. It takes money to follow minstrels around, and while it might seem that life on Dead Tour was all fun and games, quite the opposite is true.

It was hard out there. Such a life demanded stamina, and it was not for the faint of heart. A highly developed sense of adventure was key. Flexibility in the face of circumstances was required. It took a particular sort to thrive on Dead Tour; one part spiritual mystic trickster, one part intrepid seeker, and one part entrepreneur.

To sum it up, you had to be fearless to live out there.

LSD and the psychedelic experience prepared us well for the enormous, scary, and spectacular world we traveled. It honed the skills needed to navigate the chaos of existence and the vagaries of life on the road. Psychedelics however, are double-edged and not unlike staring wide-eyed at a train wreck and therein seeing the complexity, and the beauty, of the entire universe.

Grab it where you find it. That was how we lived.

The transcendent live performances of the Grateful Dead (upwards of 70 nights a year!) fueled our hearts and our souls. We guided ourselves, and each other, with the wisdom of the music, which echoed with folklore, mythology, and otherworldly knowing. In the music, we found encouragement, invitations, admonitions, and warnings. Signposts illuminating the dangers flashed like white-hot neon between the notes, but the music never blinked when things got bad. It never shied away from truth and heartbreak when such was served up. Great good things often happened, but they were not assured. The Grateful Dead never promised us anything.

No. Wait. That's not true.

They promised us it would get weird as we rambled on in our mobile community of thousands. And they weren't kidding.

Yes. I said thousands. That's not an exaggeration. We Tourheads were a transient city so large it was impossible to know everyone intimately, or even to know everyone's names, but we recognized the faces and the energies that were Us. We knew who we were, and we knew, when we looked at each other, that we had shared fates, shared futures. And we knew too, why, and how, each of us had gotten here.

Most of us didn't particularly plan to go on tour full time. It just sort of happened. An irresistible gravitational pull had a hold on us, and we didn't apply rhyme or reason. The siren song of adventure, and the grand quest for awareness and knowledge, was calling us. We had a thirst for freedom and exploration. We yearned for new ways to exist. We were misfits, disillusioned and unfulfilled at home, where the world we'd been brought up to participate in held little appeal. Eight years of Ronald Reagan, Nancy Reagan, and the so-called War on Drugs was a farce, and we knew it.

"Just say no."

"This is your brain on drugs... Any questions?"

Yeah, we had questions.

We wondered if we could have our eggs scrambled, please.

We wondered what society was so afraid of.

Mainstream America in the mid and late 80s was a world we simply couldn't relate to. A vast emptiness of spiritual meaning (in everything from consumerism to music) weighed against a surge of energy in and around the Dead, the antithesis of spiritual emptiness. The scales tipped, and the need to be there, and to be a part of it, was obvious for some of us. We didn't want to miss out on our chance to scream a resounding "YES!" to the universe.

In 1988, no other option held the least viability as a life choice.

"Great North Special, were you on board?
You can't find a ride like that no more
The night the chariot swung down low
Ninety-nine children had a chance to go
One long party from front to end
Tune to the whistle going round the bend
No great hurry, what do you say?
Might as well travel the elegant way."

And here's me, floating on this current, happily part of this growing wave. I loved the camaraderie and the "living large" aspect of it all, the audaciousness especially so. It suited me. Until I found my people, I'd been awash in pointlessness. And here, while it may have seemed I was forgoing purpose in favor of fun, and meaning in favor of the moment, what I was really doing was discovering purpose and meaning in being part of something so joyful and heart-filling, in singing the songs of the universe and dancing for the oneness of souls.

Ahhh the dancing.

We rocked the universe when we danced our tribal celebrations. Shakin' our bones was an affirmation that we were alive! And everything that was good and awful was ours. We danced for the glory and the tragedy that was our human lot (though we never actually said that). It was the place where we shook off all the negative vibes and became one with the elemental core of life energy. The self fell away, the challenges and trials, gone... leaving only bodies, music, and the shape of space between us. We danced a dance of spirit and flesh, of connection and community. Our community. Your community. The human community. We danced like it was our job.

Spending my young life with the Dead was the best decision I ever made. I learned what it meant to be a part of something, for there is a unique and special cohesion to any group that experiences life collectively. Ordinary society simply does not allow for the kind of closeness and intimacy with large groups of people that we Tourheads were able to share. The way we lived more closely resembled ancient tribal societies than it did modern-day America. We not only saw shows together and danced together, we ate together, slept together, dreamed together, traveled together, and we spent our time together between shows.

Most of that time, we talked; uncountable hours of conversation, solidifying bonds that would never be broken. We talked of our philosophies, our interpretations of the riffs we'd heard Jerry play that night, or last week. We'd tell each other what happened yesterday, last tour, when we were 12, the crazy thing so-and-so did. We'd recount the adventures and bravery of our people; how this person or that one got away, or who made a good move in our game. We'd talk about the recent art in the lot, while we listened to tapes of previous shows – we had 23 years worth of previous shows to choose from. Or we'd watch bad TV and discuss each other's love affairs, the larger societal issues we saw as we traveled, and our ability to preserve this great land. We'd talk about the size of our most recent fatty, tell of our exploits when we visited our hometowns, and share innumerable aspirations and plans with each other. Sharing our stories, growing the myths of our people, we forged ourselves into a tribe.

It was so natural and right. And it felt exalted to me. Both then and now. As if this whole coming together was set in motion long before I noticed and embraced it.

Because of course, we'd been here all along. All of us and each of us in our separate trajectories along this same path. But now, in that halcyon summer of 1988, we were one unit, one point of light. Large gatherings sprung up wherever we were, evidence of our coming together into what we called family; an infamous Lobster Bake on the coast of Maine on the 4th of July; a huge party at the cabins by the Eel River; and a positively epic party on a Northern California ranch in early August. As a family, we were coalescing. We were coming into our own and it was important. We didn't talk about it much. We just sorta nodded at each other sometimes, because we knew.

This mattered.

But none of us really know what we're up against.

We were all so earnest, and most of us, so young. We believed we were safe because we had good intentions, and because we thought it was our responsibility to spread the love and the light. We thought it was our duty to open minds to the myriad possibilities of this thing called life.

It's 1988 after all, and we consider ourselves to be direct descendants of the original Acid Tests. We are the inevitable destination of all the cross-country journeys taken by our ancestors when the Interstate Highway System was new. We are the next generation of the consciousness-raising hippie movement of the late 1960s. We are the culmination of all the cool subcultures that came before us, embodying the legacies of Kerouac, Cassidy, and Ken Kesey and his Prankster bunch, honoring their stories with our daily existence. In homage to them all, everything in our world is decadent and over the top. We are enlightened and aware, rule-bending rebels who dare to take risks. We are wild children who use outrageousness as an avenue for enjoyment. We live where laughter, hilarity, and mayhem abound. We are free and we are love. And we are unafraid.

And.

We are breaking the law with our habits and beliefs. This kind of life comes with no guarantees.

There were traps, pitfalls, and slippery slopes to navigate. But most times, laws be damned, we felt invincible.

It's true that we saw what we did as constructive – giving people the choice to disrupt their own consensus reality and find their own new ways to live – but we're still in America, and we're still on the non-subsidized side of America's War on Drugs.

☯☯☯☯☯☯☯☯☯☯☯

No sooner had all this family energy come together, than it was already falling apart. I know that 1988 wasn't wonderful for everyone. Like every cresting wave, there is a part of the whole that is already washing back in turbulence. There are personal and legal dramas playing out in 1988 for people I love, that I won't learn about for decades.

In other cases, I was aware of the difficulties some of my friends faced.

In my journals I refer a time or two to Irvine. (I wasn't there, I'd gone to the New Orleans Jazz and Heritage Fest instead.) The happenings at the Irvine Dead Shows in the late spring of 1988 had been a total shitshow. Not the shows actually, but the events that transpired for our family at a particular hotel on the morning after the shows. It wasn't a well-planned and executed raid, so much as the cops seemed to blunder upon an over-large contingent of people with money, enjoying the fruits of their labors. Lots of my new family were busted, and the sense of the safety of our insular lives showed some cracks. They were small cracks though, and for a while, we were able to go on about our business and not pay those cracks any mind.

Another thing I'll learn decades later is that the ups and downs we experienced on tour pretty closely mirrored the journey of the Grateful Dead themselves. It's the crow's story (same as it ever was) and we can't escape the story, or pay the teller off in gold to change the way the story goes, any more than the boys can.

In the band's world, things were cresting and turbulating as well. The hit status of *Touch of Grey* in 1987 was cause for media attention, notoriety, and an upsurge in the numbers of Tourheads and Tourists alike. A mere matter of overpopulation was taking its toll. *Touch of Grey* had put us all on the radar and the undertow was roiling for the Grateful Dead themselves too, as evidenced by the flyer they distributed in June 1988 with the heading, "When life looks like easy street there is danger at your door." In it, they insinuated that their problems of late were caused by us Deadheads; that the influx of new fans was our responsibility, not theirs.

They weren't right – that it was our responsibility, or our fault, but they had their own shit going on. It's understandable that theirs views on it all got a little clouded. Everyone wanted someone to blame.

We Tourheads shrugged it off, but we warriors in the War on Drugs have a lot to learn in the coming years. We're going to have to learn that freedom comes with a price. We're going to have to define and redefine what it means to be family. We're going to have to decide what matters most and what matters best.

But hey, we excelled at living in the moment. And this was our moment. So let's not worry about all that other shit.

This is life on Dead Tour.

I've heard it said that nothing lasts. I suppose it's true, but if you had told that to 24-year-old me, I would have been as inclined to listen and take heed, as the 8-year-old when told that summer isn't endless.

Were we like lemmings running towards our demise? Like moths before a flame? We didn't think so. Magic was everywhere and our love for each other was enormous. And shouldn't that be enough?

We'd found it after all!
We had created our utopia!
Nothing would ever get in the way of that.
Until it did.

Foreword

I highly recommend that you go read the entirety of this brilliant 30 minute poem, but here, to set the stage, I would like to share with you an excerpt from:

An American Adventure

Chapter One: Novus Ordo Seclorum by Robert Hunter

```
         There was no time like the time we
              thought something was happening
          which was not what we thought it was
         but might as well have been considering
              how little it was anything else.

         If what was seen is to be spoken of,
              it must be said all in a breath or
              it becomes something else: a glyph,
         a gloss, a reflection of a vase bearing
            an artificial flower on a living stem.

                                                ...


              To go back to the beginning,
                   what did we think it was
              leaked out of the sea dream
              of our age to swallow us whole
         and later spit us up on the very spot
              we'd have chosen for ourselves
                   had we known it existed?

         Behold a city half visible along
              the cloudline, studded with
         faraway spires, domes, turrets
         and other paraphernalia with
              which deep-seated yearning
                   tends to outfit a horizon.
```

A beckoning beam glimmers
across furlongs of pale grain
waving between us and what seems
our individual and collective destiny.

In retrospect it's fruitless to try to determine
if it was simply arrogance compounded
with sensory overload ...or if we really saw
something else besides, in its true and
difficult form, not always at a distance;
something not generally given to standing still
in the same spot in an attitude of welcoming.

As for entering the cloudline city,
indistinct memories tell us
we did so, although snapshots
from the era indicate that it
might have been otherwise.
The inch thick layer of immaculate
shamrock glass which coated the
pavement is shown, in the photo,
to be only unadorned city concrete
and not all that clean.

There is no evidence of spires
and the pack of gangling gawkers
posturing in the foreground --
could that be us?
Time is the great counterfeiter--
it was not like that. I know.
I was there. I remember.

MESSAGE TO DEADHEADS:

June, 1988

*"When life looks like easy street
There is danger at your door."*

Too true. The Grateful Dead has an ugly, dangerous problem at its door, a situation bad enough to put our future as a touring band in doubt. Part of our audience — a small part, but that's all it takes — is making us unwelcome at show site after show site with insensitive behavior including flagrant consumption of illegal substances (including alcohol), littering, and general disturbances of the environment.

We didn't invent Dead Heads; you created yourself. And what you came up with has been, generally, the best audience around; supportive, civil, and hip to the realities of America in the late 20th century — in other words, a crowd that treats police, local security, neighboring people and businesses like people. But the expansion of the Dead Head world on the heels of our recent successes means that there are people out there who don't understand the tradition — and they're ruining it for everybody, including us.

More security or more rules aren't the answer — you guys know what righteous behavior is about. Because you created your scene, it is up to you to preserve it. That means talking with each other and us about how to improve things. There will be a Grateful Dead information booth in the vending area at some of the shows on this tour — stop by and talk with our folks there. Or write us at "c/o Grateful Dead", P.O. Box 1260, San Rafael, CA 94915.

Remember, only you can prevent this trip from becoming a drag.

GRATEFUL DEAD

Bill, Jerry, Mickey, Phil, Bobby and Brent

~~~~~~

The above flyer was handed to me in a Grateful Dead parking lot.

1
Summer 1988
The Northwest

August 21
Washington

Zippin' up the coast on a sunny afternoon. Harsh cut hills where thousands of redwood stumps tell their story. Washington's mountains are gorgeous, except all those stumps. Looks like a dog with mange. I saw an anti-logging sign that said, "The appearance of careful management is just a careful management of appearances."

Corvette is still in Jamaica with Abe, I'm traveling with Macy and Abe's dog Seca. We left Murph and Matteo's Ranch Party two days ago and we've been following the coastal route north outta California. Currently we're driving along Willipa Bay after a stop in Long Beach, Washington for the International Kite Festival. Unbelievable! 1,800 kites in the air at once. Black and rainbow stunt kites, dayglow box kites, a spaceship with a giraffe on its string, everywhere huge spinning wind tunnels. The Japanese team had a US Navy Fleet kite performing maneuvers, dipping and flipping as one. The sky was full of color and movement.

I wanna go visit Janey while we're in Washington. I've heard it's such a small town I should just go ask people, "Where's Janey?" and I'd probably find her.

August 22nd Monday
Olympic National Forest

The coast here is rugged, serene, and magical. We're camped on some river not far from the ocean. The water is cold. Cold as when you're diggin' through a cooler, diggin' through all those Becks, lookin' for a Dos XX, and ya give up and grab a Becks because it's too fuckin cold to keep your hand in there.

Seca was freaking out when I stuck my head under the water to get my hair wet. Puppies can be a pain in the ass. We make her follow rules like – 'Puppies who hafta chew – hafta sit in the back seat.' And the obvious, 'No chewing Birkenstocks.'

later

We drove to the little store in town and asked a cool lookin' guy, "Do you know Janey?"

He looked me up and down, made cups of his hands and held them in front of himself, "Janey?" He asked the question more with his hands. Janey, forever famous for her 'Bodacious Tatas'.

We followed him to her house. He said we'd never find it on our own.

Janey isn't home, she's in Canada for a few days. Ace is here working on the house.

It's spectacular here. The mountains crawl right down to the house. There's only an outhouse (or just pee outside), but they do have a shower so I'll indulge. I haven't showered in too long.

The 24th

Corvette is headed home from Jamaica today. Hope she'll be at the Washington show. I miss her.

Me and Macy went to LaPush. It was desolate and beautiful. No Pets allowed, but we took Seca anyway. We walked the beach and layed in the sun all day.

When we left, we drove to this campground to use the bathroom, and saw a VW poptop with clotheslines full of drying tye-dyes. Dee and Oliver. They were invited to Murph's ranch party but they went to Cougar Hot Springs instead and said it was full of broke people who were ready to rip off whatever they needed.

Macy's been helping Ace on the roof but I don't dare get up there. I'm fine going up, but I get scared trying to come down.

Still no Janey. We leave tomorrow. News on Vancouver radio says we might have a big ole storm tonight.

August 25th

No storm, but Janey came home. Macy was working on the roof when she arrived. Janey yelled, "I don't know who that woman is up there, but I love her!"

We feasted on burritos and cheap beer. Janey fired up Cannibal Stew – a claw foot bathtub with a fire pit under it and a home spa for bubbles.

I love when Janey tells the story of how we met like she told it to Macy. How she had groundscored a necklace, and when I saw her wearing it, weeks later, I yelped, because it was my Yin-Yang necklace with the sticker on the back that Tanner had put there. How she said, "I've been saving it till I met you."

Spring tour 1984? Neither of us remembers exactly.

Morning 26th.

It's probably not morning anymore, but I just woke up. We're in a suburb of Seattle at Janey's friend Nanette's house. Real bathroom facilities.

On the way here we cruised by this guy's land. He carves Gnomes on fence posts, has Ogres on street corners, and a twenty-foot Wizard holding a crystal ball on his front yard. He's also building a castle. The car overheated and we had to stop and cool off. A cat came by and I made up a story about the cat being the owner guy, and how he would invite us into his house. Didn't happen though.

We got to the Tacoma lot around midnight, overheating as we pulled in.

KindBoy was the first person I saw. We ripped one. Always see lots of people as soon as ya pull in. KindBoy calls it the ten minute high. Found Doughboy making double banana rum smoothies, yeah.

Came back to Nanette's to crash.

Janey told me something horrible about Jumpin' Jack. She thinks he's one of the people who left Damien when he was dying.

August 27th

Spent most of my time yesterday in Roz and Kevin's rig. Abe and Beau are here, but Corvette stayed in the city. Dante, Anton, and Silas are here after some time back east on the islands.

Got my ticket from Gimlet and Pandora, in trade for a Snodgrass pipe. Bob and Marie gave me pipes to sell because they couldn't be here. I was trying all day, but no one was buying them. Or anything actually – everyone said so.

Once inside the show you could not get to the floor General Admission area. Or from the floor to Reserved seating. Everyone was divided and wanted to go wherever they weren't.

I mainly stayed near Murph, Amanda, Kevin, Roz, and Wolfboy Taylor. Lots of folks were scammin' to the floor. I tried awhile, but wasn't successful. Janey, Macy, Beau, Abe, Garrett, Carp, Fritz, and more were on the floor. But plenty of us were upstairs. Santa, Kerry, Jumpin' Jack, Lubba Lenny, Arthur, Jasmine.

After the show was big fun. We got out late because Santana played first and it started at 8:00. Did some drinking with Dingaling Janet, then I ended up walking around with Garrett. We kept bumping into Santa, like he was around every corner. He was busting my ass about my new driver-partner Garrett. Yikes!

Couldn't find Macy, so me and Garrett curled up in her car. There was a full moon lunar eclipse from like 3:00 to 4:00 AM. It was beautiful. Macy appeared around the time the sun came up and we went to Abe and Beau's hotel with Skip, Anna, and Janice.

Now we're on the road towards Eugene. This highway is Deadhead central.

Beau knows of a party near Eugene. Garrett wants us to drop him off so he can hitch to Cougar Hot Springs.

August 28th
morning - Eugene - in the lot

What a hell night. I'm sure Macy hates me.

We stopped at Skip and Anna's with an overheating car and the hood not closing. Garrett was freaking out and agitated because he had to get to Cougar Hot Springs. Finally we get the hood closed and get on the road again to meet Beau and company at Sunny Gas. Garrett was gonna hitch from there, but somehow I ended up borrowing Macy's car and bringing Garrett to Cougar, while she went to the party with those guys. We didn't even go to hang out – we went so he could do some business. An hour each way. While driving back, I was tired and hungry. Garrett offered breakfast so we passed the party and went to I-Hop in town.

We overheated there. Then (here's the stupid part), instead of going back to the party, we went to the lot. Garrett paid to park and we set up Macy's tent. I crashed. Garrett took off. He came back with Wolfboy Taylor not looking too good. We got stoned then all three of us crashed in the tent. Macy is gonna kill me. I was supposed to bring the car back to the party.

I wish I could do it over. But after the car trouble, and the hours of driving, I couldn't deal with driving back up that Mountain road again. Plus I probably just wanted some alone time with Garrett, which I didn't even get.

Inside

Anna gave me a ticket.

The fatties are at the back of the floor, in the breezy hallway. I'm in the stands on the shady side. Eden and Riley will be married during break down in the Fatty Zone. Kerry will be the preacher. Lots o' naked folk here. At least more than normal.

I'm pretty stoned. Met a woman from Utah – her first show. I like talking to people during their first show. – They're always so amazed.

The energy here is way laid-back. Show started at Noon. Jimmy Cliff and Robert Cray opened. Jimmy was Hot. And speaking of hot – it's very hot here. Reminds me of Buffalo and DC back in '86. The air smells of kind buds and sweat. I can pick out lots of people from where I sit. There's Riley, the happy Groom. I see Janice boppin' like mad in a drum circle out on the field, her hair flippin' and flyin'.

Last night was too tweaky for me. Cougar Hot Springs is BEAUTIFUL. AMAZING. Glorious in moonlight. But we didn't stay because I had to get Macy's car back. Why did I go at all? So Garrett wouldn't bunk his connect. What did I do? I bunked Macy instead. Sure the car was overheating, but it's no excuse. When I saw Macy, she wasn't mad. Said she had been, but she got over it. What a weird and tweaky day it was all around. Garrett has that effect all too often. I hope I just don't see him till Maryland.

Jerry just walked out on stage.

Hi Guys.

Bobby in shorts, of course. What will they play?

Mississippi ½ Step.

Somebody just put up an "*Unbroken Chain*" banner.

Above the stage, the backdrop is a mural of mountains, the moon, and a volcano.

Red Rooster. Hounds begin to Howl OOOOO

Yeah Brent! . . . . Now Jerry's rippin' it up. I can't write through a show. Yet.

~~~~~ later

OK, now it's the post-water-fight, up-in-the-stands-to-catch-the-last-of-the-sun, drums session.

Wedding during break was nice.

They're spraying everyone in the corner on Phil's side with water. There's a bunch o' folks dancing wildly under the hose.

Terrapin D – S – Other One?

Yep. *Other One.*

29th Monday 2ish?

Sitting on Ozzy's idling bus with Helena, Pandora, and Tish. (And Midnight and Sunshine the dogs.)

I stayed in the lot late yesterday trying unsuccessfully to make enough $ to fly east. I maybe had a ride with Murph, but I couldn't find him. So I went to the Hilton with Macy and Tish. Abe asleep in the room, Beau and Janice drinking in the bar. We joined them and got the DJ to play a bootleg.

This morning after fatties and bongs, Macy brought me and Tish back to the lot. Ozzy was still there.

Cool. We have a ride.

Ozzy is getting things set for the road. Garrett is at Cougar and wants to be picked up. Will we pick him up? I don't think they've decided. I want no say in that.

later.

At Cougar Hot Springs (again). It's crowded here.

So.

I'm headed cross-country on the Dead Ringer bus with Ozzy, Helena, Tish, Pandora, and (lord help me) Garrett. We're planning our route.

August 30th 1988

Woke in a rest area. Morning joint. A bathroom full of old women.

SEP field took me all night to secure. So far this ride is great. It's pretty country. I'm Lovin Life on the bus. I've gotten a couple of Garrett massages already.

We've got to make time today. We had a late start. Before we left the lot Ozzy said, "Well, I've gotten no last minute mechanic calls, so I guess everyone's out of here safely. Now we can go."

Right now Tish is asleep on the floor, Helena is reading *Acid Dreams*, Pandora's rolling a joint, Ozzy's driving, and Garrett is drawing. About as easy as writing on this bumpy mobile.

I like this bus. Painted Red, White, and Steal-Your-Face Blue outside, and light purple inside. Lots of stickers (of course) and my favorite thing – written on the ceiling, "Don't talk to my skin, Talk to my heart."

I should try to think up a sticker for New York to make some $. Maybe Garrett will draw one and we can go in on it.

Later

On the lot in Eugene I saw KindBoy acting like a fancy waiter, carrying a tray containing piles of different buds, one hand behind his back. "Which Bonghit would Madame like?"

Inspecting the goods. "I'll take one of that gooey orange bud in the corner."

"Ah. Every good smoker has correctly picked the killah Idaho bud."

We'll be crossing into Idaho soon. We've been in slow mode because it took Ozzy a long time to come down enough to drive. Murph had given him a crystal splash. All day yesterday he kept muttering, "I'm gonna get Murph for this. I'll get him."

The sound system on here is incredible. With only six of us on the bus you can dance while going down the highway. And we do. It's so empty because Ozzy said, "This trip – No Wingnuts."

August 31st

I'm not sure where we are. I'm at a shaded table in some rest area. Time is sorta meaningless. Just know it's morning. Ozzy's still asleep. He's amazing. He drove from 9AM to 2AM with only a couple ten minute breaks. Pandora and Garrett are playing stick with Sunshine and Midnight. They're great dogs to travel with. They sleep all the time.

We don't have much pot. Gimlet gave Pandora enough to "take care of the jones" with skinnies. But I just found a bud in a film vial in my backpack. When was that from?

later

Utah, 380 miles from Cheyenne, Wyoming. A while back we stopped along the side of the highway to smoke a fatty with Freddy and Dawn, and their hitchhiker.

We've been at the end of a parade of Heads flowing east. We just passed a green van with Diggety and some people I don't know. So, not only are we catching up, but we're passing folks.

Later

On the side of the road again. Mid-afternoon. Big Bertha bus is broke down – it's the drive shaft or something. They have 20 people. Yikes. Emerald is the only one I know.

These people are foolish, they should be hitchhiking already not sitting in the shade under a bush. I don't think Ozzy wants any of them to ride with us. (No Wingnuts!) But he and Helena are out there interviewing potential riders.

still in Wyoming

We've added Autumn and Troy to the crew.

Ozzy wants to make it to Iowa tonight.

Sept 1st.

Early AM. Garrett behind the wheel. Ozzy's been going since yesterday morning. Blowin' through Nebraska all night long. Just before the last stop Ozzy kinda almost went off the road. I think of it only as a small fuckup but Ozzy was really upset. "No. We almost bit it." So he's packin' a bowl, watchin' Garrett drive for a bit before he crawls in back to crash.

SEP field held up well when tested. Two cop cars at the last gas station in Wyoming left before we did. Yeah!

Another stop we had to push someone's VW bus to get it started. They said Murph was an hour ahead of us. So we're trying to catch him. No luck so far. About 60 miles out of Omaha now.

In the middle of the night, in the middle of Nebraska, at a gas station, the guy working said to me, "Wow. I was stationed in San Francisco in the 60s, we used to call those 'Hippie buses.'"

I told him, "That's what we still call them."

He said he saw 104 hippies get out of one once.

Sept 2nd

9AM. New Stanton, Pennsylvania. Four hours to Landover.

Ozzy drives great through to sunrise, then, once the sun comes up, he has to sleep for a few hours. He didn't feel safe having me or Pandora drive, so we've been here since dawn.

Most of us have washed our hair at the Sunoco across the street.

2
Fall Tour 1988
Landover and Philly

Sept 2nd 1988

We made it! Landover, Maryland. It took us nearly 69 hours. Pulled in right behind Murph, John, Santa, Amanda, and Wolfboy Taylor.

There's a short haired guy near us putting on a wig that looks like Garrett's hair. I've never seen that at a show before. Narc?

Inside

It's Taylor's B-day. I'm buzzed. A million things. The East Coast. Harsh.

Beer all day with Rum Tom. Got $5 tix from Gypsy Linda. We followed Murph into an elevator and went in through the backstage. Hung on the floor till *Let it Grow*. Find the Fat Ones. With Carp for a quick fatty, then I hear from Tish that they're throwing family out. I don't know what happened. I go to see. They chased Don (he's still inside) and threw out Jumpin' Jack. But he's back. They got JohnRay too. Then up comes security and grabs Jack again. He bought another ticket and came right back in. Again. I went with Dingaling Janet and Magoo to some seats to smoke – got told we'd be kicked out if we didn't stop.

Hot Hot *Scarlet*. WOW.

Lost Rum Tom. I can't keep my stuff on the bus, where will I sleep?

Why do I do this? This coast is so harsh.

This *Fire* is so Hot. This is why I do this. This is what I came for – but the east coast is soooo obviously Horrid.

Looks Rainy
Terrapin.
Drumz.
Found Rum Tom.

Sept 3

Me and Tish crashed on the ground – woke in the blazing sun and came towards the bus – never got back to sleep. I want to shower. At least my hair is clean. Had a few beers already. I haven't buzzed out in a while on the west coast, and I sure did it last night. Me and Rum Tom walked out on a *Black Cheesy River*. After the show I hung out with him till he left for the Ramada. I couldn't go, too much work going on there last night. Maybe tonight?

When Tom left, I went to the Smoothie Bar where it was a bit of a party for Taylor's b-day – free refills.

Hanging with Blake late night – he was tripping hard. I helped him give away boxes of bagels. Laughing so hard we could barely form words.

Later

Bad news! Skye's been busted! DEA got her for mail orders she did to N'Awlins six months ago. Yikes! They need $25,000 to cover bail (so her parents won't go broke). Izzy is trying to raise money – selling Skye's scarves and stuff. She says Skye has known in her heart for months, – that's why she quit selling drugs. Says Skye is taking it well. Says she has a good Lawyer. Skye – I love you. I hope this works out for you.

I'm broke, I'm dirty. I should blow off the show and sleep – but no – I'll probably go try to find a free ticket. Find Rum Tom and see if he'll take me to the Ramada tonight. I wish I had my Van.

Break Day Maryland

It's a Sunday. Jelly once told me she thinks of Sundays as pasty white. How could that be when you're at a show? I'm at the Ramada with Lars, Suzy, Kennedy, and Rum Tom.

Last night I was collecting bail $ for Skye. People outside really started kickin' when the show started. Puppy Pete said he needed sleep, and I should go in, he gave me a free ticket. I was walking with Rum Tom, who had no tix. After a lap around the lot, I saw Lyndelle, way-bummin' that she wasn't in. So I could stay with Tom (and get a hotel room to crash in), I sold her my ticket for $10 and put it towards bail $.

They double encored with *Another Saturday Night* and *Ripple*. I can't believe it! I thought the guy was kidding when I first heard it. That's one of the reasons I come to the shows and I blew it. Arrrgghh!

By the end of the night I had $330. Plus a pair of Tuesday tickets to Raffle off. We need $25,000. I'm sure we'll get it.

Later.

Image to remember – Rum Tom and Kennedy both rubbing their scraggly beards while talking business. Tom is flying to California and back tomorrow.

9-5-88

Went to Jerry's Sub Shop for lunch. Bumped into JohnRay and cruised the Days Inn with him. Met some guy who had extras, for face, for the whole tour. Couldn't buy any, neither could JohnRay.

later

Push-n-Shove was so much fun first set, dancing with Fritz, bouncing off each other – He's all skeletal with his gawky elbows flailing around.

China Cat Rider Playin Uncle D-S *Gimmie Phil* (now)

Sept 6th

Morning of the 4th show. Since sleeping in the lot the first night I've been here in the Ramada. Been getting free tix too. I've been broke mostly, but I saw Vincent from Atlanta, then Theo, so I made that work. Then I saw Brent from Buffalo looking for Abe.

Abe's not here, I saw Fritz and Don though. So I'm not broke anymore.

I'll tell ya, Carp is amazing when it comes to raising money for Skye. He bought a pie for $7 and sold pieces totaling $132.50. Inside the show, during a huge Fatty Circle, he made everyone who works kick a $20. I had made some money and was glad I could kick right along with everyone else. By the end of the show he had $1000. That's the way we've got to do it if we're gonna get the money.

Dancing with every one during *US Blooze* was great. Me and Fritz bumping Ozzy between us.

I have to find Justine. I'm getting a ride to Connecticut with her.

Sept 9th 1988   Philly

7:30AM. Lounged out in the back of the van. My van. Nice spot – in some park across the street from the Spectrum.

The last Maryland show was really fun. We took over a press box on Phil's side. For such a Police state we got away with doing a lot of Fatties, but the call 6-UP was more frequent than I've ever heard before.

Got my ride with Justine, and got home as Mom and Ed left for work. Slept. Showered. Went through my mail. Leo and I went over to Dwayne and Amy's new place. Came home and slept again.

I wasn't gonna come here for the first day but Amy and Dwayne had a ticket they were just gonna "frame or something."

I said, "Kick," and made them give it to me.

Afternoon

I moved the van – under a tree off Vendor's row. I have to motivate if I want to sell our junk clothes and stuff today. I'm feeling lazy. Maybe I'll set up the stuff out the back of the van and sell from here. I've got enough traffic.

Break Day

Relaxing at the Quality Inn with Judy Blue. Slept in my van last night.

Supposedly some guy OD'd – it was N_2O that killed him – he did the fish and didn't get up. Sick. The fish.

Santa woke me early. We did bongs, marveled at rocks, and took a walk around the park. I cruised the hotels and found Erik the Rude telling a maid to go away – I snagged a shower in their room. Weasel Karl, Drippy Danny, Dante and a bunch of girls I didn't know. Karl bought me lunch, and wants me to get an onion for him.

Yesterday I made $40 selling our stuff, and Jumpin' Jack bought me a ticket. Last minute – expensive – $50 each. He said, "Come on Doll, I don't wanna go in alone." Yikes. I had fun hanging with him though. Jack said, "Don't tell anyone I spent that much – tell 'em pages." Don't worry Jack, I won't tell people anything. (Who cares anyway?)

In Eugene, when Santa was busting my ass about Garrett being my new tour partner, I had joked, "I'd tour with Jumpin' Jack before I'd tour with Garrett." But damn. I wouldn't want to tour with either of them.

The show was good, but not the best.

I guess I'll finish this beer and head off to the scene. Jumpin' Jack's having a Birthday Party in the park – I should go.

Sunday morning

GratefulDeadLand – Philly, Pennsylvania. Garrett woke me with a massage and got me high. We had some fun. Now he's out groundscoring but he's supposedly gonna come back and take me to breakfast.

So I admit, I wasn't expecting much for Jumpin' Jack's party. I mean how big and cool can a party be if your whole world is a big cool party?

I went to the park with Erik the Rude. Parked in my spot and headed towards Domino's bus. We could hear the tunes coming from Ozzy's bus, from very far away.

When I got there I couldn't quite believe it. Everything was a blur of color and sound. Tye-dyed banners and flags, balloons, rainbow streamers, silly string, bubbles, – all blowin' in the breeze. Hippies everywhere – in groups all over the ground – even on top of the buses. Dancing, eating, drinking, telling animated stories over the music. A keg, and a 20-foot-long table of food. Vegetables and dips, sandwich stuff, crackers and cheese. All day long a huge Fatty Circle out behind the buses and tents. It was really loud and really colorful, – so outrageous and over the top. Santa made his famous tea.

Elsewhere, Remy got arrested. He's gonna cost a lot.

Philly Last Day

I got a $20 ticket yesterday. Show was fun. Garrett's looking like he's on a pretty steep downhill path with New York directly ahead of him. Almost too fuckin easy to go down that road. Carp is worried about people Jonesin in New York. Me too kinda.

Davy? Amanda? Jumpin' Jack? It's a part of people I try not to see. Who else is the type? Sid says, "Not me, I've been clean for five years." Good.

New shirts handed out by Carp say, "Boycott White Powders – Bring Back Herb."

We were at a Fatty Circle and a guy on the walkway went down cold. It was scary, but he got right up. Someone has died here each night. It's not an easy world. But it's ours, we made it. Some of us choose to live it full time. Why shouldn't we? – it's here, it's better than any other reality I've yet to encounter. Tour and traveling has its ups and downs, but that's how life goes – up and down – whether you're a witch in the woods, an Olympic runner, a marine biologist, or a cashier at 7-11 in bumfuck Nebraska, that's the way the world is. So maybe all the people who follow Jerry and Company for years on end have got it right by finding a corner of the world they like and following it wherever it goes.

Last night I slept at the Quality Inn with Judy Blue, Izzy, Winnie, Neil, Fritz, Don, and Karl and of course, how could I forget, Trinity. I woke to Izzy throwing dirty diapers at Don, till he attacked her, wrapped her up in his sleeping bag and sat on her.

I got an onion for Karl then headed to the lot. I'm parked near Margot, lounging out on an air mattress between the vans. It's getting late and guess what?

I Need One.

Garrett just plopped himself down next to me. I think he went to sleep. I really don't think he should go to New York but who am I to say. It's none of my business and not my place to tell anyone how to live their lives.

2:50 AM.

Sitting in the hallway at the Quality Inn, smokin' a butt.

I got a $10 ticket tonight. The show was hot.

Rumour has it Jumpin' Jack got arrested. Oh Jack! He may have had 50 pages or more. Yikes. I like Jack, but he's the type with a lot of Karma to work out.

Learned that Fritz is from South Dakota. Amazing. I didn't think anyone out here was from South Dakota.

3
Fall Tour 1988
New York

Sept 17th 1988

Corvette flew in to Hartford Thursday, Friday we went to New York. Got Free parking on the street, but tix were rough. And expensive. Fritz, Don, and Izzy got in with a backstage guy, who said he'd come back and get us, but didn't. Saw Murph while we waited – he shaved off ½ his mustache!

It was late when some guy sold us a $20 ticket. Then I met Robin, from London – he wanted hash for his ticket. "Actually, I just want to get high." So I talked him into selling it to me for $20 with a deal that if he got high he'd give my $20 back.

Headed in with Robin to section 21. *Birdsong,* then break. So many Fatties. Santa and Fritz offered him liquid or mushrooms, whichever he wanted. He gave my $20 back and wandered off after intermission.

The show was good, but the real fun started at the Penta bar afterwards. Dante standin' at the front door, directed us, "Downstairs! Downstairs! Private Party!"

Someone rented out the lower bar for Two Toke Tom's b-day. It was a swinging American Indican Party. Everyone was there – even Mark Reese who hasn't been around in a while. I used to think all these circles of people were different, but they're not. It's all one big family.

Carp said Jack's bail is $250,000 so we need $25,000 to get him out. We haven't even paid for Skye yet. They got Remy good. His bail is outrageous – one million.

That's the bad shit, now back to the good shit.

The party was hoppin'. We closed that bar. They kept telling us to leave but no one moved till Carp gave the word. Then Carp announced, as we were milling out, – "Free pitcher of kamikazes to go – for the b-day boy." They weren't gonna do it, and Carp said, "You want me to bring all those people back in?" They kicked down with the kamikazes.

We went upstairs and closed that bar too. After, we went with Tish, Santa, and Erik the Rude to their hotel on 77th and Broadway. It's a boarding hotel for actors. We had killah Chicago-style Vegetarian pizza from the Pizza Joint downstairs. We were all drunk and rowdy, wrestling and dog piling on the rabbit. Erik pulled out shaving cream. After everyone was covered with it, I tossed it out the 8th floor window.

Monday 19th

Got tickets pretty quick. I got mine from James the DC hitchhiker of years ago. I recognized his eyes.

I loved the *NFA* to open the 2nd set – so fun!

Last night was Sid's birthday party at the Marriott. Me, Santa and Corvette headed over there. As we circled for parking, Santa got annoyed because I was driving too slow. He jumped out of the van and ran off into the night. Me and Corvette gave up, parked alongside the Garden and went to sleep. Slept unbothered till noonish, when Carp stopped by the van and smoked a fatty with us.

There was a cutie on the sidewalk outside the Penta last night. Didn't like the Dead, he said. A ba-humbug type of guy. Saw him again after the show, and said, "Bet we had more fun than you did tonight."

Corvette got an onion so we're not broke anymore. And we got our Tuesday tix from some kids from Vermont.

Tuesday

The Marriott is cush. I love the elevators. Silent swift tubes of light. From the Lounge on our floor, while lying on your back, you can watch them go right through the ceiling towards the revolving restaurant above.

Murph and company have a four room suite. I slept behind the curtains, against a window wall that faced Broadway. I opened my eyes to a sea of taxis below.

After the show, shit seemed to hit the fan. There's Chris Kangaroo bleeding in the back of an ambulance. We stopped and asked what the fuck.

"Someone accused me of snitching on Jumpin' Jack!"

Earlier we'd seen Carp, red-faced and mean, 'in conference' with Family guys. Well, it seems Sid and Carp kicked the shit out of him. Is Chris Kangaroo a narc?

Friday Night 9-23

-> Take this story back to Tuesday.

No sign of Chris Kangaroo that day. Me, Corvette, and Ozzy went in together and had scam adventures trying to get to section 21. It was a really good show. Monday's was lame comparatively.

Afterwards we hung out at the Penta bar. Went upstairs with Fritz, Don, Neil, and Santa to the Roy Rodgers restaurant and smoked a fatty with Dollarbill Towerhouse who was cleanin' up. He gave us a free bucket of chicken. Something wonderful about rippin' fatties in a closed public place.

Ozzy left the city with us. We got out of the parking garage much cheaper than it should have been, but as we drove off, they noticed they had undercharged us, and a big black man chased us for four blocks. Ozzy screamin', "Just go go go!"

Run a few red lights – save $25. Good deal.

We drove up to Woodstock where Ozzy's bus is parked. Next day Ozzy took us to eat at the Pub. Delicious honey-dipped Chicken, fried mushrooms, and Kahlua Coffee. Woodstock is a cute little, west coast, hippie-type, artsy town right here on the beast coast.

We went to mine Herkimers. Went where Poet told us to go. Poet always scores huge rainbowed Herks. He said he meditates and asks the earth for its gifts. I haven't mastered meditation and we didn't score like he does, – but we did get some nice small ones.

We spent the night drinking wine, smoking bowls, and talking. We talked about our pasts, about tour, and about narcs, wondering if Chris Kangaroo is or isn't. Ozzy is freaked out by the intensity of the game lately. We mined till sundown next day, dropped Ozzy off in Woodstock, and came back to Connecticut.

Today I've gotten my shit totally together. – Packed the van. Dealt with the bank. Packed stuff to be mailed to me in California. We're headed back to the city tomorrow to try to get in for the benefit show. We hope to find one or two people with money (or bud) to drive south with. And still the major thing on my mind: Is Chris Kangaroo a narc? If he's a DEA plant, we're all in trouble. I thought of him as family. Still do, until I know for sure.

New York sadness we were just talkin' about – Wolfboy Taylor and Davy have been cracking it up. It's been so obvious. I hate that. I wonder if Garrett has been too? New York is too harsh for such a long tour stay. I never would have lasted the whole time, and I don't even have a problem with drugs.

Tuesday 9-27?

That Saturday – walking around seeing everyone (except no sign of Chris Kangaroo). We scored two tix for $64, and after a bit, we hear, "Jumpin' Jack's at the Penta bar." He looked good. His bail was lowered to $75,000. Everybody showed up, and it turned into a huge 'before the show' party.

Then – inside. Huge Fatties abounding. Tix for the Benefit for Rainforest circle thing were $250. Mirabeth had one. Blake too. Gypsy Linda and Jeanie were all dressed up. Lyndelle too. I kinda was, in my black flowery pants. Great show.

New York is done. Who will we take south? We see Q.T. brunette – the Dead-hating humbug street boy. "Wanna go south? Got any money?" His name is David. We had to wait till 5:30AM before we could get his stuff out of a Penn Station locker. Hanging on the street mostly.

Me and Corvette, going to the bathroom over at the Park-n-Lock, heard Carp's gravelly carny voice echoing off the concrete. He'd decided he needed to save the Jonsers in the Park-n-Lock, where many of them congregate. So Carp goes through the place yelling, "All you Jonsers listen up, New York is over. It's time to straighten up and cut the shit. You don't need it. It's time to go home. So get your brothers and sisters and help each other get outta New York, and if you believe you can do it, follow me." He went through every floor with his booming voice, like some sort of preacher offering salvation to the sinners. Corvette and I followed, and watched, because it was flat out amazing. He had a parade behind him. They came crawling from every corner. Maybe they all needed someone to tell them that.

Jumpin' Jack sat patiently outside waiting for Carp to be done. He said Chris Kangaroo wasn't the one who set him up. Oh-oh. What does that mean?

We went to Erik and Santa's Hotel but they'd already left. Fritz and Garrett were there instead. We (me, Corvette, and David-the-humbug) slept there. Woke up, Fattied, and tried to kidnap Garrett but didn't succeed.

David, who wouldn't talk in NY, would not shut up once he got in the van. What a young opinionated Libra. He contradicted himself often and was completely full of shit. We dropped him off in Raleigh. Good riddance.

4
Fall 1988
The Southern Semester

Sept 28th

Went to King Henry's as soon as we got to Atlanta. Ripped a fatty and got showers. Henry took us for Oyster Po'boys, and we checked out Shawna's store.

We went to Atomic Cafe and visited the house on Josephine. George's cat Kyra has two white male kittens. I'd like to take them both.

Friday 30th

At King's we met Leland, recently returned from Kenya. I've always wanted to go to Africa. I'd love to go on an out-of-the-country trip next year. But where will I ever get the money for that? I've managed to travel around our own country quite poor, but in another? Leland said Kenya was cheap because there's nothing to buy.

Henry and Leland headed to Tennessee and we went to Josephine. Jethro had Corvette's money. Vincent, of course, didn't. George, for part of his debt, is gonna make us some black leather roses to sell in Florida.

When we left Josephine we had two new additions to the Van – Kyra's kittens – both all white with bright blue eyes. They are Jake and Elwood, the Blooze Brothers.

Later

At Corvette's parent's. I feel lazy here in Alabama. Not in body, but in mind. What am I doing? – Nothing except waiting for clean clothes and to head to Birmingham tomorrow to visit Cash Hamlin. I really don't want to end up the type of person who waits for the next Dead tour forever. Right now, that's what I'm doing. It's fine on many levels. I have no real complaints. Our world is a happy one. Yet I still expect more out of life. This is the best I've seen, yet it's not all I want. Too many people I see, aren't happy. They aren't happy in Alabama, they aren't happy in Ohio, they aren't happy in Connecticut. Is it just that people aren't happy? What about me? Where do I belong? Will I ever be totally happy anywhere? Will anyone?

       Late night

We went to a bar. They sure were all happy to see Corvette. Rednecks galore. I don't much enjoy a bunch of X-ing Alabamians on a Friday night. Drug scenes with people I don't know and trust make me too Paranoid.

       October 1st/2nd
       Birmingham.
       Cash's house - 4AM.

When we got here we stormed in executing a full on silly string attack. They were dosed which made the silly string extra fun. We went to The Quick. I had the idea I might be bored. I didn't really want to go, but they talked me into it. The band was MoreMoreMore. Cash scored us a ½ gram of coke. I hate that coke made the bar more fun, but it did.

  Cash had to have more coke. So there was a runaround getting money from the ATM, and finding the guy (who was no longer at the bar when we got back). I enjoy coke now and again but I'd never Jones it.

  I like these folks. I like Birmingham. I mean, all night I dealt with trippin' southerners and I didn't mind. In fact, I'm still having fun.

  Silly string still providing a focus as it swirls on the ceiling fan.

  Note – be a Diver for Halloween – Get a wetsuit, flippers, Goggles, and a Nitrous tank.

       October 7th, 1988
       Dusk, King's house, Atlanta

Roz, Kevin, and Sid arrived yesterday. And also a package from California. Green. Sticky. Nice. Roz flew to San Francisco this morning, she'll be back tomorrow or the next day, and Skye flew in at 5 o'clock.

  Ripping fatties all day.

  Currently drinking Toasted Almonds with Skye. Talking serious matters like DEA, Drugs, and our world. *Here* is the story. Can I write about it? About the drugs, and the dealing, and the risks and joys? About what it means to be this particular family?

Oct 9th   Atlanta

Chilly Sunday morning. Cloudy. Chowing on bagels and flavored cream cheese. We've been talking family-type talk. About how good Izzy is with Trinity, about how bad some others are with their kids, and of course, about the family business. Also about rainforests, the presidential election, Buds, and Dead tour. Skye is from the same town as Kerry, Don, Izzy and Skip. I never knew this before. And I used to think that Skip and Skye were totally different crowds. Sid is from Missouri and knows a bunch of Corvette's relatives on Harleys. That makes sense, he's a solid guy who looks like he belongs in a biker gang. King Henry is from NYC – he likes his bagels and lox. Corvette busts his ass about yeast popcorn, fake bologna, and other yucky stuff he eats.

Oct 11th   Orlando

Sunday night me, Skye, and Corvette sat around King Henry's girl-talking. Skye was gonna go to Miami with us, then she wasn't, then she was. When we left, she wasn't sure if she'd go to Miami at all.

Kevin has been very nice to us. We got a little stuck. He lent us some money. They're waiting for Murph, and Matteo, in the Alpha Basil bus to arrive.

We left about 9PM. Wide awake drive (for a while) thanks to Corvette's people and the way they choose to pay their debts. Slept in a rest area a few hours this morning, and got to Wet-n-Wild around 2. We figured someone would be there. It was starting to rain, so we weren't gonna go in. We parked and almost right away Corvette points to the top of a waterslide, "Look at that hair! It's Don! and there's Fritz!"

We jump out of the Van and head for the fence, yelling to them as they disappeared down separate slide tubes. We couldn't see where they came out, then Fritz is yelling, "There's Hollie and Corvette!" They came running over to the fence. Fritz, Don, Winnie, Neil. Since it was cloudy, they left the park, and now we're at their hotel.

These guys are pot-less, so they were psyched we had Tennessee Fatties. They expect a package from Humboldt tomorrow.

Later

We went to an Arcade. I haven't played pinball in years. My first game was my best – 2½ million – Free ball, two free credits. What more could anyone want on a Tuesday than to be with friends, havin' fun in Florida? Not to mention a Dead show on the horizon.

October 13th 1988   Miami
Got tix at the box office. Met some guy from Connecticut and got a Hotel on Miami Beach with him, JohnRay, and Briscoe. We have a balcony overlooking the ocean. These are the views I love.

Oct 15th 1988
At a rest stop, 130 miles south of St Pete.

People without dreads anymore include Manny and Poet. The tweakiness felt in New York is not gone yet. Carp bitched at Johnja for Jonsin'. Murph jumped on Wolfboy Taylor for lyin'. There's still people in Jail in Philly – Remy and Chester. Nobody made much $ in Miami.

Saw Allen (the cutie). Abe and Janice. No KindBoy though, or Dante. No Rum Tom. Lars and Kennedy said he flew to California with $4800 – told them it was gone – said someone got jumped. They gave him another $1,000 and that was the last they heard from him. Didn't see Garrett, but Drippy Danny said he was here.

After the show we went to Gypsy Linda and Jeanie's friend Lyle's house to crash. Now us four women are on the road.

We took 41 instead of the highway because I always like those smaller routes. We had a flat about 50 miles back. A bunch of burly Puerto Rican guys stopped and helped us. They could barely speak English. We gave them each a hit. They didn't quite know what LSD was. We mimed putting it on their tongues and not driving!

Monday Oct 17 1988

St Pete shows were good overall. 1st night was a great show. Impossible tix, even with kind buds to trade. Me and Corvette got in on a door pop. The floor fatty scene was huge. Security wasn't sure how to handle us, so they just stood back and watched. After the show we sold black leather roses. They don't sell great, but enough to get by.

We saw Bob and Marie Snodgrass at the Salvador Dali museum. They made it into the newspaper. And in Miami an excellent TV news report showed JohnRay on a skateboard, and a bunch of Tourheads got to say a few good words.

Magoo is our rider. We left town after the show – drove from 2:30 till 4:30ish. Tried to sleep in a Holiday Inn parking lot but got kicked out. Then we got pulled over by a cop in Crystal River, Florida. He asked if I was tired. Checked our IDs (lucky it was that Magoo's ID is also a Connecticut one), and told us to sleep there on the side of the road. We got woken up in the morning by Sid, Roz, and Kevin checking to see if we were broke down and maybe needed help.

We're at Hetti's in Mobile, Alabama with Cash. Hetti let us shower. Now a fatty, then we're outta here!! We'll be in N'Awlins by midnight, Rippin Fatties on Bourbon St. Yahoo!

Inside N'Awlins

Scarlet Fire. Estimated. Hot Hot.

Getting hotter even – WOW!

We were outta hand last night. Saw Kerry hitchin' on the side of the road. Love it. He'd just finished harvesting. We drove around – very stoned like, getting lost – turning around again, and again. Kerry told everyone how I was so stoned I sat staring at a green light, and when he pointed it out to me it was too late – yellow, red again. Yep. Stoned.

"Don't worry about me, no." Go nuts Bob!

Very stoned again. The Killah P-Bud from Colorado is back.

What am I gonna do after tour? – Sell shrooms in Georgia, or go to California? Are we gonna stay for the Rads show here in New Orleans? Or are we actually gonna do the Texas shows?

Last night the moon looked like it was about to spill moon juice all over New Orleans. This morning we got kicked out of the hotel for having kittens. What about them in my wonderings of what to do?

Late night
or early morning. Whichever. I have no idea what I'm doing. Corvette wants to go to Atlanta or Alabama or something.

Bourbon street full o' Deadheads was something to see! Brent was there. I talked to him a bit. We offered to get him stoned but he just wanted a drink. Did a fatty on Bourbon street with Abe, Corvette, Kerry, Don, and Fritz.

Wed Oct 19
N'Awlins = Cajun BBQ shrimp on a balcony overlookin Bourbon St. Corvette decided she doesn't have to go back to Alabama, or Georgia. So I guess we're off toward California.

Now, the big question, – stay for the Rads, or leave for Texas?

Oct 20th   N'Awlins
Last night we did the serious New Orleans seafood meal with Roz, Kevin, Murph, Skye, Izzy, Matteo, Dawn, and Gunner on Toulouse street. What a fun time. Ten of us, fully decked out in our most glorious hippie clothes made quite a spectacle in the fancy tourist restaurant. We know we're on display in a place like that so we do our best to thwart their expectations. Especially with the size of the tip. I had a crab platter and Turtle soup – *Terrapin!*

Looks like me and Corvette are off to Texas today. Show is tonight.

Inside Houston
Someone is throwing dollar bills from the seats above. No one is fazed by the money rain. They arrested 82 people on the way here. A road block pulled over 20 vehicles between New Orleans and Houston, including Ozzy and the bus. (We missed that by leaving today and not on break day.)

Ozzy heard, over their radio, a reminder to keep a lookout for a certain RV. When they got let go, he was able to call that certain RV, and they're doing a quick paint job. They weren't coming to Texas anyway, but a paint job is a good idea. Folks said it was DEA not Cops.

I saw four people taken out of the show in handcuffs. I don't like it here.

Later
Way up on top, here inside, you can see outside through the steps. I got a massage during *China Rider* from Garrett. He's way dosed and wants a ride to Dallas. Begs me to make sure he gets safely out of Houston.

Jerry's playing something I don't recognize but I like it.

Inside Dallas 10-21

Last night was such a fuckup (as it often can be around Garrett).

Garrett put his stuff in the van and went to Drippy Danny's room "for a minute." Hours later we hunted up Danny's room at the Ramada. Garrett wasn't there. We slept in the Ramada parking lot, and I heard this morning that Garrett left on Ozzy's bus minutes after throwing his stuff in my van. Ugh.

Left Houston – quite glad to go. We rolled all our pot into one fatty so if a cop asked, we could say we only have one joint.

We've got a great corner, with a stage view. Security is letting everyone in! Huge fatties everywhere. – All around me – friends and family – Margot, Janice, Amanda, Mojo, four people I don't know (family anyway), Eden and Riley (who almost missed the show cause they thought today was a break day), Downstairs Dave, Davy, Lizette, Willow Bob and Kara (tonight, Willow Bob lights the B-day fatty) Corvette, Abe, three more unknowns, Maryland Sharon, Andre, Icarus, Red Wayne, Shane, Carp, Fritz, Don, happy-happy guitarist, Bradley, Jumpin' Jack, Rosemary, JohnRay, Beatnik Bill.

Some high guy, who couldn't maneuver through our crowd, just plopped down. He's from Memphis, with a grin two miles wide.

A cop by the door across from us looks like he's Lovin it and gettin' a contact high. When other cops walk by 6 goes up and 6 goes down, but we're un-fazed by this guy.

Everyone wants to borrow my pen.

Oct 22nd

The Dallas show was great. Just what we all needed after Houston Hell. We hung out in the lot awhile after the show and I made Garrett get his stuff out of my Van. He never got around to apologizing, but did I expect it? He's going back to California with Ozzy.

Lots of people are flying on a $74 flight special, and everyone who's driving is gonna meet at the Grand Canyon.

Louziana Steve gave Abe a hotel room – we went there last night with Janice, Andre, and his dog Shasta.

Oct 23rd

Sunday morning, rest area

In New Mexico. Made it safely through Texas – again. We went right ahead and stopped at a rest area and smoked our Texas 'one joint' fatty with Fritz and Don, just like in any other state. We saw Ozzy and company at the last rest area in Texas. Got stoned there too. Now we're parked next to Winnie and Neil – they aren't awake yet.

Later –

Old Town Albuquerque. Hacienda Mexican Restaurant. Not great, not bad. It's so beautiful in these parts. It's been so long since I was here, I'd forgotten.

This morning we fattied with Neil and Winnie. They had a guy with them that the Spinners accidently left at the rest area. Ha! The Spinners are Indicans – and obviously Spaceshots.

We saw Bob and Marie on the road just as our pipe broke, so we got a new one.

Monday   Grand Canyon

Dark. A full moon almost. A bunch o' heads at a campground Poet found. It's outside the actual park so it's free. It's made for religious revival groups or something. That's sort of us. Ozzy set up a huge Army-barracks-type tent for people to sleep in.

We're havin' a high time...

Tuesday   Nightime

Watched the full moon rise over the canyon. Breathtaking.

Someone found a fire-watchtower nearby. The view is amazing and it has a phone in it – calls anywhere in the country are free. Everyone is calling friends to say, "Guess where I am?"

Been hanging with Armand. He's a trip. Corvette thinks he looks like a Sumo wrestler. A guy who travels alone on his motorcycle, Not a Deadhead, met some heads in a step van – dosed – ended up here – and is going to California. Diggety is keeping anyone who wants dosed. Emerald is giving out pieces of Abalone. We gave away lots of our junk for sale – layed it all out and gave people whatever they wanted. The kittens are traveling well. They like it here, we've let them wander free.

Right now there's a music circle around the fire jamming *Free Bird*. Ha! There's even an organ and an electric guitar. This guy Norm does a great song he wrote called *Expect a Miracle*. Now Icarus is doing a piccolo solo.

Granny Nancy left with everyone waving goodbye like to a cruise ship. Abe left too. Took Garrett, and left Janice for Ozzy and the bus. Lots of folks still here. I counted about 50. I don't know most of us.

There's pot milk over at the Mars Hotel.

Wednesday

Motel 6 – near Tehachapi, California.

The scene at the pot milk was funny. We learned about fat soluble stuffs. THC being fat. We watched Naz boil pot, and squeeze it through a T-shirt. We also learned the qualities of cheesecloth. And we saw a dancing bear tapestry made from the colors left behind by drying Indica leaf.

We talked extensively about GDU (Grateful Dead University) having just finished the Southern Semester. Geography, Botany, and Agriculture. History, Art, Phys Ed, and Math problems – ie – If Johnny fronts David a pound, and David sells a ¼ of it, then loses the rest, how much does David owe Johnny?

After an hour of pot mushing in milk I went to sleep. I never heard if it was any good or not.

5
Fall 1988
JGB Halloween and Tahoe

Oct 30th 1988
Kaiser

    Only family types here this afternoon. The guys are having a football game –Davy, Vance, Shane, Taylor, Ozzy, Carp, Jumpin' Jack, Johnja – It's fun to watch from a Fatty Circle with Fritz, Don, Amanda, Kelsey, Lizette, Diggety, Rum Tom, and Sid.

    Gunner and them are watching a real football game on TV on the bus.

Nov 3rd

Halloween show was way high, way crowded. I was high. Ozzy hit me with the top of a vial – dammit Ozzy. But I did have fun.

The best costume was Izzy and Trinity as Wilma and Pebbles.

Spending a couple days in the city with Sid. Talking a lot about getting a house with him.

Nov 5 88   Lake Tahoe

Last night, me, Corvette, and Sid got to Tahoe just before the show started at 11:30PM.

Is it the places Jerry has been takin' us or is it us? Things aren't always peachy-keen.

After the show, Corvette slept in the van, and I stayed up late. Win some, lose more. Though I'm stickin' to nickels so I can't lose too much. Jumpin' Jack was up $1800 on Roulette. I tried to convince him to walk away and take me to dinner. "Not yet Doll. I'm not done." Next time I saw him, he'd lost it all. Downstairs Dave was stuck in a Black Jack rut with Drippy Danny. Beau was winnin' large at 4:30AM when I finally left the casino and went to Murph's room to crash.

Amanda was there. We took a walk and she told me I had just missed a pretty bad scene. Some guy named Rosario came in ready to kick Murph's ass over money that's owed. I guess this guy was really drunk, and Amanda said something about a gun. Sometimes I try not to hear the gory details. I don't need to know. But I did need to sleep.

I left as soon as I woke up and bumped into Corvette out on the street. We found Sid and headed for breakfast with him and his friend – some cute guy whose name I didn't catch. Killah buffet. That's the best thing about Nevada towns. Sid left for the city, and we spent most of the day boppin around the casino grounds with Jake and Elwood.

Late night

Outside Murph's room – new hotel tonight – only six blocks away, but in California, not Nevada like the shows.

Nevada has harsh laws. They're arresting under age folk for winning. They took Icarus out of the show for bare feet. Valentino got taken away in cuffs. I think for smoking. Then there's this chick, Layla, who has a small baby. They got her for child neglect. (While she ran inside, they took polaroids of the baby alone in the truck.) And when they came for her, they got her smoking a joint. Granny Nancy is working on getting the baby from the authorities.

Don and Fritz cleared out of their Caesars room when security told them that their room smelled funny, and the DEA was coming. Bummer. Their room was stylin, – it had a big round tub in the middle of the room. The hotels have Gambler proof windows – they don't open, so if you lose all your money, you can't kill yourself.

I kicked around gamblin with Murph awhile. He blew off both tonight's shows. $27 for each show, and each was only one set.

I got a floor seat ticket for the first show. Beau, Gimlet, and Theo were down there too. Then Hawkeye gave me a purple door stub ½ way through the 2nd show.

They've been treating us pretty badly here. As if, because of how we dress, we're not spending as much money as everyone else.

I'm tired as all hell. Didn't sleep much. Woke up to Clarity whining "ot tub, ot tub." How many toddlers have tantrums about hot tubs?

Haven't seen Ozzy. Heard he came to Tahoe but stuck to the hills. Supposedly at Spacecar Bob's house. Karl, Silas, and Dante were here, but they mostly stayed outta sight. Abe is all happy these days with Jackie. That's good to see. Jackie won 1000 nickels on a slot machine. We won enough money for a decent meal on the $1 slots with Dante, and again later with Kerry. We'd pick the machine, and wait. Then, – "You. Cute Boy. Come pull this handle."

People inside the room, before I came out here, were bitchin' about Jumpin' Jack and money. King Henry has something to do with the money Murph owes, and he might want Corvette to do him a favor when she goes back to Georgia. Everyone's broke, yet everyone (it seems) gambled right down to their last nickel. The chick who's been spare changing on Haight to get her boyfriend Maple out of jail, was there plugging quarters into a machine.

Sunday – the 6th

What a day. We're in the parking lot of a store in South Lake Tahoe. Been stuck here since 3 o'clock.

Woke up in Lyndelle's hotel room, next door to Murph's, with JohnRay, Matan and Japhy (the dog) on the other side. Lyndelle, Maria Malloy, Abe, and Beau left for SF pretty early. Me and Corvette went to Harrah's for breakfast with Murph and Gunner.

Starts off like a good day huh?

We saw Dante, Silas, and Karl in front of this store here, so we stopped to chat. As we all got ready to leave, the Van wouldn't start.

(Ozzy just got here but I wanna tell this whole story – this is too crazy to forget.)

A carful of guys stopped to go to the store. One happened to be a mechanic. – Reggie came over to see what was going on. A chick on the pay phone wandered over, said her old man was a mechanic, and went and got him from their car.

Silas was cutting it close for getting to class on time in Colorado on Monday. He gave us 20 bucks, big hugs and left.

Kathy and Gil (the chick on the phone and her old man) and Reggie stayed to help. They decided it was the fuel filter. It took a bit to get the right tools and the right size filter. Then Gil (time tells us now), forced it, and stripped the inside of the carb. It leaked – everyone thought it was the gasket.

About then a hippie bus pulled up. One I've never seen before. Hanz, on the bus, was a plumber. We bought plumbers tape and he tried to stop the leak that way. No luck.

Three hours later Gil and Kathy left. Reggie had left too. Hanz kept working on it – nothing helped. (I just lost my toothbrush to thread cleaning.)

Reggie came back with a $10 carb he got somewhere. He was with his brother who was really drunk. So much shit, two carbs, lots of opinions. Also some drunk local chick pulled up and wanted to buy pot. She didn't believe we didn't have any. She was loud, and annoying, and I wasn't in the best mood.

Reggie's brother went inside, stole a bottle of Vodka, went in the bathroom, chugged it, and got busted. Reggie let them take him away. Said he wasn't about to let his asshole brother get him in trouble. Reggie's on Probation for burglary. He doesn't drink or do drugs, but he stole something from the store every time he went in. One time we brought the carb in with us to use tools we couldn't buy.

The hippie bus was still waiting with us. They didn't want to abandon us. The store managers couldn't wait till we'd all be gone. A local drove by and said it was gonna snow tonight. Another drove by and asked why we didn't "just take it to a shop to get it fixed?" We told him we had no money. He looked at our Connecticut license plate and asked why we'd "go on a trip so far from home, with no money?"

Corvette told him, "It's better than staying home with no money."

Finally, between Hanz and Reggie the $10 carb worked! Van started! Then sputtered and died again. I was ready to cry.

With nothing else to do we called Ozzy. (Some guy on the hippie bus had Spacecar Bob's number.) The hippie bus left because the store manager was getting increasingly agitated. I told them it was okay, Ozzy was on the way.

So now Ozzy almost has my original carb back on. Cross-threaded I think, but who cares, I just want out of this fucking parking lot. The cops have been by twice since arresting Reggie's brother to make sure we're working on it and not sleeping. Van, Please. Let's get up the mountain.

Ozzy's complaining that he's broke because Murph didn't stop by to see him.

I wish I had money. It's freezing. I'm tired. It must be 10PM.

Corvette just said, "I wanna go home but I don't have one."

It's got its original carb on again but it still won't start. Ozzy is telling me I have to leave it.

Monday

Me, Corvette, and Helena slept on the bus. Ozzy stayed in the house. We were girl-talking and getting high all night. We had lots of blankets, and the kittens, so we were warm and cozy.

This morning we walked to a pay phone. There's Cake on the wire! So we hitched back to town. Up there it looked like snow, down here it's sunny. We got a quick ride from these two burly men with a six-pack and a big kitchen knife on the front seat between them. They brought us almost all the way. Then, right where they dropped us off, a VW van was going by. They were already past as we got out of the car, but we waved frantically, knowing they were our ride. They backed up for us.

Rumi, Wade, and Azado. The van was full of band equipment. We had to contort to fit in with the amps and stuff. We helped them drop off the equipment, then, on the way to my van, Rumi ran out of gas. We all had to get out and push it a ½ mile to a gas station. While doing so, the radio was on loud and a Beatles tune came on, asking us how it felt to be one the the beautiful people. We sang as we pushed. It feels great, it really really does.

Wade's a mechanic. Psyched.

later

We're alive again and sitting at Rumi's place. He manages his parent's Hotel here in Tahoe. We're in the living room, the front office is behind me.

Wade really helped us out. He did all kinds of stuff for the Van and it's running great.

We drove up the mountain to get Jake and Elwood, then came back to hang with these guys. Rumi gave us a free room and waited dinner for us, – veggie omelets and wine. Later we played kick ball, in the living room, in the dark.

Tuesday Nov 8th

We stopped at Spacecar Bob's house to say bye. Owen and Danya want to follow us down the mountain because it's snowing and they have no windshield wipers. We're waiting for them to get ready. Ozzy says he's taking Spacecar Bob to New Mexico. Helena doesn't want to go to New Mexico. Helena wants to go to Santa Cruz with Owen and Danya. They're screaming on the porch.

I just want to get off the mountain and on the road.

6
Fall 1988
In and Around the Haight

Nov 11 1988

Bush won the election. How will this affect our lives? It will definitely affect the people with drug charges and court dates coming up. Will it affect our travels from state to state? Our poor environment. The rainforests. The redwoods. The water and the air. And Star Wars. Yikes.

Aside from that, we had a relaxing couple days in Cotati. Especially after the nerve-wracking gas-leaking ride from Tahoe. Got the van worked on again, but, it still leaks.

We left Cotati early and drove to SF. We woke up Erik the Rude and he came with us to Santa Cruz. Did the Mall Crawl awhile and tried to get in to see Mickey's Monks at the Civic Auditorium but no luck so we'll try tomorrow in Berkeley.

Cannoli Ron has a room opening up in his house in Corralitos. Maybe we'll move down there. We've been looking at houses in Cotati. Found a beautiful one with a hot tub but it costs way too much.

I asked Garrett if he could help me do something about the van. He said he would, tomorrow. He's got a real job now – as a bike messenger. And he's living in Deja Dan's bus. We were making out a bit in Tanner's empty room.

Garrett still interests me but I don't take him seriously. He's got a good heart I suspect, but he hasn't much consideration for others. I like him, but I don't need the head problems. Too often he makes me feel like I don't matter. And like I need to protect myself from the wild world of Garrett.

Nov 13   Fulton St.

Morning at Erik the Rude's. (Erik's because no one else is here.)

Yesterday I went down to the bus where Garrett is living. Hung out while he cleaned, then we headed for the Haight and got into some ridiculous fight about head trips.

We bumped into Murph, who gave me a bud, and I headed for Fulton St. I figured Garrett would stay on the Haight, but he followed me up the hill. While he showered, me, Corvette, and Amanda went to the panhandle. Lots of people there. Sid, Downstairs Dave, Mojo, Vance, Denise, and Clarity, and a man in a Ford reading a newspaper that we all kept our eye on.

Back on the Haight, we ate cheese sandwiches out on the street. Jumpin' Jack said a bunch o' people were at the Full Moon. There we found Carp, Davy, Benny, and Andre. We all went to smoke a fatty on the panhandle with Bradley and Margot.

Haight was alive! Matan, JohnRay and Briscoe. Kennedy too. He was all pissed off because Rum Tom disappeared again with $1100. He got belligerent with some guy. They got in a fight and Kennedy got taken away. He was back within the hour.

We're a part of the Haight Street scene in the late 80's whether we want to be or not.

But I guess I want to be.

A guy on the Haight today wearing a shirt and tie, lookin like a young exec from the waist up, but he had on an Indian print skirt and sneakers.

Back in the bar Jumpin' Jack says 'roll a fatty Doll' and hands me a bag. I went in the bathroom and did. We went across the street to this guy's house. He's from Boston, been in California one week – in his apartment, six hours – and he knows Jack already.

We wanted to see Merle Saunders and Barry Melton at the Full Moon but when we went back, Carp wasn't being allowed in because he has a big mouth. Somethin' went down and I wasn't bummed we missed it. Lyndelle and Icarus weren't allowed in either for some reason, so we hung on the streets all night.

Garrett asked me to go back to the bus with him. I think I was gonna. After hanging out a while more Garrett said, "Wanna go?" I said I wanted to find a bathroom first. This other chick wanted to find a bathroom too, so me, her, and Garrett went to a bar down the block. When we got back out on the street, Garrett ignored me and left with her. I'm probably better off.

It's past noon. I gotta get my shit together. Erik doesn't want us here tonight, and we don't want to be here either.

Van isn't any different – still leaks. Garrett can't (or won't) help.

Late night   Abe's place

On the Haight this morning we spent the last of our money on Muffins (always from Muffin Classics), coffee, and hot chocolate. Garrett was spare-changing. We're broke so we started spare-changing with him, and as his competition. It was fun – we made it fun. We got enough to eat a Chabela's Burrito and get kitten food.

Seca just spilled bong water on this. I'm going to sleep.

Nov 14 1988

Did the shuffle today. Sad scene. Everyone lovin life – but hating the Haight. There were the nowadays usuals, Carp and Jack, Davy and Della, and Matan, JohnRay, Ori, and Briscoe. Riff Raff was there. Kennedy and Suzy too. In the 60s, the happenin' corner may have been Haight-Ashbury, but in the late 80s it's definitely Haight-Schrader.

We bought a cheap bag o' kind buds from Matan, grabbed some beer, and went over to the horseshoe tournament grounds in the park. Jake and Elwood did fine off-leash. They stayed near us all afternoon, and even followed us as we left.

Back on the Haight these two shady guys want something. Japhy doesn't like them – he's barking and wants to bite. Riff Raff goes down the road to deal with them. Not a good move. Briscoe follows "just to see." Me and Corvette walked away a block or so, then came back. Briscoe has a broken, bloody nose, Riff Raff is unhurt. What the fuck? JohnRay and Matan took Briscoe to a hospital. Riff Raff you're a dumb fuck sometimes.

He calls himself Riff Raff, like when you tell him he's a dumb fuck, he says, "Riff Raff is not a dumb fuck."

Friday the 18th I think

At Cannoli Ron's in the mountains southeast of Santa Cruz. A week of rainy foggy gray days on Haight was more than enough.

This place is gorgeous. Redwoods everywhere. It's on a private road, with a locked gate, then a steep muddy driveway down to a yard full of old VWs and rusty TVs.

Sunday Nov 20 88

Still at Ron's. Cleaning day; spider webs from the corners, ashes outta the fireplace, did the dishes and cabinets. I even vacuumed. We got hundreds of beer bottles out of the house.

After running errands Friday, we went to the Mall. The hotdog girl, took Armand home the night before. Lucky, because they ticketed everyone who was camping at Greyhound Rock that night.

We bumped into Fritz. "Meet us at the Acapulco Lounge."

Don's just back from Leggett. We found somewhere to do a fatty, then headed to the Civic Auditorium for Israel Vibration. Fritz and Don bought cheap tix, Corvette and Ron got free ones pretty easily. It took a while for mine. Once we got in it was Fatties and fun.

We were gonna put everyone in Ron's car and go back to his house, but Zia offered those guys a ride to Becky's in Aptos, so we split up.

Night time

Came up to Haight. Saw Garrett cruise by on the panhandle while we were double parked on Schrader. Took a few seconds to shake people off the mirrors and we didn't catch him. Drove up to Fulton St. A note on the door said, "No one is home so don't ring the fucking bell." Right Erik. Fuck you. –

Cruised the Econo. Hung in JohnRay's room with him, Matan, Trevor, Briscoe, Dante, Wolfboy Taylor, Davy, and Janice. Crashing in Carp's room

Nov 21st

This morning, at I-Hop with Marshal, Matan, Ori, and Fritz, everyone was throwing lemons at Fritz.

Now we're in the Continental hotel in Santa Cruz with Trevor and Fritz. We're smoking from Trevor's old bamboo bong. Trevor's on the phone saying "tell Della to get a job."

a bit later

Skye went to court again in New Orleans and the prosecuting attorney moved that three of the four Federal charges be dropped. He told Skye he went to the show when the Dead was in New Orleans and had fun. She asked if he, "felt the spirit of it all," and he said, "Yes." This is the story through Don and Fritz.

More news – Supposedly Helena left Ozzy and he got snowed in and crunched the back of the bus against a tree. Poor Ozzy. I mean that very seriously, and I also mean this. Yeah Helena!

Fritz is on the phone with JohnRay – bad news. Kennedy and Lars were talkin' too loud on the Haight. They got searched by the DEA. Lars got taken away.

I want a place to call home.

Garrett said, "I can't figure out why you don't come live in the bus with me, I'd love the company."

"Because you like the lowest of the street scene and I prefer a middle class level."

Nov 22nd   Santa Cruz

With Don, Fritz, and Trevor. These guys are raging and rolling in the cash. They looked at a house in Boulder Creek, talked to the lady tonight, and can pay for it tomorrow. They're psyched.

Today was a slow day. Went to Zack's for breakfast. Don walked in as we finished eating and we cheered and applauded. I like Zack's – great atmosphere, fantastic food. We walked to the hill path and smoked a fatty, then me and Corvette went to the library. It was rainy, so it was nice to be inside.

Later we met everyone at the Acapulco for a few drinks. Fritz got paranoid and wanted to jump on a bus to Becky's. He wanted Trevor to go with him, but Trevor had ordered dinner for himself and Corvette. "No Fritz. I just ordered food and I don't know Becky."

Fritz got all flustered and looked at Corvette and stammered, "It's… it's all your fault."

These guys seem to be short on what they need to move in. Everyone has outstanding debts – us too. I hate that. Don says he even owes his mom for the Jerry Tahoe tix.

On tour or off, life consists of spending money, needing money, and trying to get money. Not much different than life without the Dead. I could never go back to a factory life in Connecticut, doing coke to make your shit life better. Spending all your money on that nasty habit. Yuk.

Happy Thanxgiving

Cannoli Ron's, Pink Floyd, and a houseful o' hippies.

I don't think there's any pot here, and I'm not in a Thanxgiving mood. Corvette is sick and sleeping in the van, and I take too much for granted.

Yesterday, heading north, we stopped at the Pacifica pet Hospital for the kitty shot clinic, so that was good. On the Haight we found Garrett and Sid. Went with them to Oakland where Sid was working. Waited for things to dry, then went back to SF and got a room at the Econo. I curled up with Garrett on the floor.

This morning, on the van – there's a note from Jumpin' Jack to come to his room asap.

Shit! Carp's busted! Four grams of LSD.

~~~~~~~

Garrett decided he'd go south with us for dinner here. Just past Haight, on the way to the ocean to head south, Garrett said, "I

Love you, but I'm outta here," and jumped out of the van while I was stopped at a light. What the fuck? I heard *Jammin Me* by Tom Petty as I drove. That's how I feel – Jammed. Dealing with Garrett is stormy.

later

Wow, in walked a fatty with a bunch of people from the kitchen. Another fat one appears too. 25-30 people here. I only got one hit. I want to get high high high.

Armand keeps making faces at me from across the room, making me smile.

There's lots of things I'm Thankful for. I'm thankful for having a place to be today. I'm thankful for my sight, my hearing, my arms, my legs, my life, and my Van. I'm Thankful for the flowers we smoke so much of. I'm Thankful for my parents and my friends. I'm thankful to be American where this life is possible. (And I pray, it will continue to be possible in this next four year republican stretch.)

I miss Garrett. I wish he was here.

Saturday 26th

Thursday we left Cannoli Ron's house because Trevor invited us to sleep at their place, and there were too many people at Ron's anyway. We followed Trevor's directions – he said – keep left. We did. Trevor thought it was a circle road. It wasn't. We ended up at a dead-end on a mountain-top. Turned around, and got stuck in the mud. While trying to maneuver out, the back tire on the driver's side went flat. It was late, and the van kept moving closer and closer to a drop off. I finally threw it in park and slept.

In the morning, Thankfully, Corvette felt better. The guy in the closest house pulled us out of the mud, but we couldn't move because of the flat. His wife gave us a ride to Boulder Creek with the spare (unfixed from our Florida flat tire). They couldn't fix it because it was split. We had to hitchhike with it all the way to Santa Cruz to get a new tire.

Hitching back, Scot, a hippie in an old VW bug, brought us right to the van. He helped us jack it up, and get the lug nuts off. But the tire wouldn't budge. The neighbor guy had a propane torch to help with the tire, and they finally get the tire off and replaced.

It was dark by then so we just went to Don's, smoked a bunch of leaf fatties, and crashed in front of the fire. (Trevor and Fritz are in LA.) This house is really cute. A small A frame with redwoods all around. Two porches, two lofts, kitchen, LR and bathroom. The woodstove keeps things pretty warm.

Late Night   SF

At Beau's with Amanda, Andre, and Lyndelle. They're watching *Willow* on video. Garrett popped in and didn't even look at me – went straight to Beau's room. He left, without saying a thing to anyone. I understand completely that he was in the middle of business, but he could have at least said something to me. It's that Tom Petty tune again – You can walk away, babe, but that does not mean it's over.

This morning we dropped Don off on the mall, grabbed some pizza, and headed north. Beautiful sunny day in both Santa Cruz and San Francisco. Parked on Fulton St. – no Beau, so we did the shuffle. Saw Benny in the Laundromat. Janice came in to say hi, some hippies doing laundry came in. Noodle appeared with his guitar. Della stopped in with her dog, and before ya know it we had a regular old party going on.

Lars is outta jail. But alas, not Carp. Poor Carp. Margot went to see him. Della is going tomorrow. She told me Carp's real name in the strictest of confidence – it's Carol. Ha.

Wondering what the fuck is it gonna take to get Carp out of Jail? They haven't set bail yet. They might not. It's hard to think about. I don't even know what to write.

Nov 27th 1988
Fulton St.

Dante's bummin', he got stopped for a traffic violation and they may have hooked him to the extra bag, with the drugs, in KindBoy's van in Irvine last April. Yikes. He also told us that KindBoy gets sentenced today for that mess.

Dec 2nd 1988

Cotati. We come here to hibernate.

The other night we saw Zero at the closing of the Cabaret. I bumped into Skinny Jim. He gave me the address of his store in Guerneville. The store is nice, but small. He also told me how to get to Freddy and Piper's.

The mailman came – no letter. But our few days of rest are over, we've got places to be.

Dec 3 1988
Morning, Oakland

At Gimlet's warehouse with Corvette and Amanda. The show was fun last night. The Orpheum is on Market and 8th. I could see my van from inside. Hanging in the comfy lounges, doing mega-fatties. I loved Bobby's acoustic version of *Throwing Stones*.

Carp's bail is one million dollars. Mojo is in jail for pot in Barbados. KindBoy is serving time in Irvine, but he gets out before Xmas.

Seems the LA Jerry shows were fun and I haven't heard of anyone going down. So that's cool.

Something to remember from yesterday – when we pulled into the lot Fritz and Don saw us and ran away – exaggerated and cartoonish – even jumped over a fence.

Night   SF

Ozzy was at the Orpheum tonight. His bus is dented, and without a few lights, but it's not too bad. Pandora was walking around with "hang in there" cards for Carp and for Bradley in jail.

There was no getting away from the fatties – huge ones. A Fed sat by the women's room and watched us in our Fatty Circle. What could he do though?

Right now I'm sitting on the fire escape outside Abe, Jackie, Andy and Chloe's new apartment on Willard North.

Sunday Dec 4th

Listening to Joni Mitchell. Everyone's awake. Double bongs.

Karl and Jackie are off to get Bagels and try Bass for tix for tonight's Bridge School Benefit show in Oakland. $27.50 each. Bianca is drawing buds for us for the t-shirts we want to make. Her buds look psychedelic. She didn't get in to either Jerry show at the Orpheum. I hope she gets in tonight.

Dec 5

Yesterday was outta hand. We got up early so we could do something. Yeah we did something alright, we did bongs until 2:30, then smoked a fatty and left for the show in Oakland. Gates closed till 5:30. So we parked the van there in line and went cruisin. Got back after eating at Denny's with Benny and Anjalee – everyone was driving around the van. Oh well.

We came in on Neil Young doing *Sugar Mountain*. After him, Nils Lofgren played – he was rockin – really fun. Next was Billy Idol. He was lovin it, said how this was the closest he'll ever get to warming up the Dead, and thanked people for listening. I like that. He was actually good.

At the Fatty Zone in the hall, Becky had a huge blow-up heart and we played volleyLove. "Hit Jack in the head!" Fritz was shouting between cackles. Some guys stood outside our family circle waiting for chances to spike the heart into the middle of us.

During Bob Dylan we fattied inside, on the stairs, with Karl. I looked over a section and watched Taylor and Davy dancin. After Dylan it was Bob and Jerry and a stand-up bass (probably Kahn but I couldn't tell). They played *Wang Dang Doodle, Friend o' the Devil, Throwing Stones* and *Ripple*. Excellent, and way hot.

Next – Tom Petty and the Heartbreakers – acoustic – wild pedal steel guitar. Then Tracy Chapman. All alone on stage with her guitar. Really moving. After a break, was CSNY. They ended with a sing-a-long *Teach Your Children*.

Afterwards – outside, walkin' around with Jumpin' Jack, I said, "Jack buy us a beer."

"No money Doll." Then he turned around, real smooth like, and said to the first guy he saw, "Yo, cuz, buy me and the Doll a beer."

And the guy said, "Hey Jack, how ya been? Sure, I'll buy you beer."

Another time I was talkin' to Big Brian (the guy who stays with Camera Aaron in Cotati) and Jumpin' Jack walked up. They knew each other. Small world. Either that or everyone knows Jack.

Della said Carp was bummed we didn't come to visit yet. I miss him, I want to see him. I don't really want to deal with a jail though.

7
December 1988
Long Beach through New Year's

                Dec 8th   Long Beach

A nice low-key hotel with Camera Aaron. – There's a Metallica Monsters of Rock concert tonight at the Arena, but supposedly we have a lot out there somewhere.

                Later

Cruised the scene with Cute Allen. Saw Two Toke Tom, Ozzy, Boots, Sid, John (without Murph), and heard rumours of King Henry. Fritz is outta hand – "Monsters of the Lot." Ragin through the heavy metal lots. – Movin fast on his skateboard. Now you see him, now you don't. Crazy.

~~~~~

I went down to room 22 for balloons and a fat one. They're going back to the lot. Not me. I'm kickin back and gonna get some real sleep.

Oh! Big news I forgot to write – Carp is out, but he won't be here. There are two stories, #1 says one of Carp's and Jack's brothers put his house up for bail. #2 says Carp only had 50 hits and someone else was holding everything else, meaning the charges are not as bad as people thought.

                Dec 9   Long Beach

Riff Raff is supplying the Nitrous – wing-wing-wing-wing-wing-wing. Paranoia talk. Not really paranoia, just realistic. DEA taking our pictures? Probably. Riff Raff says he's a flaming lesbian trapped in a man's body. Don says – "Riff Raff's the type of person you feel many veiled about." Everybody has layers, some are just more visible.

After the show

You can tell we're in LA. During the hottest part of *Estimated* some drunk dude was screaming, "isn't this fucking great?" I've never really liked LA. Though tonight's show was fun. Tight, great song choices.

Bob and Marie Snodgrass, and their daughter Ginny, are here. As soon as we saw 'em I traded in my blackened bowl for a new one to resinate. He likes when I give back a used one so he can show off the way the colors change. The Spinners are back from India. They're glowing. Good to have 'em back. I guess. Mojo is out of Barbados jail. They gave him a horrible haircut and sent him back to the US. Sid was way dosed. By accident I think. King Henry has been lovin the sushi for sale in the lot. Yikes! Raw fish is bad enough, but raw fish from a Dead lot?

I was hanging with Jumpin' Jack. He had me rollin' fatties all 1st set. He said, "Here Doll, wear this." It's a beautiful beaded agate slab with a quartz point.

Corvette's headed to a Jägermeister party at the Hyatt. Do I wanna go? No thanks. I'm in no mood for crazed LA partying.

Dec 10

I told Corvette to send someone cute back to the room. This morning I couldn't figure out who was on the floor. It's Dimitri. He's going to Australia for Xmas, but he'll be back for New Years.

Aaron has the tape from last night. It's the kind of show you go on tour hoping to see. Could tonight be as good? We always hope.

Rumours abound that Brent wants to leave the band. Maybe he gets all drunk and blubbery thinking, "Deadheads don't like me." But I think he's staying.

Noodle just came in to grab a shower.

Late night.

The show was good, but not as hot as last night.

I wasn't in the lot five minutes when Jack appeared – "Merry Xmas Doll," – and gave me a gorgeous necklace. (I thought the one yesterday was nice, this one's even better!) It looks like a butterfly – looped purple and white beads, with hematites interspersed. It's the most beautiful thing anyone has ever given me. I was blown away. He told Corvette to wear the agate one till he figures out who it belongs to.

Inside, the Fatty Zone was huge and many flowered. Seriously unstopping Fat joints. Fatty Zones have turned football like. Forward laterals, and interceptions. Today two strangers got in the circle, one of our chicks reached in for the intercept.

Everyone cheered and someone nominated her for MVP. Fritz and Taylor were going for touchdowns. Taylor and Davy are a way-cute twosome, but they jones. Not often (I think), but they do jones. That cuts the cute factor.

Everyone was bustin my ass that me and Jack have a "thing." Skip is amazed Jack lets me disappear with his pot. I haven't forgotten what Janey told me, but I like Jack. How could I not? Many veiled for sure.

Dec 11

I happened to be there to see Murph pay off his debts, somewhat, to Rosario. Good deal. (Did I ever even mention that weirdness? When Amanda told me that story, in Tahoe, about Rosario making a scene in Murph's room? How next morning I went to breakfast with Sid and a guy I didn't know? – that was Rosario! Yikes!)

I've been selling photos for Aaron. Tix were expensive last night but I traded three pictures for one. Not selling so well today.

Dec 12 1988

Driving out of LA on 405. Smoggy, brown yuk-clouds.

Last show was fun. But, the first night was the one.

During the fatty session JohnRay told us Matan is in jail. Bail $5000, so we need $500. People started kickin. I helped collect the cake. Hanz also got arrested so when we passed $500, the rest went to Hanz. Five minutes and both of them were covered.

As Skye says – We're getting good at this game. We know what we have to do, and we just do it. Help out the team members. The fact that, with all this bullshit, we're still Lovin Life and havin fun, is what makes it game-like. We were so large a crowd last night, I'm willing to bet more than one someone was taking our pictures from across the Arena. Telephoto lens.

Without Carp around, everyone intercepts fatties. They go as they will, with no director. Carp used to put a bud in every joint so he could direct where it went.

I came upon Rosemary, Skye, and Corvette with a garbage bag full of popcorn. "We're trying to decide if we should dump this on Fritz."

"I'll help!"

When Fritz looked up, he saw only me and threw a soda on me. It was cause for much laughter, wrestling, and a chase scene. But really it was a sticky mess.

later

Driving up Route 1. The sun is even with the car on the horizon. What a great video it would make as the car's silhouette jumps back through a ravine, then slides to the bushes in the foreground. It looks like bad trippy animation as it distorts and bends with the landscape.

Dec 16

Told Leo I need the $60 he owes me. Corvette is leaving Sunday and I'll be broke. We owe Beau $225 and only have $60 of it.

Dave Gooden and Jim Avery in Cotati, have been helping us out quite a bit when we need to make money. Also Randy's roommate Perry. We visited them all yesterday. Jim brought us to smoke a joint with his mom. She was amazed to hear that we follow the Dead. Said, "I used to see them in the 60s, but after Pigpen died, I never saw them again. Why bother? He was the heart of that band."

We're headed for the city to see the Vicious Hippies at the Full Moon.

late night

No sign of Jumpin' Jack or Carp. Fritz said Carp was at the Pall Mall the past few nights, but we didn't see him there. What a sleaze bar. Fritz insisted, "It's a great place. Owsley's original hangout."

Bumped into Beau and heard very bad news. JP went down in Oakland on Tuesday. One million dollars worth of LSD. Arrested as Lee S. Diamond. (More in a bit.)

On the panhandle we saw an RV that looked familiar, although a different color. We knocked.

"Well shit, it's a regular party, come on in."

Hadn't seen Roz or Kevin since N'Awlins. It was with them we saw the article with bold headline, "Speeding chase leads to biggest LSD bust in Northern California." JP thought he was being followed so he speeded up – it <u>was</u> cops. They pull him over and notice the bag o' pot in his pocket – flashlight to the back seat, another bag. Search the car. The trunk full of mushrooms, coke, and mega doses. He's been a fugitive for years. (I didn't know.) Yikes.

If I were traveling with lots o' stuff, I wouldn't have pot laying around the back seat – that's for damn sure. Sounds dumb all around. You would think people would be smarter after decades in the business. Was he being followed? Or did paranoia lead to this? I'm sure this will affect the family business. There's such a demand all over the country. And with President Bush, I'm afraid the worst is yet to come.

Speeding cars lead cops to cache of LSD

By Harry Harris
The Tribune

What appeared to be a freeway drag race ended yesterday with Oakland police making their largest seizure ever of LSD — dosage units and powder worth at least $1 million, investigators said.

Police said it was one of the largest LSD seizures ever in Northern California.

The LSD was found in a foot locker in the trunk of a car driven by a Chicago man police believe intended to sell the drug at an upcoming Grateful Dead concert.

Also found in the car were quantities of marijuana, cocaine, and psilocybin, commonly known as psychedelic mushrooms and peyote, police said.

The drugs were found after Officer Charlie Jones saw two cars speeding in the southbound lanes of Interstate 880 with one of the vehicles trying to catch up with the other.

Jones was able to stop one of the cars, a 1985 BMW driven by a man later identified as Lee S. Diamond, 43, of Chicago, near 16th Avenue.

As Diamond was reaching into his back pants pocket for his wallet, the coat he was wearing opened and Jones said he could see a "baggy" of marijuana in Diamond's shirt pocket.

Jones said he could also see another bag of marijuana in the back seat and arrested Diamond.

A subsequent search of the trunk turned up more marijuana in a cardboard box and the footlocker, which police said contained the LSD and other drugs.

Police said there were more than 100,000 manufactured dosage units of LSD and enough of the drug in powder and pill form to make an additional 900,000 dosage units.

Police placed the value of the LSD at $1 million and the other drugs at several thousand dollars.

Diamond, who declined to give a statement to police, was booked for investigation of possession of dangerous drugs, cocaine and marijuana.

On a request from the Alameda County District Attorney's Office Major Narcotics Vendor Program, Diamond's bail was set at $500,000 by Oakland Municipal Court Judge Courtland Arne.

We smoked a fatty and Roz came to the Full Moon with us. They still wanted $6.50 cover, even though it was almost midnight. Us three talked the door guy into letting us in for the price of two, just as Deja Dan, and Ozzy showed up. They let us in 5 for 3. Full Moon isn't usually so cool. The Vicious Hippies were great. The guitarist is quick.

Now we're at Beau's doing bonghits and watching Fred (the cat) freak out about Jake and Elwood. Seems Fred might be pregnant again. And it seems Jake is a girl...

      Dec 18   Boulder Creek

At Don, Fritz, and Trevor's. Santa's cookin' spaghetti. We made a pretty bowl of colored condoms, with a bow, to put under their xmas tree. (Thank you Planned Parenthood.)

Yesterday we checked out the Telegraph Fair then went to Berkeley Community Theater to see Steve Miller. I got a free ticket from Dante. Corvette traded for hers. Beau got one in the 3rd row for smokin' a joint with the guy inside.

Got stoned with two older ladies. They told me and Corvette we should go to a Grateful Dead concert someday. Ha.

Fattys during break out on the balconies with Two Toke Tom, Downstairs Dave, Riff Raff, and lots of Spinoffs.

After the show we took Dante and joined Lyndelle and Fritz at Chi Chi to see Martin Fierro's band. Judy Blue was there, and Andre and Mitzi. We had a blast, got stoned in the men's bathroom – that was a first – and stayed till they kicked us out. Afterwards we went to Lyndelle's.

Woke up next to Fritz. Blanket fighting to start the day. He told me about the new girl he's crushing on – Mavis.

Out of Lyndelle's by 11:00 so she could get Mitzi to the airport.

We keep hearing that Carp's around but we don't see him.

No one on Haight, no one in Santa Cruz either – where is everyone?

Fritz rode to Santa Cruz with us. We got pulled over in Felton, by a female cop, because of the peace sign on my front license plate. (In Connecticut you only have to have a back plate.) Fritz asked her, "Why do you always pull over vans with hippies and stickers?"

I snapped, "Fritz, shut your face."

She looked at me with raised eyebrows and ignored him, thank god. Time to reinforce the SEP field. She gave us a fix-it ticket for our bald tire and let us go.

Me and Fritz have been at it all day. One time that I said, "Fuck You Fritz," he goes, "You shouldn't say fuck you to your closest friends."

And Corvette says, "Whoa! You consider her one of your closest friends?!?"

And he goes, "Well, yeah. We're always hanging together. She must be."

Late night –

After dinner we gave Fritz a ride to the pay phone in Boulder Creek. We bought Kahlua and headed back to the house. Santa, Don, and Trevor were going off – jumping on each other, jumping off the lofts, wrestling. We brought the kittens in, – said we'd get them out before Fritter got home.

Bonghits and Bullshitting. Time drifts by. The door slides open. Don coughed, "Kittens."

Everyone got quiet. Fritz stepped in slowly, and looked at us all one by one. We waited. Somebody snickered. Santa said, "Relax," and handed Fritz the bong. As Fritz was doin his bong he looked at me, the kittens, then Don, and raised one eyebrow, but he said nothing.

Now we're back at Beau's. As we parked, this whole crowd was piling out the gate headed for a bar called The Armadillo. A blond man, in a hat and trench coat crossed the street and watched. How closely is this place watched? What do they think goes on here? It's just a hippie crash pad where people come and go. Nothing happens here except minor bud deals.

Two different rumours regarding Matan. #1 – he's out and so is everyone who got arrested in Long Beach. #2 – $500 wasn't enough, and he's stuck there, and JohnRay and Ori are staying in LA to be near him. Which is true?

Judy Blue says she wants to tour but is afraid to. She doesn't want to endanger anyone by being seen with them. She thinks the reason Skye and Murph aren't in jail is because the DEA gets more out of 'em by watching who they associate with.

Beau didn't score any buds so I've got to figure out where I can get some to sell, otherwise I'll be potless on Xmas.

Dec 19   SF

Corvette's lucky she left this morning. It's cold and pouring. I want to head back to Cotati, but I want to have pot. I thought I'd cruise Haight before I left, but the rain.

Erik the Rude is gone for Xmas. At least I don't have to listen to him. I should head out, but I'm waiting for Beau to wake up so I can ask him to sell me a bud.

Watching cartoon Xmas specials that I'm not following, and listening to the pacing of the speedfreaks upstairs. The kittens ripped apart yesterday's paper and are now sleeping on it. I'm hungry.

24th

Leo finally sent $ on the onion. He sent $40 extra for an express-mailed 1/8, so I went and visited Piper. Gooney Bird bit me on the cheek as soon as I walked in. Thanx Goon. Freddy wasn't around. There are three Xmas trees in the house. "Because Freddy wanted a huge spruce that barely fits in the room, and I wanted a medium sized pine so I can reach the top of it. We couldn't compromise."

"And the small one?"

"We figured if we each had our own tree, Jillian should have one too."

Dec 27th

On Xmas I called the Santa Rosa radio station for a request. Told the DJ I was alone on xmas. He said, "come on down, I'll make you a tape." I went. He was the program director and I probably have a job there in January, if I want.

Next morning I picked up Corvette at the airport. We thought Beau was coming in at noon so we waited with a rainbow welcome banner. No Beau. But Kerry stepped off that plane. Yahoo! Picking up Kerry is like hitting the jackpot.

We're at the Sixpence in Oakland – in a room with Jumpin' Jack, Kerry and Santa.

Gotta make a run to the onion.

January 2nd 1989

Yesterday we couldn't find Janey's B-day party, but we saw Inspiration Bus on the side of the road. They told us where to go. Miranda and Nanette (from Seattle), were there, and Garrett. He looked good – showered and shaved, but quiet. I think he was with Nanette.

So let's see. What about the shows?

Our room at the Sixpence got taken over by babies, but it was cool. I Love Trinity. She's the most well-adjusted baby out there. Corvette was saying how all the new parents we know hope their baby will be as good as Trinity. The Fatty Zone too is full of kids. Carp has his kids now. Heidi, his wife, is supposedly losing it. We haven't seen much of Carp these shows, been hanging with Jumpin' Jack, Davy and Taylor mostly.

Denise and Vance were staying down the hall from us. Denise is pregnant. She has five weeks. And Becky, whose boyfriend Mitch is finally out of jail, is due soon too. They stayed in our room. Mitch makes beautiful barrettes. He made one for Becky with green beads and a malachite heart. KindBoy was here! So good to see him free!

Jake and Elwood have been great. Elwood we keep tied because he wanders, and he's deaf. Jake we let run free. She stays close and can hear us when we call.

Sid was in the room next door with a chow dog named Aloysius. One night Jake was outside the room going to the bathroom and the chow chased her. Someone yelled, "Aloysius has a cat!"

Sid jumped out of his room, yelling, "Oh no! Not that cat. I Love that cat!" Jake got under a car, Alo couldn't fit.

Lots of fun dancing with Fritz in the hall all week – as usual. Especially when they played *Push-n-Shove*, and Becky goes, "Oh no – look out for these two." It's true, we get a little wild. I like Fritz's new girlfriend Mavis. She seems to have picked up on how me and

Fritz are. On New Years Eve – Don at the top of a massage chain, Fritz at the bottom, Mavis kept motioning for me to sit in front of Fritz. (I did, and I even got a good massage.)

One night Fritz stepped on my foot and leaned all his weight on me. We fell on this poor couple who were laying there. Fritz jumped up quick, and Hawkeye pulled me up. It was hilarious how they didn't even move.

Everyone got in New Year's Eve except those who didn't want to. Like Ozzy. He's a god in the lot on New Year's Eve. Helena came in for Tom Tom Club and the 1st set, but went out for Midnight in the lot. Yes, her and Ozzy are back together.

Me and Corvette got our New Year's tix for $50 each, but Jack didn't have one yet. Kerry found a guy with tickets from backstage and brought us over there. At first the guy wouldn't sell me one because I didn't have exact change. I wanted him to keep the extra ten – he wouldn't. I had to get change, then wait for him to come out again.

We sold beers all weekend. Heineken, Becks, and St Pauli. Getting supplies was a bitch. One time we went to Spaceway in Berkeley, and managed to get four free cases because of a long line, and good beer positioning on their part. We stayed in the lot till very late on New Year's Eve, selling Becks for a buck. After leaving the lot, we went to Davy's room. He had a gram of coke he'd saved for doing with us – just like he said he would. Wolfboy Taylor slept all night, and the whole next day. He did some coke with us too when he finally woke up. Me and Corvette were wrestling with him. Taylor's brother Nicolai was here for the shows. He told us Taylor used to be a surfer, and a Junior Lifeguard in LA.

Taylor and Davy went through a friendly divorce this morning. Davy is off to Hawaii with Boots. Taylor's off to Colorado to grow mushrooms. They sold their car to Matan and Ori for $200, and a ¼ ounce of buds. Ori had a vision which told him to start learning, and Matan has a warrant in Long Beach so they're off to Mexico.

8
Winter 1989
SF and A New President

Jan 4th 1989

We got to Fritz and Don's in time for Santa's lasagna. Lots of people slept here including JohnRay, Justine, Puppy Pete, China Sue, Two Toke Tom and more. It was like a crowded hotel room, except it was cold like hotel rooms aren't. Poor kitties had to stay in the van because of Fritz.

It's colder than normal all over California. Before the New Year's shows people were getting snowed in in Leggett, and they closed Rt. 9 in Boulder Creek because of two inches. I don't think there's any snow today, but there's lots o' frost.

9PMish.   SF

Sitting in the Pall Mall Grill watching Jack play pool. We met one of Jack's nephews on Haight and transferred Jack's stuff to his car. Saw Davy, he couldn't get on the same plane to Hawaii as Boots, – he flies out Sunday.

Oh man, there's guys about to do hubbas right here. Yikes.

In Santa Cruz this morning we saw Ori walking down the mall Chanting. He stopped for a second and said to us, "My life has become one long intense trip. I never expected this." Before we could even answer, he started chanting again and moved on.

We stopped at a thrift store. The lady before me bought three books. Two were bibles. Books were 50¢. The lady at the desk charged her 50¢.

"Oh?"

The lady behind the counter said, "I don't charge for religious things." Jack put his stuff on the counter, one thing was a rainbow scarf. She was ringing up the stuff, and held up the scarf. "Wow, I don't even know what this is." She said. "You can have it for free." She gives away religious things even when she doesn't consciously know those things are religious to those people.

The hubba folks left. The seller, a middle-aged man with short curly hair, the buyer, a young blond in tye-dye and a Guatemalan sweater.

January 7th 1989
13 days till Bush.

At the Beach Motel in SF with Jumpin' Jack and Corvette. Today we sent out for Kaiser tix – mail order, then took Clarity to the Zoo. She was psyched. Oh how she loves Jack. Clarity crashed on our way back to the Haight. We parked, found Vance and Denise, gave back the kid, and saw who – but Garrett. He was in the mood to be nice. We went to Full Moon. Carp came by. They played pool. Then we all went to Garrett's bus and smoked a fatty. Garrett asked me to go to Big Sur with him. Pulled a real romantic scene. I told him we had planned to hang with Jack and that was what I was doing.

Jan 9th 1989

At Tina and Keith's on Fell St. We've seen them around but never really met till coming here last night with Jack and Carp. These guys work for Greenpeace so there was lots of earth conscious talk.

Jack wants to get a house with us. We've looked for houses and thought about living with so many different people lately. A place in the city would be nice. There's a $1200 place on Potrero with two fireplaces and a jacuzzi. Maybe we'll look at it today.

Tina and Keith are house hunting too. Would we like to live with them?

We cruised to Page and Baker to check out Beau, Amanda, and Janice's new place. Not bad, but small. Amanda lives in the living room. Janice the small bedroom with attached bathroom, and Beau the big bedroom.

evening

Santa Cruz – the Pacific Inn with Jack, Old Sam, and a young couple, Sapphire and Billy. They have the home-finders guide. There's a house on East Cliff with lots of good shit. $3000 to move in. Do we want to live with Billy and Sapphire? We're talking about that, and about New York, and about Jack's Philly bust, and Sid beating the shit out of Chris Kangaroo. What a world we live in. Money and business.

Saw Fritz on the Mall today. He's bummin there's 15 people staying at their house. All broke and potless. I'm glad we're not there too.

What am I doing anyway? I don't want a job. Radio wouldn't be bad, but I don't want to be held down. What if the most fun thing happens, and I can't go because I have a job? I can't even believe I'm thinking like this. What am I doing with my life? Why am I so against a job? Even in Radio? Do I want to work my way back to the society of real people, or stay in this world? Jack says he hasn't had a job in eight years, has never filled out IRS forms, and except for arrests, the government wouldn't even know about him. How many folks on tour don't exist? Am I getting too deep by wondering what existence even means?

late night

Jack can't read or write. Says he learned to hustle before he learned to read. Says he tried to learn, but it's a brain thing that he can't. Old Sam says, "bullshit."

We've been talking lately about Damien. Damien partied with so many people the day he died. I know from Janey that lots of people said things to her like, "If it was coke or heroin that killed Damien, then it's my fault." It was nobody's fault but Damien's. He overdid it. Maybe I was trying to find out if Jack did leave Damien, but I didn't learn anything. There's something important about forgiveness here, but I'm too stoned to put my finger on it.

Vance was in the room when Jack said, "I haven't done dope since."

Vance said, "Jack you've come a long fuckin' way since that day."

Even though I didn't know these guys then, I do believe that. I like Jack. I hope he goes further on a good path. He has that potential, but, like learning to read, I'm not sure he'll put in the effort.

Jumpin' Jack quote of the night – "LSD blows everyone's mind but your own."

Jan 10th 1989

Saw Carp when we dropped Jack off at his and Carp's brother's place in Concord. Carp's not allowed to party at all if he wants to live there. And he can't really go anywhere else – he's got the kids. He's as broke as everyone is these days and needs diaper money. He wants to get a place in Santa Cruz with Heidi (the mom of his kids) when she gets out of the psych hospital.

He jumped in the Van and demanded pot. We shrugged, "Carp, we're potless." So he smoked a bowl with us. Constantly looking over his shoulder. Poor Carp.

Jack's been talkative about Damien's death lately. It upsets him that Janey feels like she does. He loved Damien. Whatever did happen, Jack changed, and was affected and hurt by Damien's death. Janey gave me a raised eyebrow from across the street when she saw me walking with Jack during the New Years shows.

Jan 12th 1989

Spent the night with Garrett. Sitting on his bus now as he gets ready for court. Trying to get his license back. Corvette is crashed in the van next door.

Yesterday on the Haight, Davy was still there. No Hawaii for him, instead he got a place with a hot tub, six blocks from Haight.

I met Crafty Adam yesterday – the guy who made the necklace Jack gave me for Xmas. Told us Ozzy's parked on Berry St. So we bought some beer and headed there. That's where I found Garrett parked too. Kinda under the highway, with a view of the Bay Bridge and downtown. Mostly truckers sleep here.

night

On Haight today Sid got mouthy with some big dude in a pink shirt. Vance said it had something to do with Sid raiding a crack house a couple weeks ago. We grabbed Clarity so she didn't have to see it and took a walk. Came back and the big guy was in cuffs.

Clarity asking, "Are we going to see the animals?" And starting in with "Hey Ho." (We had watched TV with her the other day and a cartoon put forth the call and response rhyme "Hey ho, where do we go?"

"Nobody knows but we're rarin' to go."

"Hey ho where have we been?"

"Nobody knows but we'll go there again."

This reminded us of our Dead wanderings and we sang it a few times, laughing. She picked it right up, and whenever she said 'Hey Ho' we'd do the whole bit for her, so now she does this a lot.) And of course, "Where's Jack?" A constant refrain of hers.

Later me and Corvette found a bunch o' people with buds and two N_2O tanks in their van. We drove around with them while they smoked us out. We got out before they broke out the balloons.

Sid took us to dinner at an Italian place on Stanyan, then we walked up the hill to a schoolyard to get stoned. He had to go get some work done, but he said he'd come back and make sure we're not on the street tonight.

Friday the 13th
Cotati – 7 days till Bush.

Last night, at the Pall Mall, Garrett was tweaked. He'd backed into a car and was terrified to drive back to Berry St. He was convinced that us following him was the only way he wouldn't get busted. So after another round of beers we escorted him home.

Me and Corvette retreated to Cotati to get some real sleep, and take real showers.

Jan 14th 1989.

Back to the city. – At the Pall Mall. As we cruised the Haight this morning, the guys we met the other day in the N_2O van were surrounded by six cop cars. Yikes.

Also yikes – There's bugs around.

Lice.

That's mine and Corvette's tour nightmare.

Later.

Everyone is worried about bugs. Jack bought a bomb for the van. Vance was giving us bombing tips. Apparently Jack was afraid to tell us. I'm sure that's because we told him we'd quit tour if we ever got bugs. Vance told Jack, "Ya gotta tell the girls as soon as you see 'em. They both have long hair and a lot of hot spots." Yikes!

We've seen nothing, but we're bombing the van nonetheless.

We're still at the Pall Mall. Jack went to get a cake for someone's B-day, – someone he just met. He always does shit like that.

January 18th, 1989
Skinny Jim's, Guerneville

We lounged here all day yesterday. This chick showed up, "Hi I'm Mandy. Jim said you're in need." She sold us an 8th of bud grown in Forestville. It's pretty good.

Went over Freddy's with Jim. Freddy's on roach motel stash so we smoked some of ours with him. When Jim, Corvette, and Piper went for a munchie run, me and Freddy got to talk. He's almost broke. Says he'll have to get a job soon to support the kid. He's sad that he spent too much of his money along the way to do anything legal with it now. What he has left is not enough. A job is his only way, he's sure. He straightens his shoulders when he talks about it.

It goes against our whole world for him to get a job. But what else can he do? What are the options? If we change our way of life because of our fear of them – Are they winning?

Thurs. Jan 19 89

Noonish – Saint Randy's house. The Program Director at the Radio Station called. He wants me to come in and cut a demo tape for him. He actually wants me to work there. But... I don't want a job.

I've done it now. I've become one of those Deadheads who has nothing going, nothing to look forward to except the next tour. I'm sure next tour will be a blast. But... I'm even shying away from a job that wouldn't be hateful. What will I/we do for money? We can't even afford the shirts we want to make. Unless maybe I take this radio job. But how can I work without a place to live? And why do I so often go through life not knowing what I want? And even when I think I know, – why is it I'm usually wrong?

Tomorrow – Bush. And I don't even have a passport. Randy joked to try spare changing on Haight for a passport. "Spare change so I can leave the country?"

Jan 20 89

Oh god, a new president. Please help us, as a nation, through these next four years. Ron and Nancy are on a plane and outta there. Good riddance, but I don't welcome Georgie.

There's a protest in the city today. If the onion for Corvette comes in, we'll go.

Jan 21   Willard North

We went to the Haight. Saw no-one. Off to Berry St. Garrett's not home, but there's Jack with Yes Ma'am Sam.

The Anti-Bush Rally was something. We marched from the UN Plaza to Union Square. Lots of cops in full riot gear, with tear gas ready when folks wouldn't move into the park. The crowd turned and we marched right down Market St. with cars and busses getting caught in our parade. It was chaotic. We left when the parade got back to the UN Plaza. As we walked to the van, we passed close by three cops on motorcycles. Sam, trying to be friendly and fuckin human, asked, "Are you having a nice night?"

And one cop growled, "Fuck you scum. If I found you alone, I'd fucking kill you."

It was really time to get outta there. There were a 100 or so cops in parade rest and riot gear standing behind my van. We pulled out real slow and left.

Went to the Full Moon for the Return of John Cipollina. He's been in the hospital since September or so.

Last night was one of those nights where everyone arrived buzzed and in a good mood. Davy bought me and Corvette beers all night. Inside we took over the new area. – They moved the bar back and it's got great dance space now. Beau thought John Cipollina's return was too soon, but he rocked out and was havin fun.

Red Wayne was arrested in Santa Cruz, with mega doses, but he said he stashed them in the cop car – charges dropped – because when they searched him at the station, he had nothing. And supposedly Crafty Adam was arrested, but that's all anyone knows.

During break we walked to this guy Art's house on Page St. One of Cipollina's roadies was there selling pot. Nice.

2nd set was hoppin'. Merl Saunders showed up. The encore was a very long '*Mona!*'

Jack moved into Maria Malloy's place. He wanted us to go there with him, but Maria didn't want him 'bringin a party home.'

9
Winter 1989
Super Bowl, the End-of-Fulton-St., Kaisers

Jan 22   Willard North

Poor Dandy Andy. The Super Bowl just began and he's in a house with a bunch of women who don't care.

Later

Did the Shuffle and popped into the Full Moon. Saw Davy and Rockefeller. And Crafty Adam who's out of jail on OR. Now we're at Art's with Jack. Listening to Reggae and watching the silent Super Bowl.

Jan 23rd 1989

Went back to the Full Moon for the end of the game. Cincinnati was winning by 3 points with 1 minute 30 seconds left. SF got a last minute touchdown.

The bar, the whole fucking city, exploded with excitement. Drinks ½ price, and people poured into the streets, cars beeping all night, Truckloads of people screaming and cheering. Back at Art's we smoked a couple of Super Bowls then me, Beau, Corvette, and Jack went off to jumpstart someone's car on the panhandle. We got in Beau's car and looked for the people we were supposed to jump. Didn't find them, but we found some others who needed a jump.

Jack wanted to go downtown, or to North Beach. Beau wanted more coke. Jack said, "No, no, let's eat. We'll buy food instead of drugs." Beau agreed to food and we went to Clown Alley.

It was way, way outta hand downtown. People screaming and cheering and partying like the game had just ended. We parked near Broadway and hung out on the street awhile. Saw some asshole beating on his girlfriend and threatening to beat Beau and

Jack if we didn't keep on walking. He'd let up on her, so we moved on. As we drove away, we saw three big guys giving him shit.

We dropped Jack off at Maria Malloy's, and Beau dropped us at Willard North.

Jan 24th　　　Fulton St.

Me, Corvette and Rockefeller swung by Maria Malloy's to get Jack. Maria bitched at me for telling Vance to meet us there. – Her house is not a meeting place. – I wasn't even the one who told him to meet us. Then she bitched about Thorin out on the stoop. Jack grabbed all his stuff and told Maria to fuck off.

We're at 2332A Fulton for the beginning of the end-of-Fulton-St. house Party. This house will be history as of Feb 1st. What a history it has.

Conversation on one side of the room with Beatnik Bill, Jumpin' Jack and Tanner, is about the DEA – their culture vs ours, and on the other side of the room, Marshal, Erik the Rude and Rockefeller are discussing Pitbulls on tour.

Jan 26th 1989

Yesterday we did the Shuffle. The weather has been beautiful. Me and Corvette walked with Sid to his truck and got stoned. Hadn't gotten way-high in a long time. He loaned us 20 bucks to take care of the bald tire problem. (I got a letter at Randy's that said if it wasn't fixed, and signed by a uniformed cop, by 1-26-89 it would be a $252 fine.)

Me, Corvette, Rockefeller, the kittens and Thorin drove to Santa Cruz during a gorgeous sunset. On the Mall we saw Old Sam who told us a good place to fix the tire. We did that, then went to the cop shop, got told to wait and basically, I was ignored. I asked a cop I saw outside, and he said they'd all be busy for at least an hour, so we went to Upper Crust Pizza. They had all-you-can-eat Spaghetti so we ordered that instead of Pizza. But they ran out of food after we each had one plate. They wanted to charge us for Al La Carte – 49¢ cheaper than all-you-can-eat. "No way. We can't pay that much for one plate of spaghetti each. That's not fair. We're poor hippies, we only bought that so we could eat a lot." They were cool about it – so we all ate for $5.

We walked with Armand, looking for a cop to sign this stupid paper. Never around when you need 'em. Went back to the station to try to catch a cop after roll call. I finally found a cop to sign it for me and we dropped off the envelope at municipal court – stuck it through a crack in the door, – at midnight.

It was too late to go to Don and Fritz's budless, and Rockefeller said he didn't always get along with Fritz anyway. So we drove all the way back to SF to crash at Willard North.

Abe says he isn't going to either of these Jerry shows. He's harboring a Ba-humbug attitude towards Jerry Band.

Friday 27th

Jerry Show was hot. Amanda and I got down to the 8th row.

Fulton St. now – The party is raging. People everywhere coming through the door. JohnRay and Briscoe. Drippy Danny, Janice, Beau, Amanda, Andre, lots of people I don't know.

We ate at 1705 Cafe with Hawkeye and Rosario. Hawkeye was totally incognito in tye-dye and Guatemalan clothes. Sid got popped. 2½ grams. Hawkeye wants me to bring money to the jail for his books tomorrow. I don't like the idea of dealing with Jail, but for Sid I can't say no. I met Calico tonight. She recommended, to Della, a Lawyer for Sid. I can't believe Sid has gone down.

Someone told me tonight that Murph turned state's evidence just before JP went down. Wondered if this is what happened to Sid too. I don't believe any of that.

Corvette bought Abe a ticket for tomorrow's show – we can't let that attitude stand.

January 28

I went to the Berkeley Police station to bring cigarettes and candy to Sid. Beatnik Bill brought me down there in his van. I tried to give $ too, but they said I couldn't. Said he'd be outta there tomorrow.

Inside. Jerry. Orpheum.

Drumz. Lots of people. Very crowded. Kerry doesn't smoke pot? What? Still, though, he helps break buds and roll fatties. Allie and Silas are in from Colorado. Just got way high with them. Mavis dressed in black and wore leather for Jumpin' Jack. Too bad he didn't get in. Right now she's kicked back in Fritz's arms. They're cute together. She's got that long, curly hair, and him with that fro-mop.

Tina sat down with us. I bummed a butt, she offered Corvette one too. Corvette said, "I don't smoke. Got any chocolate?" But of course! She did!

Hawkeye is looking like himself again. Gimlet looks like he has been doing drugs that aren't always good for you. Shame that. Carp is here. Patty and Hinch. Margot. Zia too. The Spinners are back from wherever they were. This one chick is spinning obnoxiously close.

Sittin' next to Izzy and Don. Don accused me of being his shadow because I show up every time he rolls a fat one. When the music plays Trinity gets to crawl around the rug and everyone watches over her.

Don't Let Go. I Love this song.

Mavis was showing me pictures of her family at Xmas. She's the oldest of I don't know how many kids. She said, "My parents were broke this year. I spent $1200 on presents for the kids."

"Where do they think you're getting the money?"

"Swinging LSD. They worry about me, but they know the money is good."

Jan 29th

At The Stone in SF – a benefit for someone. John Kahn, Nick Gravinitis, Merl Saunders, and more. Beau, and Amanda are here. They're quite the couple nowadays.

Did the shuffle with Rockefeller and Thorin this morning. Not too many people out there. Rockefeller was looking for Lars. Maybe if he makes some money we could take him cross-country with us? We met up with Hawkeye who gave us a bag of stuff to bring to Sid, who is not out yet. The jail would not let him have kool aide or soap or shampoo.

Back on Haight, as we drove by the Full Moon, there were lots o' dancin' hippies in the street and tunes crankin' from the apartment above. A few days ago they hung a banner from their balcony, – "We support you in your Haightness."

Trevor was on the Haight this morning looking for a ride to Santa Cruz. He was still out there when we drove by while it was rockin' out. Trevor's a spaceshot and sometimes doesn't get things done very well. Fritz called him "100% Lame".

Tonight's music is great, but I'm tired. We just smoked a skinny here inside. Amanda and Beau are totally molesting each other.

There's only one week till the first Kaiser show. I hope we find a way to make our shirts. My van insurance runs out March 20th. My van registration runs out in March too. I need to get to Guerneville. Freddy has some extra tires and I need to see if they'll fit the van.

After tour I'm gonna have some decisions to make. I don't want to live in Connecticut, I don't want to just do Dead tour for the next uncountable number of years, I don't want to live in a cheap house with no sun, I don't want a real job, I don't want to start swinging again, and I don't want to be broke. Sounds like I need a rich guy to take me traveling and buy me a nice house in the sun where I can sit back and write a book.

Now it's Barry Melton and I think Merl is gonna join him.

I have no energy to dance. I want a beer. I want sleep. I want someone to Love.

Jan 31st AM

I stayed at Fulton St. all day helping Tanner clean while Corvette did errands. I scarfed a bunch of leftover stuff for the Van thrift store. No money from RAD Leather. The guy told Corvette he sent us a check to the address we gave him. (Randy's.)

We just smoked the last fatty of the Fulton Street house.

evening

Saw Santa on the Haight. – Headed North. We actually flipped a coin to decide which direction to go. South won. Santa Cruz. Did the Mall Crawl a bit and came here to Fritz and Don's place.

Feb 1st

We brought the cats into the house last night after Fritz crashed. I woke up and knew they weren't in here. I ran outside and they were both up a tree with two big dogs waiting below. Fuck you Fritz. It's like 10AM. We're outta here.

Feb 2nd

At Dave Gooden's house in Cotati. Last night we drank wine with them and watched Daffy Duck cartoons frame by frame. Today we did Laundry and acted lazy all day. Preston stopped by. Jim Avery too. Once we leave this time, we won't be here for a bit, so they all want to see us.

Mom sent a package to Randy's. It's not there yet. And RAD Leather's check isn't there either.

Feb 3rd

Sunnyvale – at Mercedes' Uncle's condo with pool and steaming hot tub outside. It's 2AM. Mercedes and Eddie are crashed. They're Atlanta folk. We came here after picking them, and Leland, up at the airport.

This afternoon we went to Guerneville. Said our goodbyes to Skinny Jim, then cruised by Freddy's, but he was in Oakland getting a good parking spot for the Hearse for the shows. We cruised by the vet's to get the receipts for the shots the kittens had last month, and who saunters up but Mutz. He's a friend of Rockefeller's. Mutz has a cottage across from the vet's. We went over and got stoned. They told me all kinds of Rockefeller horror stories. About how he stayed in Rhode Island with them and about how much money he made and the dumb ways he spent, and spent and out spent them as if it were a competition. Stuff like that.

On the ride from Guerneville to Santa Rosa we saw the best Rainbow I've ever seen! It started as just the right ½ of the arc. As we drove, it reached further over towards the ground. We passed under trees and when we came out it was one solid rainbow – end to end. As we drove more, its left side got very intense. The colors so sharply defined you could even see Indigo separately from the purple. The spot on the ground got closer and closer to the road. It was like 20 feet to my left and it stayed even with the van for nearly a minute. I could see the colors running over the ground. It was beyond spectacular.

We ate at Rafa's, then finally caught Freddy.

He and Piper think the 'heat' is in the middle of the family. They think it's Murph. His history is sketchy, they say. But anybody's history could look sketchy. The rumour on Haight St. was that Murph and Skye had turned state's evidence. That's more likely than that Murph has been a narc all along. But I still don't believe it.

Feb 4

Don't like to write details about all the stuff in our world but I've got to mention that I don't feel right about Vance right now. The cost has gone up, and I can't explain why, but I feel like we should stay away from him today. We'll have to find someone else.

Is Freddy's paranoia rubbing off on me? I hate when it gets like this.

Feb 5

Sitting in the Kaiser park, not selling any cheap clothes. Traded a purse for some Indica brownies though.

Elwood is playing with the clothes hanging in the tree.

Everyone is swinging carefully and heavily.

I need a ticket. So does Rockefeller. Corvette's set.

Inside

Back o' the floor, Phil's side, doing bongs.

Janey sold me a ticket. Rockefeller found his own. Then Corvette scored – she got two more tix. We sold one to Freddy, cheap, and one was for Jack – he'd given us money, but we missed the first four songs looking for him. – We even had Willie yelling through his megaphone, "Jumpin' Jack. Where are ya Jumpin' Jack?" Finally we sold it to Tavi for what Corvette paid – $40. Yikes, I hate the prices nowadays. (I haven't seen Jack inside yet.)

Came in during *Althea*. Nice decorations – balloon bouquets with streamers.

Feb 6 1989

Morning in Skip's room with Anna, Fat Matt, Magoo, Rockefeller, Corvette, and Mark Reese. Magoo is telling the story of how he carried a broken bike tire all the way from Leggett. We're going to the Hyatt to shower because there is no hot water in the London Lodge.

Inside

KindBoy just walked by with his shower cap on. Ha! He did a comic pivot and came back to sit with us. Silas had been lookin for Gitch all day. I only met Gitch once, last year, but, "Isn't that him?" I pointed to a guy over aways. It was Gitch! I love when shit like that happens.

It feels good in here tonight. Gunner is dressed in his bunny suit. Denise looks ready to pop. Della and Dawn are raising bail money for Sid. Sorry, not bail money, lawyer money.

Looks like most everyone got in except I don't see Justine yet, and I know Garrett didn't. We had to flip a glove between Garrett and Jack with our extra. (Yes a glove. Thumb up for Garrett, thumb down for Jack.)

Break –

Went to the bar during *Tennessee Jed*. Lots of room for dancing and it sounds great. Speaking of sounding great, the Chinese orchestra was wild. Renaissance – medieval sounding.

On the floor, Phil's side, with Mark Reese, Anna, Skip, and Corvette. They decorate more each day. There's a huge dragon, the colors of a Steal Your Face, hanging in the back of the hall. Macy just appeared. Lights out.

Later

The hallway is such a great place! It's my favorite place ever – everyone so near, and dancing. Jack, Skye, Fritz, Mavis, Andre, Benny, Kennedy and Suzy, Jeanie. Carp rolling fatties. Huge, pregnant Denise, dancing like a wild-woman during *Hell in a Bucket* was a sight to behold. The hallway has a rhythm and a pulse all its own.

There's a wingnut on Haight lately with twinkling eyes and the biggest smile. He shines. Tonight, he had a bunch o' papers arranged in front of him. He came up and gave me one of those papers. It said 'I Love You' on both sides. I wrote 'too' on one side and sneaked up to him a few minutes later and gave it back.

Tavi just pressed a fistful o' buds in my hand – I've got a job to do.
Later
I missed the drum Dragon on stage, while rolling the fatty, but during space the Dragon came and snaked through the entire Hall.

Hot *Other One*.

Fatty Circle. Sitting near Carp and Jack, Dreadless Manny, Matteo, Kona Paul, Hawkeye and Adrienne, Ozzy and Helena.

Lovelight..... Danced with Jack and Mavis.

Black Mud.

Feb 7
Fat Tuesday. Woke at 12:15. Supposed to be out of the hotel at 12. We smoked a fatty and got out right away. Me, Corvette, and Jeanie went to eat. Rockefeller, Mercedes, Leland, and Eddie went to the Hyatt to sleep more. That's where we are now. At Denny's we saw Mavis and Justine. Everyone's begging for Ibuprofen. I know that feeling. I'd love to sleep more but instead we just keep getting stoned.

King Henry just got here, – Walked in with a fat one, imitating Groucho Marx with a cigar. He went to some Costume Ball in New Orleans – people dressed in Saran wrap and such. He said it turned into an 80s group grope. And now, here, King stepped into a harem. Me, Corvette, Jeanie, and Mercedes. He wants to Group Grope. I say, "It must be addictive."

He shrugs, "I'll eat some tofu, it'll pass." A quick phone call and he's off.

Almost 3 now – sometimes it takes so long to get motivated. And there's always that weird hippie time warp thing where if you're not moving by 11:00, suddenly the clock jumps to 1:00.

We're gonna run up to see Kennedy and maybe stop by Mavis' room.

Feb 8th 1989

Yesterday we left the Hyatt finally, and went to the lot. Horrid parking scene. I found the best creative parking spot, but a cop nixed it as we were leaving the van, so we drove back to the Hyatt, and took a cab.

I went right in because I hoped to claim a section for the lot of us, but it was too late for that. I got stoned with Mutz up near the top. The decorations inside had tripled. Weird and wonderful stuff. Out in the hallway only Don and Justine were there. But soon the whole circle materialized.

Corvette sold the extra ticket to Garrett last night. Jack didn't get in. I think he didn't try. He was way drunk after the show and wanted to go to LA with us. I can't bring myself to travel with Jumpin' Jack. Garrett said he was going to LA, then he said he wasn't, then said he was, so who the fuck knows.

Back at the Hyatt – room 1227, with the Atlanta folk – Mary, Eddie, Leland, Mercedes, and Ryan.

To Silas' room – Lots o' bonghits.

Then to 1411 to visit Mavis and Justine and them. That was the munchie room. Don put his palms up and looked away, "Go ahead. I'm about to puke." Pigged out on cookies, potato chips, and string cheese. We told them we'd be leaving as soon as Fritz arrived. When Fritz got there, we actually did jump up and leave. We were ready to move on anyway, but the effect was nice.

To 1601 – Dante's. A corner room with a fantastic view of Oakland and SF.

Back to 1227 – Rockefeller was there with Thorin. He wants to ride with us to LA.

1620 – Silas again. Hung out there very late. Jeanie – running around with us all night, says we're crazy, and we keep her guessing.

We decided to take Rockefeller with us to LA. So... back to 1227 to give him the # at Willard North, then off to London Lodge to see Skip. He upped the price, so we blew that off and went back to the Hyatt – sucked in to the party scene like a whirlwind tornado.

Finally me, Corvette, and Jeanie went across the bay at 5:30AM. Got donuts in the Mission, then came here to Willard North.

There's been no sign of, or call from, Rockefeller. We hafta go to RAD Leather, call Freddy to see if we can look at his Hot Springs book, call Mavis, and talk about buying her plane vouchers. I already called Randy. My package from mom is there. So it's North before South.

10
Winter 1989
LA to Connecticut

                        Feb 9 '89   Cotati

Getting ready to hit the road. Mom sent my mail – a card from James the gorgeous hitchhiker says he's sad and wants a hug. Hopes to see me on Spring Tour. What could have happened to make my gorgeous hitchhiker with the beautiful eyes so sad?

                              Feb 10

Sunny morning in LA, and the birds are just singing away. It feels like summer. Sleeveless clothes, bright sunshine.

                              Later

The lot is cool. $5 regular parking, or $10 Vendor. Parked near Zia. Sold clothes and hung in the sun with the kittens. Bianca sat with us and had clothes to sell too.

                              Later

Ya know, we have our own way of life. We know how to make it work the way it has to be. Some places don't let us be as we are. It's funny watching us work around the obstacles they present. We're actually quite easy to accommodate and if they'd just pay attention to that we wouldn't have to scam them so often.

                       Inside   LA Forum

Balloons strung in Rainbows on the ceiling. No speakers in the Hall. There should be – the halls are huge. And crowded. We're near the back o' Jerry's side where the sound seems to be best. This corner is full of Spinners. Speaking of Spinners, when we came in we had to find Nonnie and tell her BethBeth got arrested. I hear it's a bogus thing. Probably get let go tonight.

TAYLOR'S here!! He makes quite the entrance. Everyone screams and yells and cheers and jeers.

Break

It's dark here behind the stage. I can't even see the words I'm writing.

I went into some seats to smoke a fatty with Jumpin' Jack, Wolfboy Taylor and Davy. I got to roll it. I Love buds – green, sticky, sweet, crystally, Buds. And I love that I get to roll fatties.

Then it was break.

Looking through the stands I noticed King Henry sitting with Kerry, Winnie, and Izzy. I turned again and saw Tavi, Mavis, and Don. Each had fatties in their hands, holding them up, waiting for me to notice.

Later

Saw one guy break in. He blasted through the hall and directly inside with guards hot on his heels. We followed through the door to watch. Impressive the way he ran over the tops and backs of the chairs through half the place till he melted into the crowd and even we could no longer tell which guy was him. They didn't have a chance catching him. Saw three others try the same sort of thing, but they were too slow and got kicked right back out.

Hot *Wharf Rat*.

Late Night

Best Western with the Dingalings.

After the show they wanted us out of the lot right away. I took an N_2O detour with Silas and when I got back to the van there's eight people who want a ride to the hotel. So we all pile in and leave the lot. There's a long line of traffic and as we're crawling along, a rolled blanket hits the windshield. It's Beau. He wanted a ride too, but it was him, Amanda, and Big Doug. We couldn't fit them. Traffic started to move. Corvette stood with the door open, yelling to Beau the hotel and room #. Off we go.

We get to the hotel – No Jake.

We went back to the lot. It was desolate, kinda like I feel. We parked and looked for Jake everywhere by where we saw Beau, and a block in both directions. Garrett stopped to see what was the matter. He parked and helped us look for her.

Oh Jake kitty, come back.

I hope Beau has her. What a shitty section of LA.

I'm hungry. I want to get stoned. I want Jake back.

Feb 11

Denise had a baby boy in the lot this morning – Ryder Orion. The lot wasn't open yet, and Vance said he had to drive the RV over barricades, screaming to security as they chased him, to fuck off – he was having a baby – here – NOW – no matter what they said.

Later

There's a jock type guy across from us with ripped tye-dye long johns, playing bad air guitar. Another guy is trying to trade a wave-trip-watcher thingy for a ticket. We're doing well selling our used clothes.

No sign of Jake. Beau doesn't have her. We'll do the newspaper/pound trip tomorrow.

Ryan just showed up with plum wine.

Inside

China Rider of course! For little Ryder Orion. Welcome little one. You are the newest member of the Fatty Family, the nomadic tribe of the American Indicans.

Everyone got a ticket tonight easier than me.

Women R Smarter

Taylor is such a wild man hanging off the stair rails, hair flinging in all directions. Holding on like it's the only thing keeping him from dancing up to the ceiling.

Standing on the Moon. Smokin' a bowl with Jack. I really like this tune. It's sweet.

Estimated.

I'm ready to go east. I've had my winter fill of Haight St. Hippie bullshit. California is the best, but it's time for Spring Tour! Rockefeller is going east with us.

Gettin' Spacey

Later

In Hawkeye's room with Adrienne, Della, and Dawn. This is the number we put on our lost cat flyers but there's still no word on Jake.

I lost my bowl in the show. I need a new one. Bob and Marie aren't here. Word is they're broke down in Arizona.

Feb 12

I hate bitch desk ladies who call and say, "It's 10:19 are you checking out? Check out time is noon." And her voice was so loud we all heard it.

Elwood's missing Jake. He's not as brave without her. He's asleep still, under my blankets. Being deaf, he doesn't know we're awake.

In the lot

I brushed out Shane's hair, then wandered the lot with him, lost him, found him again, got more beers. Now I'm sittin' with Ryan and Atlanta Mary.

Jack gave me a new pipestone bowl made by Socrates!

Inside, Break

Smokin' first set. Spencer Davis made an appearance.

Everyone is in, and all the right people (the Indicans) have found the Fatty Zone. We're behind Phil. (Me, Corvette and Mavis just put on matching Fire Triangle bracelets. Aries-Leo-Sagittarius. Mavis said it was the most interesting thing all night.) I see the Spinners in the section to my left. Heard BethBeth actually got arrested for X. Her bail is $1,000.

Ha – Godzilla and Gumby are fighting it out in front of the stage. Godzilla won.

Later

Wild 2nd set with Dylan – so far *Aiko, Monkey and the Engineer, Alabama Getaway, Dire Wolf, Cassidy* and *Memphis Blooze* with Dylan singing a line or two.

Drumz ... Space

Other One – Brent was a little late. Lights are really great for these shows.

Stella Blue

Taylor is a wild man at the railing again – or still.

Foolish Heart

Encore with Dylan

Not Fade Away

Knockin'

Carp is having a party at the Sheraton or it's a party for him. Something.

Later

Tasty buds at the Sheraton. – Fatties flowing.

Carp, Shane, Taylor, Hinch, Patty, Rockefeller, Jeanie, Shaleigh, ten people whose names I don't know. $120 room, two full coolers. Smoothies on the way. What a Party! Old Sam went to get more Beer.

King Henry brought a CD player – playing Professor Longhair. Taylor's rolling a fatty. Bianca is high high high. And it's a grand entrance for Davy!

A small bit later.

We got a bigger room, a floor lower. Everyone who came into the first room said, "Oh my god, there's a cloud in the hall." Then tried to open the window. No luck, they don't open.

We left the cloud behind. But this is LA – is this cool?

Please SEP us.

Carp, doing what he does best, collected money for the adjoining room. Doughboy's here – Lots o' rum on the table for smoothies. (His specialty.) Fatties everywhere I turn, and it's getting cloudy in this room too. Mavis and Shaleigh wanna throw Fritz in the shower. I won't help. More people I don't know squeezing through the door. Della, but no Dawn. Now Shane is collecting money for more beer.

Unbelievably Hannah Banana announces, "We've got a bigger room next door."

~~~~~

This room is huge, with a table and living room chairs. NOW we're getting somewhere. Carp growls, "Don't trash the place." Time to roll a fatty...

~~~~~

We're raging! – Mega-cases of beer being passed person to person towards the tables because there's barely enough room to walk. Enough with the book already.

Feb 13

Carp tried to make a serious speech about Love, and fighting for what we believe, but he was really high and he couldn't find the words he wanted. He kept mentioning his kids. I'm not sure what's up with him. It was a solemn atmosphere, like he was headed for jail or something. He talked about how right now – there's over 100 of our good friends in BIG trouble. It's true. It's outrageous. It was a sad speech and very hard for Carp, but we all knew what he meant. When he was done we all told him how much we love him, and we're with him, and don't worry, we'll never give up, and we won't forget, and all the things he needed to hear.

When the speech was over Della jumped up and called for attention as everyone was beginning to talk again. "Hey everyone, don't forget Sid. We need $4,000 more for his lawyer by Wednesday." It was like a council meeting of a big corporation.

Soon the party began to rage again. King kept turning the tunes up louder and louder. Someone would turn them down, he'd turn them back up.

Then... suddenly... there came the Ominous Knock.

Some knocks are friendly, some casual, some frantic, some even pissed off, but everyone seems to have an instinct on certain knocks. It took a minute to get everyone's attention and tell them the manager outside the door said he'd call the LAPD if we didn't leave immediately.

Had we actually thought we were moving fast enough through rooms that we'd be safe?

Carp got animated – started insisting everyone stay locked in the room. Sorry Carp. I don't think so. I Love you, but we just picked up an ounce of kind that we want to keep. LAPD? No one has to tell me twice.

We still have Jeanie's stuff in the van. Couldn't find her as we left pretty fast.

Don took us to the Days Inn to crash. Mavis and Fritz were shower fighting when I woke up. Now they are just plain fighting.

Feb 14

In the desert, at a little restaurant called Oasis. A guy in cowboy boots, in a rockin chair in the sun, with a 10 gallon hat over his eyes. Elwood on the van roof, surveying the territory. Rockefeller drained the radiator and refilled it with Anti-freeze.

Feb 15

Sedona yesterday. The psychic vortex of the world. Beautiful Bright Red Cliffs. 89A wound down into Oak Creek Canyon – all twisty and curvy. I loved driving it. We got an $80 room at the Best Western – not worth it, but Mavis wanted the hot tub.

Started today fighting with Rockefeller about Thorin. The dog deserves better.

We went into town – Onion, bank, Post Office, Chamber of Commerce. A pleasant lady told us the "cool" places to go. We went to Airport Mesa looking for this particular vortex. We went too far at first but on the way down we found it. At least we think we did. The energy was different there. We hiked over the hill to another cliff – there was a medicine wheel made of rocks. We brought Elwood. We forgot pot. But we made a peace sign out of rocks to the left of the medicine wheel.

2-16-89

At a pizza place in Oklahoma. They gave us a free chocolate chip pizza because we've never heard of it. It's got vanilla pudding. Not bad. But I'd never order one again.

We drove through the top of Texas all day. Grey, wintery, dull. In Oklahoma the weather is no different.

Dave and Mavis stop to eat too much. And they're the ones who say they want to make time. We traded Rockefeller and Dave for an hour or so. That was nice.

Dave's always saying, "It's cool, It's cool," whether it's cool or not.

Feb 17

At Dave's Mom's house, in Ohio. Nice house, set high on a hill. I'd like to see this house in Santa Cruz full of hippies.

Drove last night till 1^{ish}. Today – Gray Gray Gray. Flat, dreary, Middle America. Drove all day without shutting off the van because it's leaking gas again. For a while Rockefeller bailed and rode in Mavis' car, because he thought we might blow up. We didn't, and he got back in the van.

We fight a lot. He's a dick.

We went by Mavis' house when we first got to town. Met her Dad and step mom. And Jagger. He's Mavis' best friend.

I don't know whether we'll get the van looked at here tomorrow, or if we'll push to get it to Ziggy in Connecticut.

Rockefeller and Dave went to some party. I'd rather shower and sleep.

Later

Dave's mom gave me and Corvette the 20 question treatment about the Dead and the scene. I hate that. What do you tell someone else's parents? When Corvette was in the shower, Grandma asked me in a whisper if I've accepted Jesus into my life. She told me musicians can be saved. Like Stryper. She asked me to save Dave.

Feb 18

Morning at noonish.

I love *Beat it on Down the Line* into *Promised Land*. Rolling 'cross Georgia state... and ... smokin' into New Orleans!! Mavis has a pink and purple orb that hooks to her stereo and pulses to the music, and a stuffed Pink flamingo that everyone's having fun with.

Talking politics. And Guitarists.

Supposedly there are Jerry shows on March 2nd + 3rd in SF. I'd like to go, and we have plane vouchers, but it's not on the hotline so we don't want to make reservations yet.

Later

Me and Corvette just wanted to hang at Mavis' and smoke and drink and look through her closet. They wanted to have a party but no house was big enough. Dave got us motivated and we're at the Residence. $115. Two floors, Fireplace, Kitchen, two bedrooms.

Mavis is a phone head. She may as well keep a phone attached to her ear.

Roll a fatty, – They're about to play quarters.

19th

The game got wild. Lots of yelling and wrestling. We crashed about 4:30. Now it's checkout time.

Mavis, "Should we leave the Cuervo for the maid?"

Definitely.

Feb 20th
Monday Morning

It took 10½ hours to get to Binghamton. For the last hour I was dizzy and sick. I figured it's from sniffing gas all day. Driving felt like the van was standing still and the world rushing along under us. Sometimes I picture the land as a map. Cruising along a blue line, no cities or towns, just green bumps, white dots and tiny black dots on a map.

I don't know what time it is. Those guys partied late. I came in Jeanie's room, – feeling sick all night. Jeanie made me tea before she left for school, and we just noticed it's snowing. We're outta here.

Feb 25

I haven't been writing because Connecticut is still just a pork chop on a map. And Rockefeller's a pain in the ass. So is his thick-headed dog.

Elwood got neutered yesterday, and today we went to Ziggy's. Smoked a roach fatty and played video games on his TV while he worked on the van. (God damn, Rockefeller is worse than... never mind.)

11
Winter 1989
A Quick Trip to San Francisco

March 1st   Atlanta

Rockefeller is gone (thank you universe).

Shawna called Daybourne house. They said Rockefeller and Thorin could stay there. So we dropped him off, and he was like, "What? Now? I thought it wasn't until tomorrow." Sorry bud – I've had enough of you.

Shawna talked us into letting her take care of Elwood instead of smuggling him onto the plane. He's entranced by their fish tank. King Henry took us to some t-shirt printer friends of his at a place called Magnitude Ink. He's financing six dozen Indican Shirts for us and they've begun work on the art. Psyched. We hung at his house, scaling down to one back pack and talking about the 700 Club, the axis shift, and religion in general.

March 2 1989

Ta-da. San Francisco! The Full Moon Saloon!

The flights were long and bumpy. As we were landing I saw a full circle rainbow.

Murph met us at the airport. (We brought a package for him, from King Henry.) We had drinks and bullshat. His Dad is in the hospital in LA for open heart surgery. He flew up to meet us – flies back to LA tomorrow. He got on the Santa Rosa bus, and we took a shuttle to Willard North.

Good to be home. They never imagined it was us when the bell rang.

So... a bit of gossip. Amanda's pregnant and so is Janice.

And Becky had her baby – a boy. Murph didn't know the name.

We came down to Haight to do the shuffle. Saw Marshal. He went to court the other day. He was convicted, and he'll be sentenced on May 8th, so at least he'll be able to do tour. Carp has court tomorrow. He might have to go to jail tomorrow. No word on Sid. Jumpin' Jack's on the East coast. Flew back for a court date but it was cancelled 'till March 7th.

March 3rd

We bought a 6-pack and went to Page St. No one was home. We sat on the porch drinking Dos Equis and watching the gorgeous guy across the street leave and come back, leave and come back. We yelled hello to him and he ignored us. Corvette was like, "Hey, what? Do you like guys?" just as some innocent walker came into view.

That guy looked around to see who she was talking to, then said, "I do!" as if he'd win a prize. Another guy came by doing high pitched bird calls. He gave us a huge smile and waved.

I was very much enjoying the city last night in all its weirdness.

After a while Art and Pinky came home. We went in and smoked some Fatties. A bunch o' people came over. They were all upset about a Nazi skinhead concert in Napa this weekend. Their house has way too much traffic. In and out way too quick. We left and went to Haight again. Met a bunch o hippies keeping warm in a van. They were bummed we didn't have a shower to offer. We went to Cala Food, bought munchies, then went back to Willard North.

Andy and Corvette went to ticketron to pick up tix for Jerry tonight. Before they left we were talkin about Seca going into heat, and cats spraying, like Andy's ex-roommate's cat spraying his Albums. Andy, "What if humans were like that? 'Nice to see you guys,' squirt squirt. Jerry tickets! Splash."

"What would a show be like?"

"Galoshes."

"Plexiglass in front of the stage."

"Windex men during break." Gross but funny.

Inside the Jerry Show

Sittin' on the window seat, 1st set. Carp next to me. Tavi wearing a great Rainbow skirt. Lots o' babies. Betty-Ann, pregnant and moneyless on the street all winter, had a baby girl two weeks ago – still unnamed. Cherri's baby Bonnie, – lurching around the Fatty Circle with an orange. And Trinity of course.

Amanda and Beau are psyched about being pregnant. Amanda picked Beau (said Beau so proudly) because he's got good genes. Janice and Tanner are psyched to be pregnant too, but I wouldn't want to be in that house in eight months or so.

A few minutes ago Fritz offered a free high to anyone around. Some kid said yeah, and it splashed out – he got way way way puddled, it was dripping down his arm. The kid gave some to his friend and they rubbed it in like hand cream. Have a good night guys.

In the lot we smoked bowls with Domino and (Murph's) John. The joke became John's hairy butt and how Corvette doesn't like hairy butts. It's still the joke now as he came and sat next to me.

Cherri was handing off a fatty, I missed it. John was bummed. Marshal got it. I said, "Don't worry, Marshal likes me. And I like Marshal." Marshal grinned as he handed me the joint and pinched my cheek.

Mutz is here, and others who laugh that we just left Rockefeller in Atlanta.

Davy, Don, and Fritz, are dancing in front of me. I love to watch my friends dance and move with each other.

Kennedy was sitting with me earlier. He lost his van – went to Mexico, and coming back, it got confiscated at the border for 1.2 grams of bud. He'd have to pay ridiculous fines and tickets to get it back, and probably won't bother.

Della and Dawn are here. They had a hard time getting in. Ozzy and Helena are in. Ozzy has a remarkable new jacket with an embroidered version of his bus.

Outside we did balloons with Munch at Hawkeye's van. Amber (Adrienne's dog) was being bad. Munch was giving pointers, – he went to school to be a Dog Trainer! Lovely vision, big bully biker being sweet and patient to dogs.

Hawkeye says the guy who narced on Sid is here. He says Munch is 'gonna get him.' I'm not sure how I feel about that. I just can't get behind the violence. Sid has been sentenced to one year, which probably means six months.

Fritz, Don, and Trevor bailed out of their Boulder Creek house when someone turned state's evidence on Trevor. I'm not sure exactly what happened but Trevor just walked in, maybe I'll find out.

Carp didn't go to his court thing this morning. Says he's gonna turn himself in on Monday.

           Break.

On the window seat. Everyone sitting on the floor below me. My friends.

I see lots o' fatties lit, and fatties in progress. The breaking of the buds, our ritual sharing, treated with reverence, always giving thanks. Seems almost religious sometimes. Many people hold the fatty to their third eye before taking a hit.

Don just intercepted a fatty from Carp, yeh!

Outside Clarity told us about her brother. She was excited that she'd watched him being born. She invited us in to see him. Open-mouthed, head-bobbin, black-headed cutie.

Now Don's lighting one. We're trying to convince him to turn around and pass it to us. Instead he forward laterals to Fritz across the crowd.

It's so fatty-smokey in here. I just saw Kerry smoke – yeah, he's back!

Poet is looking happy and vibrant. Says he's been in Tahoe composing music. Neil and Winnie look so cute and peaceful. Santa lights a fatty.

Pregnant Janice just came and lay down next to me with her head on my knee. And there's Eden. She's glowing. She's pregnant too.

The music begins. Helena is telling me how wonderful this all is. This life. This scene in front of us. We all get overwhelmed sometimes by the beauty of it all. She's glad I'm writing it down.

Mojo's hair is getting long again. Cannoli Ron is here. Benny has a new tattoo, a small pink heart with lightning bolts. Ozzy's way dosed. He just came and put his head on my shoulder.

I've been here most of the show – on this window sill, writing.

I should dance some. Stretch my muscles.

After the show

Me and Corvette learned to do round peyote stitch. I'm doing one on a bic lighter. I was working on it just now, but light got voted lower, and I can't see well enough.

The big news tonight was that Dragon Dave was back. BACK! Sparkle in the eye and everything! He said he just walked into the woods and found himself. Yeah! He says he remembers everything from the months he was gone, and as proof he proceeded to tell us about both times we found him, wandering in the lot, got him a ticket, and walked him inside. He says he has lots of people to thank. I never wrote about any of that because it was too uncomfortable to contemplate. Uncommunicative, and staring into space, while everyone did their part to keep him safe. I probably didn't write because who knew if he'd ever come back? He was gone a long time, like, since last summer.

I saw Garrett tonight. I asked him to give us a ride, he thought about it, one hand on his chin, the other holding his elbow. In the end, he said no. I'm trouble he says. I say he's trouble. It's all true.

Saw Willow Bob and Kara after the show. Before he left for his court date, Jack gave Bob his big bracelet to hold on to. Dammit. I don't want Jack to go to Jail.

3-4-89

Beading. It's a tin imitation day in SF. This couple Carmen and Jason from Arizona are here. We're rockin out to 12-27-83 show on the tape deck. I was there. It was my first New Year's run.
Inside.

I like writing during a Jerry show.

KindBoy was the first we saw of the crew from Colorado. Then Silas and Allie, and Karl with his finger in the air. (As Fat Matt runs a monologue, here beside me, about fingers in the air.) We came in and fattied on the small 3rd floor platform. That's where I'm sitting now and some guy just took my picture.

"Oh man. You shouldn't have done that."

He said, "I'm sorry. Why?"

"I don't like my picture being taken."

"But you look wonderful sitting there writing in the middle of a show." He said he only keeps the pictures for himself. He was dressed in leather and didn't have a narc vibe.

Kerry is dancing in an usher's face. Marshal and Beatnik Bill are here on the landing with me. Silas went to check his floor seat.

There's some drunk long hair next to me, "I'll bet it's nice in that book you got there." He's wide-eyed by all the people who follow Jerry now. "It was better before so many people knew about Jerry." "It was better before they let alcohol in."

"I want to say to my sisters and my brothers, Keep the faith!" (My favorite tune!) "We can walk together little children, We don't ever have to worry, through this world of trouble, we got to love one another. Let's take your fellow man, by the hand, try to help him to understand. We can all be together, for ever and ever, if we make it to the Promised Land"

I hope China Sue is in – she really wanted to hear this.

Deal. Must be the end of the first set.

~~~~~

Still *Deal*. I've moved to the Main 3rd Level.

Domino's in. Adrienne and Hawkeye, Carp, Ozzy and Helena too. Helena has Rosemary's #! (I've been trying to find it all night.) Watchin Fritz and Don and Izzy and Trinity and Kerry and Santa dance.

Justine is here, and Wow, there's Pandora – haven't seen her in a while.

Just as I wonder if Silas is back on the landing, I look over and Corvette's there, she shakes her head no.

Riff Raff is here, trying not to be scary, but it's not too easy a thing to reverse.

Davy is high. He just took a long time making the ashtray into a chair using his shoes. Kerry is being a Fatty Factory in front of me. There's Gina. She and Andre are having a party for Carp tonight.

Music starts and everyone is up and dancing. Davy wants to borrow my pen.

~~~~~~~~~~~~~

Santa drank too much of his own Mushroom tea. He yelled at Izzy, threw water on her, and left the show. I got a half-assed massage from Fritz. Leaning back on him, he's almost comfortable sometimes. Adrienne's moaning in the corner. Hawkeye's holding her. Apparently she spilled a vial on herself. Skye has some Niacin for her.

At the Party

I told Carp I'd drive his van to the Party. It was just women and Carp in the van. Kara, Helena, Tish, me, Corvette, and a few more. As we gathered the vanful, Fritz and Don wanted a ride. Carp barked, "No!" Said he can't let the hottest things on Dead tour get in his special, women-only-van-ride. Fritz and Don didn't mind hearing that and happily went to find another ride. While the door was open, some guy came and started talking to the chicks inside. Carp stepped in front of him and said, Carp-like, with his gravelly voice, "Wrong door." And slammed it, shutting the door in the guy's face.

We all giggled, "Tell him Carp."

Later

Carp did a planned beer spill on Fritz. The party is raging. The major Fatty Zone is in the kitchen, but the whole place qualifies. I came back into the living room. Sitting near Garrett. He's massaging some blond's foot. So many people there's barely room to move. There's been no sign of Santa since he ran off. Kestrel Jim from Santa Cruz is here. Hawkeye just walked in. Adrienne's feeling better.

Later

Fritz wanted to get Carp with whipped cream, so they rolled a huge Goodbye-to-Carp fatty and went up on the roof. I went to the top of the ladder to watch. Carp was doing a speech and saying something about he, "can't read or write very well, and people who can... well..." But I didn't hear the rest. People wanted to go up and I had to go all the way up or down. I chose down.

Fritz said they missed me on the roof party. Why? Would I have been whip creamed too? Hawkeye, Adrienne, and Dawn waved at the room and left. I might have been the only one who saw them wave.

Someone stole all our stashed beer.

Trying to write about a party. What a joke. Can't be done afterwards and it's pretty hard to do during.

March 7th

I'm gonna miss Carp. He was emotional and loveable at the party. Too many family going to jail.

March 8

We decided we needed beading supplies before flying back to Atlanta. Spent 50 bucks at General Bead. Boots got on the bus at McAllister, also on her way to General Bead. It's where hippie girls spend their money.

Me and Corvette went to Beau's. Janice and Amanda were headed to Oakland to the jail to visit JP, but Gimlet called and said JP was "out." Ah the importance of a good family lawyer. Janice and Amanda being pregnant together is a thing to behold. Beau says he's learning a lot.

We went to the Red Crane for Chinese food, then to Willard North with some movies borrowed from Beau. I finished my first peyote stitch necklace.

This morning we talked the logistics of Karl's coming trip North, wondering if we have time to profit from it.

March 9th

We met Beau and Amanda for dinner at Padrino's. It's Karl's favorite place, but as we left Willard North for the restaurant, me and Karl got in a pretty bad fight, so he didn't come with us. He's always got to have the last shot. And he doesn't know when to quit.

Dinner was pleasant. We talked about the doings of all our friends. And we talked about JP, Sid, and other jailed family.

Afterwards at Beau's, we bought pot from his neighbors, and watched Amanda nervously clean the rug with her fingers. Her parents have just flown in and called from their hotel.

Back at Willard North, Karl and I smoked a peace pipe, and spoke not of our regal differences.

12
March 1989
Georgia and Alabama

March 10
Went to Shawna's when we landed. Some guy rides up on a bike the second we get out of the car, "Rockefeller wants to see you before he leaves tomorrow." He was at Daybourne house, so we went over and smoked a skinny. 'Leaving tomorrow' was said like a threat – like, that's what he'd do if we didn't take him back. We only stayed a minute and nixed the idea of him coming with us when we left.

Today Rockefeller drew his hitchin' sign, and Shawna brought him to the highway – 15 miles – a good hitchin' start. He's headed for Ocala, Florida.

We went to King's. He bought Chinese food. ("You fly, I'll buy.") During the after dinner fatty, two of King's Rainbow friends came over – Cooper and PineCone. Cooper walked in chanting, "Rip a fatty, Rip a fatty, Rip a fatty."

Later
- to write someday on how what one person says, in a corner, or in the hallway, or all the way up top of the place, can affect and/or change the whole show!

Saturday 3-11
At Shawna's, listening to the benefit show (9-24 in N.Y.).

Mavis called. She has Louisville tix, and will get Cincinnati tix for us.

I called Rosemary's. She wasn't home, but her mom said, "This is what Rosemary thinks you want to know, – Jack doesn't have a phone, – he went to court and it got postponed again till the 14th of April."

Morning 3-13

What a wild, out o' hand, party we went to yesterday – 45 minutes East of Atlanta. Widespread Panic was the band. It was big land, with cow facilities and ponds, major field parking, and a little house. It felt like a show – groups of people gathered around open trunks, lawn chairs, crankin tunes, tye-dyes, long hair. Elwood got videotaped while two dogs barked at him, – he just blinked at them.

It was a dose party more than a mushroom party. (Which is what we were told.) We left Elwood in the van when the sun went down. There were some pretty weird vibes going through that place. The band rocked out. We saw three sets. At one point though, the guitarist shook his head, put his guitar down, and walked off stage.

King was pretty high. He had the "light" with him at all times, in the form of a gallon jug of water. Victor wore the 'hat of foolishness' all night. Mercedes was unhappy with her name so we changed it to "Face." Victor, looking for Carlos, "I gotta find him, he's got the keys to my beer."

The cops came a couple of times, drove across the field with their lights spinning slow. I felt a bit paranoid and trapped. Like, how the hell can we get out of this party with a stickered van from Connecticut? (Yankee!) The cops are probably waiting for people leaving the party. So we stayed a few more hours.

It was 3AM when we finally left, following Carlos and them. They decided they had to stop for cigarettes, or munchies, or something, so they pulled into a 24-hour convenience store. I didn't like that, right off. Two cop cars pulled in. I felt, for a moment, hopeless and said aloud, "This is how it happens. Middle of the night, backwoods Georgia…"

Both Corvette and King yelled, "NO!"

And brought me back to my senses and I agreed, "No, they won't bother us." And they didn't. They drove off without looking at us at all.

Later

We called Hawkeye. Psyched! We'll have something any day now.

We're at Josephine. These guys are all impressed, like, "Look at the color of that pot in the bowl!"

Last night I watched the Orion constellation travel across the sky. Orion is like a guardian for me somehow. Which seems silly so I don't mention it, but I look to him for insight and messages. Makes me think of this quote, – I don't remember who originally, but Ken Kesey quoted it in *Demon Box*. "When the best student learns about 'The Way' he practices it constantly. When the average student learns about 'The Way,' he believes it sometimes there, and sometimes not. When the worst student hears about 'The Way' he laughs. If he did not laugh, it would not be worthy of being The Way."

Orion is part of 'The Way' for me.

3-14-89   Alabama
Corvette's parent's house

We smoked a joint in the backyard. Elwood loves it here. I love it here. It was 86° today. We caught the local Salvation Army on a ½ price sale and bought all the cool hippie type stuff to resell on tour.

Alabama, might not be as far in mileage as some of the places we go, but as far as state of mind, you can't get any further from California.

March 16   Alabama

Actually it's midnight so Happy Saint Fatty's Day!!!!!

We went to the post office – sent a money order to Hawkeye, and more black leather roses to RAD Leather. Drove to Huntsville, to Kirby's. Rusty called, and we asked him to bring us Chinese food, – said that if he wore a sumo-wrestler's jock strap, we'd smoke a joint of California kind with them. That's how he showed up.

March 17 1989

Another Rusty came over Kirby's this morning. At first he looked narc-like to me, but what the fuck, this is Alabama, everyone looks like a narc.

We copied some tapes from the second Rusty. The first Rusty came over on his Harley, dressed in leather fringes. Certainly a better look for him than the jock strap was.

We left as the sun went down, towards Birmingham. Corvette had called Cash Hamlin at work and told him to be home tonight, at 9:00, for a delivery. They were quite surprised the delivery came in person. We drank green bottled beer, and smoked a fatty for our patron saint.

Cash wanted to go to The Quick. He tempted me with, "the same motivation he had to use last time." Coke. So we went to some guy's house before The Quick. Cash expected us to spend our $. We didn't, and he didn't turn us on. Neither of us cared.

The Quick was a typical Friday-night-Alabama bar scene. The band, Ladybug Highway, sucked bad, doing lousy blues. Man, I get disgusted watching these oblivious people, dancing their asses off to lousy music. I could never live that fake a life. How could you fool yourself into thinking that's a good life? Or am I totally fucked in my thinking, and it actually is a good life? Maybe it's good for some people, but not for me. I feel like I'm getting old. I don't always feel like a party animal. I certainly don't like the idea of chasing coke all night. Maybe it's just that yucky coke vibe.

Monday 3-20-89   Atlanta

We stayed at Cash's all day Saturday, – had a cookout, and played with super elastic bubble plastic. Next morning we headed back to Atlanta.

First stop, King's. "Rip a fatty. Rip a fatty. Rip a fatty." Went to Magnitude Ink. The sketches were done – we figured out the color scheme, and the colors/sizes of shirts to order. Total estimate – $850. King bought Chinese food, and told us he thinks his house is being watched. (Great.)

~~~~~

Fuck. The Feds picked up Jack night before last. On charges that have to do with the guy who set up Carp at Thanxgiving time, and something from July 88, in North Carolina. Something about cross-country trafficking and racketeering.

Oh Jack.

Rosemary said the lawyer is saying 10-20 years.

NO! That's not fair.

<p style="text-align:center">March 21</p>

We're at Atlanta Mary's. Un-fucking-believable – the decadent riches. They have a jungle-like atmosphere throughout the house, and a waterfall in the living room. A waterfall in the fucking living room. So cool! Mary's dad does car dealings – she drives a Jaguar. She says he doesn't really work, he just invests well. Stylin'. We got stoned and helped her clean out her closet. We got some great clothes – for wearing and for selling.

<p style="text-align:center">March 23rd 89
Atlanta</p>

Center Stage at the Neville Brothers show. Sometimes I hate being in a place like this. All these stylee women, and I'm wearing painters pants and a tye-dye. They look at me like I'm so much lower than or less than they, while I think many of these people have no fucking idea what the universe is really about.

Wow. I smell kind bud. I've actually seen it a few times here in the South.

Went to Magnitude Ink today. Bullshat with 'em and got high in the darkroom. They were like, "Do you have that same polio-weed Henry smokes with us?"

Jack called last night. Said where he is is pleasant enough, for a federal jail. Said they're gonna ship him around to face all these charges. He thinks they're trying to slap him with some of Carp's charges. His bail is $250,000, but he doesn't even want to bother with that. So it looks like tour will be spent trying to get lawyer $ for Jumpin' Jack.

Yuk, now I smell dirt weed.

I do hope tour is good to us. Don't know what I'm doing after. Corvette has all kinds of plans that I'm not sure I'm into. I want to find a gorgeous guy to massage me all day, a quiet mountain cabin, and pounds of green bud – relax a few months, and spend time actually writing in book form instead of just these silly notes.

Hey baby, come find me. I'll be on tour.

Later

Mercedes came dancin' up to us, "Let's go to the Grapes!" The Grapes are fun. I like the way they rock out old Dead classics like *Hard to Handle*.

'Who are the Grapes and why do they stay in Atlanta?'

Corvette is friends with the backstage bouncer – this chick Letty. She was glad to see Corvette. Ha! Everywhere we go these people are glad to see Corvette.

March 24

Grapes on stage at 'Tango'. Rockefeller is here. He wants us to pick him up at his hotel tomorrow. I said NO. Also a vanful of hippie boys from the Bay Area. I recognize them, but I know none of their names. They had no $, so Corvette gathered some spare bucks from people to get them in. They were psyched.

I went with the owner and King to smoke a fatty in the walk-in. King's rainbow friend Cooper was in there doing whippits.

March 25

We were lazy at Josephine 'til Magnitude called. They had some shirts done. They're great! We've even got some proofs, which are pretty much like felt wall hangings.

We cruised "The Lot." – It's there. It has begun!

People were arriving at the rate of one or two a minute – laden with backpacks, or in vehicles trailing dust from the west. Bob, Marie and Ginny were there. Bob gave us a fatty smoker. We ran to the store and got him some beer, then came back to King's to show off our shirts and break in the fatty smoker.

March 26

Cruised the lot again last night. Mavis and Shaleigh came runnin' at us all hair and skirts and arms. Went to Fritz and Don's hotel room for a Fatty. They followed us to the Cotton Club for the Widespread Panic show. They wanted too much to get in, so we went next door and drank. Mavis wanted some guy's wizard shirt. She didn't get it, even when she offered to pay for it. Apparently she's not used to being denied. After a bit we got into Panic for free thanks to Letty. The place was packed. They rocked.

Afterward we all headed for King's. When we got there – gone were his CD player, all his CD's, an ounce of kind, and a full set of tour tickets that were on the table. King had been feeling something wasn't right earlier and had had all his cash on him, so he was calm.

It was morning when we went to Josephine to crash. Leaving King Henry's – I raise my arms and say, "Corvette, look at all the sparkling morning dew." Then my Birkenstocks slipped on the sparkling morning dew, and I was flat on my back on the hill in his front yard, laughing my ass off.

Later

Went for a birthday dinner with Justine, to "the old spaghetti factory," which was elaborate, with purple velvet couches, and cheap, with good food.

We set up our stuff today, but sold only one American Indican shirt – to Blake.

Gypsy Linda and Nina set up their tent near us. Saw Tavi and Santa. (Santa had a rough night running naked through the Panhandle that night he ran off from the Jerry show.) Izzy and Trinity didn't come east.

It's 3AM. We're at Jeremy's workplace. The restaurant is long closed, but he's making cheese sticks for us. We left the van in the lot near Bob and Marie, – we're crashing at Jeremy's.

13
Spring Tour 1989
Atlanta to Louisville

March 27
Atlanta. Inside. Break.
Show's good. Lotta new stuff.
We've not gotten much money for Jumpin' Jack. Haven't sold many Indican shirts either, but we're doing ok on used stuff.

It's Poet's b-day. He got a huge Birthday song sung to him.
We got some Fat ones going – some kind, some not, – but there are no buds anywhere to be bought or sold. Seems no one was

brave enough to bring quantity across country. Leandro appears, "What are ya havin' – a shwag circle?"

Marshal's here. Patty and Hinch. Hinch looks pretty high. Red Wayne's here. Mindy too. She bought a lot of our stuff today, and traded us a dress. Dawn and Della, and Dragon Dave! Suzy and Kennedy. And now I see Hawkeye. He threw pennies at me till he got my attention. Taylor's here. I think I spent most of first set watching him dancing on the stairs. Briscoe got busted in Arizona for two grams of kind. He got out though. A cutie named Grayson, that I met at the Grapes, got arrested last night and bribed a cop to get out. The venue here is in the same building as the cop shop.

There's been some big door pops tonight.

Cops just came in and got Mavis and Fritz!!!

~~~~~

It went like this. Six cops came storming in through the Fatty Circle, right to Fritz and Mavis. I saw Fritz say, "Unh-un, not me."

And he melted away as someone yelled, "Stand-up!"

Everyone stood. The cops surrounded Mavis. They had her. Me and Corvette each grabbed our Fire bracelets and said, "Fire Power NOW."

We followed the cop procession around the corner and there they all were, standing there looking confused. She was gone. It worked! Yeah!

They opened 2nd set with *Scarlet FIRE. Estimated, Eyes.*

I was weirded out about how they almost had Mavis. Shaky for a while there. Till *Fire* actually. If this is an indication of tour, I'm worried.

A lot of people won't kick for Jack, because Chester said, a couple o' tours ago (was it the south tour?), "Either get me out, or I turn state's." Apparently Jack collected enough bail money, but spent it? I don't know. I didn't see any of that.

I truly hope tomorrow is a better day.

March 28   Inside 2nd set.

Maybe I'm paranoid.

Ship o' hit hard – "Don't lend your hand to raise no flag atop no ship of fools".

Corvette said during break, "Yesterday was a warning so we're not so blatant this tour – sitting in front of a plate glass window not even looking at what's outside."

Mavis said, "I never look."

The Omni is octagonal, which is cool, but it's been too weird. The boys have been playing great here, but I'll be psyched to leave.

Last night, Eddie from Atlanta got busted and taken downstairs – where the cop shop is. He told them the cubes were for sugar energy for dancing.

Today in the lot was hot. Temperature hot. We made some $ on clothes, then totally invested when KindBoy and Silas hit the lot. Yeah!

Drumz

The keef is around. I never saw it before, it's pure THC powder. We're smoking some now. There's a nice rainbow around the drums.

Fritz, leaning against me, "Are you really writing a book?"

"Yes."

"What's it about?"

I was like, "Fritz! It's about us. Somebody's got to tell the real story." He sometimes objects to my writing, but today he just seems curious.

Stoned. And happy about it. Intense space
Late

The Atlanta skyline is all Billboards – in the Omni hotel, on a balcony overlooking the lot.

March 29   Greensboro

Last night selling buds, we got rid of everything we had at the Omni – friends of Hinch and Patty. Nice we didn't have to drive with it. Did some N_2O and watched the lot seething below. That high above the lot all the music melted together and became a whole new Dead tune.

Found Murph's guy John as a rider. We took 441 and 23 North to 40, because I didn't feel like going the obvious route. Got here about 10. You can't get in the lot without tix to both days so we parked across the street in a lot for "Coke" employees. We walked over to the lot and scammed tickets to walk in.

Skye and Matteo, at Murph's bus, told us the place was way hot. They saw ten people busted, in view of their bus, in four hours. We went walking. We saw cool-looking local-type young kids getting instructions from cops. We saw 16 and 17-year-olds in Tye-Dyes pull out badges. One aisle we turned down some guy said, "Don't do it, this aisle is a trap." They busted one guy, circled the onlookers, searched 'em all, and busted accordingly.

Back across the street we saw Auguron and Lizette. We warned them. Word was spreading fast – this place is hot.

We saw Pixie and June smoking a fatty, so we sat with 'em, and discussed this sad state of affairs. Davy and Wolfboy Taylor joined us. Taylor was even more tweaked and paranoid than me. He saw a vanful of narcs jump out and circle a smoking crowd – all busted. He was spinnin' around wild-eyed, "Dude, let's go to a hotel – let's get the fuck outta here."

KindBoy rode up on a bike and we walked around with him. Every conversation I overheard was about the busts people have seen. We went to Silas' truck. Smoked a fatty, and Leland and DebbieJo came by. They heard the cops are writing down the plate # and state of every car going into the lot.

I was too paranoid. After the fatty I had to get outta there. This other lot was starting to fill up and I did not want to get blocked in. We got a hotel with Leland and DebbieJo.

I hated how the lot was tonight. That's no fun. It's not how it should be. Atlanta wasn't either. I don't want all tour to be like this.

March 30

Woke to a wakeup call so Leland could try to get tix at the box office. I went back to sleep till I heard a knock.

It's Leo and Deek! They're gonna go in on the room with us. It's pouring outside.

Later

The sun came out and we went to the lot. Didn't take the van. Easier to scam in walking. The lot is a lot cooler today, and the weather is great. We tried all day to get tix – no luck. Came back to the hotel an hour ago.

I wonder what they played?

Morning 3-31

When the show ended me and Leo went for a walk. We met our wingnut quota for the night and headed back to the room. Karl came over, smoked some keef with us, and crashed on our floor. Seems to have been a smokin' show. I want in tonight.

Late

Spent all day lookin for tix. I was in a pretty bad mood. Willow Bob got busted with shrooms. Diggety got busted liquefying someone. Poet was collecting bail for seven different people.

It was windy, and cold, and I didn't want to be outside. I spent $40 on a ticket. Corvette spent $35. They were tour tickets – with Bears on them. They were both counterfeit and got confiscated at the gate.

FUCK.

It's hard to describe how I felt. I really wanted in. I wanted to be with my friends. I even thought I was on my way. Last night too! Why didn't we get in? We never get shut out – let alone two nights in a row. So what if it's Friday!

Part of me wanted to cry, part of me laughed at the part that wanted to cry, and another part was mad that I cared at all. A band shouldn't be that important. But it is. Even Nonnie, who is a Spinner-type, wasn't inside. Fritz went up to the door and said, "Look – I <u>need</u> to see the Dead." And just walked right in. The invisibility trick.

We left towards Pittsburg. Without a rider because of when we left. We passed an Atlanta car – stopped and ate with them. There was a huge scary American flag – snapping whipshots in the wind, sounding deadly and threatening.

Rumours of a blizzard are true. 2AM snowing hard. We got a room in West Virginia. Some heads checked in next door. At least I think they're heads. I peeked out. They were laughing, had eight people, couldn't get the key in the door, and one was singing, "Good Golly Miss Molly."

I'm not too happy with this tour so far.

April 2nd   Pittsburg

After a bitch of a time getting in the lot, we parked near Murph. Skye is collecting $ to fly Izzy and Trinity out here for Trinity's B-day. Kara stopped by – Willow Bob's still in Jail. Fritz swung by and smoked a bowl. And Gunner bought a couple of Indican shirts from us.

Tickets are seeming really hard. Corvette just brought back four big N_2O balloons.

Later

It started to rain so we packed up the sale stuff and walked. Didn't get far. Hung out by Kennedy's van with Rosario. Silas got us high and we went looking for tix. Corvette took one side of the street, me the other. She didn't come back. I circled the doors as the rain started really coming down. Mavis kept telling me to go to the Spinners, but tonight I couldn't even find them.

Aiko – Red Rooster – Dire Wolf. I could hear it. I kept circling. No sign of Corvette. She must have gotten in.

As I gave up and headed for the lot, I heard my name. Skip, with Anna and Justine. They didn't get in either so we're in Justine's room, about to go eat. My feet are soaking wet.

This makes three shutouts in a row. There's way too much bad energy here.

Things are not right – something has got to change.

April 3

Silas and Corvette got in on door pops. Everyone got in on door pops.

Just saw Trevor and learned that, because of the guy who turned state's on him, we have to call him Rick now. I can write that, because this notebook will soon be filled and mailed home. So it won't be around. I'm always cautious about what I write here in case it ever got found by the wrong people. I never really say what goes on, unless sometimes if my book isn't going to be in the van with me, but I expect I'll remember it all.

We tried to get this room again, but today they want $129. Suzy, Nicholas and company got wrongly told by the front desk that they were paid for the night – so we're with them now – yeah – Free Marriott.

Later

Inside finally. Fritz gave me a ticket first thing this morning.

This place is wild. Great Halls. Break now on Phil's side with Silas, Corvette, Lubba Lenny, Hackmen, and Gitch. Eating m+m's and smoking keef. It feels good to be inside.

Today is Trinity's B-day, she's one. She took her first steps three days ago. Everything about her shines. I'm glad she and Izzy are here, but still this tour is lacking. I miss Sid, and Kevin and Roz, and Carp, and Jack.

Rosemary is bummed at the spirit here. She says people don't seem 'together' enough. That may be one way to put it.

April 5 1989

In Silas' truck outside a University Union while they run in to the box office to get tix for tonight. Ann Arbor seems cool. Small townish and college-y. Not Stressful.

April 6   Ann Arbor

Last night's show was short, but fun. Everyone had tix early so there was no worrying.

We got a free parking pass for two days, – "One time parking for $5, or a two-day-in-and-out pass for $12."

Silas said, "How 'bout an in-and-out pass for $5?"

Guy said, "No can do," handed us a two day pass and said, "Get outta here, you're holding up traffic." No problem dude, we're already gone.

We parked near Silas' friend Dodd. Went bud hunting and found Skip and Anna set up behind Mavis' car, selling Espresso and Hot Chocolate. Mavis is selling Jewelry. Fritz, Tavi, Two Toke Tom,

Pixie, June, and Newburgh were there. Everyone was waiting for Kona Paul. When Paul showed up, he needed a ride to his hotel. I borrowed Silas' truck, and me and Corvette helped him weigh out the buds, then came back to the lot.

Did a bunch o' nitrous then went back to our hotel to get show clothes, leave this huge ¾ oz bud in the room, and feed Elwood.

This is a nice place – college kid ticket takers letting in anyone who asks. But too much blatant stuff everywhere I look, has been freaking me out. This tour I prefer smoking fattys inside where you can see the band.

April 7   Ann Arbor

It was harder for folks to get in last night. Thankfully we had tickets already. Inside we did the hallway rounds. Fritz looked great all in turquoise – new pants – our Indican shirt. Him being nice to me all night was a plus. He hooked me up with buds for Silas, after the show. I had to wait for him a long time by Mavis' car, so I was drinkin' a bunch o' coffee at Skip's espresso stand.

This is a nice place to see the Dead. Even the cops are pleasant. Janice is here. She's getting bigger. Pregnant Eden and Riley are here too. Gimlet's here. He's still doing nasty drugs – it shows and he doesn't deny it. Rosario went through the snack line across from the Fatty Zone and threw munchies to us over the crowd – flying peanuts, popcorn, and candy. Of course this started a food fight.

We saw Chrysalis being carried off by a straight-looking woman. They thought she was an abandoned child in the hall. We found out where they were taking her, told Chrysalis she'd be safe, and we'd find her mom. Armand knew where mom was.

I'm slowly getting motivated. Corvette is looking around the hotel to see if there's anyone we want for a rider.

April 8 '89   Cincinnati

Loungin' at the Residence Inn. Nice room – two floors. Like an apartment.

We didn't end up getting a rider. The only people needing a ride were too dirty for us to consider. I still think about bugs when I see dirty hippies. Yuk.

The drive was short. We were the first to get here, so we rented the room out of shirt $. Came in and made ourselves at home. Silas, Nicholas, Laney, and Dodd arrived soon after. We did a housewarming fat one and those guys headed to the grocery store, while me and Corvette went to Goodwill. We spent way too much money. $127 too much. It also came out of shirt $. When we got back, we feasted on spaghetti, bread, and salad. I did some beading – working on a peyote stitch necklace for Murph.

This morning Dodd rolled a joint for a pre-wake bake, but Nicholas delivered OJ in bed to everyone so no one went back to sleep.

Fritz came over to borrow Dodd's ID so they can get a room here. Fritz is so immature sometimes – it shows he's only 18. Silas says, "quote me on this, – Fritz is bunk. $70 a ¼. Ha."

Later –

Outside is cold rain and snow. We decorated the room with the rainbow banner, the Mardi Gras face masks, t-shirts hung over the paintings, and we draped Mexican blankets from the bedroom balcony.

I said, "Man, I wish we had tickets – all you guys have yours huh?"

Dodd, "You guys don't have tickets? I have two Extras."

Inside –

Hot show.

Talking with Skye as they broke into *Don't Ease*, she told me all the things she worries about about jail. "Every damn thing but the jail house key." I wanted to tell her not to worry – but I didn't.

Break

Fatty Zone is on a platform in the top back corner. We're on a "smoke-no-pot-in-the-hallways" routine. Lots of very fat ones. Lots of coughing. Not too many people seem to have tour flu though. I see Eden, Riley and Marshal over aways. I'm near Janice, Rick, Hawkeye, Mavis, Fritz, and Mutz. Close by is Boots and Benny, Spyglass Michael, Don, Tavi, Washington George, Santa, lots more. Someone wonders where Davy and Lizette are. And a joint is put out and shunned by the Indicans because it is purely chemical pot and outdoor is preferred.

Lights out.

China Rider Looks Rainy Eyes drumz space *Wheel Fantasy* – and now, *Jude*.

Miracle!

I like to watch people dance – Bianca flows like water.

April 9
in the lot – Louisville

Today has been a good day. Started with a fatty, then KindBoy, Gitch and Dante showed up. Nice green suitcase! Two more fattys and we hit the road with Dante and Ohio Dave. Sunny, short ride – 1½ hours. Two more fattys on the road.

– "I smoke two joints before I smoke two joints and then I smoke two more."

The whole highway was Heads. Every car. That's always fun.

It's a nice feeling that a bunch o' good bud is hitting tour and it stopped in our room first. We just got fronted a QP, and we're selling used clothes.

1st set

Nice Hallway. Found the Speakers and the Fatty Circle as soon as we got in. Fritz announces, "Chef Ra from High Times will be joining the Indicans during break tonight for a fat one."

When we weren't here some undercovers came into the hallway and got Neil and Winnie. The Spinners followed as they were escorted away. Lots of shady types around. Lots of picture takers. Willow Bob just walked by – yeah – he's out of jail! Also we saw Chris Kangaroo (who got beat up in NYC by Carp and Sid). Good to see him. He mentioned that karma would get them. Who's to say? But... They are both in Jail.

Izzy is throwing cigarette butts at some guy who won't stop taking our pictures. King Henry's here in the hall. So are Skye and Murph. Skye goes to jail in the morning. That's so sad.

Word comes back that Neil got away, but they have Winnie still.

The picture guy left. I would too if a woman with a baby started throwing cigarette butts at me. They just ended the set with the first two notes of *Help on the Way*.

2nd set

Estimated Prophet. Yes! "California."

Bad news between Cincinnati and here. Someone stole the bail $ for Diggety that Kimmy had collected. Also Dragon Dave is still in Jail in North Carolina, and Jean Claude went down in Cincinnati.

We are people just trying to live peacefully, be good, and believe, and we get persecuted for drugs. It's ridiculous. Some people learn a lot from drugs, and use, not abuse, them.

Late night.

After the show we hung out doing balloons with Tish. She's traveling with a chick who got in by giving a backstage guy a blow job. She laughed, "I hadn't done that in a while." I never thought Deadheads were like that, but we're all kinds, aren't we?

I went runnin' around the lot while Corvette waited for Hawkeye. I ended up finding him and bringing him back. Once we got our shit together, Corvette went to find balloons so we could take some back to the hotel. Tish and her tank were already gone.

So we bought three huge balloons and hit the road with Ohio Dave. We got kinda lost. It's a hard Residence to find.

Chef Ra did come to the Fatty Circle! I wasn't there. Fritter said he was amazed by the quality of the pot, and the size of the fatties – To think, the Indicans can amaze even someone who works for High Times... Yah mon!

Thinking of Skye. I can't yet accept she's going to jail in the morning. In the hall, I was watching her – I burned an image of her into my brain, – so strong and beautiful, dancing in her Indonesian dress. I'll miss her. She's the closest person to me going to jail in this way. – Knowing in advance the exact day you'll be going.

TV news, – There's Winnie on a patch of grass being angelic, as the announcer says, "There weren't many arrests at all."

14
Spring Tour 1989
Chicago, Milwaukee, Minneapolis, and Colorado to SF

        April 11   Chicago

  When we got here around sundown yesterday, parking was already a bitch. The lot was across the street from the place, and way too small. We bought fresh hot donuts from the tent next door and hung out in the van – it's fuckin cold here in Chicago. Don was out cruisin the lot – he stopped in and we smoked. He told us Winnie is free, and talked us into going to the Sheraton Bar. We left a note on the van for Silas.

  When Dodd appeared, they hadn't gotten a room yet. So we asked the front desk. All they had left are 'parlor rooms' for $75 – and a normal room for $120. We took the Parlor room. It's so close to the lot, it's great. Me and Corvette found King, Kerry, and Jeremy in the restaurant. King bought us an expensive and delicious dinner.

  We went back to the lot to get our shit. The people who own that lot across the street, went home when it was full. They left one cop, told him, "anyone with a pass can come and go as they please." People were pouring in by the second. More cars than passes. As I look out the window, I can see the lot is jammed full.

  Everyone is waking up. Bud tips for breakfast, and we got the room again. The first time I went downstairs I was barefoot and had only ten feet from the elevator to the front desk. Three Security guards jumped in front of me and pointed to my feet, "You have to have shoes." They were so vicious looking.

  I was like, "Dudes, I just wanna pay for my room."

They wouldn't let me go ten feet barefoot. I got shoes and when I came back one guard bowed big, made a flourish with his hands, and said, "Thank you." I curtsied in return.

Late night

It was so cold and windy in the lot we didn't set up – just carried around sweatshirts. Got cheap tix – two for $25 and went back to the hotel. No one home and Silas has our only key. Back to the cold lot. And into the show pretty quickly. No speakers in the hall. *Shakedown* opener. And for some reason I'm thinking of Jumpin' Jack.

The Fatty Circle began up high on the 2nd level, but we experienced too many 6-ups, so most people went down below. Corvette came back (from following the Fatty Circle to see where it went), and had Jack's new address. By the end of the set I'd found paper, and during break I had lots of people write to him.

Rippin' show. But when I got to the hotel – A semi-tweak scene.

Silas (on valiums) went back to the hotel alone, and left the key card stuck in the door. Security walked right in. They wanted to know what the towel was by the door for. And what the smell was. And why the smoke detector was in pieces. They saw pot on the table and made him flush it. Then they called the front desk to check the number of people supposed to be in the room – One. Me. When I showed up things were basically cool but they wanted only me in the room. Silas was calmly tweaked as he packed up and left (with a way dosed Dodd in tow). I walked them out.

There was no talking him into staying. "Dude, don't worry. I'll get another room, then we'll check into the Residence tomorrow." I told him to drive safe and when he hugged me he told me to open the smoke detector when I went back upstairs. I just did and it's filled with pot!

Me, Corvette, and Ohio Dave went to the Ramada bar. Great dance floor, and high/drunk heads dancing madly to Prince and other stuff.

April 12 1989

At the Residence – smoking our first joint of the day. It's all Hawaiian Indica tips. Smokin it out of the new Fatty Smoker Bob Snodgrass gave me.

What a crazy morning. Woke at the Sheraton to Nicholas and Laney knockin, then Dodd appeared. Him and Silas slept in the lot. Dodd wanted to do bongs. We decide no, it's almost checkout time. This room got weird last night. Let's just leave.

Dodd goes to get Silas and the truck. Nicholas and Laney go upstairs to get their stuff, while me, Corvette, and Dave waited out front. Hackmen appeared. We told him to go get his van from the lot, and get ready to go. Then Dodd drove up in the truck, without Silas. Silas had stayed in the lot to look for Hackmen. When Hackmen pulled up, Corvette went to the lot to find Silas. It was as confusing as it sounds.

Silas was way fucked up last night. That's how he left the key in the door. But when the guard told him to flush the pot, and put the smoke alarm back together, he was smooth enough to stuff most of the pot into the smoke alarm cover without the guard noticing.

We've all been hanging pretty tight and I'm realizing how it affected the group with two of us being so high. We all had to make adjustments. But we minded not at all really, 'cause that's what it's all about. Sticking together and Caring. Think of us as a group mind with parts running slow, and other parts handling the overload with love. Isn't that part of the point! I think yes.

Back to the story.

The Residence rooms weren't ready. Everyone was hungry, so we decided we'd go shopping to fill the time. Off we went to the Jewel Osco. Debating the merits of products – squeezing veggies, doing like we always do in a store – filling a huge grocery cart. Suddenly some asshole in ½ a suit comes up to me and Dave and says, "You guys are gonna have to leave." He's holding open cookies, open sandwich baggies, and an empty box of nail bond hardener. (Of all things!)

Dave goes, "What?" Truly not getting what the guy was implying.

"You guys are gonna have to leave." He looks around and says, "Obviously you are the ones doing this. I want you all to leave."

Dave gets it now and says again, louder, "What?"

I've always been the type to get upset when accused of something I didn't do. I went off! "What are you talking about? We didn't do that. We didn't eat any fucking cookies, and we certainly aren't the type to use nail bond hardener. We came to shop and spend $ just like every other person in here."

"If you don't leave I will call the police and I will have you all arrested."

Corvette grabbed Dave's hand and he followed her away like a puppy dog, Hackmen, Laney, and Nicholas took the cart to checkout, and Silas dragged me outside while I was still trying to bitch.

April 13 1989

Yesterday's show was way hot. I liked the *Smokestack Spoonful* combo especially.

After the show Silas bought a nitrous tank. Balloons, Balloons, and more Balloons. Late night, smoking a fatty around the tank, Dodd fell asleep with a balloon in his hand. I went into a back bedroom to sleep. This morning Silas and Corvette woke me up jumping on the bed with a fatty and a balloon. This can't be good for your brain. But it sure is fun.

Late night

Fritz wants my Yin-Yang lighter case. Don says I should hold out so Fritz will style me out awhile. Fritz, doing just that, cleared a seat for me in the Fatty Zone during break, and gave me a big roach.

April 15 1989

We were gonna stay in the Residence again but when I woke up there was weird news. After I crashed, three different people came by – All hitting the wrong bell at 4AM. So security came by too. They saw Glenn's dog and demanded a $50 deposit in cash, right then and there. Silas paid, and somehow got rid of them, and then he slept in front of the door. We packed up and left pretty early.

Outside – Weird vibes. Narc cars all over the hotel parking lot. Turns out the front desk people offered some heads a free night at the hotel for a couple o' sheets. The heads kicked down with the sheets and got busted.

Suzy had just flown in with product, and they were here in the hotel. The narcs were watching everyone so we left without visiting them. We went and got a cheap hotel – one with a kitchenette, so at least our food won't go bad.

While I finished Murph's peyote stitch, me and Silas had a long discussion about strengthening SEPs and cops and Karma and friends.

Everyone wanted to go out last night so we went downtown. Two small Reggae bars, a block from each other. Both bands were fun. We did a fatty out back, laughing about the crowd in the alley smoking better pot than the Reggae bands backstage.

When the bars closed, Silas took us to the shore of Lake Michigan. Beautiful view of the shimmering city. He smiled telling us of hot summer nights hanging out on that shore. We smoked a few bowls but didn't stay long, – it was the exact opposite of a hot summer night.

Getting ready to head to Milwaukee. It's Saturday and there's a show tonight!

Hackmen will be back today, – returning empty because he didn't want to wait longer and miss another show.

Late night   Milwaukee

Drove here with Laney and Nicholas. Got a hotel and went cruising. There's no real lot, so we parked in a garage and wandered. I traded kind for a ticket, and Corvette got one from a tourist. Then she got a Spinner ticket, so that left us with an extra. There was Justine, and Weasel Karl. Justine got a Spinner ticket, so I gave the extra to Karl. Lenny was like, "I don't understand things sometimes." Looking to the stars, proclaiming, "Hollie just gave Karl a ticket." I told him to stop spreading rumours.

Today was a rumour day. When we got there Granny Nancy was crying about a recent bust. Someone we didn't know. Then Fritz came up and said, "They got Rick." Thank god that turned out to be a vicious rumor. Trrrrrrick – that's what Puppy Pete calls him (it's hard to remember to call him Rick). Later I heard they got Newburgh. But he was inside, so that was a rumor too.

I got inside during *Franklin's*. Fritz, Don, and Mavis had just gotten in too. Fritz had on his satin pants and his hair in a bitch handle because I said those were two things he had to do before he would get my lighter case. Someone ran by, telling us about some room downstairs.

The moment of just getting in is super charged. Always such high expectations and a rush of energy. So we all come laughing into this room, and start peeling off layers as Jerry breaks into the one I've been waiting for all tour. *When Push Comes to Shove*. We slam danced. Me, Fritter, Mavis, Don, Patty, King, and some folks we didn't know joined us.

(Pizza break – I'm starving...)

So this room downstairs at the Mecca is huge with five big speakers. It's there just for us. One end had pictures and portraits of Deadheads from Alpine. There was one of Macy's friend Zorba, one of Dimitri, and one of Poet, Lizette, and Kelsey. There was a picture of the Spinner lot set up, with Jonah in it. (He's long gone, and his parents have a court order on the Spinners to stay away from him.) There was also a picture of the photographer. It was the guy who took my picture while I was writing at the Orpheum. So that's cool.

During break the whole room was a Fatty Circle – no cops, and hardly any shady-looking people at all. As we fattied, broke buds and loved life, Tavi put on a bitch handle, then Santa did too, and Butter Bob, and VW Walt, it was hilarious. JohnRay kept laughing at Fritz for doing whatever I told him to.

Back at the Ramada now. Everyone winding down.

Fritz got the lighter case tonight. He owes me a ¼ oz of kind.

April 16   Milwaukee

Waked and baked. Laney came back from a walk, "You can smell pot all the way down the hall." So we put out the fatty, lit incense – the whole bit. I hate that we have to be so paranoid about the way we live. We don't hurt anyone. Yet we live like we have to be scared. It's just not right.

Afternoon

We paid for the room another night, but we've decided we don't wanna stay. We're gonna drive some after the show, since it's six hours, and no break day. We'll sell the room to someone in the lot.

April 17   Minneapolis

Last night they played *Saint o' Circumstance*! I loved it!

The lot in Milwaukee wasn't any sort of real lot. It was small, and it was rainy and they were busting people for selling shirts.

When Mavis told us Jerry's room was right next to Don's in the Windham, we decided to slide an American Indican High Council wall hanging under Jerry's door. On the elevator, we couldn't remember what floor Don was on. We headed to the lobby to ask. The elevator went up instead. The door opened. Jerry, Manash and the baby got on. Our mouths must have dropped open. Jerry smiled at us and pushed the baby carriage on. We smiled back and at each other. "Jerry we have a present for you."

He was so cute close up, and taller than I thought. He asked if he could fold it and Manash said, "Jerry, you want me to put it in your suitcase so it won't get ruined?"

"Good idea."

Some guy got on on another floor. He was stunned and the doors almost shut before he remembered to get on. When we landed in the lobby, Corvette and I said, at the same time, "Hey Jerry, Thanks...... for... everything."

As we all walked through the lobby, that third guy hopped across the room on one leg, playing air guitar. "I feel good!!"

We walked back to the lot, smiling in the rain. I was so high from meeting Jerry. Such a regal presence.

But news in the lot was not good. Rockefeller, the rider from hell, got popped in Milwaukee. Thorin is in the pound. Mutz is trying to get them both out. And Andre got busted while selling shirts – but he was holding a backpack for someone else, with major amounts of LSD in it. Enough to make Andre the biggest bust this tour – and it wasn't even his!

I saw Blake in a Paddy Wagon, but I saw him later inside the show. They thought he was selling LSD, when all he did was give some girl a ticket – he got released when a search turned up nothing illegal. They tried to tell him he had too much money.

Nina got busted for trying to get in on a fake ticket. It cost $130 to get her out. Stupid shit.

We sold our hotel room to Mojo and hit the road. Hawkeye and Munch passed us – Waving and grinning – in a pick-up truck, with two Harleys in the back bed.

We slept in a rest area, got up and came to the Marriott – right across the lot from the Met Center. Me and Silas walked over to the Box Office. Hooked up with Benny and Kennedy on the way – we all got tix.

Inside

Estimated.

They had to play this for us all who'll soon be headed west...

This place is huge! Sounds like the Dead is playing in a bubble.

"Might and Glory gonna be my name!"

The last night of tour. Yes. California. Of course.

"My time coming any day. I ain't in no hurry no. Don't worry 'bout me NO."

April 18   Minneapolis

Working towards extended checkout.

Just saw Mutz and Thorin. Rockafucker costs $10,000. That sucks. I have no idea how anyone would be able to come up with that now that tour's over.

Currently fattying in our room with Glenn, Hackmen, Mavis, Fritz, Don, Tavi, June, Pixie, Newburgh, Silas, and Dodd.

Mavis can't go home because her friend Jagger's mom is telling the whole town that Mavis is a drug dealer and a heroin Junkie. (She is not a junkie.) June and Pixie are looking for hot springs to hit on the way west.

We've got Fritz listening to David Peel's Fuck song. Because Fritz's motto has become, "Don't say 'fuck you' to your friends."

Later

Murph's guy, John, just bought the Hilton's football team school bus, for only $400. Stylin'.

April 19   Colorado

Drove all day, Major Mountains. The highest point was Monarch. We got high there, and let Elwood run. Now we're at Silas'. The town is new-looking old west, if that makes any sense. It looks like a fake town some old man in Maine would set up in his back yard.

There are huge snow covered mountains all around. There's even snow drifts on the shaded side of the house that reach the gutters, but it's warm. KindBoy says everyone in this town smokes bud and knows the real deal, so it's cool here.

As I drove today I gave thanks for some of my favorite things – One is that I love being in the hallway, with the smell of Indica blanketing us, dancing, and seeing all the faces of people I love, as they dance. Sad that each time more faces are missing.

April 21

The waiting game has ended and we're getting ready to go. We packed the two N_2O tanks under the bed in the van. Silas had just finished packing the truck and paneling everything away when a cop came and parked right in front of the house and set up a speed trap coming down the hill. At least he waited till everything was done to show up.

April 22

These roads are so long and straight, I'll attempt writing as I drive Rt. 50 across Nevada. It's 8AM. I've been driving for 16 hours. We're two hours from the California border and Corvette can't even stay awake.

Last night was a warm, heavy night as we drove through Utah. Sunrise was wildly beautiful. A full moon going down over snowy mountains at the same time.

A while back I saw a mirage. I saw it out of the corner of my eye, and in the rearview mirror too. It was a parking lot full of heads. Impossible right? But it was there. A mirage. No Deadheads in the desert.

Met a woman truck driver on one of our stops, "Wow, you're hippies. Oh! I love seeing hippies in 1989. You're so beautiful. And you're young too! That's so great. You've made my day. Don't let anyone stop you from doing what you wanna do."

I don't much like Nevada. Not sure why, because it sure is beautiful. Maybe it's the harsh drug laws, or maybe it's the karmic energy of all the underground Nuke tests. Scary place.

way later

I drove straight through to SF. 25 hours. I almost thought I was too old for that shit.

We cruised Haight St. – Saw Wretchy Richie. He waved at us. Something about him rubs me all wrong, but on Haight today we had to acknowledge each other. Same family. He's a bad Joneser though. Not our style.

We went to Beau's. Allie lives with him and Amanda now. Until tour, she'd been in Colorado with Silas.

April 23, 1989

Hanging with Silas is like having rose colored glasses. We're pretty broke, but now we have a ½ lb. We're gonna head to Cotati and make some money.

April 25th

We didn't bring enough pot. Sold everything we had and almost ran out of head stash. Thankfully we each got a hit on the bridge on the way back.

We re-upped this morning and Crafty Adam brought us to a house full of happy souls. When the door opened, there was the smiling wingnut from Haight and the hallway. Smiling as big as ever. Like someone turned on the brightest lightbulb in all the world.

We had pot to sell, and this house wanted some. As we walked down the hall, he was bouncing and radiating energy. When we entered the room full of people, he announced to them, "For so long I have had a love connection with her in the hallway, and..." he turned to me, "and now I get to meet you. I don't even know your name."

We formally introduced ourselves. Bill. He bought a ¼ pound. "I know I want to buy pot from you. I always see you in the hall, smoking the kindest fatties, with the kindest people."

There was a girl getting massaged by two guys in the middle of the floor, a guy who barely moved, standing in a shaft of sunlight grinning out the window, and hippies draped on all the furniture. We knew none of them. Bill declared with a flourish, "Bongs for all!"

15
Spring Tour 1989
Irvine and Frost

April 28

Checked into the Hyatt Lodge, below Irvine. Considered the Marriott with Suzy, Nicholas, and Laney, but decided against it. It's too close to the infamous Embassy Suites, where everyone got busted last year.

You need tix to get in the lot – of course we don't have any. We've got to get in there to make money.

Later

$25 vendor parking. It was still a scam-in lot though. We got in showing Silas' Frost tix. As we're parking, good news – we see Diggety. Yeah, he's out! Then, seconds later, Shaleigh yells to us, "They just got Fritz!"

No! Not Fritter!

We set up our stuff and started collecting bail $ too.

Later

We're selling some stuff, but not much, and even the Spinners are kicking down bail money for Fritz.

Silas had Wretchy Richie in the van. I bitched about that. He says he's not comfortable around people he thinks of as shady, – says he got chills one day seeing Carp standing outside a hotel. How he can be weirded out by Jumpin' Jack and Carp, but not by Wretch, is beyond me.

Corvette's on a ticket walk, but I think the Spinners are gonna offer her one. A Security guard just asked if I was writing about him. Ha.

Inside – Break

It's the first outdoor show of the year. Some parts feel good. The air, the breeze, a new Bobby tune that's not half bad. Some parts suck. Gestapo scene. Fritz in Jail.

As the set ended, some chick accidently hit a guard while dancing. He punched her and tried to restrain her. Everyone lost it on the guards till they let her go. It was a bad scene.

Later

Oh Fritz. You were supposed to be immune. I feel like something broke. Suddenly I feel straight, and I want to be high. I could cry when I think of Fritz with court cases. Fritz should have been like a core of Safety. He melts away So well. But. Have they got us? Are we doomed? I don't want Fritz in jail. Hell, I don't want Jack in jail either, or Skye, or anyone. But no matter what I want.

Damn.

Uncle John's.

Jerry's licks rolling up the hill – so peaceful.

Nice rainbow lights on stage, – not just a rainbow of lights, but rainbows in each light bulb. Silas is rolling the *Terrapin Station* fatty as LA is teeming, gleaming, and steaming off to our left. LA people talk too much. *Terrapin* – beautiful, sweet, soft, and these people are loud and obnoxious.

Drums.

The word "Fatty" is used by everyone lately. They say Fatty Circle as three of 'em sit and smoke a skinny. So wrong.

Ahh. Stoned again.

Damn. I keep thinkin' about Fritz. I feel tight. The fatty's done and I'm not stoned enough.

Great Space. But it's cold.

Fritz Fritz Fritz. Damn it.

Gettin' colder. Jer ya better heat the place up.

Sounds like a *Wheel*. (That's an early call) ... Yep.

"Wouldn't ya try just a little bit harder, couldn't ya try just a little bit more!"

Need a Miracle. Yeah I do, every day, and I don't think there's anything wrong with expecting one.

Standing on the Moon. I Love this tune – I watch it all roll by....

Silas has the moon ball crystal out.

Standing on the moon, but I would rather be with you, somewhere in San Francisco on a back porch in July – just looking up to heaven at this crystal in the Sky.

Sugar Mag. Dance for it all!!!

Later

After *Sugar Mag* was not *SSDD,* but *Touch o',* with a *Quinn* encore.

Hawkeye rode back to the hotel with us, and bought us dinner. – Only thing open was Jack in the Box. He and Corvette are in the hot tub now. I could join them, but Dodd went to get balloons, so I'm waiting for that.

The courts won't let anything happen with Fritz till morning. Oh! I love Fritz and he doesn't deserve this. At least the $ is already collected.

29th

Tavi wants to buy land, or go to India. He was there when they got Fritz. He's upset. Like I feel. This is the best we can do. Trying to be real. Trying to help friends. Wanting Peace.

It's almost noon. Fritz I want to see you <u>today</u>. <u>Soon</u>.

in the lot.

Saw Rockafucker as soon as we got here, – looking for Thorin and Mutz – we all fattied with Don and Santa. Fritz's bail has been paid at $2,000. Now we wait.

Crafty Adam did a beautiful piece – a Malachite ball with crystal points sticking out – a wheel. Same purple as the butterfly necklace. I traded a ¼ oz for it. He laughed, "You're gonna end up with all my best pieces."

Inside.

Break now, in the Fatty Zone. Fuckin Hawkeye, pays $5 for the last chipwich. Decadent. Everyone's attitude when they're rich is, 'what the fuck, it's only money.'

Fritter is home. He came dancing up to me in the lot. I'm glad to learn he did not use his real name. But he better never get caught doing anything in California.

(Lights out.)

They have the Yin-Yang lighter case. Damn. I have one chance to get it back, by going and saying I was from the car next door, and I don't know who this asshole was, but he borrowed my lighter, and I want the case back. Maybe I'll do it Monday.

China Cat.

Tavi bought the huge rose quartz crystal ball I was drooling over in the lot, and he's letting me hold it tonight.

Hawkeye is falling asleep on my shoulder. He says Sid got his jaw broken by a bunch of black guys in Jail. Youch. Wretchy Richie is raging about drumz and bells inside the show.

He's Gone melts into *Spoonful.*

It's good to have Fritter back. While sitting with him leaned back on me, during *Lullaby*, I had the rose Quartz in my hands, on his chest, and the ball was beating. I could feel it strong on my fingertips. Fritz's heartbeat, or my pulse? Having him back feels Safe. Somewhat. But. It's not right. Something has been broken.

April 30

I gave a ride back to the hotel to Tavi, Santa, Della, and Spyglass Michael. Tavi got beer and we partied. It was a tired, late night. Nicholas and Laney showed up with 10 big balloons. That about signaled the end of the party, and everyone went home, or to the hot tub, after that.

Me and Silas talked a long while in the dark. About tour, and life. Once you start "touring" there are only two ways to go. One is to eventually burn out and leave, the other is to make a career out of it. Whether a tye-dyer, or a wingnut, – being a tourhead is a full time Career.

Tavi gave me the Rose Quartz ball!

Inside – Break

Still light out. 5:30 show. There's a huge fatty being rolled in one Big Bamboo paper.

"We need more buds." Fritz, Don, and Tavi are the official rolling team.

"Buy pot and kick a lot."

We tell passer-bys – "Do not attempt this at home, these people ARE professionals."

This corner is all us – on two levels. Around me – Newburgh, Corvette, Mavis, Fritz, Pixie, June, Mutz, Don, Tavi, Shane, Gimlet, Santa, Lizette, Fletcher, Rockafucker (everyone calls him that now), Benny, Hawkeye, Allie, Mojo, Dawn, VW Walt, used-to-be-Dread Manny, Domino. Justine sitting on the fence staring off into space.

Above us is Dave Echo, Patty, Hinch, Granny Nancy, Davy, and Taylor bent over the railing yelling encouragement, and instruction, to the engineering project.

Tavi finishes rolling. Huge Cheers and fatty cries.

We are Indicans! Everyone screaming, "Send it this way."

We have crowds around us, waiting for a hit.

We joke about who does, and does not, have an "Inner circle gold card."

The chipwhich guy scored big. Hawkeye bought everything he had and tossed them among the crowd of us, then the guy stayed to get high.

I suppose a fatty like this qualifies as flagrant abuse, but I bet no one will get more than one hit.

~~~~~

We've all gotten it once. Now it's gone to the outer circles, and the joint is running, and the masses don't know how to fix it.

"Get a fatty doctor."

"Give it back to a pro!"

Hawkeye got a hold of it. Whoa – Dave Echo intercepts from above. Now the action moves to the upper level.

Sounds like 2nd set's starting. And it's getting dark.

When it gets dark it gets weird.

May 1st

Bob's Big Boy, Laguna Hills

Boots and Santa were gonna go North with us, but Boots found bugs and wouldn't get in the van. I appreciate that. Me and Corvette get freaked at that thought. We told Santa we wanted to do something alone, so he left hitchin'.

This morning was weird in 309. Tavi counted his money, then went to eat. Came back, and the money was gone. That happened to him just recently too, and now he's way in debt. Poor guy. It's not even his money. He was tweaking. Seems the guy who called himself Kokopelli, and the Governor wanna-be that we met in Tavi's room last night, left and said they'd be right back – but haven't come back. Tavi doesn't want to think they took it. But what else is there to think?

I'm ready to get the fuck outta Hell A.

Later

Carpenteria Beach. Stopped to smoke a fat one.

Poor Tavi. He was raging and screaming about why the fuck does he do this Dead shit anyway? Said he doesn't have fun anymore, – He's in big debt, so all non-show time is spent hustling, and he just gets ripped off again and again – getting further and further into debt – and the thing he loves most is the dancing, and there's no room for him to really dance nowadays.

I love Tavi. Especially when he's doing 50 rpm's in the hall. I feel the same way sometimes though. In Greensboro I was ready to give it all up. It's hard on tour now. Used to be everyone was swinging and raking. Now everyone is broke, and not into swinging, or in fucking jail.

I blew off the lighter case the cops have. If I went there I'd be fucking crazy. Besides, it was in Fritz's fanny pack with nine (as yet) unnoticed things.

Wonder what's up with Andre, and Jean Claude, and Dragon Dave?

Too many oil rigs on this beach. Too many people in jail.

May 2nd

Morro Strands Beach. We scamped here last night. It's nice waking up a few feet from the ocean.

There are kittens living in the bushes. Afraid of people, but they'll eat Elwood's food as soon as I get outta the way.

I liked the way we heard the story of the Irvine Super Fatty 89. Hippies we don't know told it to us – one of them was on the top tier and watched some guy say to a guard, "I've gotta get down there and put pot in that joint."

The guard looked down at the rolling process, and said, "Don't look to me like they need any o' your pot. They doin' just fine by theyselves. Why don't you go smoke with those people over there – they don't have any pot." And he pointed to Taylor, and everyone else hanging along the rail.

I hope Santa got a good ride. I feel bad we blew him off when Boots said she had bugs, he's been lookin' kinda sad lately. I guess we're all sad, deep down, when we think of what's happening to us. Rumour has it Dragon Dave only costs $500. Yet there he sits.

I should be writing postcards to everyone, but I never seem to have the time, or the cake, to do so as much as they deserve. I love you guys. I don't know what to do about all of this.

Later

Walking on the beach this morning, some hippies told me Santa was out on the Highway, hitching. We decided to go get him but he must have already gotten a ride.

May 3   SF

Saw Don and Taylor on Haight and Schrader. Taylor, on a bike, played chicken with us. We parked and hit the street. There's a lot going on in the city tonight. At the Fillmore, David Crosby for $20. At Slim's, Bo Diddley for $12. And at the Full Moon, Zero for $6.

Right now, we're at Don and Justine's hotel waiting for Chinese food. Seems it's been had out with Mavis. She insists Fritz stop selling LSD, and wants Don to stop too. She tells them mail is ok – but nothing else. Don says him and Fritz can't be partners anymore, because Mavis won't allow it. And she was supposedly screaming about it all, at the top of her lungs – which is totally not cool.

May 4   Willard North

Everyone waiting for Hawkeye on Haight yesterday, Don was gonna go check his hotel, but kept missing cabs because of mine and Taylor's antics. Then Hawkeye showed up, so hey, we saved him the cab ride.

We picked up cards for Jack, Skye, and Sid, for everyone to sign at the Frost.

May 7 1989   Frost

Yesterday I kept wanting to write, but starting out the day with Indica brownies, and eating them every time we got hungry, really got me fucking high. So high I didn't know they had already done Drumz and Space.

Hardly anyone got in. Spinners didn't even try. The scene outside is very cool. No charge to park, park anywhere you like. The show was broadcast on the radio, so there was no real need to get in. We had a Fatty Circle under the eucalyptus trees. Suzy and Laney sold beer right close to us. Becky and Mitch were here with baby Devon. Macy's here. So are Arthur and Jasmine. Ozzy's bus is here – without Ozzy. It's owned by the Hog Farm now, and they don't know how to put up the speakers for the right effect.

Fritz and Mavis got a puppy. They named him Cabaret.

Right now we're in Freddy and Piper's room at the Stanford Inn doing keef bonghits.

Current subject – the biggest problem is that "they" have fucked up our trust. That's where they've got us.

Inside Frost

I got my ticket thanks to Silas. Just about showtime, "What! You don't have a ticket? Got any pot? Got an 1/8?"

Garrett was with me and he had one, so I grabbed it, and Silas went looking for his friend Apollo who had the extra. He couldn't find Apollo, so we gave the pot back to Garrett. Went up to the stop sign, and there was Apollo. Race backwards lookin' for Garrett again – gone. What a hassle getting it all together. But as soon as I got my rose quartz ball off the dash, in hopes it would bring some magic to the process, there was Garrett, and there was Apollo, and I got in for the beginning of *Aiko*.

We saw a bad scene today. On the side of the road three heads were on the ground in weird positions – like they had been running or something, when they stopped and dropped. There was one cop standing over them, and another with a gun pointed at a car full o' hippies. Heard just now it was Butter Bob, the guy who had the Big Bamboo paper in Irvine, and five others.

Also Marshal goes to jail tomorrow. That sucks.

So far *Aiko, Red Rooster, Bertha, Me + Uncle Mex. Built to Last*.

Mavis didn't get in. She was shrieking at the gate as I came in. Without her around, Don and Fritz are hanging together inside.

Did I write about how when Santa was hitchhiking at the beach – Catbird and company drove by him and said, "A blue van is coming to pick you up." They meant us, because we'd decided to go get him. Two minutes later some other blue van picked him up. Santa just thought it was one of those cosmic occurrences.

Later

If you took the background, and knowledge, of everyone who is a Head, you would come close to knowing everything about everything. Wouldn't it be great to have access to a group mind without all the chaos? We'd know every trade and skill and craft and service, and we'd know every social level, and we'd be fair. But now... – There's just too much noise.

Later

A shirt I saw today – "Spring Tour isn't over till the DEAD melt the FROST."

16
Spring 1989
Life Between Shows

                       May 10   Cotati, Randy's

Perry is cooking himself breakfast. He's so self-sufficient. He eats every meal – balanced and on time. Says he's gonna be a doctor. Preston is going to be a physicist. He wants to design a safe Nuke plant.

Working on Auguron's peyote stitch necklace – thought I had that spinning pattern figured out, but it tricked me.

We stayed here two days so Jumpin' Jack could call, but he never did.

                               Later

Keef is so strong, some call it the crack of the pot world. We're in Fritz, Mavis, and Ohio Dave's hotel room in Guerneville, joking that Fritz will be the first keef casualty.

In town we saw Rockafucker and Mutz. They pointed out Judy Blue's store. She got a bunch o' stuff from Bali today. That's the new rage – Bali Clothes. Fritz, and them showed up. We went to Judy's apartment upstairs, and out onto the deck. Saw Pixie and June below, they came up too. A whole family party here in Guerneville.

I'm writing shit. Stupid unimportant shit. I need to write about what's important.

                       May 11   Guerneville

Have I ever mentioned how Elwood sings in the shower? We figure it's because he's deaf and probably likes the way the sound reverberates back to him. He gets in there and starts making loud howling-meowing noises that sound like he's singing scales. We woke this morning to him doing that and Cabaret puppy-jumping around like he was dancing.

We took our time getting out of the hotel. Mavis is so demanding sometimes. It's hard to watch. Dave came with us, because Mavis and Fritz are headed north and he wants to head for civilization.

We decided to visit Pixie and June. (They have one of the cottages near Mutz.) Saw Newburgh on the payphone. He smiled and mouthed, "#12." There's Tavi lounging in the sun! Everyone is in Guerneville it seems. Also everyone is short on buds, but we just did a fatty, then had cheese sandwiches for lunch. June, trying to change her nose ring, dropped a sapphire through the porch slats.

May 12   Saint Randy's

Preston saw Holograms being made and he's excited by the process. He says he might head in that direction. That just tells me college boy doesn't have any more idea of what he's doing with his life than I do.

Late

On our way to the city we smoked our last skinny, it was 5th generation roach weed. I threw the itty bitty roach out the sunroof – "to the gods."

We cruised by Dodd's and got excited when we saw Silas' truck. Went inside hoping for a fatty. No fatties. Took Silas to Beau's, thinking KindBoy might be there. He was. No buds though. KindBoy is so animated and quick with the lines. He keeps us laughing.

Margot called, inviting us over to smoke some keef – Yeah!
Back to Baker and Page, – all night on a major bud hunt.
Beer.
If we can't find pot, we'll drink.

Art and Pinky have a new apartment with a hot tub. That's where we are now. This place is kind. Huge bathroom, artsy bedroom, and big built in couches. Dave whispers to me that he saw a mouse in the kitchen.

May 13th

Corvette flew east this morning. I sat on the porch in the sun and called Mom. While I was on the phone Elwood started hopping backyard fences. It took an hour to find him. He was out on the Haight.

At Keith and Tina's I managed to score some keef. Had some stimulating conversation there and headed back to Art and Pinky's thinking how glad I was to be alive and seeing and walking and hearing and high in San Francisco on a sunny Saturday.

May 15

Went across the bay with Silas and KindBoy. Score! Finally! Silas was a bit on the tweaky side till we got stoned on the bridge. We paid the toll of the person behind us. KindBoy decided it's good luck. I think it'll become a new tradition.

Evening

At Abe and Jackie's. Clayton here is weird. He calls motherhood a disease that turns beautiful warm people into flaming bitches. He's also the one who says he feels in-valid on tour. That when he's on tour, he's not doing anything for anyone but himself. Wonders why us Tourheads don't notice we're in-valid.

Abe says Dragon Dave called last week from Jail. His bust was for trying to trade acid for coke. Bad move. No wonder he's still there. He probably hoped Abe would help, but Abe was just mad he called this house from jail.

Monday May 22

Inside the LBC. Stevie Ray Vaughn show. I came here alone tonight.

I asked a yuppie if he had a free ticket for me. He said he'd rather walk in with it. Fuck-you. That's what's wrong with yuppies – $ is everything to them now. Most used to be hippies. Where did their hearts go?

I got a free ticket from some bikers. Smoked a fatty with them when we came in.

May 24

I got a package from Mom with three letters from Jumpin' Jack, and one from Skye. Bradley has been moved to the same jail where Skye is. She's very happy about that.

May 26th

In a cheezy hotel in Berkeley. Long day. Visited Garrett and wandered Telegraph. I found Boots. We hunted up Tilden park, got stoned and hiked around a bit before heading to the United Fellowship Unity of Universalists – the church where the Prankster movies were being shown.

We got in line. Freddy and Piper pulled up with the Hearse. Along comes Don and Justine, then Tavi comes down the street playin' guitar, then Santa. Neil and Winnie. Pixie and June. And Cindy, the loud chick from backstage.

The line was long. The place looked small. They didn't sell tix. You paid and went in. So you couldn't buy extra tix for people who weren't here. It filled up quick. They added a second show and that sold out too. Fritter, Mavis, Kona Paul, Hawkeye, and more, didn't get in to the first show.

Pot is in short supply among us family folks. Just before showtime I ran outside and there was Fritz. Right then we traded buds for the Yin-Yang lighter case I remade for him. I smoked 'em all inside.

The evening was hosted by Ken Babbs. What they had for footage was not too impressive. It's still unorganized, nowhere near what I'd call done, but Babbs was fun to listen to.

Between shows I saw Auguron. He gave me $150 for the necklace. Yeah!

The second show went in, and I went to eat at LeValle's with Freddy, Piper, Downstairs Dave, Domino and Maureen, and Kevin. We went in the Hearse which is always fun. Lots of talk about kids, lawyers, laws, Jails, Paranoia, Tour, and leaving Tour.

We smoked a big ole Fatty on the way back to the church. When the second show got out, I followed Mavis and Fritz to this motel.

Mavis is a tyrant to Fritz. It's kinda funny. (And kinda sad.) They fight a lot though. For real. And that's not funny or fun at all.

May 27

The AIDS Benefit was tonight. I had cards for Sid, Bradley, Skye, Carp, and Jumpin' Jack. I got lots of folks to write little notes of encouragement. Tracy Chapman played a somewhat pertinent song while I was doing it. About souls being all we have.

The best part of the show was the John Fogarty set. Bob and Jerry played with him. No Phil though. Mostly Credence tunes. They did *Down on the Corner* – my personal favorite, but I wanted to see Phil do that bass line. We joked about putting up a "Where's Phil?" banner.

2nd Dead set – *Hell-Fire* with Clarence Clemons was nice. The Fatty Circle was on the field edge, close up on Phil's side (of course).

Skye sent me a wonderful letter about how it felt to her, to think about dancing in the hallway with all of us. I let everyone read it.

May 28th

Sunday. Memorial Day weekend. At the San Gregorio Music Fest. Maria Muldaur is doing *Promised Land* JGB style. She used to be a Jerriette.

The festival sold out, so they opened the gates and let everyone in free. John's Hilton bus is here. It looks great filled with Matt Ackerman's curtains – the inside glows purple. Not too many cops here, but the few who are are mean.

A point to remember – That lost feeling. People don't know where to go from here. There ought to be a better/next earthly step... from the Grateful Dead to... What? Where? How soon? And how do we find it? (Or make it?)

later

Since the gates were wide open, Fattyland included all the dogs. Hawkeye brought in a blow-up lounge chair and acted like a king. His roommate kept letting the air out. Hawkeye never caught on and kept looking for the leak.

People were collecting money for Andre (still in jail in Wisconsin).

May 29th

Silas' truck got broken into outside Margot's. They put a brick through the window and there's shattered glass everywhere. He's cleaning it up now as I sit on some neighbor's stoop. At least they didn't take his wallet full of credit cards, or the Jar of Life. A fad phrase applies – Shit Happens. I wonder why Margot lives in a neighborhood like this? Crack is the worst.

May 30th   Willard North

Hawkeye hasn't called. I don't know what to think. Dealing with Weasel Karl all morning puts me in a bad state.

later

Karl's keef made me paranoid. Paranoid mostly for Hawkeye, but aware that it was just general paranoia, because I also thought Karl might read my notebook, in which I wrote that he's a weasel. I know it's just Paranoia – Hawkeye is fine even though he hasn't called.

May 31st

There's sad news in our hippie music world. John Cippolina died. I hope there'll be something which we can attend and show our love.

June 1st   Santa Cruz

Came here by myself to meet Hawkeye at the Rads show. We cruised town in his new car and smoked ½ a fatty. Not sold out and tix only $5. I gave my extra to a wingnut. "Sometimes giving tickets to wingnuts is good luck."

The RADS rocked.

Afterwards I went to the Continental, to Fritz's room, to crash.

Morning now – Sunny and hot. I'm off to deal with the municipal court system.

June 3

Played with Trinity and smoked a fatty before going to the court. This all goes back to the bald tire pull-over. They said I have to go to actual court. Ugh.

I went to Zak's and got some breakfast then left Santa Cruz.

In the city I saw Janice on the Page and Baker front porch. Gave her a buck. She's broke, living with Tanner and Beatnik Bill. I don't like seeing pregnant Janice broke.

I went right on out of the city and came to Cotati. Been doing beads for days. I think a lot when I bead. I think about Jumpin' Jack. I think about Skye, and Carp. I think about friends back in Connecticut. I think about tour. I think about wanting a place of my own. I still don't know what I'm doing or where to write. I'm procrastinating to the fullest. Maybe I'm avoiding writing because I don't know that I'm actually capable of it.

June 9

This morning Corvette and Jeremy flew in and we headed North, towards Jerry on the Eel. Got to Piercy about dark, got a spot in the KOA, then went across the street to French's Camp. Some guy lit a firework – it started a small bush on fire and he ran off! Jeremy put it out. What if we hadn't been right there? It's too dry for stupid shit like that. Later the guy found us and thanked us for putting it out. We joked about Jeremy slapping at it with his big ole feet.

Tuesday June 13th
Willard North

What a lot to write about JGB on the Eel. Arthur sold us two tix for $20. Heading in, we stopped to rearrange the beers in our packs. My ticket was in my hand when we stopped – Gone. Just gone. Either I'll find it someday in my stuff, or someone groundscored it and was psyched. It was easy to get in though.

People were makin' bracelets all over the place. Cindy (who is now calling herself April Flowers), walked me in through the backstage camp lots.

Abe and Jackie shared our camp spot. Abe's big thing this weekend was magnifying-glass bong hits. We claimed space under one of the pavilions that had a hole on top. The sun beamed through in a perfect pinpoint. Abe held the magnifying glass, and we took turns on "a spot in the sun."

Margot's dad was here. He's a professor. He looked intrigued by the way we did solar bongs, but he wouldn't do one. Margot said he ate a cookie though. Abe had cookies, and Skip had kick-ass brownies. I ate too many of both.

Under the other pavilion were the birthday boys – Fritz and Hawkeye. Don was over there. And Kerry, Mavis, Justine (she's pregnant and starting to show), Santa, Becky and little Devon, Rockafucker, Mutz, Pixie, June, and Newburgh. (Newburgh bought the musical note lighter case for $10 plus buds!) It was a fun day. Hot. Good show. I was very high, and by nightfall, lethargic.

Allie, Beau, and Amanda camped across from us. Silas and Karl and Silas' friends Jimmy and Patrick were hanging out with us till way late, even though they were camped a mile up the highway at a state park.

Everyone was starving. The store was closed, and there was no food being sold anywhere that we could find. We walked over to Hawkeye's RV and snagged some frozen chicken from him. Went back to our place, and went through hell to thaw it and cook it over the fire. It was very very late. Amanda and Janice, the two pregnant women, were hungrily waiting for that chicken.

Later

Yesterday when I woke up here at Willard North, I opened my eyes at the same time as did this guy who had been asleep on the chair when we came in. I like days that begin with a smile shared with a stranger. We quietly got stoned. Said no words at all. Just smiled and smoked till others awoke.

His name is Parker. He's a friend of Clayton's, traveling with a guy named Alex.

June 15

Night Court in Santa Cruz dismissed my case.

17
Summer 1989
Shoreline and Oregon

June 18th

We left SF because Karl bothers me. Been in Cotati two nights. Today we drove the coast to Shoreline. Sellin' postcards for Aaron. Got in for $8. Inside now, hanging with Arthur, KindBoy, and Anton (who just graduated High School!) Preston found us, we led him to June. She did him up good. The screen is playing wild patterns. Hawkeye wants me to roll a joint.

June 19

Morning in Cotati. Preston left the show with us last night and we ran out of gas. He and Corvette walked for some. I stayed and dealt with the cops who stopped. I forgot I had glowing blue rings in my hair. Didn't even notice until long after the cops were gone.

Hung out with Kevin inside. We talked good, deep talk. He's gonna take the addresses of jailed folk and make copies to pass out. We'll get strangers to write to them – such a fantastic idea.

I didn't see Mavis or Fritz for a while at first. But I saw Fritter during break – he told me Mavis is pregnant. Wow. I saw Mavis during 2nd set. She told me right away too. I hope all goes well for those two. I love them.

Tavi wasn't here last night. Mavis said he had court in LA.

In other Tour news; Lyndelle graduated from College in Pennsylvania. Great accomplishment. And word is Jean Claude's parents got him out of jail. And Andre is no longer in jail, but he's still in forced re-hab.

All vending at Shoreline is inside. It costs $100 a day and includes two tix per day. A decent deal, so there's hardly any lot scene. Me, Preston, and Corvette hung out selling postcards at the crossroads awhile, then left that lot and went back by the front of the place. Some guy we passed said, "Anyone need a ticket for tomorrow?"

I said, "Free?" But kept walking 'cause people usually laugh at that thought nowadays.

"Could be…"

I stopped. He was with two girls. They wanted to trade beads. Unbeaded beads, because Heather (the blond) was learning to bead. I didn't have any on me. She saw Jumpin' Jack's peyote stitch, which I was wearing, and asked how I made it. Francis (the guy) said he'd give me a ticket if I told them the secret to my slinky stitch. No Problem! As I talked beads with Liza and Heather, Francis fed Corvette and Preston living, sprouted bread. Heather has started making beaded fringes on the sleeve of her denim jacket. She won't be at any more of these shows but someday I'll notice her again, especially if her coat is done. We bullshat, sitting on the grass awhile. They're from Davis, California. Great people. We're set on having some $ and now I had a ticket too. I said, in random conversation, "Too bad we don't have a bridge bud."

Corvette said, "We should have gone spare budding. We still could."

Preston laughed and told these guys that if we didn't have something to smoke over the bridge we'd die. Heather pulled out a small purple tin and gave us a little piece of a bud and said, "She's very nice, this bud. We call her the Princess." I love buds with names. It was so good to meet them. Refreshing.

June 20

As we left Randy's yesterday, Dave Gooden called from Palo Alto – he wanted to go to the show with us and see the fatties we always talk about. We cruised into Palo Alto to pick him up and saw Bobby Weir and some chick riding bikes. We even turned around to drive by again and confirm it was him.

The show was hot – the dancing was especially fun.

Push-n-Shove – I always enjoy that. I was in the far corner when it started and I went dancin' fast – back up the hill to jump on Fritz. Mutz and Hawkeye had a wrestling match. Fritz was jumping up and down on them as they rolled around. I think it scared the locals.

I loved it when Tavi showed up – right off the plane, at break time, with not a care in the world now that he's here…

This morning we brought a bunch of Muffin Classics to Hawkeye's. A new flavor is Jerry Cranberry. Hawkeye's jingling change like a mad man. He quit cigarettes today.

Corvette and I had to go back to Hawkeye's tonight. We took a cab. He asked us if we were being careful.

June 22

Yesterday we got to Shoreline in time to get in the good lot. It was hot hot hot – hanging out on a used-to-be landfill. Hilton John, Murph, Vance, and Domino were parked in a nice little line along the grass island. Clarity had a bunch of kids in a blow up pool to play with. Trinity can run now and she does. During the show she ran and ran and ran, then stopped for no apparent reason – Izzy found a twenty where she stopped. McNeel was wearing our Indican shirt as he worked security at the front of the venue. We stopped and talked with him a few times throughout the day. He's so damned good-looking, cute isn't even an acceptable word.

Tickets weren't easy. I lost Corvette and she was holding all the money. The show started on time, because of TV. Winnie and Neil gave me an unused Sunday (1st night) ticket and I got in on that.

Saw KindBoy right off. He grabbed my hand and dragged me into the middle of the crowd – we did a fatty with a bunch o' strangers. Next Kona Paul got me nice and high. (Yesterday we bought buds from Tavi, Skip, <u>and</u> Kona Paul. Variety is the spice of life!)

Made my way up to the Fatty Zone. Hung there during break with Don, Santa, and Hackmen.

2nd set, me and Corvette went by Matt Ackerman's stand. He's set up with Oliver and Dee (who me and Macy met at LaPush last year). It took us a while to scam down into the seats but we managed it for the last part of the show.

Clarence on *Lovelight*! Yeah! Then a *Brokedown* encore.

When we left the show we had a pillowcase full of clothes from Matt Ackerman that he had tye-dyed for us. I must have left it outside either Domino's or John's bus, because we didn't have it when we got to the van.

But that's not the worst.

Weasel Karl's story is worse. JT (Andy's friend from LA), was here at Willard North. Karl rode to the show with him and left his stuff in JT's trunk. JT left immediately after the show to head back to LA. So we're all bustin' Karl's ass about spacin' his shit. Not something he'd typically do.

And. Not what actually happened.

This morning Karl calls JT to start the process of getting his shit back, and JT tells him – he left it in the lot with people he didn't know. That's a fuck-up on JT's part – big time. Ya don't go leaving someone's shit with strangers at the end of a show.

Karl's bummin'.

Big goodbyes last night. Overwhelming trying to remember who's going where. Rainbow Gathering in Nevada, Oregon Country Fair, Tour. I wish I could go East in John's bus. Don says he can't believe we're not going on summer tour. I can't quite either. Fritz says he'll miss me. Ha!

I hope everyone is safe and careful.

This is a tour many of us aren't going on. That's a little weird. I guess it's tour graduations, or generations more like.

Picture Grateful Dead Tour. Some folks come and visit, we call them tourists. Others of us find our way to living here full time. We stay. And there forms a hardcore group. Not only are we "on tour" together, we hang together off-tour too. We are family. Some tour for only a season or two. Of course they alter our chemical makeup while they're here, – Everyone who is on tour alters us, changes us as a whole.

But I'm looking at family – I'm looking at those who take up residence and call this place home. Every tour we gain new full-time people, and they will always slightly change the shape, but not the mission, of the hardcore group. Then suddenly (like now?) a bunch of the hardcores say, 'Enough!' 'I've had all I can take!' Because tour is not easy. It requires stamina, flexibility, resilience. Every tour we lose a few. But sometimes it seems excessive.

New people will appear and fill the gaps. They always do. Every tour we lose and gain. Every tour more drop out. When ya just can't deal with it all – with friends on Drugs or friends in Jail; when everything is harder to accomplish and the band doesn't even seem to be on our side any more, it's not fun vacationland, it's work, it's hard, it's sad. It wears ya down.

I take heart that some of the hardcores are still out there on tour. My people. Some will never give up. That's good. And it's good that there's new tour blood every season. Some of those folks will become important and essential to the family. Soon there will be a whole new bunch of family to carry on distributing the light – a continuous stream of us – always filling the same functions. Like cells in the body – new cells, same job – be a Deadhead, dance for the universe, spread the love, and the light. Ten years from now it'll be the same scene with all new people. That's important. And it matters.

– I won't reread that just now, – I'm afraid the exact concept I was trying to put across got incredibly lost in my stoned words.

The controversy over JT's vs. Karl's stupidity, rages on here at Willard North.

June 24

On the afternoon after my last entry, as we sat at Willard North, the phone rang. I heard Jackie say, "Abe, hurry, it's Skip calling from Jail."

Fuck.

What about Anna? And weren't Don and Justine with Skip and Anna? Abe tells us Skip got busted with buds and Justine got busted too – but Abe didn't ask what's up with her.

We went to Hawkeye's. He called the jail. Then the Lawyer. Justine had 20 sheets I guess. The lawyer's gonna fix it up. It was good to see how fast Hawkeye helped. Good feeling. To see that family backing again.

Before we left the house I had to remind Karl that he had wished Skip into jail this very morning. Probably exactly as it was happening. Now it's not that I blame Karl, – not really, – but I see the universe as all connected. I imagine that in the scheme of things, Skip's encounter with a police officer could have gone either way. It was a moment in flux and it was at that very moment when Karl said, "After all the shit Skip has done to me, I'd love to see him in jail." Karl made up the universal mind. The situation went along the path of Karl's statement and Skip went to Jail. Karl got defensive and said it had nothing to do with anything he may have said this morning. "Completely unconnected." But he was agitated enough that I suspect he partially believes it.

Nothing in this universe is unconnected.

Anyway, Skip's bail is $3,000. Anna's been found, and she's working on it. So far, there's no bail on Justine. Don wasn't there, he'd already left with John's Hilton. I don't know if anyone's gotten through to him yet.

Corvette flew back to Atlanta last night, and I came to Cotati.

June 26

John Cipollina Tribute show. Tickets were hard to get. I got mine from Rosario. It was Hawkeye's ticket, but he wasn't here when Rosario was ready to go in. Hawkeye got in by paying a scalper $75. Yikes.

More people still in town than I expected. Marshal, out of jail, was there with Hana. Weasel Karl got in a fight with Bill Graham. Ha.

June 27

Saw Justine at General Bead with her mom. She was buying Justine new beads because her pack got stolen from the car when they impounded it. Her mom is great. She's insisting on dealing with Justine's arrest herself. The Lawyer says Justine got busted in a bad place. Says she should get a job right away, or she may end up in jail and lose custody of the baby.

6-28

Visited Kevin. We smoked a fatty and bullshat. Kevin has lots of state of the art stuff. This massage chair he has is incredible, – it does an almost real massage. He has great pictures of Sid, and an older beautiful pic of (in the foreground), Vance and Denise holding Clarity blowing out her 1st B-day candle, and in the back ground, Damien. On the wall over Damien's shoulder is a John Lennon poster.

We talked about Damien and Janey, and the old days. Not sure how it was that I didn't yet know Kevin when Damien was alive, but I'm sure glad I do now. Kevin's one of my favorite people. He has an idea for the perfect defense for Sid. When it gets to court, Sid says, "Not me man. Not drugs. I was just there to steal the $ once the deal went down."

Kevin is a pretty smart guy. He's got an outlook on things that's good to hear. Things aren't hopeless. I mean here's an idea – In the lot, take pictures of the obvious narcs – 1 hour developing – copy and distribute. Within three or four hours, well trained narcs would be rendered useless.

Kevin is always refreshing to hang out with. I don't think he'll ever burn out. I love him for that. I can't say that for sure about others. Myself included.

He gave me two Foxboro tix (for July 2nd) – Yeah! Now how the fuck am I gonna get there?

I cruised by where Domino and Maureen are parked off 101 in Larkspur. They had our pillowcase of stuff. Psyched!

July 2

Dante flew to Massachusetts yesterday. I gave him the Foxboro tix.

> **NEW LETTER FROM THE BAND — JUNE, 89**
> Dear Deadheads;
>
> We're going ahead with camping and vending this summer, full of doubts as to whether we can continue them — Summer '89 will be a last chance to find out whether this scene can govern itself and make it work. Pittsburgh, Cincinnati and Irvine are clear warnings — we're running out of places to play, and we're running out of ways to say the obvious:
>
> **This is a music scene first, and camping and vending have turned it into a largely social scene that is potentially a real and ominous threat to the future live performance of the music itself.**
>
> As a result, there will be only a limited amount of on-site camping available at each gig, and you should give serious thought to staying at hotels/motels or other campsites. As far as the vending goes, a LIMITED number of small spaces (the size of a table or blanket) will be provided on a first-come, first-serve basis — no more tie-dye corporations. Also, the vending area will be shut down and packed up each day as soon as the Dead hit the stage.
>
> It's a game to travel through America, and we don't make the rules — after all, we're just passing through. Deadheads have to control this scene so that local people — police, merchants, neighbors — can be comfortable with this traveling circus — and that means the obvious, like not trashing up where you go, not using people's lawns for bathrooms, not violating local laws (whether you agree with them or not) — or the circus won't be able to travel no mo'.
>
> Nothin' but footprints.
It's that simple.
We're not kidding.
Bobby, Phil, Billy, Brent, Mickey, Jerry
>
> P.S. We've got great opening acts this summer. Please come early and enjoy them.

July 3rd   Cotati

Randy asked me, "When was the last time you weren't at the show?"

"Pittsburg. I didn't get in."

"No. The last time you weren't there in the lot?"

"Four of the nine New York shows last September."

"Nope. Doesn't count. You went to New York. What city?"

It took me a few to think of October, Shoreline, and June, Rochester both in 88.

But I didn't care about those. This one I cared about – Foxboro's practically a home show for me.

I gave Hawkeye a ride to Kevin's. On the way we talked about business life. How the top position is a helper more than anything else. Being good to those around you. That's all it takes. When you start fucking up basic goodness (in the tiniest ways), you start losing it. Like when ya charge 11 bucks per couple to smoke one of your fatties. (Yes someone did that recently.) You may be beginning to lose it. Or when you start spending other people's bail money. You <u>have</u> lost it.

What our family does is a good thing in the scheme of humanity. As long as it continues to be good... well then – it's good. But when it starts to go bad... shit... anything can happen.

Keep thinking and doing good out there on tour, my friends. I Love and miss you all.

July 4

At Beau's doing 9-foot Keef bongs in the sun. The very tip of a bud put in the bowl, drizzled with hash oil, and sprinkled with keef. You need someone else to carb the bong.

Keith points out. "If ya get caught doing shit like this they put you in an asylum, not jail." I'm still coughing.

I'll be hitting the road soon with Keith and Tina for the Oregon Country Fair, then picking up Tour for Indiana and Wisconsin.

So it's the 4th of July. Whoopty-doo – Ya-fuckin-hoooo.

July 5

I guess you could say I pray a lot. I don't pray to the pope's God. Or really to Jah or anything like that. It's more like my own spirit guides and even trees and natural stuff. I give thanks for things gone right. I wish good will on the people I love. (And sometimes on people I don't even like much.)

I saw a young girl pray on tv and I remembered that I grew up praying each night.

"Now I lay me down to sleep / I pray the Lord my soul to keep / If I should die before I wake / I pray the Lord my soul to Take. God bless...." and a list of the things and people I loved.

Now my prayers sound more like this (in my mind), "Thanx for everything. Thanx for keeping the Van rolling. Thank you for the beautiful land around me, I love this country and I love what it means to be free. Please make this a safe and happy trip for everyone concerned. Make things safe and happy for all these people in cars here on the highway with me. (I often seem to pray while driving.) Please let Jail be easy on my friends. Please keep the rest of us safe from whatever. Please let this trip be free from mechanical problems, and SEP me heavily, it's 1989. Thank you for all these friends I love, and for my parents. They are the best I could want. And Elwood. He's the best I could want too. Thank you for the buds. Thank you for the sun, and the trees, and the rivers. Thank you for everything."

July 7 1989

Veneta, Oregon at the Country Fair. It began as a grower's gathering. I've never seen anything like it. The atmosphere is incredible – people are so friendly. Wooden structures tucked into magical spaces and large paths winding under gorgeous trees. The coolest stuff for sale – velvet, leather, fringes, feathers, glass, and wood. It's too hot for animals in vehicles so they set up a dog pound in the shade. They took Elwood, but I warned them he'd be more work than a dog.

July 8

Yesterday was incredible. Not a cop to be seen or needed all day. People loved the jobs they did to make it all happen – even the toilet cleaning women were joking, and singing about cleaning toilets. Such a joy to see so many people with their minds in the right place and the Dead are nowhere near.

Walking along I smelled buds. Up the path, in an alcove half hidden by draping branches, there's Murph, Matteo, Rosario, Shaleigh, and Santa. Santa looked great. Fresh from the gathering. He said on the 4th, 7,000 people held hands in a circle around a valley.

July 10

Everyone needs a ride to Alpine – June, Cannoli Ron, Allie, Eden and Riley. The van is so full of shit, but we told Santa and Kerry they could come with us.

(There's been only one bit of bad news from tour. Mavis had a miscarriage in New Jersey. Mavis I love you.)

18
1989
The Tail-end of Summer Tour

July 12, 1989

Not quite to Missoula, Montana. Santa is with us but Kerry is with KJ (Kestrel Jim). Anna made a face when she heard that, – like Corvette made a face when she heard Kerry was traveling across one time with Wretchy Richie. But I think Kerry is probably great for people who might be losing their way.

We drove along the Columbia River between Oregon and Washington. We took a smaller road through Walla Walla, following Rivers all the way. Mostly backtracking the Lewis and Clark trail. It must have been gorgeous for them – it's still pretty special now.

All day on the map Jerry Johnson campground was calling to me, but these guys didn't want to stop there. Santa saw Lolo Hot Springs right over the Montana line, so we went there. Me and Keith got out by the pool that said Hot Springs and asked this chick behind a counter where the actual hot springs were. She waved her hand at the pool, "Hot Springs are right here, we close in ½ an hour."

She was saying more but me and Keith both said, "That's a pool."

"We pump in the hot water."

Keith asked, "Where's the spring?"

She shrugged. "Up the hill?"

"It said Lewis and Clark took a bath here – where's that?"

She said slowly and laughing-like, "That was a looooong time agooo."

So Keith asked, "Are there any Hot Springs, around here, – real ones?"

And she goes, "Jerry Johnson campground has a nice one."

I could have screamed.

July 14

We picked up 90 in Missoula, and drove through Montana. At one rest area we got a flat. When we got it fixed, and back on the road, we ran out of gas. But we managed to push Van up an exit ramp. That was all near Billings. We drove through the top eastern corner of Wyoming, stopped right over the South Dakota line, and crashed in the van. Yesterday we drove through South Dakota and Minnesota, to Bluebird Springs Campground (exit 4), just outside Lacrosse, Wisconsin.

Elwood likes camping. He entertained us last evening chasing fireflies.

Chicago

Silas wasn't home when we got here. We sat on the Condo porch, looking at a duck pond in Suburbia hell, till him and Allie got home. As we sat there, everything I heard was stressed, or mean, or both. A lady bitchin at her kids over unimportant stuff. Another mom screaming timeless complaints at her teenagers. Two boys (one in tye-dye even) telling their dog to eat Elwood and harassing three little girls on bikes. These little girls were bug eyed that we had just come from San Francisco.

Indianapolis is six hours away, and tomorrow.

July 15

I feel pretty good about the fact that I blew off Indianapolis. I didn't feel like dealing with it – a six hour ride to get to the place just in time to spend $ on a ticket, then turn around and cruise back to Alpine. Fuck that.

One of the little girls here loves to talk to me. She looks about 8 or 10. Wondering where I sleep, where I'm going, do I camp, is driving fun? She has rainbows in her eyes.

I called Ziggy and told him I might be there next weekend needing van work. I hadn't planned on Connecticut, but now I think I will.

July 16   Alpine

Met some bikers on the way in – they sold me a Monday ticket, which you had to have to get in to the lot. Drove in right behind Hilton John. They're giving him shit about parking where he wants to. I'm relaxing a bit instead of running right out to see who's here.

July 17

Morning. Hot Hot Hot here at Alpine, but not as dusty as last year. When I emerged from the Van, I saw Newburgh and walked to the phone with him. Don cruised up on his purple bike. "We missed you on tour."

John's Hilton is quite the energy center. It's the only great bus out here now. Judy Blue and Tavi are traveling with him. I love Tavi. I was talkin, telling some story or another, and Tavi blurts out, "Hollie I love you," and engulfs me in the biggest Hug. It's SOOO good to be back in tour world.

Everyone last night was waiting for King and the Tennessee buds. I was psyched when Corvette got here – she's traveling with King. And suddenly – Tennessee bud was everywhere. Karl got the last of it ten minutes ago. That went fast. King was Jammin loud Reggae from the Motor home till all hours. No complaints though. Folks are mostly mellow.

I saw Rockafucker and Mutz, Raging. Rockafucker bought Bob Snodgrass' standing dragon pipe for $300. He gave me a huge hug looking like he's on top of the world. "Say... Where have you been? I thought you'd be there! I missed you."

Mavis and Fritter don't look very happy. Mavis scratched up Fritz pretty bad.

Gypsy Linda and Corvette are setting up on the main row. I'm about to bring shit down there to sell.

Inside 2nd set

Standing on the Moon. I love this song.

Hawkeye's here with Munch. Blake works the lot now like Calico does. Izzy and Trinity. Nicholas and Laney. Lyndelle. Garrett. Rosario. Everyone I haven't seen before now is here in the Phil Park.

Some asshole just stepped on Trinity, and while trying to apologize, stepped on Ryder Orion. They're both OK, but we all flipped out, "Don't touch our babies, Man."

Garrett is pretty high. I feel it coming through his fingers as he gives me a massage. Lots of folks are way high tonight.

Dante is telling us that KindBoy broke his foot jumping over a fence in New Jersey. Tavi has a girlfriend named Michelle. He seems psyched. And Andre's here! He's living in a Rehab here in Wisconsin!

Saw Kara. Willow Bob got busted in Deer Creek with 20 pages. The only Tour bust I've heard of.

Mavis and Fritz are radiating sad. Both, when I tell them (separately), that they look sad, say, "I just don't feel good."

I asked Fritz, "Have they played *Push-n-Shove* yet?"

"No, I don't think so." Like he was in a fog.

Two songs later – *Push-n-Shove*.

"Yo Fritter, it's our tune. They waited till we were together again." We danced, but it was low energy. His heart wasn't in it.

In the lot I saw Red Wayne walking fast, so I fell in next to him and said, "Where're we going?"

He raised his eyebrows. "Can't ya tell?" I looked up and saw Kona Paul at the center of a crowd so I ran up to say Yeah! Hello! Scored some of the last of the way kind.

Saw a great shirt – Grateful Dead written like Overnight Xpress on the front and on the back it says, "When You Absolutely Positively have got to be there Every Night."

July 18

Yesterday everyone woke up at the same time. – When the sun came over the trees and baked us all in our tents and vehicles.

Today when I first opened my eyes it was quiet and not hot, I went back to sleep. So must have everyone else because you could hear cries of surprise an hour later when mother nature dumped on everyone. Now it's pouring.

Later
It's raining harder and harder each hour. Allie brought me a Coffee from Domino and Maureen's. They're good people. They sell Tapestries along the side of the bus, with Lemonade, Teas, and Coffee sold via donation cups that are on the honesty side and actually seem to work, whereas Bob and Marie get a pipe stolen at least once every show.

July 19
The show last night was good, but the first night I heard everything I could have wanted. *Push-n-Shove. Good Times. Built to Last. Standing. NFA. Gimmie Some.*

Last night though, they did a better *China Doll* than the one I missed in Indy. A b-day fatty for Santa was bigger than the Irvine fatty I have pictures of. It was a mob scene for the joint. I hung back. It was really too crazy.

It started to rain again as I was talking to Hawkeye during *Throwing Stones*. It rained harder and harder until it was a downpour as everyone left.

July 20
Waking in the muddy lot again. Gotta find Blake. He's riding East with me.

It rained all day yesterday and downpoured most of the first set. We had an Indica bubble – Blake took plastic from the speakers and we huddled under it. Don was the center umbrella holder. Dave Echo was tweaking. He popped under the bubble babbling about hiding from someone. He disappeared. Then came back again, panic in his eyes. Security followed him into our bubble. Kennedy got involved. It got really weird for a minute. Silas took my hand, and pulled me away from the weirdness. I didn't stay gone long. I had to get back to the bubble. They were waiting for me because the pot in the fatty was half mine and half Blake's.

Some chick OD'd in the lot 2nd day, and last night they played four heroin tunes in a row.

July 21   Connecticut
I drove all day and night. Dropped off Blake at 6:30 this morning by Albany and came here. I haven't slept yet.

I think a lot when I drive. What a book this would be if I could capture all that.

This journey has me thinking about Silas. I love the light that brightens his eyes when our eyes connect. We never would have found ourselves hanging with Silas if Jack hadn't been in Jail. He's not comfortable around warm (as in almost hot) people. But yet, he always asks about Jack. It's sweet – he knows I care.

Speaking of Jack, I've got two letters from him that I'm about to read. I thought about him too, as I drove. How we said we were gonna hang on spring tour. Instead, Jack went to jail. I miss him. And the old cliché, 'Absence makes the heart grow fonder,' seems to be true here. His Philly charges have been dropped. Now just North Carolina charges. Please let them drop too. Blake says there may be something hanging over Jack's head from Alpine last year. Please no. Just drop it. I haven't even heard his voice since April. But oh my god, I'm talking about Jumpin' Jack? Yikes. Truth is, I look forward to hanging out with him again when he gets out. He can be fun. And did I mention how cute he is? I love the way he mixes dyes and leather. It appeals to the heavy metal side of me that existed before I found The Dead. What will he do anyway, when he gets out? I hope not swing.

Night

Still no sleep. After an all-nighter I don't usually sleep the next day, and I certainly don't sleep more the next night. I don't think there is any such thing as 'catching up on sleep.' If I lose sleep, it's gone.

Spencer and Deek smoked halfway good brown buds with me. I'm on very low rations, but while cleaning the van I found two bud scores that Silas must have known he left. Thanx Silas.

July 25   Upstate NY

I'm at Rosemary's. Hoping Jack will call.

Ziggy fixed Van up good. My gas mileage should be better on my way home.

I'm psyched to head towards Silas and Allie. I'll leave tonight to avoid driving in the heat. I feel as though I'm floating, like my existence is nothing but hazy and humid. No plans. Headed west because it's the home coast now. I want to get a house. And I want to feel loved. I want to <u>feel</u> it, not just <u>know</u> it.

Evening

Carp just called. So good to hear his voice. They moved him to North Carolina and

~~~~~

Yeah! Jack just called too. They're in the same jail. He bribed the three guys in line after Carp with cigarettes so he could get to the phone. Everything looks like he should get out soon, which is better than Carp's situation. Carp's lawyer says – plead guilty and get 12 years, or plead not guilty and maybe beat it, or get as much as 148 years. Hell of a choice.

July 26

If I drove far enough alone I think I'd either figure out the world or end up in a straightjacket.

My theme song this trip is Peter Tosh – I can't find love – or sympathy. I've no idea what kind of love exists for me.

July 27   Chicago

Lazy day spent with Allie. Magic talk, life talk, occult talk, Dead talk. I love her. It's good to have days like this, though I still feel like I'm floating in nothingness. It's the void. This is why I smoke – because I want something... something... and I don't know what it is, so I have another cigarette.

July 28   Midnight(ish)
(Near Madison, Wisconsin)

Silas broke into The Jar of Life before I left. Big beautiful Buds! Yeah!! We smoked a nice fatty and he gave me a bud, some keef, and a citrine point for the trip. Allie gave me the beautiful Yin-Yang barrette for my B-day. (The one Santa thinks looks like something smokin' a fatty.)

19
Summer 1989
Cal Expo

August 4 1989
Sacramento
Morning at the Executive Lodge with Rosario and Hawkeye.

Yesterday, Don and Justine brought me to their Residence room for a baked Ziti B-day dinner. The room smelled green and delicious. We spent the evening boppin around, – visiting Mutz and Rockafucker, – Mavis, Fritz, and Izzy. Izzy looks like she's doing good. Fritz too. Mavis looked like a Zombie.

Later
Rosario brought back a letter he got in the lot from a "Concerned Head."

It's harsh and heavy. Saying how the Dead created an influx of 80,000 people then they blame us hardcores for the problems. They're not spending any money on making changes to deal with the problems. This person suggests all day trash cleanup might equal one ticket. The lot would be so fuckin' clean.

The letter also says "don't tell us not to travel with you, don't tell us it should be for locals only – expecting those without tickets to stay home is not at all realistic." It ends by saying "We didn't build this bus, it just came by, and we got on."

4AM
I'm trying to see exactly what's going on here in our world. And I don't like it.

Alpine was bad. This has improvements, but yet it's worse.

I set up in the vendor's lot by Domino's bus with Maureen. They were assholes about letting anyone into the vendor lot without tix. Thinkingly or not they funneled people past the vendor lot. People paid $100 per day to park in that lot and barely any traffic comes through. It's like you need a passport to get from one lot to the next. And either you belong in the Vendor lot, the camping lot, or the tourist lot and they don't want you mingling. I made $28 but the scene was lame. Not like the vendor lanes we used to make for ourselves. One, maybe two, main lanes of people who were into the massive selling scene, and lots of cool shit on the smaller side streets.

Near the end, 'the letter' says, "If what you want to do is end it all and shut it down, just do it, don't ruin it first." It's being handed out mostly by Garrett. Freddy wrote it, but that's a secret. Some are upset that it's anonymous. Everyone has an opinion about it, and there's much talk about the issues it brings up. The Hog Farm isn't happy and it names Calico. It isn't the most tactful letter, but a lot of what it says is true – this breakdown isn't our fault.

People seem, mostly, to be doing good. Eden is due in three weeks, Janice in 2½ months, and Amanda in 3 months. They all look healthy and happy.

Hawkeye seems weird. He said he had a ticket for me, but then he forgot and sold it to Eden. Right now he's doing a split between Don, Fritz, and Kennedy while I watch. Like a father doling out favors to his sons. Who does dad love more?

I couldn't even buy a b-day ticket. None to be found. Even Willie, the old Security Guard, was trying to find me a ticket with his megaphone. Finally, during *Queen Jane* while I was talking with Willie, Two Toke Tom gave me a ticket.

In Don's room, after the show, Fritz calls – Izzy and Trinity are in the lot needing a ride, will I go get them? Me and Mavis' friend Jagger made an adventure out of it. Had to Scam and Bitch to get in there "just to get a mom and a Baby and leave." Ridiculous hassles but no real problem – more of a fun game I knew I could win and I enjoyed showing Jagger how it's done. Izzy was exed and Trinity was way overtired.

Now I'm in Fritz's room, about to crash hard. Jagger's talking in his sleep – lots of fast talk, #'s and plans, then more clearly, "Come on man, come on, they're not cool."

August 5

It's ticket time and I'm broke. Sat around the room all day with Izzy, and Jagger. Came here late. The vendor's lot is empty and dead. Outside of it is packed, and pirate vendors are raking. Calico cornered Garrett this morning demanding to know who wrote the letter. He wouldn't tell.

Night

Not in. Didn't really try. With Lyndelle and Tavi. Garrett was gonna hang with us but he's too flighty to stick around while we figure out what we're doing.

I'm not happy here. It's not a nice place. And I'm not actually having much fun. I wish Garrett had come with us. I'm bored. I don't just mean for the moment. That hazy nothingness is still with me. I can't seem to grasp what it is I don't like or rather what it is that's making it all feel like this? Is it me? Well partly, sure, but I think what's going on here goes much deeper than me.

Late

I feel like I'm just going through the show motions. Not feeling the good energy I'm trying to put out. Is it me or is it tour? <u>Or</u> is it Cycles that go through tour and eventually everyone burns out? OK, not EVERYone burns out. But the Cycles – Yes.

And the reason Hawkeye's being such an ass is that he's been Jonesin'. Disgusting. I'm not even talking to him right now. And he's not bothering to talk to me. I'm not someone who does hard drugs ever, so he wants nothing to do with me while he does. Fuck him. Heroin gets in the way of everything.

Jagger came back earlier than the rest – said it was the 'best show of the century.' *Hey Pocky Way* and *Standing on the Moon* I'm bummed about missing. When Fritz got here, he said it was, 'Good. But nothing special.'

See? – Fritz and I, and the folks we tour with, are in one cycle, and Jagger and young tour folk are in a different cycle – not yet noticing the bad shit.

8-6   Inside

Eden had a little girl this morning at 4:12AM. Ruby Claire is her name. Can't wait to meet you Ruby.

Today is a much better day. The lot was how it should be – the vendors just up and moved to where they should be. Ha!

Just now someone wrapped rolling papers around a bundle of sage, and for a minute we thought someone had a bigger joint than us. (Not likely!)

Hilton John's here (just back from Reggae on the River), Mutz, Skip and Anna, Weasel Karl, Red Wayne, Rockafucker, Suzy and Kennedy, Amanda and Beau, and Gypsy Linda too! Janice is so beautiful pregnant. Everyone is thinking twins for her, she's so big.

It was laughable how long it took me to find singles for Saint Randy. No one had anything in their pockets. I suppose that's good.

A lump near the Fatty Circle just sat up and said, "What the fuck Wretch. I haven't slept in three fucking days." And he thunked back down. It's no-one I know.

8-7

Today was a B-day party in the city for Don. I remembered the address (the corner), but not what apartment. I saw Don's car, and Fritz and Mavis' new camper van, but never got to the party. Instead I drove off. That Nothingness – I feel like a stranger wherever I go. I don't feel like I belong anywhere I've been since I got back to California.

I want my own house.

8-9-89

I drove to Clearlake to look at a place. $450 a month. It was big, but the yard was all prickery things. 2½ hours from SF. Pretty drive though.

August 12 1989

I feel stagnant. And I'm getting broke so I'm gonna work the Sebastopol Flea Market this weekend. I've been driving all over Guerneville and Monte Rio looking at places. I want to get out of Randy's. Please let me get a place soon. Please Please.

8-13

Looked at a place 15 miles past Jenner – On top of a mountain – almost perfect, but too far out in the nowhere zone. I wanna go see the place in Ukiah with the Hot Tub.

And I wanna do Jerry tour (most of it anyway) – like Hartford on September 5 to Chicago on September 16. And I want somewhere to come home to.

I still feel like a stranger.

8-14

Corvette won't make it for the Greeks – bumming. I wish shit would work out better for her. Don finally wrote to her last week. But too late for the plans we had... so... slowness.

August 16, 89

Still at Randy's. Looking through the paper each day. Calling about houses. And beading. Did some lighter cases, and another stick wand, and another necklace.

Got mail from Mom with letters from jail folk. One letter from Jack, dated 8-1, said, "My lawyer says I should be out in two weeks." So maybe he got out today?

I looked at a house in Forestville that's perfect. Decks all around, big rooms, above flood level, fireplace. I hope this one works. It's exactly what I've been looking for.

Greeks are tomorrow. BFD? Not really, but I'm finding it hard to get psyched.

I hope it's better than the Cal Expo scene.

20
Summer 1989
Greeks, more Greeks, a House, and The Who

August 17
Outside the Greeks

There's no vending and no "scene" other than the sidewalk. The tennis courts are ripped up for renovation, but I heard there may be speakers in a soccer field behind the theater. When I first got here I found Tavi tryin' to park his new van and not doing it too well. Auguron and Shiny Bill (the smiler) were sitting on the wall. They smoked a much-appreciated skinny with me and Bill gave me a bud. Just saw Beau. He's a BGP Gopher for these shows and Amanda's working pack-check. Mutz bought Garrett's small bus for $1200.

I hope someone trades me a ticket for one of these lighter cases.

Inside

Tickets seemed hard. Cyrus offered me a ticket for face ($34). I didn't have it, but I hooked Rosario up with him. Amanda had face tix too, but I'm broke, and no one wanted to trade. Then King Henry *ran* up to me zig-zagging through the crowd and put a ticket in my hand. He gave me a handful of little buds too in my other hand. He didn't say a word. Just smiled and ran off.

Sittin' on the top of the hill near Fritz, Mavis, Lyndelle, and Judy Blue. Heavy clouds overhead and light fog on the city, with a perfect opening to watch the sun go down. Clear skies over Marin.

Davy and Lizette are here, Janice, Boots and Benny, Lubba Lenny – just back from Alaska. Tavi and Michelle are getting married. They're gonna ask Elijah to perform a ceremony. King Henry, Matteo, Murph, and Jeremy have joined us. Pauper Paul has hash oil.

Skye, from jail, wrote an answering letter to the Sacramento letter. Hers says that the first letter was too harsh – says, "I've seen Calico up to her elbows in garbage..."

Break

Tricky saw Yes outside in Ohio last night while the eclipse was happening. Someone told me that in '84, when the Dead played *Darkstar*, there was a lunar eclipse the night before. So – High hopes for a *Darkstar* tonight.

Big Fatty Circle. Kerry is the fatty factory – he just keeps rolling 'em.

It's getting dark, I see Kevin coming this way in his velvet beret.

August 18
Outside the Greeks

Got a halfway ok parking spot near the sidewalk, with trees for Elwood. Tricky gave me a letter to mail to Skye as we shared veggie sandwiches and berry seltzer. Garrett stopped by – gave me a foot massage and tried to talk me into going to Chico with him after the shows. He took off to get milkshakes.

Bad news. Mindy and Leandro went to trial. The jury found them both guilty of LSD possession with intent to sell. They'll be sentenced in September.

August 19   Morning

Tickets were hard yesterday. I got offered a few, but I was broke. As the show began, the cops swept by to kick ticketless folks out. I refused to be shut out. I went past Willie the Guard. He didn't ask me for a ticket. McNeel said he could walk me in, but not till later. Some guy found a wallet with a ticket in it. He was asking McNeel what to do with the wallet. He gave me the ticket. Funny. Sometimes, right in front of the gate is where you need to be to get your ticket.

About a ½ hour before the show Fritz came by and pointed with his chin, "They've got Blake – across the street." Four or five cops around him. He was selling Margot a ticket and they swooped and searched because they wanted to know what the money exchange was about. That's the same basic way he got picked up in Milwaukee, but there he had nothing. Though they tried to tell him that 2,000 bucks in cash is against the law, it wasn't. Yesterday he had hash oil. That's potent. Worse than pot as far as the law goes. They took him away. What the fuck. Margot called the cop shop. $1575 by midnight, they told her, or they send him to Pleasanton. I'm sure it got taken care of. Margot was sitting with Murph,

Gunner, and Hawkeye. They won't let Blake just sit there. Hawkeye's being himself again.

Fritz sat on me during break. I couldn't flip him over me because there were folks right behind us, so I put my dirty feet on his pants.

He's like, "What're you doin'?!?"

"Listen to you Fritz. You come up and jump on me, and ask what I think I'm doing?" So I wrapped my legs around him and would not let him go for a bit.

Walked out with King during *Mud*, but we stopped by the gate to listen to *Bid You Goodnite*.

1st set

Sitting with Kona Paul by a BGP Speaker truck. I'm caught without a ticket and writing beneath a truck. Today is Tavi and Michelle's wedding. It's being held out here – lots of people stayed out for it.

Garrett, inspired I suppose by the upcoming wedding, snuck up behind me and whispered in my ear, "Marry me." I merely laughed at him.

All day Santa's been collecting pot pastries of all sorts for the wedding. Alongside the truck is an ivy-covered hill with an altar set up: A big beautiful Buddha, ringed with flowers, sits at the top of intricate blue tapestries.

It's Break. I've gotta get a wedding seat.

~~~~~

What a crowd! We forgot to reserve family seats for the wedding. We should be closer. Mavis, Fritz, Lyndelle, Don, Justine, Becky, Rockafucker, Santa. There's a wingnut next to me I've never seen before. Babbling babbling slightly.

OOhm's. The sound of the chants crawls up the hill like an approaching cloud of bees.

I have a perfect view of Tavi's face. Can't hear anything though. Fritz is loud. Everyone is here. Memphis Mike, Gracie, Vance and family, Abe, Jackie. There's a cop behind us, on the other side of a fence. Cannoli Ron was talking to him. He doesn't seem to be a threat.

Huge Cheers. Congrats Tavi. I hope it makes you happy.

There's Theo. I never see him anymore. There's Tricky. Neil and Winnie. Everyone stands up – both directions – up and down the hill, yelling.

"Tavi! We love you."

"Speech! Speech!"

"Roll a fat one!"

Tavi is a married man! Lots of balloons are caught in the trees.

Shaleigh, Suzy and Kennedy, Atlanta Angela, and Pauper Paul just sat down here. Kennedy gave a counterfeit ticket to an 80-year-old lady and watched as she got in on it.

"Buds build better babies." We believe this. Trinity is proof.

Keef cookies?!? Izzy and Santa trying to distribute the wedding "cake."

Garrett, Dante, Cute Allen, King, Briscoe, JohnRay, Tibbs, Kerry, JoeJohn (he was the best man). Wretch, and Benny, who tells me the cop bummed a cigarette off him.

Tavi's coming to see us.

a bit later

Nicholas says, "We'll go get buds during Break." Hey Nicholas, it IS break. Ha! They're looking for a house in Oakland. No one cares about electric bills in Jokeland. I'm thinking about us in that house with all the porches. Visualizing it. It's so perfect for us. I'm forcing myself to wait till Monday to call.

August 20   Cotati

I saw KindBoy yesterday – cast and crutches. Eden and Riley didn't come down from Oregon. No sign of Hilton John all weekend. Wonder where he is?

Mavis was her wild self again. Fritz threw Sativa Slim's hat up on the truck and he grabbed Fritter's Guatemalan hat and went to throw it. Mavis jumped on him screaming, "Don't you dare! I'll kick your fuckin' ass!" Fireball. She yelled at me and Fritz for horsing around. Fritz goes, "Awww, Mave, we're only playin'."

Speaking of playing with Fritz – I was flippin' him on my hip when Randy came up behind us and tried to catch him, which only made Fritz land on his ass. Perfect! I brought Randy for a walk and hooked him up with Murph. He didn't come home last night.

Still laughing, picturing Santa tip-toeing through everyone trying to pass out the wedding foods. Holding a bag, giggling, and wagging his finger. "Now ya gotta share."

As Don, Fritz, and DigDoug are pleading, "Come on Santa, kick down."

Michelle looked blissful during the wedding, – she mostly seems to look detached and confused at the same time. Like whatever's happening isn't really happening to her.

I find it hard to write what I really think about people.

I believe that if everyone could read everyone's mind – people would hate each other. Everyone thinks horrible things about the people they love once in a while. There are so many things that would hurt if they were known, dumb things that don't deserve to hurt.

I'm hyper-conscious of what I write. I don't want the things I write to ever hurt anyone.

I saw a movie once where a writer in the Navy left his journal out. His musings about a friend's homosexuality got his friend kicked out of the Navy and other life-changing shit. Yes, only a movie. But its moral hit home. Don't write shit that could get anyone in trouble. The responsibility is too great.

later

Oh and I got $38 worth of parking tix...

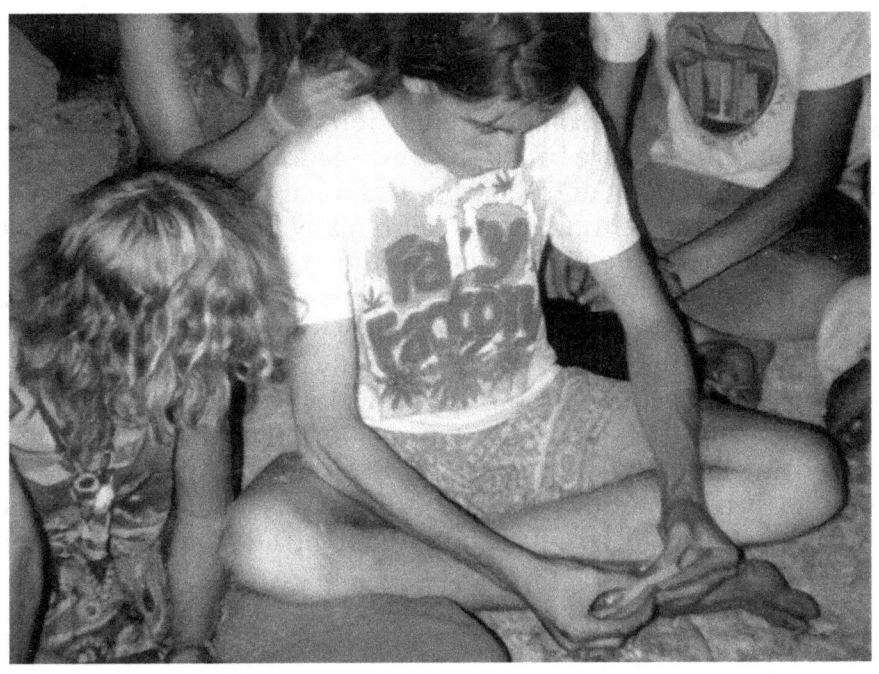

August 21

I don't disagree with the things that are bad about buds. Izzy, in the hotel room in Sacramento, "I used to have a memory that scared people." It is undeniably true that the memory system is altered. Ken Kesey put it best. "When you live a life of drugs, it has its drawbacks. You make certain tradeoffs for it." But it's a good life.

America, the land of drugs. Drugs keep us all pretty much immobilized while the leaders of this country run rampant with evil power lust. Even me. I'm sitting here letting it happen. At least I don't partake of government sanctioned drugs. My drugs are grown organically in mountains all over America, and in basements you'd never imagine.

August 24

Corvette is getting used by folks she works with in Alabama and Atlanta, so she calls Don. He waits. And I'm waiting too. We're racking up some phone bills these days.

It's hard for me to bead lately. I don't feel very creative. I've gotta fix two lighter cases. One started undoing at the top, and the other one broke when Fritz sat on me in the Fatty Circle. Instead, I'm just sitting around waiting to hear if I got that house in Forestville.

8-27

Got to the Greeks for the JGB show later than I wanted to. Tix impossible. They sold out day before yesterday. I saw lots of folks when I first drove by, but by the time I parked most everyone was inside. DigDoug and Katarina had a hard time getting in. He was bitching and ranting. "I smoke so many Fatties with everyone and no one cares when I get shut out." For a while me and Katarina tried eight or ten different names on the will call list – no luck. DigDoug got tickets somewhere and they went in.

Jimmy Cliff was over when I finally gave up.

I went to a hotel room with Spyglass Michael. We drank a six of St Pauli Girl, smoked a fat one, and talked about how 'all those who should get in' don't always anymore. After the show I went to Fritz's room at the Bel Aire. Mavis was asleep on the waterbed. Fritz looked relaxed and happy. Did some bongs, then went to King's room.

In the back room! It was a bud bath! A great huge pile of kind buds in the middle of the bed. King called for a pick-and-weigh your own. I went off. Karl was goin off too. Hell, everyone was going off. I got ¼ for myself and ¼ for Jim Avery.

Henry made it stop when he saw my bag. "That should be my head bag. This is over."

From there he just weighed out handfuls. I helped – in trade for getting to buy the bags I'd picked. It was the most fun way I've ever bought buds.

8-28

I got the house!! I put $950 down on it. I'll give him $800 more on Friday.

Move in one week from today!!!!!

8-29

I drove to the city and parked near Suzy and Kennedy's new place. Marble steps, nice building. Classy. Nicholas and Laney were there. So were DigDoug and Don. The guys were with Kennedy working in the other room. We've just smoked a fatty and we're getting Pizza. We're gonna try to get in to the WHO tonight in Oakland. I read in the paper that Pete Townsend rammed his whammy bar through his hand. Smooth move Pete.

I just asked, "Did Fritz and Mavis already go East?" Yes, they flew. Santa and Kerry took their van. And I hear the news – Santa and Kerry got pulled over, or broke down, or something. Where? We don't know. They got searched. Cops found roaches and doses. They also had a bong and a bowl. Please let them be in California not Nevada. Please let them be ok.

Fuck...

late

Went to the show in Kennedy's van. Fun navigational confusion. Sometimes I wonder how we get anywhere. There were $5 tix all around! Everyone had an extra. We were just in time to be stepping to the top of the stairs inside – making our dramatic entrance – as they opened with *Overture*.

What power!

For a bunch of old men they sure can Rock. Pete even windmilled, however cautiously.

21
Summer 1989
A Quick Trip to Connecticut

Sept 1 1989

I signed the lease today. We're $300 short, but that should come on the wire from Alabama Kirby tomorrow. I'm broke. Not a dime over 3 dollars.

Sept 3

Today was Bob Dylan at the Greeks. I didn't go. Didn't want to spend any money. Called about a "Best Offer" plane ticket to JFK in the paper. Offered low. It leaves SFO Tuesday morning.

Sept 4

At my new house. It's so huge and empty. Elwood loves it here – he's bookin' around outside. I have a plane ticket to NYC tomorrow at 8:15AM. Cost $20. How could I refuse? Plus, I'll get there in time for the Hartford JGB show.

Night

At Randy's. Packed and ready to fly. There was some controversy about money, but these guys agreed to watch Elwood while I go east. So off I go, not knowing how I'll get back, but I have faith. This is too perfect not to go for it.

Sept 6 1989

Dateline Connecticut, but not for long.

Landed in NY at 4:15PM. Got on Connecticut Limo at 5. Got to New Haven at 8:06 and Leo, and Dwayne had left! On the board was a message scrawled in chalk, "Hollie your [sic] late, find another ride, we missed Bob don't wanna miss Jer too." Leo always lets me down when I need to be held up most.

I called Mom. It took her and Ed an hour to get there. When we got home I borrowed the car and raced to Hartford. Got a free parking space and walked around trying to get in. Got my fingers slammed in a door. Welcome to the Beast Coast.

Fritz saw me and tried to bribe a guard to let me in – No go. He slipped me a $20 through the door, "Go buy a ticket off a hubba freak." No luck with that either.

I was raging! "My home show! I got stood up! Let me in!"

Finally someone opened a door where there was no guard. *Evangeline, Gomorrah, Don't Let Go* and a Killah last song – I don't know the name.

When I first got in I saw Dwayne and Leo. I reverted to my East Coast Attitude. "Fuck You both," I said and turned and walked off.

I went by the Spinner crew and gave Ethan's message to Memphis Mike. After the show I went to Tavi's van and had a beer with him, Michelle, Pixie, and Newburgh. They saw Jefferson Airplane at Lake Compounce last night. Found John's Hilton. Erika was asleep. Me and John bullshat awhile.

Two guys knocked. "We live right there and we've been jokin' that this must be Jerry's bus. Can we see inside?" So they came in to hang.

It got bad when McDonald's came up. They said I couldn't prove McDonald's had anything to do with the rainforests being destroyed. Conversation turned to Rainforests in America: Like up by Janey's in Washington. These guys swore I did not know shit, and there are absolutely no rainforests in the U.S.

Next subject Buffalo. Endangered or not? Buffalo burgers?

"No Way."

"Yes way. We travel – in the mid-west, some places do serve Buffalo." And John's friend paints Buffalo hides for a living.

"No Way."

One guy eventually said, "I like good conversation as much as the next guy..."

And John interrupted, "Well, we're not havin' one."

I mentioned being tired and they got the hint. As they left, I shut the door and it clipped the guy's foot. John yelled, "Don't let the door hit ya on your way out!"

Today was spent packing – pots, pans, towels, rugs, kitchen stuff, and dreaming about a U-Haul. Leo came over, apologizing. At Dwayne's, we laughed about me screaming at them. Talked about Bush's new drug laws. The first thing they ought to do is separate, in laws, marijuana from the nasty drugs – coke, crack, and the new designer killer – ice.

Sept 8 1989

Checked out Leo's pot plants and we walked out by the waterfall. He kept stressing how much he likes it here in the New England woods. Weird. Like he was trying to convince himself. We got stoned out in the barn like old times.

Sept 11 1989

Leo drove us to Great Woods. It took a long time to get in the lot. We borrowed tix to get the car in. Later I got mine for $5 and Leo's cost $2.

It was hot and muggy – for a while we sat in King's air-conditioned RV. Don was happily surprised to see me. I hadn't seen him in Hartford.

It's a scene like Dead shows used to be. Vending happens on its own, tickets are easy like they should be. That's not just my word from one night, that's the general word I've heard. Fewer undercovers too. Nonetheless, Rockafucker told us how an undercover had gotten Jean Claude and someone. Jean Claude ran, and the cop had the other guy on the ground. Scary Jerry (who I don't know) kicked the cop over. Everyone watching jumped on the cop, all got away.

This isn't normal. But what else is to be expected? At this point even buds carry the same bails/fines/sentences as crack and coke. Let alone Acid. So if you're goin' down (or a friend), Go Kickin, and fightin' and runnin' cause ya got nothing to lose. You may get away. This is war. They declared it on us and we are not even the correct enemy. If "they get you," you aren't a criminal, you are a prisoner of war. Skye even writes POW after her name on her envelopes. Good thing "we" aren't still in Boston. But Woostah cops will be pigs tonight.

Fatty Zones aren't like they used to be. Everyone's all spread out. Don's Fatty Zone was on Jerry's side with DigDoug, Katarina, Poco, Rockafucker, and Mutz. They were smoking some sweet Oregon buds. King Henry, Fritter and Mavis, Kerry, Izzy and Trinity, were on the other side. Trinity gave me a big hug when she saw me. King Henry was waltzing around with her.

Saw Neil and Winnie. And Gimlet. (Someone said Gimlet had a b-day card for Jumpin' Jack but I didn't see it.) Vance and family look happy and healthy.

And fuckin Wretch. The port o' let in the lot – I'm in line, one has been occupied a long time – I'm up – Wretch comes out of that one – he left his 'tye' in there. YUCK!

Santa was bumming. A runner lost 300 dollars – sounded shady. But he made me take $10 towards a ticket. I didn't use it so I gave it back. He bought me a soda on purpose, and a piece of pizza accidently. As we went through the line, Santa got a piece of pizza and chowed it right away. When we got to the checkout guy he said, "Give me another one please." The guy yelled over his shoulder, "Two pizzas," as he rang it up, and another guy gave us two slices. Nothing like the old 3 for 2 Pizza scam.

Talked to Corvette. She's almost ready to roll. We want to have a party in our new house. I made a quick list, and came up with 35 people. (25 of whom have their own houses, which is important. You always have to consider how many people won't leave.)

King gave me his travel agent friend's phone #, so maybe I can get a cheap ticket back to San Francisco.

Sept 14 89

Corvette fronted out to a couple o' junkies and now she's fucked. I'd never trust junkies like she does. I guess one of 'em got caught by his Dad and is headed for rehab, so no cake there. The other seems to have blown her off and is headed for Alpine. So is she, but she's broke. May her travels be safe and happy.

From the Great Woods show I wanted to write down the new little trick that keeps strangers away from our fatties. When they come up and say, "Can I have a hit of that?"

We say, "It's got DMT in it."

I really wanted to go to Maine. I bet it was great fun. I don't feel the urge to "go on tour" anymore, but I still wanna see the kind shows. I'll probably get over that too someday I suppose.

Sept 17 1989

Talked to Corvette this morning. Bad news. Pony OD'd last night in the lot at Poplar Creek. That sucks, I hate Junk. Our world is so full of it.

Santa is ridin' west with her, they're caravanning with Don, DigDoug, and Katarina.

I called Kennedy looking for a ride from the airport but he's up in Oregon at Hawkeye's new place. He says it has potential but needs a lot of work. That's cool. It should keep Hawkeye busy and out of trouble.

Sept 18th 89

I brought all my old notebooks west with me. They're very heavy. But perhaps, with a house and my notebooks, I can begin to write my book. It has to be a good book. A book that explains why we do what we do; what it means to us, to be here, now, and to be family; how our economy rules us just like that of the 'real world'; what we're all trying to accomplish – not just Indicans, but all humans I think. In the end it's a universal story. It'll show that when it comes right down to it, tour is very much like the 'real world' – the ups and downs, the learning, the loving.

Clayton's talk of "being in-valid" on tour has stuck with me. I don't believe most folks on tour are in-valid. Tour is just as much a valid thing as being a dishwasher, or an advertising agent, or a night watchman, or an assembler of junk products no one really needs. What's more valid – picking up garbage in a Dead lot, or trying to sell newspapers over the phone? Helping to spread a little light in the world, or campaigning for a political candidate (helping to spread a lot of bullshit)?

Now I'm not saying there are no in-valid people on tour. I'm sure there are. BUT, per capita, the 'real world' contains a lot more invalids.

Sept 20 1989

Yesterday I went to Food For Humans, used the phone, and dealt with utilities. PG+E wants $180 deposit. Yikes.

As I was leaving, Roz pulled up. She's been staying with Judy Blue and says Judy's gettin' flaky. She wants somewhere to begin her hypnotherapy trip. Said she'd been praying for magic as she drove down the road – "then there was your van."

She followed me to the house and we hung out all afternoon. Kevin is in Australia visiting with a certain famous Personage whose name every educated hippie would recognize. They're broken up and we talked about her moving in with us. We also talked about Jumpin' Jack. (His last letter was upsetting, – about other lives, future ones, because he feels doomed in this one. Fuck you George Bush.)

Skinny Jim moved out of his place and he too wants to move in here. Went to Santa Rosa with him, so he could put all his shit in storage. He gave me this desk for my notebooks. Its drawers lock!

Sept 27 1989

Roz stayed with us till she went to pick up Kevin at the airport. We haven't seen her since. Freddy came by this morning, raging about paranoia awareness. He's scared. Jah knows we all have reason to be.

We were outside, sweeping and raking, when Lee, the landlord, and this guy Gary came over to survey the house. They were funny. Pointing to the pictures on the wall, going, "Look! It's Jerry!" And talking about, when they were kids, sneaking down the river on canoes to get an eyeful of naked folk in Guerneville. I'm glad our landlord is so cool. I love this house.

Sept 28 89

Jefferson Airplane last night. We got in for $6, which is good, because we don't even have rent money yet and it's due next week. Tickets for Airplane were harder tonight, so we left with Silas and came to Beau's for some 9 foot bonghits.

It's nice to know that a bit ago I was feeling lonely for Corvette and Silas. Now they're both here.

22
Fall 1989
Shoutin' and Shakin'

Sept 30 1989

That was a funny note to end on, considering what's happened since.

Yesterday, we got to Shoreline early enough to get in the good lot. I went on a bud hunt. Found Ethan, who had Santa Cruz outdoor. Got an ounce – ½ for Freddy, and ½ for Silas. No scale, so Silas held onto it. Saw Janey and Garrett, and Eden and Ruby Claire. Lots more, but no time to write of those things now. (My loss, it was a good day.)

We paid $19 to get in. The show was weird.

We hung in the Fatty Circle 1st set. During break we found Silas and Nicholas. Smoked a Santa Cruz outdoor fatty, and the boys did *China Rider* and *Blow Away* then took a break again. Tech difficulties or something.

There's some very bad news. Kennedy went down in New Mexico. 50 lbs of pot and mega doses. Him and three other people. Hawkeye and Suzy were especially upset because they think New Mexico has his prints. Please help Kennedy get off these charges.

We saw Camera Aaron and Big Brian as we left. We should have gone with them, but Silas had Freddy's ½. He wanted to give me some other ½ that wasn't as good. I said no. I wanted what I got for Freddy.

Silas and Karl decided to get a hotel room for breaking up Buds. We went with them. Benny was near the truck as we left and invited us to go with him. But again, we didn't.

Karl and Corvette rode in back, and Silas drove his truck as we went to look for a hotel by the airport. The cheapest was $63. Silas started to tweak, demanding money for a room and saying,

"Well, where are you gonna sleep?" I stayed calm, even though I was getting really upset. I said we'd get the buds, then leave his hotel.

"No."

I have no idea why this wasn't good enough.

"Then bring us to the airport and drop us off." I just wanted to get away from him.

"That's cruel."

"Not as cruel as driving in circles screaming at me."

"I hate driving in circles – you're gonna get me busted."

"I don't want you to be driving in circles – just bring me to the airport."

"No."

"Then let me out here."

He stopped – I got out and started getting my stuff.

He flipped! "Get back in the truck! There's a fucking cop over there!"

I got back in the truck. There was no cop. It was a tow truck.

I was very upset – intense yelling with groundless points. There is no defense. It's what I grew up with. I don't react well. He continued to drive in circles that consisted of highway, and the same two exits. It was literally sickening. I felt like I was gonna puke. He went back to the $63 hotel. It was sold out.

I got my stuff and got out. He insisted I get back in the truck. No way. I kept seeing his flip out as the type of tweak scene that does indeed get people busted. I didn't want to be blamed, if anything happened.

I don't know what triggered it. It was so sudden. I stayed so calm – tried to say anything to calm him down. (So reminiscent of my dad when I was young.)

It was lame. I asked, "Why is this happening?"

He said, "Ask Corvette."

I was like, "What do you mean? – She's with me – broke, and dealing with you tweaking."

And he said, "Yeah. You're both too dependent on me."

Me and Corvette got the Hotel driver-man to bring us to the Airport for free. Then we convinced a super shuttle driver to bring us, two-for-one, to Willard North, which is where I sit now, on the porch. The free show in the park begins in a few minutes.

late

At the Free Show we saw Kevin and King Henry and learned that, last night, "they" got Kestrel Jim, Wretch, Santa, and Tavi.

No!

It happened in Burlingame. They went to a hotel – no rooms – ok, they go to leave, cops appear. "This looks like a stolen van." Search. Mushrooms, and an assortment of other things. KJ had crystal meth on him. $5,000 each. It's especially scary because Tavi just got done with all kinds of court, and was on heavy probation. I seriously hope we don't lose Tavi. But it looks like this will be bad.

Fuck.

Airplane at the park was good. We saw Tink from older days at Fulton St. Went for Chinese food at the Red Crane with her and her roommate, then they gave us a ride to Shoreline. They had Big Sur outdoor. Yum.

Got to Shoreline late, rough traffic, hard tix. We didn't get any. Just kept walkin' and tryin'.

Of course we saw Silas in the lot. He gave me Freddy's buds and said, "What happened last night?"

"You were screaming at me."

"You can't depend on me like you were."

Obviously.

During break McNeel came and found us, and walked us in.

Saw Big Brian inside, arranged a ride home tonight – supposed to meet him at the Greenpeace table during the encore.

In the Fatty Circle it was mostly talk of how to afford to free those guys. Poor Tavi, and Santa, and Jim and yes, poor Wretch too. (Just because I don't like him doesn't mean I want to see him face this.)

Later we bumped into Silas and KindBoy. Silas asked me to roll a fat one. Still smoking it, and suddenly, it's the encore, we gotta go! I gave KindBoy a hug, and Corvette hugs Silas. I started to leave, but I turned, and gave Silas a hug. He wouldn't let go for the longest time, "I dreamed, this morning, of hugging you," he said.

We raced down the stairs, zig-zagged through the hall to the Greenpeace table, and Brian was gone. We looked for him outside, in the far lot, – no luck. Sold some postcards out there though, and ta-da, there's Andy and Chloe. So we're back at Willard North again.

Didn't hear anything about Kennedy today.

Oct 1st 1989

Haven't sat around a morning with these guys in a while. Chloe's satin pjs, Corvette's satin sheet, Parker's very bad coffee, Andy's habit of showering with the door open.

I'm worried about all the busts this week, too many close people, too much seriousness due to past charges. It scares me. Not for myself, but for our world. There was a huge empty space – our circle is large, and when a light of rainbow energy is removed from it, we who are left must fill the space with our energy and keep the circle. The more people we lose, the thinner becomes our energy layer which encloses the circle. – Yes that's exactly what I meant. – It lost nothing in the written form – unlike so many other of my cosmic oriented ideas about exactly what's going on.

No. 13C — Shoreline
Sept 1989 — Free Handout

NEW MESSAGE FROM THE GRATEFUL DEAD:
Dear Folks:

When we sat down to organize the fall tour, the venues we have worked with for years gave us a simple message — if we want to tour, we've got to cut camping and vending loose from our scene, despite everyone's very fine efforts this summer. We've all seen how the camping and vending have attracted people there for a party, not for the music. We like parties, too, but first we're musicians — If the outside scene interferes with the music inside, it's gotta go.

AND IT'S GONE: THERE WILL BE NO VENDING AND NO CAMPING ON THE FALL TOUR. There will be security people representing the Grateful Dead who will tell you not to sell anything outside, (or inside, for that matter); listen to them. The parking lots will be cleared every night.

The music and the dance is important; being able to buy a t-shirt or camp out are not. If you are a Deadhead and believe in us and this scene, you will understand what the priorities really are. Thanks for understanding.

Best, Bobby, Billy, Brent, Mickey, Jerry & Phil

THIS IS THE DEAL. NO VENDING, NO CAMPING, NO KIDDING! GDP is hiring people to walk around the parking lot to be a buffer between Stadium Security, The Police and the Deadheads to try to keep the calm. This is serious business. Please, if you really do love the Dead, please help us all out.
DON'T SELL YOUR WARES IN THE PARKING LOT. If you are caught, and the odds are heavily against you, your stuff will be confiscated, you could get busted and thrown out. As well as the bad reflection on the band.
DON'T EVEN THINK ABOUT SETTING UP THAT TENT. At the end of the night, the parking lots will be cleared.
DON'T STOP ON THE SIDE OF THE ROAD AND SLEEP IN YOUR VEHICLE OVERNIGHT. The New Jersey cops will be happy to give you a bed for the night.
THE DEAD NEED VENUES TO PLAY IN. HELP KEEP THE SHOW ON THE ROAD! LET'S GET INVITED BACK. PLEASE! WE NEED YOUR HELP!!!

Oct 3rd 1989

The 3rd Shoreline show was good. Corvette got walked in with Shaleigh. I got a comp ticket from Miranda.

In the morning I called Big Brian to see if we could hook up for a ride home. He said they weren't gonna do this 3rd show, because it's confirmed, and tix are already on sale for the Warlocks in Hampton. See, the Dead is banned from Hampton, but the Warlocks have never played there. Andy didn't believe us till he made many phone calls.

We told the Fatty Circle and it changed everyone's plans. It got exciting. Hampton again! Change plane flights, hurry vehicles. It's next weekend – the 8th and 9th – to start tour. Ahhh, Hampton. I wanna go!

Everyone kept telling us we, "Have to go."
"This is History."
"This is not the time to give up tour."

Big Brian told us about $99 flights to DC on Braniff. We made reservations, just in case, even though it's unlikely we'll be able to pull this one off, – but who knows, right?

The Fatty Circle was two. One circle was Arthur, Jasmine, Karl, Eden, Riley, Ruby Claire, Allie, Abe, Jackie, KindBoy, Anton, and Silas. Another circle was Don, DigDoug, King Henry, Izzy, Trinity, Boots and Benny. DigDoug and Don were trying to find someone to go sign Santa's bail ticket. Someone who's not one of us.

Oct 7 1989

Went to Cotati yesterday. No mail. (Overnighter from Cash with our money in it supposedly got sent back!) Not much luck on the phone. So we headed home, out of Buds, and fucking broke too. Get home. There's a blue van.

Texas plates. Kennedy and Suzy!

"We're here to smoke big fatties with you." Yeah!

Kennedy got out on bail. State charges. Day after he got out, they made his charges federal. So he probably has a warrant. They laughed at our bare cupboards, then went shopping. They went off and totally stocked the house. We drank and smoked and ate all evening.

Oct 9 '89

I woke to Suzy and Kennedy quietly leaving. "Monday." They said. "We have shit to do, money to pay, lawyers to talk to." Jah look upon them please.

I haven't been thinking too overly much about the fact that today is the second and final Warlocks Show in Hampton. How is it all, I wonder now?

Oct 10

Just the facts – no emotional comments.

We found out from Remy. 1st night Hampton – lame 1st set, then *Help Slip Frank*! 2nd day *Dark Star* and *Attics of My Life*.

They've supposedly added another Warlocks date in Florida, after Miami. I'm torn between "oh well" and "Fuck!" It's certainly not the end of the world. But to see those songs would have been Grand. Magical, Joyous, Uplifting, Enlightening, and High High High.

Oct 13 (Friday) 1989

Gary (the realtor) came over. Lee can't afford to fix this place up, so he's gonna sell it. Fuck. We told Gary we were gonna hang him from the rafters as a conversation piece. "Oh that? That's the guy who came over to tell us about selling the house." He said we'd get a $50 rent break. BFD. $50 isn't enough to cover the inconvenience to us as possible buyers come through.

And right on the 1st day – intrusion – as they show up to put up the For Sale sign, and put the key box on the door.

Oct 14 1989

I don't like waking up to strangers walking through my house.

We looked at a bunch o' houses yesterday. Nothing perfect. Many places around here are small and ugly, or moldy and dark, or too close to neighbors.

later

I'm in a horrible mood. Corvette too. We both have such an attitude. Every time we talk, we bitch at each other. I mentioned possibly leaving and forgetting about having a place. So now she's fucking packing. My main reason for wanting a house was to write. I'm not writing though. Should I give up the idea, and just keep living as each day presents itself?

I want to get high, but guess what, – we're budless, and money won't be here till Tuesday.

Oct 16 89

As we sat around yesterday, bored and bitching, we decided to go to Sebastopol. We stopped in the middle of the road to wash the windows and who cruises by but Kennedy and Suzy! Nicholas pokes his head out. "Where ya goin? We got a case."

"Well! I guess we're headed home!"

We needed company. They brought Nicholas to check out our 'underground room.' He has some extra plants he was gonna give us, but with the place being for sale, we can't do that now. They had news – Tavi is free, but that's all they knew.

We sat around drinking St Pauli's and playing Grass (the pot smokers Uno game), then they headed back to Jokeland. Nicholas has a seismographic foundation inspection tomorrow morning. Not ideal, but somehow it'll be ok.

We're headed for the city today. And we gotta find out if another Warlocks show is happening.

Yes... I miss tour.

Oct 17 1989   SF

We're at Beau's, and Elwood is being an asshole. Literally bouncing off the walls. At the park this morning he was awful too. He climbed inside a hole in a tree and Corvette had to climb up and pull him out. He scratched her up pretty bad.

Beau is taking bets on Amanda and the baby – when, what, how long, how heavy, what color hair? Winner gets a kind fatty, others get shake fatties labeled, "It's a boy," or "It's a girl."

Janice hasn't popped yet either.

~~~~~

Just heard – Meadowlands 2nd set was *Dark Star Playin Uncle John's Playin'* D–S *Take You Home Miracle Dark Star Attics Playin'*.

Fuck. This obviously was not the tour to give up.

The thing we used to do – the world we used to live in – has gotten intense and exciting, while our new house is being ripped out from under us. Maybe I'm just homesick? Maybe I'd like to move from Forestville back to the lot.

Oct 17 5:15PM

Left the city, mostly because Elwood was out of control – now we're at the house.

We just had an Earthquake. Long. Rolling. I watched Corvette's car shake. Wow. Only one radio station is on the air. Said it was felt as far as LA. Airplanes are being directed elsewhere. Kinda glad we got out of the city.

~~~~~

Part of the Bay Bridge collapsed. Holy shit.

Oct 18 1989

Stayed up late doing beadwork and listening to earthquake details on the radio. We went out around 9:30 to make some phone calls. Couldn't get through to the Bay or to the East Coast. "All circuits busy." Word is Santa Cruz is horribly ruined. The Pacific Garden Mall is flat. Jah I hope everyone down there is ok. Really, please, let them all be fine.

Oct 19 1989

Folks in the city heard from Janice and Tanner. They're in their house, cut off from civilization, and Janice is five days overdue.

The Quake was 6.9. The Bay Area is basically closed. It's the biggest Quake in the continental US since 1906 in Santa Rosa. We saw some TV at Remy's. It looks horrible. The Marina in SF is flattened and burned. Both 9 and 17 into Santa Cruz are impassable. The mountain towns are burning. The Mall was on the news.

Our people in the city are all ok. Except we don't know if Justine was here or on tour. We've been calling her every time we get near a phone but there's no answer.

The biggest news is that Amanda was in labor during the Quake. She had a little girl at 11PMish. What a day to be born, little girl.

Nov 1 1989

Traffic was hell on the way to the Jerry show in Concord. With the Bay Bridge out, everyone uses the San Rafael–Richmond bridge. What a mess.

It was great to see everyone, but I felt a bit out of place, like I didn't belong because I didn't see the Warlocks shows. Lots of people though, only did Hampton. And Don left tour after New Jersey. The scene must not have been too great for so many to leave.

King's broke, and knowing we don't have his money, says, a lesson was learned in the lot this tour. The lesson – Everyone owes Everyone for something or other, but go ahead – have a good time, do what ya can.

Some guy won the stage costume contest with a Gorilla suit, carrying a guy in a cage.

Benny was Dick Tracy. Mavis was almost hard to recognize as Pippy Longstocking. Kerry was a cheer leader with pony tails, pompoms, and a big K on his chest, – "One! One! I need only One! / One! One! I wanna have some fun!" He bought my Jerry barrette for ¼ of his harvest. Looks great in his hair. Trinity was a fairy. So cute when she fell asleep with her huge wings on. Don had a short beard and a top hat. Roz was a 20s flapper chick, and Kevin a Jester. Tavi was dressed as a Sgt. Pepper cover guy. I walked up to Becky and heard her saying. "I didn't recognize Santa."

"Why, where's Santa?" He was standing right next to me, clean shaven with short hair. Wow.

Tickets were so hard to find even Rosario didn't have one. (Eventually though, he got 2nd row.) The show had started and lots of us were still without. I finally traded the twisted Rainbow barrette for my ticket, from this random couple. It'll look great in her black curly hair.

Cops were coming and Corvette didn't have one. We tried getting us both in on my one ticket. No go. As I walked up the hill, inside, Santa came wriggling in under the fence, and Jerry broke into Promised Land. "I say to my sisters and my brothers – keep the faith." I love that tune.

Inside I saw Abe dressed as a hippie with long black hair, and Jackie as an Indian. Beau in a three piece suit. Saw Tanner. He said Janice had the baby last week. A big boy named Timothy Tanner. More babies for the fatty family!

Mindy has to go to Jail for three months starting Monday. The jury decided she was more than just Leandro's girlfriend – she was a partner – to jail with you, little girl. That sucks. And I learned last night that the Kaiser has structural damage from the quake and will be coming down. Gone. History.

Kona Paul has a huge peace pipe he calls Bob. The stick part was wrapped in Seal skin, and the bowl covered with a Bobcat head skin. I thought it was beautiful. Mavis thought it was gross. Paul wore his huge African mask and Mutz was excited. "I saw that mask dancing wildly at my 1st show. I was so dosed. Thank you."

Skip and Anna both go to school in Santa Cruz now. Their house is ok. Lou's isn't. He got red-tagged and had 15 minutes to go in and get his stuff. KindBoy, Fletcher, and Gitch got in a bad accident in Arkansas. KindBoy's here. Gitch went home with head injuries. Fletcher is in intensive care in Memphis (but should be fine).

Corvette got in with a pass as 2nd set started. As soon as I found her, we stumbled right into a keef circle with Fritz, KindBoy, and Don. I hadn't keefed in a while.

I got really high off all the fatties, and I felt really weird; like I didn't know something everyone else did. Because of missing *Help* perhaps, or the *Dark Star*? Like a native San Franciscan who arrived home the day after the quake said on the news, she felt like she missed something that affected everyone so much.

The show ended with *Werewolves of London*. Outside in the lot, the night ended with Speakers on top of the hearse, and a party outside John's Hilton.

23
Fall 1989
House Party and Turkey Day

Nov 2 1989

Yesterday Mavis, Fritz, Shaleigh, Kerry, Izzy, Trinity, and puppy Cabaret, were first to show up. Trinity was a cranky one, so whenever she screamed, I'd scream back at her louder. She was amazed. Next was Tavi and Michelle. They aren't getting along very well. Right now, outside my bedroom door, he's mad because she's been drinking already this morning. JohnRay showed up with Ike and Paige. Mavis, and Shaleigh went to Guerneville (Shaleigh lives in Guerneville!) and brought back Judy Blue, Newburgh, and beer. Don and Justine showed up on their way home to Leggett. Late night, in comes Boots, and Benny. Boots falling all over the place – Benny had been feeding her Stolis all day.

I came in here to crash. As I'm falling asleep, I hear everyone calling my name because the fatty's about to be lit. I smiled and went to sleep.

Judy Blue took Kerry, Izzy and Trinity home with her. Fritz and company went to Shaleigh's, but I heard them come back early this morning – they're supposed to get Boots and head north. I can hear the morning scene, with CSN playing in the background.

1PM

Santa is on fire detail. He's chopping logs with a too-small, blunt axe. Kennedy and Lars are sawing wood. Benny (way hungover) is helping by watching.

The house is warm with people in it.

Nov 3 1989

After making a huge woodpile, we way baked. Benny keefed everyone, and turned us into vegetable material. Silas, KindBoy, and Hackmen showed up, and Kennedy got the whole room playing Grass.

I can hear someone playing guitar. *Peggy-O*. Is it Tavi?

Noonish

It was indeed Tavi jamming earlier, but KindBoy took the guitar. (We'll forgive him, he left us buds to sell.) Lot's of folks left. The only people here now are Tavi, Michelle, Santa, and Newburgh. Corvette is out checking the mail.

Amanda called. They're coming up tonight. Their baby's full name is Chaya Truth Kimberly Colburn.

Izzy had a good story when she was here. They flew to New York and got on a Greyhound to Hampton. It got stopped by cops. They walked right down the aisle to her, and said, "Come with us." They took her off the bus. "What's your name?"

"Izzy"

"Are you sure it's not Lisa Hirsh?"

"No. I'm Izzy Morgan."

"Are you sure?"

They were looking for Lisa Hirsh and her child, whom she had kidnapped. Izzy fit the description. They hassled her a bit, not believing her, and she didn't have ID. Then they heard Izzy refer to Trinity as a girl. They made Izzy prove it, so she ripped off Trinity's bottom and waved Trin in their faces. The kidnapped kid was a boy. They had to let her go.

Lucky.

Nov 6 1989

This morning we're babysitting Jillian.

During the cleanup scene, Hawkeye showed up. Vance and family came over for an hour or so, and Mavis and Fritz swung through. They've moved in with Shaleigh.

We went to Cotati and tried to hook up with Jim Avery, to make some money. Instead we found Perry, who wanted more $ for the phone bill. I told him I went through and marked off my calls – it equaled $8. I gave Randy a $10. Perry says he paid $60 that wasn't his, – said there are more pages, and perhaps I'd soon give him 10 or 20 dollars more? I told him, if I'd seen all the pages, I'd have paid my whole bill. I tried to give him a $5, but he wouldn't take it. 60 bucks couldn't have been all my calls. But why not take the $5, and another $5 or $10 next time I see him?

If I was rich... Ah what a stupid way to start thinking. But it's true. Money is a very serious problem. Hawkeye was driving King's van. Everyone owes everyone. Just like King said.

We didn't make any money for KindBoy. His buds were too expensive, and harvest products abound. He'll be hatin that. I wish he'd call.

I wish I had a typewriter and a chair.

I wish I had rent money.

I wish Jack was out of jail.

Nov 7 1989

We're kind of up the creek. Rent is three days overdue, and we're totally broke.

Nov 10

Lee called the other day. We told him we'd have the rent today. We don't. Cash says we'll have it on Monday. We are seriously considering winery jobs.

On the day we babysat Jillian, later that afternoon, Hawkeye and Fritz came over. Hawkeye gave us 5 bucks to bring Fritter home. We joked it was like getting paid to babysit twice in one day.

I woke up yesterday to a call from Fritz, screaming about voting and elections. What he actually wanted was to use me and Corvette as his and Mavis' taxi for the day. When you're broke, you do what you gotta do.

Corvette brought Fritz to the city. They hung at Benny's, waiting for Hawkeye. I took Mavis to Santa Rosa to buy a futon. We ran out of gas, got pizza and beer, then made it back in time to meet Roz. (She lent us $200.)

Roz and Mavis didn't really know each other. Mavis spent most of the time in the doorway screaming for Cabaret. He'd come back for a second or two, and leave again, and she'd scream again. I think Roz understood her own question (after the fact, when she learned Mavis was his girlfriend). "What's up with Fritz these days? He always seem so sad, never happy-go-lucky like he used to be." Mavis squinted. I shrugged.

I told Roz how Jumpin' Jack still has no charges, no upcoming trial, and no rights. She says she cares and will try to do something.

Roz brought us a High Times magazine. Chef Ra wrote about us: "The greatest ganja groupies of all time, the FATTY CLUB of CAL." Says, "These hippies don't fuck around. They roll joints as big as a swollen peepee." What a stupid analogy. When he came to the Fatty Circle, what he actually said was, "It's un-natural to smoke pot this good in joints that big."

Nov 17 1989

We went over to Mavis and Fritz's. Fritz wasn't there, and Mavis was slow on moving the syringe. Well. Now I have no doubts about Shaleigh and Mavis. I had no reason to doubt it before, but doubt it I did, because I didn't want to believe it. Mavis looked like shit, saying, "Lookit me, I'm a dreadhead, I look horrible." True all her beautiful blond ringlets are clumping together, but that's not why she looks so horrible.

I'm afraid that probably means Fritz does it too. Jah I hope not. Not Fritz.

Because he wasn't there, I can still doubt that he does it. Oh shit though, he probably does. Boycott that shit. Whatever happened to that attitude? He knows how bad the energy from Heroin is. So the fuck does Mavis. I don't want all these people I care about doing hard drugs. Everyone we tour with probably does it. Keeping it hidden from me and Corvette.

When I say that, Corvette tells me that when she was at Benny's with Fritz, Judy Blue came in and said, "What are you all doin'? Heroin?"

Benny looked at Corvette all shifty eyed and said, "Not with this crowd."

Heroin energy is so ever-present lately, even some of the fine upstanding Dingalings were talking about wanting to try it.

later

On the phone with Fritz.
Him, "I was just spacin out."
Me, "Oh yeah? What are you on these days?"
"Absolutely nothing. And I heard about yesterday."
"What'd'ya mean?"
"Nothing. Forget it. I only do THC and LSD."
Is it true?

Nov 18

Late last night, Roz calls. "Come do the Sausalito Flea Market with me tomorrow."

So we're rollin' – Off to Judy Blue's to get our Jewelry, and some of Judy's Bali stuff. Got to Larkspur by 2AM.

Woke to a line of speed in my face. Roz said, "I told Kevin I wouldn't do any speed today, but you two are here, and we need it." We both told her that was a lame excuse.

Better clientele here than Sebastopol. $30 for a table though, so I hope it pays off.

An old gypsy woman read our palms. She told me I'll write a book, it'll be good if it's written for others. I'll own a store someday.

Turkey Day '89

Rosemary called, with Jack on the other line. Yeah! I told him to write a sob letter to Mavis. If Mavis starts screaming about a lawyer for Jack, it'll probably get done just to shut her up.

late night

Pulled up to Freddy and Piper's with Kevin and Roz, Garrett was there. I'd asked them days ago, "You guys aren't springin' Garrett on me are you?"

"No. No. Of course not." They both said.

He looked like shit. I hate to say that but it's true. He gave me massages all day. I kept telling him I wasn't gonna spend the night with him, but he kept on with the massages. He begged me to come live with him, – said the first day I don't get a nice long massage, I can leave. He'll keep the cooler stocked with Becks, keep the bong full, and not complain about me smoking cigarettes. Why on Earth, Garrett, would you want to go to such lengths for me?

Nov 25 1989

Fritz and Briscoe came over last night while we made black leather roses. Fritz started raging, and suddenly we were deep in a pillow fight.

Fritz made a point of bringing up the Heroin subject. Saying he doesn't do it, and what we saw was Shaleigh's. She does it a lot, he said. Nobody said anything about how much Mavis does, or doesn't, do it.

Nov 26 1989

Earthquake Benefit day all over the Bay. We're at Willard North watching Santana's Simulcast on TV. He's in Watsonville at the high school. Quicksilver and more are at the Kaiser, – that's happening now. We're gonna go to the Cow Palace – at 5 – to see Neil Young and CSN.

Reading Skye's letter in Golden Road. I don't think admitting (or even offhandedly saying) that one was an LSD dealer on tour, "snug in family," is very smart. But it's her whole point.

I think Europe is a good plan.

America doesn't want us, and we need new horizons!

Let's go!

Nov 28

The benefit at the Cow Palace was great. Me, Corvette, Pixie, and Newburgh sat down together, and the whole Fatty Zone materialized. Santa, Kerry, Izzy and Trinity, Fritz, Shaleigh, Briscoe, Kennedy, Suzy, Hawkeye, Benny. Even Gunner, Roz, and Kevin were there. And let's not forget Rosario.

It was such a long show, most everyone's buds were gone by the first half. It started at 5, and ended like 12:30 or 1:00. We felt like we'd found the never-ending show. After Neil Young everyone came out to Jam together. Steve Miller, CSN, The Chambers Bros, Jessie Collin Young, and even Santana showed up!

Slept till 2:30 the next day. Hawkeye called at like 10 wanting to know if we had anywhere he could store four Harleys. I was too asleep to think.

Briscoe and Laurie moved in with us yesterday.

Something must be done about money. I can't miss a European tour.

We got the electric bill the other day – $136 Yikes! $200 to Roz (what she lent us), $100 to King (for my plane ticket in September), December rent, LA shows, Xmas presents, water bill, food, Elwood vet and food, tires, a typewriter. Let's not forget wood – we only have about 20 pieces left.

Fuck. I need something to happen.

Nighttime.

Went selling roses. The Harley shop on 116 welded a bouquet of our roses onto a friend's grave. That's the coolest thing ever.

Came home to Fritz here visiting Briscoe. He said Hawkeye wants to have a meeting with all the guys. A lecture sort of, about how it's not very family-like nowadays. Ha. I knew that. I know it because Jumpin' Jack sits in jail, when the cheapest lawyer could probably get him right out. Family is a term that means (to me) that you're connected by things that go much deeper than likes and dislikes. You might not always like your brother, but he's always your brother. You might be incredibly disappointed with something your sister did, but you don't disown her. She's your sister. You don't write off your brother because he's fucking up, you try to help him, and if you can't help him, Oh well then, he's your fucked up brother. But he's still your brother.

That's my point.

Family.

What does it mean to others? To Fritz? To Hawkeye? To Don? Kennedy? Benny? I bet that right there is the crew Hawkeye wants to meet with. I'd love to see/hear this meeting. But alas, it's none of my business.

Dec 1 1989

King Henry called. He's headed south, and gonna stop by. He goes, "You know who else I'm gonna visit?"

"Judy Blue?"

"Yep. I'm gonna clean out her store."

Do I wanna help? Not really Henry, thanks.

Dec 4 1989

At Judy Blue's, King took everything in the store that belonged to her. We haven't been by since. Judy must be bummin. Fritz said the rumour is that she's closing up shop and leavin' town. I've gotta go and get my shit back so I can try to sell it at the shows.

We didn't get into JGB the first night at the Warfield. We blew off the 2nd night and did beads instead. Briscoe and Laurie brought home another couple, and yesterday Boots dropped off Maryland Sharon, and Ike.

I talked to Rosemary. No good news. Jack's lawyer is a dick. Mavis and Izzy both say they are gonna do something for him in LA. I hope that's true.

Dec 5 1989

I'm hatin' my whole situation. I had a broken lighter case that would have taken ten minutes to fix. Someone fucked with it, and now it'll take me an hour. I can't afford more beads, even though I've got lots of custom orders. There's a houseful of hippies. And I'm fuckin sick of hippie food. And the people here are drinking Red Tails and not giving us any. We've made all our phone calls with no luck. No $ comin' in except some roses money in three fuckin' weeks.

Zia said she saw Fritz comin' out of the van bathroom handing Shaleigh a straw as she went in. Ugh.

We expected Boots to pick up Sharon and Ike on her way south, but she blew it off, and went straight to the city. Lame. Sharon was mad. On the phone Boots told Corvette, "It'll blow over."

later

Mavis called and made a phone-scene. Said everyone thinks all they do is sit around and do heroin because folks heard about a syringe on the couch. And she thought we were spreading that rumour. I guess King heard it here, and told Don, who told – who the fuck knows?

Our whole scene is fucked. I'm thinking about blowin' it all off – but what else would I do?

King Henry talked about taking me and Corvette to Australia with him. Ticket prices are pretty expensive, but what Kevin said is hard to forget. There's good money to be made.

24
December 1989
Shows and Holidaze

Dec 7 1989

Yesterday at the Oakland Coliseum tix were hard, but I got a free one from Gunner, and Corvette got a free one from Aggie. We got in late and missed a *Shakedown* opener. Every time I appeared in the hall Garrett followed me. He's in Pepé la Pew mode, so I retreated to the horseshoe seats with Silas, Dodd, Margot, Nicholas, and KindBoy. Met Little Timothy Tanner finally! He's is a big chubby kid. Janice was beaming. And Macy was there too! She had a bud box with a picture of King Henry VIII. It totally looked like King!

We're at Willard North, waiting for pizza, then hitting the road to LA. I got pulled over, drivin' here in Corvette's car, because I didn't have the headlights on. Very lucky he didn't search us, only told me to turn the lights on and let us go.

Dec 8 1989

We went to leave, and didn't have the car keys. Last seen by me when I was waiting for the pizza guy. I've never lost keys in my life.

We had AAA break into the car. No keys inside. No one would (or could) give us a ride to our house to get Corvette's extra set.

Around midnight I thought of Roz. She wanted to help without question. She'd come pick us up in Kevin's car, we'd go back to their place, take her VW van to our house to get the keys, and bring the van back to her tomorrow. She came to get us at Willard North, and off we go to Kevin's in the Mazda, Kevin's sporty new car. So we're sociable a while, then we go get in the van. It won't start. It's very late, and very cold.

Kevin's bitchin under his breath, "How do I get myself into these situations?"

"Kevin, I'm sorry you got into our Hell night."

The only other car is the Mazda. So Kevin lent it to us. Oh! Thank you Kevin. Off we went, through a solid bank of fog from Novato all the way to our house. It was so thick, and hard to see, following each white reflector. The car wanted to move. But I was good, even when I could see, and stayed at the speed limit.

We got the keys and got back to Kevin's at 6:11am. (Oh let's not forget – as soon as we got in the Mazda, we pulled over to roll a joint, and a cop stopped. Told him we were switching drivers, and I was figuring out where everything was. Lucky again – he let us go. I would have hated to have to mention that to Kevin. Or worse if we'd been caught rolling a joint.)

They looked so relieved when we got back. Kevin, had to put a lot of trust in me to let me take the Mazda.

All night we're thinking – "Maybe this means we shouldn't go to LA." But not really believing it I don't think. And also thinking – When Ken Kesey makes decisions like 'whether or not to go', he always says, offhandedly, "I threw the I-Ching and it said _____, so I did that." Thinking – I wish I knew about the I Ching so I could try it. I can't decide what's the right thing to do. Lost keys, a van that won't start, two cop interactions...

Kevin, "Maybe it means stay home."

Parker, "Maybe you shouldn't go."

Hackmen, "Losing your keys means something. You obviously aren't supposed to go yet."

Yet?

Today we awoke still asking ourselves and each other, "Should we go? We've had so many things try to stop us. But we want to see special songs badly, and we have so much to sell. We need to make money. What should we do?"

So, it's getting on towards noon – we still don't know what to do, and I voice my earlier thought, "I wish I knew about the I Ching so I could do like Ken Kesey."

Parker pulls out a small red I-Ching book! It says if you don't have anything to throw, you can flip through with closed eyes, or open to any page. I sat outside with the book. Thinking on this major dilemma. I flipped through to #62. The Hsiao Kuo Hexagram.

"TIMING. Do not take action prematurely. IGNORE WARNING SIGNS AND YOU WILL OVERLOOK DANGEROUS SITUATIONS AND YOU WILL BE HURT. Use self-control."

Youch.

Corvette, grounding, centering, and meditating, opened to #58. The Tui Hexagram.

"BALANCE AND PLEASURE. Sensual pleasures tempt you. SUBMIT TO PLEASURE AT THIS TIME AND MISFORTUNE WILL FOLLOW."

Well, I guess we're not going. It would be folly.

Dec 9 1989

Not going yesterday was a hard decision but a smart one I think. We're headed down there today.

Dec 10

Morning at the Marriott with Benny and Rosario. They played *Help on the Way*. Mavis literally screamed at us for missing it. Please Mavis. I missed it, don't scream at me.

Anyway. We're here. It's all cool. Paid for Postcards with what we sold last night and today is all profit. No vending on Forum grounds, but there's a lot across the street that rages. I sold a $25 lighter case. Corvette sold a $25 pouch. And we sold a shitload of $40 1/8s. And we managed to trade one 1/8 for two tix. Psyched!

Dec 12 1989

That last day in the lot was too much! Fritz traded for a tiny motorcycle. Me, Corvette, and Cannoli Ron were getting high, laughing at Hawkeye, and then Kennedy riding it. Then the news – Fritz got hit by a car. Off to Seth's RV to find out what's going on. Fritz's ankle is huge, – off to the hospital. (It's just a bad sprain.) Then we saw Hawkeye almost drive into the back of a van. I declare that thing dangerous.

Was talking to Kevin about Australia. "If you go, I'll call and tell 'em you're coming. Family will pick you up at the airport." We're seriously considering it. We could set ourselves up for a while.

We got into the show with one Comp ticket, and one for $7, plus ten postcards.

Found Silas during *Sugaree*. In the usual spot, with a fatty in hand. The show was much better than Saturday. Special guests Bruce Hornsby, Spencer Davis. A way funky *China Cat* ragin' Jam. A real good show all around – no *Dark Star* though.

We hung out in the lot until the guards got too thick to move through. We drove halfway home, slept, then finished it off yesterday.

We're gonna go to General Bead and spend some money before we have none again.

And we made enough to pay all our bills!

later

Matt Ackerman was getting shit from a GDP merchandising agent in the lot. This guy tried telling Matt that the harshness of the vendor scene at the coming New Years shows will be all his fault. He is a pretty high guy in GDP, and he told Matt his dyes are no good, and he should go get a job at McDonalds. That's fucked. If this guy is who he is, he knows Matt's stuff isn't "no good." Why would he say it? Matt was hurt. I don't blame him. This guy is obviously an asshole.

Dec 15, 1989

Dear BGP,

I get these handouts from the Dead, asking me not to come if I don't have a ticket. I come anyway. Sorry. But I want to be here, and I almost always get in. Ticket magic is a big part of the scene. When you have an extra, give it, when you need one, you'll get it. What would all this be like if the real hardcore tourheads did all that BGP has asked? What wild dancers would first timers see in the hall? The hardcore tourheads who follow the band around, well, the Dead needs them. They would not have gone so far, would not be a musical phenomenon without the tourheads.

The Dead are our lifeblood, working, living, with and around such an intense light. Why would ~~you~~ anyone want to take that away from us for lack of a ticket?

☮ + ♡   signed, A Tourhead.

PS. See you at New Years – I'll be the one without a ticket.

Sunday Dec 17 or 18th

I haven't been writing much. This is the season for "rush rush – no time." I finished Roz's lighter case. It's good. Got more to make. We're working the flea market again today. Made only $7 yesterday, but today will be all profit. Hopefully it'll be a good day even though it's cold with heavy fog.

Rosemary called with urgent advice needs on Jack's part. Kevin stopped by last night to smoke a fat one with us, I asked his advice. He said he'd put up the $ for a lawyer visit for Jack. Thank you Kevin.

Crafty Adam called us. He needs a place to go till New Years – A place to make beads and tye-dyes. We told him he could come here.

Thurs 21st of Dec 1989
Winter Solstice – Oakland

At Nicholas'. Good energy here with 59 vibrant plants. We helped trim. Great way to spend the longest night. I had never seen the grow room with full power lights on. As I rounded the corner, a sharp blue-white light shining out the door edges. Sort of eerie or UFO-like. In the room, – the pungent smell, the heat and breeze making the shiny walls breathe. It was a sensation not unlike tripping.

We heard a gunshot as we trimmed and watched the news to see what our country is doing now. Georgie and friends have "invaded" Panama. Looking for Noriega. They say, because he's a drug trafficker. Ha! They've known that all along. They are after him now because he either, a – cut them off, or b – ripped them off. That's how the drug world works.

Monday we brought Crafty Adam home with us. He needed to be saved. I like Adam. Feels good to have him around. (And he cooks!)

Dec 24 1989

King Henry was here for a couple days. When he left he said goodbye and Merry Xmas to us each, and Corvette said, "What about him?" pointing to Elwood.

Henry picked him up, held him high, and danced around the room singing, "Have a white Christmas Elwood."

I woke to a call from Ma. She's bumming it's only her and Ed for Xmas. I told her about the Dead possibly going to Europe and she was like, "Well if you're ever going to go to Europe, you should go while all your friends are going."

She said there's a letter from My Beautiful Hitchhiker. Yeah!!! I've thought of him often these past few months. Bummed I lost his address. I'm so glad he wrote again. Last time I heard from him, he was lonely and depressed. I often think of him when I'm feeling alone.

Dec 25 1989

My day to cook. Dinner came out perfect. Turkey, stuffing, gravy, sweet potato and marshmallows, rolls, mashed potatoes, peas, steamed broccoli, and carrots. Yummmmm. Briscoe made Apple Pies – threw 'em in when the Turkey came out.

Adam kept taking over the sink for tye-dye production (which is behind schedule). Laurie and Corvette beaded all day. Josh (a kid Briscoe brought home) was just lazy mostly, with good reason. I talked to him a lot. He's trying to get over, and off, drugs – hubbas or heroin I'm not sure. I didn't ask, I just let him talk. He doesn't think he can hang without going back to doing drugs. He's 22, quiet, with kind eyes. He oughta be the sweet kid type, not looking sad and tired, half beaten, and afraid of the next confrontation. I gave him a massage and tried to pour good energy into him. I hope he can make a life without drugs. He wants to go home. He's worried about these shows. If his mom will send a plane ticket, he'll leave before them. If not, maybe he'll hang with us.

Oh and Jumpin' Jack called. He wants a box of presents. Of course he does.

Dec 30 1989

Day after Xmas, we cleaned, and beaded. I started another Jerry barrette. Hopefully to help us get a ticket or two on New Year's Eve. Adam tye-dyed like crazy. We didn't leave the house till the afternoon of the 27th. Briscoe and Laurie left without cleaning. Lame. At least they'll be moving out when we all get back. (They're moving in with Fritz.)

Stopped by Aaron's in Cotati. He had six extra tix to each night except New Year's Eve. We bought them all with Nicholas' money. Great feeling, having tickets. Got to town just in time to get a room and get to the show. Tickets were easy the first night, – we had to sell the extras in the tourist lot.

Inside, Nicholas tells us 'they' got Silas on the way in. WHAT? Not Silas! The gate people thought Silas had something in his pants. He did, but he tossed it before they got a good hold of him. Hackmen caught it, and disappeared. They searched Silas, found nothing, and let him go in.

Walked with Xmas Josh a bit now and again. He was doing good that first day, it seemed. 2nd day, I wasn't so sure. Yesterday, he looked a wreck. Some guy died in the slEasy8 parking lot. It was a friend of his, Stumblin' Kenny. Heroin and N_2O. Our hotel room is way mellow – Just me, Adam, and Corvette, but Josh wouldn't join us. Said he had shit to deal with.

Skye was here for the first two shows. She was so bubbly. She had to go back to jail yesterday. I'm not sure how that worked. We missed the goodbye breakfast party, where I might have found out.

Fritz is in a wheelchair, with his fucked up ankle. Don's pushing him around. I keep asking if I can take him for a walk, but they both shout, "No way." Ha!

Justine had her baby a couple days ago. Indigo Morning, a girl.

I've got more to write, but another eventful day is moving by outside my hotel room. I think I'll take Elwood for a walk to the Holiday Inn – but first a P-bud bowl.

December 31

Lights off. What will they open with? I'm so glad to be inside. Energy is very high. Fuckin stoned. Fatty's everywhere.

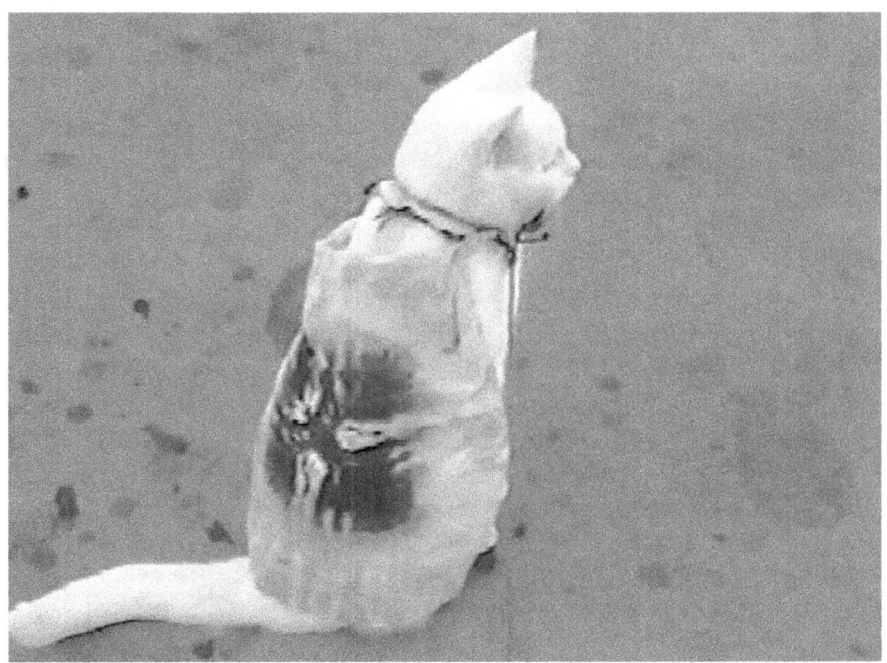

Jan 2 1990

Sat around the hotel lot, on the 31st, with Tibbs. He told us about his next big project. He's gonna get a huge crystal cluster, and put beaded people all over it. Call it a Rainbow Gathering. That'll be wild.

I saw Freddy, taking Jillian to be babysat.

On the 30th, while hanging in our room, He asked her, "Do you want to go to Grandpa's tonight, or to the Grateful Dead?"

A triumphant yell, "Grateful Dead!" But for New Years, she was off to Grandpa's.

When I gave Izzy and Trinity Trinity's Xmas present (a dress), I was holding the postcards, Trin points to the cards, and says, "Bobby! Bobby!" Ha. That's gonna be her rebellion – to be a Bobby Kid instead of a Phil or Jerry kid.

Talked with Calico when we 1st got to the lot on NYE. Asked her if she had any tickets. No, and she was surprised we got into the lot without tickets. Oh Calico, be real. The guy at the gate didn't even ask us.

Looking for tix was hard, expensive, and scary (to think one might not get in). I had face cash, and/or my Jerry barrette. I talked to a guy early on, who said he might come find me later. Corvette paid $35 for one stamped "Comp – not for sale." I also tried carrying around the last High Council American Indican sweatshirt. I would have let even someone who's not on the High Council have it, but, No luck. Later, I found that guy again. He looked, and thought, and decided to walk away. "No!" I pleaded. "Please." I talked him into it for the Jerry barrette, and $40. Then he shrugged, and gave me a $20 back. Yes! I'm in!

Crafty Adam didn't get in. Neither did Garrett, but I heard they all had fun in the lot.

Many people had huge buds to trade. Laney had a 25-grammer. She didn't get in. They got one ticket and Nicholas used it because he missed the past three New Year's shows. Santa had a juicy-looking bud, and some staff-pro came up to look, broke off the top half, and walked off. Asshole. But Santa got in.

Silas and company all had tix. Suzy and Kennedy only got one, so Suzy went in. Hawkeye, frantically running through the lot, waving three hundred-dollar-bills. Telling us, "Someone out there needs $300 more than they need the show." A Spinner sold him a $300 ticket. He promised not to tell, but he told. Sort of. Though he wouldn't tell us which Spinner.

Nearing showtime, walking around selling postcards, already got tix, but still looking, because we always know someone in need, and Cindy/April came up to us. "You aren't in yet?"

Not lying, "Why? Can you do anything?"

"Only for one of you."

Corvette slipped me her ticket and went with April. When they got to the gate, the ticket taker ripped it up as counterfeit, but it actually came straight from backstage. April was pissed. She went to people in charge of security. "No problem, we'll walk her in." (Meaning Corvette.) But then, two major door rushes happened. The first almost trampled Corvette. And the security guy said, "I can't do anything now." So Corvette comes out to the lot, screaming my name at the top of her lungs. Thankfully I hadn't gotten rid of it yet.

I was talkin' to a 60s hippie-activist-bomber while watching the door rushes. We talked about Abbie Hoffman, and he told me about Earth First.

We went in as they were clearing people from the lot. Saw a few tunes by Bonnie Raitt. Wish I'd seen her whole set.

First set was great. It seemed to me a list of tunes they wouldn't be doing at midnight. *Sugar Mag, Touch,* closed the set with *Shakedown.* Bonnie Raitt joined them for *Big Boss Man.*

At midnight we had a mega-fatty, Bill Graham came out as a Chicken on an Egg and nest (we had hoped for a spaceship), and the Dead broke into a relatively lame *Aiko.* The other night the *Aiko* was much better. Then *Victim,* and I joked, "1990, the year the Dead let us down."

But... after *Victim.*

Ba-nar,nar,narw. Ba-nar,nar-narw, Ba-nar nar nar nar nar nar nar nar nar nar narw.

Darkstar!

Long, spacey, excellent, but only the first half. Then Drums.

(On the 30th, and on NYE too, they had this big guy in a green sweatshirt, on drums with Billy and Mickey. On the 30th he did incantations, but I don't know who it was.)

Outside, after, was really fun! Dave Echo gave me a Red Tale Ale. Someone else gave me a Becks. Then there's GreenMan Joe, selling iced Champagne for $10 a bottle. What fun going through the lot with Champagne in the crook of my arm.

I raged on postcards, especially near the end of the night, while looking for a final beer with Crafty Adam. We left the lot late. I'd missed hooking up with Nicholas for buds, so we cruised by his house. A crew was there, still awake, drinking Champagne.

We got home at 7:30AM, fucking exhausted. Slept till 3:30. Was lazy for a few hours, doing shit like trying on all the clothes we got from Pixie and Newburgh, getting high, putting Jack's present box together, cleaning the glass for our new flea market display, getting high, eating Mac and Cheese, and getting high. Then I crashed again till this morning.

Hawkeye called a few minutes ago. Said Fritz's phone is disconnected. We have to go relay a message. He wants to take Fritz to Oregon. I didn't know Fritz and Mavis broke up, and she's off to Santa Barbara with Shaleigh.

Happy New Year.

25
Winter 1990
It's Like This...

Jan 8 1990

Beading. Beading. Beading. Adam and Corvette too. The shit Adam whips out is Amazing! Corvette is working on a beautiful Rainbow Crystal, for a woman in LA, who sells custom bead and leather stuff to rich ladies. I've been goin' off on custom lighters.

Adam invited this guy, Tarnowski, over for a few days. Tarnowski cooked us Chicken Cordon Blue. It looked like it came from a restaurant, and tasted even better. Having Tarnowski here was interesting. Who is he? He has lots of money, and bought everything we needed around the house. Says he's from Colorado. Says he's got a bus. Says he'll front us cheap pot. Then Adam tells us, he's only known him since LA. Fuckin nice.

When Freddy came by though, it seemed that him and Tarnowski had been acquainted some time ago by the way they talked.

1-9-90

Adam left this morning with Tarnowski. He's flying to Maine for a week or 10 days to make some $.

Jan 14 1990

When we paid rent, Lee said the house is almost sold, and the guy who made the offer is interested in keeping us as tenants.

Silas is at Margot's place getting ready to head east. We asked him to come up here first. He asked would it be worth it. I said I'd make some calls. When I called back – no answer. Next morning, the truck is in the driveway.

There were three, cheap, QPers. We called Kevin, in hopes of borrowing $. It got a little complicated when we got to his house.

It was the first time we'd really met Joelle. She's been around forever. Has lots of beautiful Owsley Jewelry. She knew who we were because Gunner bought her one of our Sweatshirts and she loves it. Anyway they wanted half of it for themselves. We agreed to that, and borrowed $ from Joelle to make the whole thing happen. Went down again yesterday to pay her back, but we still owe Silas $250 on Monday, by Onion.

Spring tour is almost completely planned. They announced Landover, Ontario, and Albany. And there's three shows at the coliseum in February. No Chinese New Year's show though.

Just talked with Fritz. Mavis is in Santa Cruz with Becky, not in Santa Barbara with Shaleigh. That's good. I was worried about her going to live with Shaleigh.

Jan 19 1990

Adam's still on the east coast. Me and Corvette are still beading like crazy. I finished a wand made with Goon E Bird feathers from Piper. This one pretty much made itself.

Sucks having both vehicles incapacitated. Corvette's water pump isn't fixed yet, and the front end of the van started to shake on our way to San Rafael to see Zero last Sunday. I'm hoping it's just that maybe I lost one of those balance pieces in my tire. Haven't had any money to fix it. Maybe today.

We've been working to pay back everything we borrowed (mostly from ourselves) when Silas was here. But we're on top of it all again.

Briscoe told us Fritz and Mavis are fighting really bad. (Yes, she's back.) She threw Fritz's Glass Graphics bong against the wall. Yikes. They keep trying to split, but can't get away from each other. It's harsh.

Roz stopped by yesterday. Here's a disappointing story. Let's go back in time a couple days, to when we went down to Kevin's place. She said she couldn't afford to pay $70 for the lighter case she requested. She thought the lighter was a present. I said, "Roz when I gave it to you at New Years I told you what it cost. $70, or trade for ¼."

"But, I said we'd talk. I thought it was a gift."

"I don't know how you could have thought it was a gift, when I told you the price as I handed it to you."

She wanted to give me $40. Now it's not like she has to put out any cake. I owe her money, so I figured we could take it out of that. We finally (that day at Kevin's), agreed on $50 of the money I owe her. So I gave her a deal. Fine.

Now she says, when me and her are alone in the room, "Um, about the lighter. I can't afford to pay that much right now."

"Roz, nothing has to come out of your pocket, it's from the money I owe you."

"Well, that's not important, you can pay me back whenever."

"I'm trying to do it soon."

"I'm in no hurry for it, but I just can't pay that much for a lighter right now."

"Well if you don't want it, give it back, and I still owe you the full $200."

"It's not that I don't want it. I do. It's really Killah. I just can't afford it now."

I'm like, "What'd'ya mean? You don't have to put out cash, and you keep saying don't worry about what I owe, right away, so what's the problem?"

"I can't afford the lighter at that price."

"Well if ya don't want it, give it back."

"But I want it."

She made me say, harshly, "Roz, if you don't want to buy it, then <u>give it back</u>. I'll sell it to someone else, and give you the money towards what I owe you."

She left with the lighter, deciding to think it over more. The princess is used to getting what she wants. What she wants, is for me to give her the lighter case – Free. And she won't be happy till it happens like that.

Corvette made these earrings with Fairies on them. They were $35. Roz, asked, "How much for me?"

Corvette said $25.

On the day we went to her and Kevin's, Corvette brought 'em. Roz said, as if she'd never been told, "So what'd'ya want for 'em $15?" Corvette got $20 in the end.

Jan 20 1990

I woke up this morning to a great phone call. Jack will be a free man on Wednesday!!! It's about time they let him go. They don't have anything on him. He says he wants to put his time into keeping in touch with those in jails who need it. He and Skye have talked about it and he's gonna work on making Rainbow Communications a thing – a newsletter to distribute the addresses of jailed Heads.

Jan 25 1990

Freddy told us some family news. Seems Hawkeye wasn't happy about something, and ended up going after Joelle with a gun. Not good. Wonder what repercussions that will have for him? There's no need to get violent. It's happening everywhere. I don't like it. It's not where it's at.

Spacing out. Thinking of Tour.

I do wanna do tour, but I don't know how that'll work. We still owe $400 for the electric bill. I need brand new tires before we can go cross country again. That's at least $200. It all seems so overwhelming when you look at it like that.

So.

I'll stop looking at it like that, and just go to sleep.

Jan 30 1990

Beading, Beading, and more Beading. Low, low, bud level. Could be making money, but no sign of Silas. My bead projects of late include, a lighter case with dancing men, one with a lighthouse on it, a rainbow pen for Tish (came out great!), a small green velvet pouch with a beach-jade piece inlaid, and a glass wand. My next project is a big one – a peyote stitch bracelet, in the pattern of a thick knot bracelet. I saw one on a woman in the grocery store the other day.

I was answering the phone all day, asking – before they could – "Got anything yet?" – because that's what we all want to know. – Whose got the kind buds?

I answered it that way when Jumpin' Jack called. He's Free! They gave him $56, and a plane ticket to New York. He says his hair is really long, and that he's looking gorgeous.

Crafty Adam's not back yet. He called yesterday. Somehow he lost $2000. He was pretty buzzed, and adamant about us keeping the house. Nice thought, but January's rent is still short. And February is due right after the Jerry shows this weekend.

We've had Skinny Jim's VCR for a few days, and one of his tapes is a Public TV broadcast called *The Secret Government*. It says shit I already knew, but it's great to see it in documentary form. It amazed me to learn that the CIA tried to dose Fidel Castro. What did they think that would do?

That phrase makes me think of Hawkeye. Pulling a gun on Joelle – what did he think that would accomplish? I've heard of people pulling guns on folks below them, or even on the same level, but it just doesn't make sense to pull a gun on someone above you.

Feb 1

Zia, on the phone, "Did Judy Blue get her phone hooked up, or is she still playing poor?"

Me, "Her phone's not hooked."

Zia, "Why doesn't she just jump in a ditch?"

I say, "Anyway, call me later." Zia cackles, and hangs up.

I relate the end of the conversation to Corvette.

Corvette says, "Why doesn't Judy go jump in a ditch? She's never gonna go to another Dead show, because she's afraid to show her face…"

"Ah no, that's not what she said. She said she'd lost her faith. But I can see the misunderstanding – face-faith"

We're laughing, and Corvette says, "It's all the same thing."

Feb 4 1990   morningish

Friday we got to the Warfield, late-ish. I got a ticket from Matt Ackerman. Psyched!

Mavis bought the ticket I found for Corvette and couldn't afford. Mavis sold that ticket to Anjalee. Anjalee then decided she needed money to go east, so she sold us the ticket, cheaper than the first time it came our way.

The show was a ragin' one. The Warfield is beautiful. The upper lobby was fatness overload. Eventually went inside, and Suzy stubbed us down near the stage front. Jerry played a tune no-one was able to identify, or even to claim having heard before.

Sold postcards afterwards. Made enough to eat with.

Saturday I went with Parker to get the keys to his new place. It's in Oakland. The building is a little scary. It's tilted, but that's not the scary part. The scary part is the Earthquake cracks, fixed with different color plaster, so you can still see them all.

I did not voice any of my opinions, but he kept saying, "You don't like it."

"I never said that! It's… it's…."

"You don't like it."

We laughed a lot.

We got to the show late last night, again. It was raining and ugly. We thought we'd get in, but no. No luck scoring buds yet either. Maybe I'll see Hackmen today.

Crafty Adam flew in yesterday. Just days before he flew back, he said he had $400 towards the house. Yesterday he said he was flat broke.

Feb 7 1990

We didn't get in. I didn't even see any tix. Silas, going in, gives me a hug, and says, "You'll get in. I know it." Mavis and Becky heading in at the last minute, "Don't worry. You'll get in. You always do." Bullshit. We always get shut out of JGB shows on Market St.

Sucks we only got one ounce at the shows. It's already gone, but it covered rent.

Haven't heard from Jumpin' Jack since he got out. I hope he'll still find time to write to all those people he promised.

Adam's in big debt and has no money, and he's not telling us what the story is, or even who he is in debt to, but he's agitated about it.

Feb 23 1990

Atlanta Mary called, saying, "Not gonna roll for a while." Meaning most likely, till she straightens up this morning. She's tweaked because her Dad's in Jail. He got busted with his car import system. (And she lost her Jaguar.)

Feb 24

Got woken up at 4:30AM. Freddy – bringing some boxes here to stash. It was scary energy. He's movin' just ahead of the storm. Things are not good with Piper's situation. A total set-up. And let's hear it folks – do not forget – The first three letters of DEAD are ...

Poor Piper. I hope everything works out as best it can for all concerned. Jah be with them – especially Jillian. This sucks bad.

Feb 26 1990

Jasmine got a table at a high-class Art show at one of the Hotels during these shows. She invited us to work it with her. We were told Jasmine got the only bead booth. But we're not just the only bead booth, we're the only other artists besides Stanley Mouse. It was Mouse's Art Expo and some guy talked him into giving Jasmine a booth.

A woman came through buying stuff for a psychedelic restaurant her boss is opening in Japan. Must be great to come into a place like that, and rage, spending other people's money. She didn't buy anything of ours though. I had hoped, being an "art" show, that people would buy from Corvette and me – all our weird, high-end, artsy stuff. No. They bought other people's jewelry we had with us – earrings, barrettes, bracelets. There's a difference between beaded Jewelry and beaded Art. It's harder to sell Art. Sigh.

Justine and Don stopped by. We smoked a few bowls out back with Don while Justine watched the booth. We were talking about the upcoming tour and how he and Fritz will be traveling together again, and how maybe it'll be fun again. We agreed. Maybe it WILL be fun again.

Corvette stayed at the booth during the show last night and all <u>we</u> sold was her rasta guy necklace for half price. I went off to the show long about 5^{ish}. Inside I went to the usual section to look for Silas and found only Karl. He got me stoned. We got along nicely. Karl almost took a ride with us back to Willard North. But he changed his mind. He's probably glad, seeing as how JT, the guy who gave away his stuff in LA, is here.

I didn't go near the Fatty Circle except to throw my shit there. Fritz was being a dick, and kept either giving me weird looks, or ignoring me completely. I didn't much want to deal with that shit. He hadn't even said "high" to me all day. When he walked by, ignoring me for the hundredth time, I said, "Well, fuck you Fritz."

And he goes, "What? What'd'ya want? Do you want me to walk by and say 'Hey Hollie, you got great fuckin tits'?"

What the fuck?

Anyway, it was a very good show. And I saw the best something I've seen in a while by the Dead. *Last Time*. Strong and powerful, with a message. Well practiced too.

"Well I told you once and I told you twice, but you never listen to my advice, You don't try very hard to please me, with what you know it should be easy... well this could be the last time, this could be the last time, may be the last time, I don't know..."

It was way raging.

Jeanie's here at Willard North – just back from Israel. It's soooo great to see her. We're about to head to the show. Gonna stop by to see if ticket master still has tix.

March 4 1990
Flagstaff

On the 2nd day of Mardi Gras shows, we didn't do the bead booth again, because during the show, that 1st night, Dave Echo was visiting Corvette at the booth. Some drunk guys came in and talked to Dave. Some drunk chicks came in and talked to the drunk guys. One of the chicks spilled a drink on Mouse's stuff. He decided they were our friends, and we were not invited back. Fuck you – you lofty fuck. He knew that wasn't true.

Oh well. I'm not upset, but I'm afraid Jasmine might be. Fritz came up to me 2nd day in the lot after the show – all nice, and asked for a ride to his hotel.

"I don't think so Fritz, you've been a total dick to me all weekend, and this is the first time you've even talked to me – and, that's only because you want something." He said that wasn't true and gave me a hug, but I still wouldn't give him a ride.

So as me, Jeanie, KindBoy and Corvette are pulling out of the lot, Fritz is in the van to our left. KindBoy called out the window telling Fritz he's a dick. Fritz yelled shit back, and KindBoy jumped out like he was gonna do something. Fritz jumped out too. It was all done as if in fun, but had serious undertones.

"You're nothing but a bunk-ass motherfucker." Said KindBoy.

"You're nothing but a fat fuck with stinky feet."

After KindBoy's back in the Van, we're crawling along in traffic, still next to the van Fritz is in. I say, "Fritz, got a bud we can bum for the bridge?"

"No. I only got 2 grams of pot."

"Oh."

"Why? You guys have none?"

"Nothing."

"Here." He gave us enough to get over the bridge that night, and back again next day.

The Mardi Gras show was fun, and musically, really good. The parade was the best yet. A huge blow up skeleton puppet, dancing and bobbing over the crowd.

Out in the Fatty Circle there were two big fatty costumes – Tricky and Kestrel Jim. They had dry ice, so they smoked throughout the night. Looked fuckin amazing. They tried to get in the parade. But they were late, and stoned, and got behind the last float. That float got lost in the crowd, and Tricky and KJ did too.

We blew off the first JGB show to get our shit together and left our house Friday morning. Stopped to see Roz. She told us Piper's out on bail, but in lots of trouble. That situation sucks so bad.

The show that night was one of those Totally Amazing Jerry shows. I was so high, I felt like I was dosed.

After the show, on the drum circle sidewalk corner, some guy stepped off the curb and got hit by a rider rent-a-truck. Not a good scene. He was unrecognizable – his head just mush. I didn't mean to look, but I still kinda saw. It was gruesome. It took the cops 20 minutes to get there. Some people said he was a street person, others said it was a tour dreadhead. If it was a head, I hope he at least saw the show before he died. The Rider truck took off – making it a hit and run.

At the last Warfield JGB show some chick jumped off the top of a building and died. How does this effect you Jerry?

~~~~~

Jeanie decided to drive east with us. Perfect. We needed a good rider.

Got to Carmen's house at 4AM. We've had a Kahlua morning. Showered and did laundry. We're headed for Sedona.

March 7 1990

At Corvette's Grandma's in Missouri.

After Sedona we drove to a Hot Springs north of Albuquerque, in a valley with painted cliffs all around. The Holy Ghost Warm Springs came bubbling out of the ground, traveled along a stream to these pools. When sitting in the pool, our heads were at ground level – such an interesting perspective, eye level with the desert floor. The bottom of the pool was thick, soft, silt that was grey until you touched it, then it clouded up black. It looked like the universe.

We drove the rest of New Mexico in daylight. Then Texas and a large part of Oklahoma at night. Tuesday, we came to Grandma's house by a lake in Missouri. Corvette's uncle is cool. I gave him those long-johns Crafty Adam tye-dyed. Her Grandma made dinner. There were issues around Jeanie being a vegetarian. Grandma said she would cook plenty of veggies. And she did, but she put meat in every veggie dish. She just could not understand eating <u>only</u> veggies. She'd never heard of such a thing.

26
Spring Tour 1990
Landover, Hartford, Canada

March 14
Dateline Landover – 1st show.
Jeanie came with us to Connecticut and we've been kickin' around with the homescum for a few days. Word had gone out that Hartford tix would go on sale Tuesday morning at 10. We were bummin' about the fact that we were leaving before that, and gonna miss ticket sales. I decided to drive by Peltons to see what the scene was on tix. Lottery or line? And the radio DJ says, as we're driving, "That's right folks, Dead tix are on sale now." Score!

Everyone was leaving work and vehicles would screech into a parking space and people were jumping out as the wheels hit the curb. Dead! Hartford! Everyone got tix! We didn't have enough money to get all that we should have, but we got some for Hackmen, and Benny, and Don, and Jumpin' Jack.

It was 80° when we left Connecticut. Hot drive through New Jersey. Got here late. Got stoned with Hawkeye at the slEasy8, but we're staying at the Knights Inn. The 6 across the street is raging too hard, the 8 feels too shady, and the Days is too expensive.

I woke to GM Joe at our door. Mmmmm Morning fatties. As I've been writing, the room has filled up. First with Atlanta Mary, Neil and Winnie, then Kestrel Jim, Santa, Hawkeye, and King. King's RV is blaring reggae outside our room.

later
Ragin' hotel scene. Fritz and Don got here and tackled Hawkeye to the bed and pummeled him. So many people coming and going. We're all pretty high, and the room is extremely smokey – set the smoke Alarm off – twice.

Knock knock.

"Who's there?"
"It's a gas gas gas."

Ahhh!! Jack! What a surprise. Everyone was psyched. Even Hawkeye gave him a low five.

March 15 1990

Didn't get in last night. Neither did Corvette, Santa, Mutz, Two Toke Tom, or Icarus. As a crowd, we tried for a long time to bribe guards with all the money we could spare between us. No luck. They played *Loose Lucy*. We could hear it.

Finally, I just went back to the lot to sell postcards.

After the show we came back to the room we're splitting with Santa and Kerry. Silas and Hackmen stopped by to get us stoned, even after I warned them Jumpin' Jack might be here. They left late to go back to their campground. I didn't crash until sunrise – After showering and walking Elwood. (Wingnut watching isn't as fun alone.) I woke up when Jack came over. Domino grabbed a shower, while I got a great massage, and coffee!

The weather is gorgeous. 20° above normal, breaking 100-year-old records.

Word is Andre is out of rehab, but not allowed to come home. Dawn got busted. Her friend since elementary school rolled over on her. Youch. Poor Dawn. And yesterday in the lot, Briscoe's girlfriend Laurie got busted for selling to a narc. Anybody working out there is fucking nuts.

Inside – Break Time.

(I hope Corvette got in.)

Bubbles all around me. Phil's side. Phil's 50th B-day.

We rode to the show in King's RV. I raged on postcards. – $42, when I counted.

Sun was going down – NO Tickets. Please! I got shut out last night. Please!

I saw none all day. Finally, "$50."

"$42?" It was all I had.

"okay."

But then, "You have a ticket?" from some approaching young urban pro asshole.

"$50" he said to the new guy.

"Ok."

"Sorry." He said to me.

"Yeah right, thanks dude."

Gettin' down hearted – got my finger in the air.

Phil's 50th. *Unbroken Chain* perhaps?

Please Please let me in. There's only about 2,000 other people out here looking.

I'm feeling low.

Another chance – "$50."

"42?"

Another yuppie – "What?!? $50? Okay. Here." Once again. NO way, this can't be.

"Please, I need a ticket. I got Shut Out last night."

"Looks like you're out here tonight too ha."

"FUCK YOU Dude. I hope you have the worst show you EVER had." And I can't believe I said that to him, and I can't believe I'm so close to tears. It's just the Dead. Just a show.

Upset, I walk off, as his girlfriend is saying, "What did you say to her? What did you SAY???"

I don't care this much about a stupid show. With every finger I see held high, my eyes are getting more teary. I hate it when I get close to crying over something like a show. So what if I don't get in – it won't kill me.

But I wanted in SO bad. Why does someone like that guy get a ticket, and not me?

It's so mean to tell a Head they won't get in. Malicious almost.

Please lead me to my ticket, I don't want to be Shut Out again. All alone, feeling bad – finger in the air. Hackmen walks by, almost doesn't see me. I reach out and touch his arm.

"What's wrong?"

I can't even tell him. It's so silly. "I don't have a ticket." And the water in my eyes is welling up. Such a dumb thing to be so upset about. I walked away. I didn't want Hackmen to see me cry. Or anyone for that matter. It's not something to cry about.

I stop on the corner, wipe the tears from my eyes, lean on the wall, and raise that finger.

"It's not too late," Hackmen says in my ear, "Hold this." His backpack. And off he goes.

"Please I need a ticket." Says me to the passing crowds, and Hackmen appears smiling, and nodding. The tears increase, this time for happiness. He did it for an 1/8. He'd only take $30.

I felt saved, relieved and drained all at once. We ran to the truck together – dropped off his stuff, and got inside as *Jack Straw* started.

Everyone wants Phil tonight. He looks to be in a great mood. Lights out.

March 19 1990
Connecticut

Been a while. Start with 2nd night Maryland. Corvette didn't get in that night. They played an old Brent tune, *Easy to Love You,* and encored with *Revolution*. Great stuff.

That night, Jack stayed in our room. I like having him back, but he started drinking again. I can see the difference.

Next morning me and Corvette went to breakfast with Jumpin' Jack, Two Toke Tom, and VW Walt. Terrible restaurant, but we had a nice time with them older hippie boys.

Hawkeye didn't come around anymore after he saw Jack. Corvette said he'd just smile, or stick his tongue out from afar. King's RV was quite the lot scene. Blaring reggae, Rads, or Red Hot Chili Peppers. Lots o' nitrous. Fritz grabbed my ass as he was wah-wah-wingin. He gets so weird sometimes. Corvette says Benny's bein' weird. He's been hanging with a cute redhead. It's bummin' her out.

Inside I was talkin with Riley. He sold five to his long ago friend, who, he thinks, gave 'em to the DEA. She wanted more. He blew it off because of a bolt of truth – DEA! Perhaps he was right. It's good when we follow our gut instincts. Intuitions are the things we must pay attention too in our world. The important awarenesses come through, if we listen.

Me and Corvette both got in 3rd night. I got a free one, and we got one for face. They broke out *Black Throated Wind* – so so good! Encored with *Last Time*.

Martin and Dave Echo had a great story from outside, 3rd night. They didn't get in. Martin had a fake laminate. He tried to get in on it. It got taken away by a Yellowjacket. They ended up talking with the guy. He told them he'd been pretending to be a narc all day, and showed them how much LSD he'd confiscated, and was now trying to sell.

A bit later, they saw some kid with Martin's fake laminate, asked where he got it. He said he bought it for $80, from a guard. Martin told him it was fake, and he wouldn't get in. He tried anyway and got thrown out. He was pissed. So Martin went to the scammin' guard, and said, "Dude, we know the deal. Give this guy back his $80, and all this ends now."

The guard said, "No."

Fool.

The bunked kid went to the cops, and when they got to the guard, they searched him, busted him for 15 pages, and stripped him, right then and there, of his Yellow Jacket and flashlight.

Sunday! Yesterday! Heads in Bushnell park! It felt great – all the colorful crowds lounging, and playing on the lawn in front of the Capitol building.

Lots of people looking for tickets last night. Me and Corvette traded our extras to Suzy and Kennedy for a Saturday, Albany, and Corvette's B-day in Hamilton.

Ragin *Shakedown* opener, definitely one of the high points of the show. Weird 2nd set. *Wharf Rat He's Gone Truckin Spoonful* all before drums. *Spoonful* was another highlight.

The Fatty Zone was inside the back upper section. King and company in the purple zone. Fritz, Don, Rockafucker, and company in the 1st red section. Silas, Hackmen, Kennedy, Suzy, and our homescum – Leo, Jesse, Amy, Dwayne, and Spencer, near us. Homescum didn't get too many fatties, but they got a few.

Walking with Leo, we passed Fritz and I hip-flipped him. He put his arm around me, danced me around to face the opposite direction, and said, "Come on."

"I'm walking with Leo." I said.

Fritz goes, "Ok. Fine." And makes a big deal of pushing me away. Fritz gives me the weirdest looks these days.

After the show. Silas crashed in the van, and we tried to sell postcards – sold very fuckin few, not good at all. Drove to Mom's, with Silas still asleep. Hackmen stayed to look for Jimmy and Patrick, who were lost, no doubt. Suzy and Kennedy drove their Uhaul to Mom's, and later, Hackmen showed up in Silas' truck.

March 20   Connecticut

Suzy and Kennedy left early, – decided to blow off the show and go to Cape Cod. Jimmy and Patrick showed up and we went to the top o' the Mountain. So ugly up there now. Garbage everywhere, – when we used to hang there we used to keep it clean.

Neil and Winnie had another magical getaway. Daytime, in Bushnell park, smoking fatties – seen – caught – cuffed – blocked, covered, hidden – and got away with the cuffs on. Someone had a hacksaw blade and they got them off before the show started. She was smiling all night! Winnie is a beautiful spirit, meant to be smiling. They can't have her for such a silly thing as buds.

We traded an extra ticket for two killah batiked tee-shirts with Phil's silhouette. Purple. Subtle. So well done.

Currently the Van is ½ hour back, at Rosemary's. Me and Corvette are in the back of Silas' truck, Hackmen's driving, and Jimmy, Patrick, and Glenn are in the car behind us. So nice not to be driving for a change.

On the way to Rosemary's, a toll taker offered me tickets to the show because some kids had wrecked their vehicle. She was selling their tix for them. I hope they're okay.

We had a quick little snowball fight outside Rosemary's. There's about two inches on the ground. Jimmy and Patrick say they aren't going to Canada but they're still behind us!

90 West towards Buffalo. Time to roll one.

March 21 1990

Morning. The snow stopped. The sun is out, but it's fuckin cold. I hope I brought enough clothes. I'm sitting outside, in the sun. They're smoking a fatty upstairs.

We don't know exactly how we're getting to Canada. Our original idea was the train, which doesn't leave Buffalo till 4:30PM, and gets to Hamilton at 7:30. That's way too late. I don't even have tix yet.

They're trying to talk Patrick into renting a van. I'm not involved in that conversation.

Man it's cold.

Let's see, what tour news have I yet to document?

Murph is here. Murph himself! Playing or being poor – I can't tell. He passed up what I had of the nicest buds, in Maryland, making me believe he actually had no cake. Said, with so many friends in jail, he's too afraid to work. I must admit, it's enough to scare anyone.

I heard of two busts in Hartford. One Young Evan for all naturals, and the other Francy. I have no idea what they got him for. Probably all natural also. I hope someone is doing something for him.

We're almost totally broke, and I get worried about Silas tweaking on us for cake again. We have no idea how much it'll cost to get over the border. And I'm hungry.

later

Outside the Buffalo airport. Silas and Glenn went to find the FedEx office. Glenn's wallet was sent there by the health food store he left it in, in Pennsylvania.

Hackmen, Jimmy, and Patrick went to rent a van. It was nearly done, but they noticed Patrick's license is expired. So now we're trying to figure out what to do.

later still

Jimmy and Patrick went through a lot of 'should we? shouldn't we?' type stuff. 'We're going. We're not going.' 'Work, or the show?' They even flipped useless coins. Abbott and Costello, Corvette called 'em. Hackmen, ever practical, says, "You know you're going. You should just face facts and concentrate on other things. Trying to fight the inevitable wastes energy."

We rented a van, with a driver, to bring us to Canada. Now we're on the road.

5:52 PM

Just crossed the border. The toll guy sent us to a secondary inspection. We got out of the van and went inside. ID check. US Citizens. They told us our driver looks exactly like Bernard Getz. Yikes! We had to wait for this lady in a uniform to check the vehicle. When she got to us, she only went through my backpack and let us go. Too bad we're all so clean. Jimmy's jokin' that he's got an ounce of gak.

There was a bus there at the border – The Peace Train. What a load of hippies they had. As we were leaving, a dreadheaded rasta guy was walking back over the border, – his stuff in a pillowcase over his shoulder. Entrance denied. Don't know who he is, but I've seen him all over this tour.

Listening to the blooze. 43 miles, sorry that's kilometers. 20 miles to Hamilton.

Middle of the Night

Got to the Victor K Copps Arena – looking for a place to put our stuff – found Lubba Lenny and tossed our shit in his van. And we saw the dreadhead who'd gotten turned back. He said he just jumped the fence. Crazy mon! I heard of one chick who smuggled in 10 pages and sold it for $1500. Some friends got buds through. Said it was easy.

I got a ticket right away, for free, from Young Dread Jamie. Been a while since I saw a show with such easy tix. Corvette paid $15 for a ticket. Silas did a lot of quick trades, and got some hash. Lubba Lenny had smokeables and there's even word of buds in the lot.

1st set raged. *Loose Lucy* was GREAT! It's a really nice place. Clean floors, polite ushers, but lots of cops and undercovers.

After the show we had trouble getting it all together. We lost Jimmy and Patrick (what did we expect?) We got the last room at the Royal Connaught.

March 23 1990.

In a hotel in Buffalo. The Royal Connaught had a great pool and a 30-foot spiral water slide. Hackmen and Glenn were hilarious – fighting, and wrestling, and racing down the slide.

Later, me and Corvette were walking through the streets of Hamilton with Santa, plastering the place with Glenn's stickers – "The Drug War is Immoral." Corvette got caught putting one on a city bus. The driver made her take it off.

The guy directing pedestrians out front was fun to toy with. He'd page people for you with his bullhorn, and people were having him page – Jorma Kalkonen. Jack Straw. August West.

Sold out of postcards and had our tix already, so we went to the Sheraton Bar, 'cause it was rainy and windy.

I was in a weird mood. Corvette's B-day ya know. She collected back massages and drinks all day. Yeah, that's part of what was making me down. I'd be a liar if I said different. On my B-day there was no bar, no party, no back massages. And no ticket till 2nd set.

They opened with *Feel Like a Stranger*.

No doubt.

Walking down the street with Don, Fritz (who was being a dick), DigDoug, Katarina, Kestrel Jim, and Mirabeth, I felt like I didn't belong. I didn't get high at all yesterday. The smell of hash so pungent and prominent. I really don't like hash all that much. I didn't even go over to the Fatty Zone for Corvette's B-day. I wasn't in the mood.

2nd set I sat next to Lubba Lenny's girlfriend, Brenda. She asked if I was alright. I said yeah. "Well, you're usually dancing, instead of sitting there looking sad." We talked a lot. I'm not even sure what we talked about. Life. Death. (She had a friend die on the way to the New Orleans show that October Southern tour a couple years back.) The good and bad of the Dead. I ended up giving her one of my Yin-Yang earrings.

As I was starting to feel better, the Dead broke into *Hey Jude*. And they did *Dear Mr. Fantasy* in the middle of it, then back into *Jude*. With the audience chanting Hey Jude refrains low and deep, and Brent singing the words to *Fantasy*. Really Really nice. Peaceful. Sweet. Relaxing. Restoring. The whole show was Hot Hot Hot. I can't think of the last Bad show I saw. The Dead is so smokin' these days.

After the show – to the Sheraton Bar for Corvette's B-day party. Disco lights flashing, the place packed with high people, wearing after-show glows. We got yelled at for getting stoned in the corner. I helped the DJ to play the right sort of music to get the heads dancing. Talking Heads, Thomas Dolby. (Hyperactive!) Someone requested Little Red Corvette for her b-day. One waitress kept grabbing cute hippie boys to dance with. She got Tricky dirty dancing with her, while everyone cheered them on. We danced wildly with King, and Fritz, and Don, when the DJ played B-52s' *Love Shack*. I love a good after show bar party! Fun Fun Fun!

We had rented a limo to pick us up at 1:30, outside the Sheraton. The car he was in barely looked like a limo. We asked if we could puff in the car. He said no. "Well then, wait a few minutes, you're early." While Big Donny stood with our luggage, we booked up around the corner with Fritz and Santa to smoke Corvette's last two b-day fatties.

Most of us passed out till we got to the border. Putting out the vibes that say, "It's 3AM. Please don't make us get out of the car." We got waved right through and went to the Buffalo airport, to get Silas' truck.

We packed the seven of us into the truck, and came to this Hotel, here in Buffalo, that some friend of theirs parent's owns. We got a friend-of-the-family discount.

This morning we went to a health food place and pigged out. Now we're back at the hotel with a late check out. Silas and Hackmen went to do laundry. Corvette is getting a foot massage from Glenn, who's looking for the bliss spot on her foot.

We're broke, and need to get to Albany. We're willing to hitch, but Hackmen doesn't want us to. I don't want to be broke around Silas, and head for a tweak on his part.

later

Movin down the road.

We sat around awhile, waiting for Silas and Hackmen to get back, but when the chance arose, we took a ride to the New York thruway, and got dropped off. Right away a Rider truck pulled up and we got in.

27
Spring Tour 1990
Good Cop, Bad Cop – Albany, Atlanta, and N'Awlins

March 24
4AM – Albany(ish)

At The Swiss Chalet. What a night.

The folks in the Rider truck were cool. Morty, a Chicago taxi driver who wore his sunglasses the whole time. Some chick Elise, and another named Maria, who carries a Jerry doll everywhere, like a teddy bear. Drippy Danny was there with some girl Wilda, and Ryelle, from Jamaica. It was a cold ride, in a big box truck, but we were piled under lots of blankets.

Morty brought us right to Rosemary's house. It was midnight. They left, and I realized I needed a jump. While wondering what to do, a drunk neighbor came stumbling out of his house, so we got him to jump us. Sat for a while warming up, charging up, and smoking the last of our roaches. No sign of Rosemary, or any life in the house. I expected her to leave me directions to Jumpin' Jack's house, but she didn't. We went to a phone and called, – woke her parents up, – but they said Rosemary wasn't home, Jumpin' Jack doesn't have a phone, and they didn't know where he lives.

So we headed for Albany – Swarmed by three cop cars.

Lights everywhere – they were excited. I didn't do anything to make them pull me over and they wouldn't tell me why they pulled me over. Said things like, "You're going to the concert huh?" Kept circling the Van, shining their lights on everything. Told me the stuff on my dash was obstructing my view. I told them it wasn't in my way. They said, in New York state it is. Gave me a ticket for obstructed view. No cost until the judge decides.

So I think, 'OK, that's it.'

Then he says, "Would you please step out of the van so I can search."

I'm like, "I see no reason for you to search me, or my van. There's nothing to lead you to want to search."

"Would you please step out of the van." It wasn't a question.

"I don't think this is right. You have no reason to search."

"Please step out of the van. If you have nothing to hide, there's no problem. It'll only take a minute."

"I don't think this is right. If you search, you'll find nothing, and I want to know now – when that's the case – what can I do about the fact that this isn't right?"

"If you have nothing to hide, they'll be no problem. Please step out of the van." He was getting mean. He acted like I didn't have a choice about stepping out.

I got out. He checked my pockets and fanny pack. Then told me to go stand by this other cop car – where Corvette already was. So I go over and say to that cop, "This doesn't seem right to me. He has no reason to search my van."

"Well, you gave your consent, didn't you?"

"Not really, why? Did I have a choice?"

"By stepping out of the van you're giving your consent."

"Ya mean I didn't have to!?!"

So I go back to the cop searching the van, and I say, "Sir. The officer over there just told me I didn't have to consent to this search. And from what you've seen so far, I'm sure you can see, there is nothing illegal in my van, so if you'll get out of my van, I'll be on my way."

He got out. He had been looking under the driver seat – in the door – under the dash. But he got out. Told me to clear everything off my dash before leaving. Then he asked me what concerts I go to. What kind of cop question is that?

I said, "Well obviously I'm going to the Dead this weekend."

"We always ask that question. Because if you fail to mail in this ticket, or appear in court, a warrant will be issued for your arrest, and we WILL look for you at concerts."

That sounds fucked to me. I'm glad I stopped the search before he found our stupid little bowl. Yikes.

So we're outta there, and we cruise to Knickerbocker Arena. Nobody. Nothing. Only the Hilton in sight and Dead band buses. But no heads. No other Hotels. It was eerie and weird, so we went back to East Greenbush to find these guys.

Ryelle has a newspaper. The small front page headline says, "Narcotics officers ready to be busy."

       March 25   Albany

Or the 26th cause it's 2:30AM.
Albany got a bit better from there. After lunch, we headed to the Preserve. That's where Albany is letting people camp.

We got in during *Slipknot,* and missed *Help on the Way.* Missed it. I had a ticket all day. And I missed the *Good Times Roll Help* opener. NO Way. Why is it I keep missing *Help on the Way*? Silas and company missed it too. They were outside waiting for Karl, because things that are sticky, and green, are scarce. In fact, most every tourhead missed it. The crowds at the doors, and the inefficiency of the staff, didn't help. This place is brand new, and not good at this yet.

Inside, I was standing with Rockafucker when we saw an ice-cart guy ram his cart into Briscoe, snarling, "<u>Excuse Me</u>!"

This ice guy's boss got to him in front of us – "Hey guy, relax."

"I'm gonna kill 'em. They're in my way. I'm tryin' to do my job, and they're all over the fuckin place. I'm gonna fuckin' run 'em over."

I said to the boss (very nicely), "Maybe you should get someone else to do his job tonight. He's already tried to run a couple people over."

He snapped, "Fuck you baby, mind your own business."

Wow. Uptight.

Silas and company were psyched to see us. Silas goes, "Dude, you left me. They had X. I had to drive with that energy. I was tweaking, and you weren't there."

I said, "I think you might have tweaked on me if I had been there."

"No Way. It would have helped me to have your energy."

Glenn was like, "There was ice inside the back of Silas' truck – I was so worried about you guys."

Hackmen was bummed that we left. He said, "If it ever comes down to finances like that again, you'll deal with me, and not worry about it."

I was in a weird mood till, during Break, I was in the bathroom, and I heard a middle-aged woman say to another, quite animatedly, "This is worth anything!" I needed to hear that just then.

Shows are still amazing. High Quality shit. And worth ANYTHING. All the bullshit we deal with – on the road, and from each other – it's all so fucking worth it. This is the best life I could imagine.

~~~~~

Sold a lot of postcards today. But saw no tickets. It was getting colder and windier. Me and Corvette decided, we're going in. Just gonna walk in. So we got past the first ticket-checkin' guys, and we're up by the door, puzzling, "How are we gonna do this?"

"Maybe they won't even see us?"

"Maybe last night's stubs and $20 bills?"

So we're talking like that, inching towards the door, and the two guys behind us are like, "That's not gonna work."

We're like, "Yes, it is. If you guys believe we can get in like this, then we can."

They're like, "I don't know..."

So the line's movin, and we got our stubs and $20s, and we're hoping...

It's too fucking cold outside. We have GOT to be inside.

We get like two feet from the door, and the guys behind us go – "Here – buy our tickets – we're gonna blow it off." Yahoo we're in! Early even! They opened with nothing too great, though it was a good *Greatest Story*. What a great way to get in!!!

Cruised the halls a lot tonight. I miss the section where we all used to be – Knowing everyone dancing around you. That was always so electrifying.

March 26   Albany

Drinking Kahlua coffee. Called Spencer first thing this morning to make sure he wasn't selling our tix to anyone else. He had two for us yesterday too, but sold them before he saw us.

It's snowing. Just started when I was out having a cigarette.

Nighttime.

Sold postcards at $45 per 100 today. Sold a bunch, we needed to. The show was fun. I gave Glenn a massage during Space, *Miracle* and *Fantasy*. I like giving massages to music.

Before we left the lot, we hung in King's RV (waiting for Fairy Mary to get back and buy postcards). Fritz, Don, Kerry, and Santa were there. I already can't remember what had us laughing so hard. Fritz was in rare form. It's nice to see him and Don raging together.

We're not going to Nassau. No way – that place is evil. But you know they're gonna rage there. I just hope that's not where they decide to bust out *Unbroken Chain*.

Word in the Hallway says, they've added Miami shows after Atlanta. I've heard it all – 'It's on the Hotline,' 'It's not on the Hotline,' 'It's confirmed,' 'My backstage people say no,' 'So-and-So has seen tix.' But who knows.

March 29 1990   Albany

Next morning, Isaac came in on the train with what we've all been wishing and waiting for – sticky, gooey, beautiful, green.

Word travels fast. Soon our room was full of Indicans jostling to get nearer the buds. Fatties being rolled and passed in every direction. Tunes cranked and everyone's in a joyful mood, talking over everyone else. A bustling morning.

March 31 1990   Atlanta

Stopped in South Carolina for gas. Murph was there – Hoping they'd cash a money order for him. They did, and he gave us $10, because we didn't have enough $ to get a full tank. We smoked a skinny out behind the place with him and Domino.

Got into Little 5 Points about sunset. There's a street fair this weekend and it was packed with people. Went by Josephine – saw Jethro and Vincent and a new roomie. Had to be sure they knew we were gonna bring a bunch of hippies here. To Shawna's a bit, where Atanta Mary appeared with piles of Greek food. Yum!

Back at Josephine now. Our express mail just got delivered at this hour, because I called and bitched – the signature waiver was signed, specifically, so it would get here today.

King Henry's having a warehouse party the night of the 2nd show. His b-day is the 4th. Trinity's is the 3rd. And Jeremy's is the 1st. But Henry says Jeremy has to kick some $ or it won't be his birthday. Funny – King can take away Jeremy's b-day. Such power! Ha!

April 1st   Atlanta

Went to Little 5 Joints with Simon, the new Josephine roommate. We ate at this Jamaican restaurant he turned us on to called Bridgetown Grill. I could live on food like that. Wandered The April Fool's Fest a little. There were two stages. One by Fellini's Pizza, and the other in front of Crystal Blue. Totally a happening scene as far as Atlanta goes, but we didn't stay – We knew where it was really happening. Down by the Omni.

We brought Simon with us. Found Ryan – he had our tix. Then we had to get one for Simon. No Problem. Some chick sold him one for $20, and two postcards. Silas and Hackmen managed to trade buds to some of Corvette's local friends, for tix. Inside we found Karl, Lenny, and Brenda for a Smoke Out. Simon told me he just got over a pretty bad bout with dope. I'm glad he's back to the purely marijuana state of mind.

And Mavis is here! She's off the dope too! She told me she died on it one night out in SF, got lucky, and came back. Next night – high again, she called her Dad. He told her he'd had a dream about her, that made him wake up crying. That was when she quit. She went back to Ohio and dealt with the withdrawals without the methadone clinic her parents wanted to put her in. I'm glad she realized she was strong enough to do it.

After the show we were totally hungry – strangely, it seemed like no one was selling food. Just as the helmeted, billyclub-carrying army came through, we found a guy who was giving away bag lunches – veggie sandwich, fruit, and a juice. I gave him postcards as thanks.

April 4 1990

Atlanta was fun. 2nd day another *Last Time,* and a *Death Don't Have No Mercy.*

I was talking with Freddy, about Louziana Steve, telling him about walking into Steve's apartment with Abe, and not remembering where me and Steve had met before. Telling Freddy, "Steve knew right off. Said, 'It was in Damien's hotel room. Spring tour 1986.'" And as soon as I said Damien's name, it coincided with the 1st note of *He's Gone*. Freddy loved it. Shit like that happens a lot.

That was the night of King Henry's party. It was one of those ragin', over-the-top parties we do so well. Fritz was makin' bad margaritas, and everyone was downing them anyway, while joking about his complete and total lack of bartending skills. A funk band called Cool Joe, and some pickin' and rockin' band.

Everyone was there! Really. Everyone. Hilarious happenings in every direction. I wish I had time to write some of the party realities, but I don't really. Well. Just one hilarious one – Domino had had a spill on his bus that soaked the dog biscuit box. They looked like little cookies. He dumped them on the counter, and went to try to find a plastic bag to put them in. Got back minutes later and they'd all been eaten! Ha!

Next day I found Louziana Steve with an extra. He invited us to N'Awlins to see the Rads this weekend at Tipitina's.

I gave out a bunch of massages in the show last night. Everybody I saw got a few moments of finger attention. I love it when they play *NFA*. Wooooo!

And there it is – another semester over.

Last night the big joke was me and Karl, congratulating ourselves about making it through a tour with no arguments.

We did just okay, financially, this tour. Didn't make enough money to totally pay off Aaron for the postcards but so it goes. However, in Little 5 today we got four stores to order postcards. That's nice. It gets us money on future orders that we don't really have to work for. We need to do more of that.

April 7 1990   N'Awlins

Got to Louziana Steve's about 10PM and headed right to the Rads. I had forgotten how far it was to New Orleans from Slidell. We got there five minutes before the Rads went on stage. Fat Matt and his crew showed up. I like Tipitina's, and the Rads raged.

We had a major dancing corner – balcony, Phil's side. (Because yeah, it's Phil's side even when it's not the Dead on stage.)

After the show, we tried to meet someone who might get us on the list for tomorrow. Eventually we met Lemon. Never figured out exactly what he did for them but he had a backstage pass.

April 8 1990   N'Awlins

Karl, Brenda, Lenny, and Marcella (Brenda's sister) were at the Rads last night. Marcella goes to school here. I kept saying how much I liked New Orleans, and she told me about getting mugged, at gunpoint, in front of her own apartment, with a cop in sight up on the corner.

Me and Karl made a great show of seeing each other.

"Oh I've missed you since tour," etc.

Totally easier to deal with than the usual.

Today, we went to the French Quarter. Got a nice shady parking spot for Elwood, and tried to sell postcards to stores. After 8 or 10 rejections we're like, 'well Fuck it, let's get one drink, and head back to Slidell.'

We got a huge Pina Colada in a bucket, and there's this cool-looking guy with a cardboard placard over his shoulders selling Mardi Gras posters. We fell into talking with him. Mirro. Told him we're broke (I suppose it always comes up in conversation), and he offered us jobs silk-screening. "Come, let me show you the warehouse."

After that we walked through Jackson Square. It's the French Quarter Fest, so the place was ragin'. We asked him and his friend if they wanted to get high. Mirro said he quit smoking in 1969, and his friend said, "No way man, this is New Orleans." Yeah, New Orleans has the free flowing party mode down – cops smile and watch, as everyone drinks in the streets, but if you light up, look out.

We went and got Elwood out of the van. There was a concert going on, so we wandered over there. It was Charmaine Neville – she was great. Elwood likes N'Awlins. So much to watch. Little boys with bike tires spinning on their heads, tap dancers in sequins, a parade of feather-hatted trombone players, horse drawn carts, flamboyant cross dressers, and fireworks. He loves fireworks.

28
April and May 1990
JGB, LA Three Times,
Garrett's B-day, and a Dead Car

April 13 1990   SF

    We slept at Carmen's in Flagstaff, left early, and drove all day through the desert. Hot Hot. Crossed the Bay Bridge around 6^{ish}. Still hot as hell, sitting in traffic. Came directly to the Warfield. JGB. Got a massage there on the street corner scene from Garrett. He wants me to go on a date with him. Jeez, he never lets up. Maybe I will. Man, he gives a great massage.

    Good Friday the 13th, and we couldn't find tix.

    We kept looking a long time. Garrett offered dinner so we went down the block for Pizza and beer with Deja Dan, Skinny Jim, and Lyndelle's friend, Danni. Tasty, and fun, but I can't believe we didn't get in. Race across the fuckin' country to sit outside, again.

    Danni was there in Nassau when Wolfboy Taylor got arrested. Taylor was selling hash. Two narcs bought some. Everyone around thought something felt shady, but when they walked off, everyone breathed a sigh of relief. In an instant they were back, and all over Taylor. He fought them off and got away. Other narcs in the crowd grabbed him. He fought them off too, and sorta got away again. But there were too many, and they swarmed him. Some nearby heads jumped in to fight – the cops maced everyone, and finally got a solid hold of Taylor. He's being held for resisting arrest – thankfully, he had nothing else on him. But they've still got him.

    When the show was nearly over, we went up by the door. This guy who had almost sold me a ticket was outside. I asked him how it was, "You didn't get in?" He gave me his ticket. "They didn't rip it when I went in."

I'm like, "Dude, you should have passed it out to someone a long time ago."

"Aw, Go in and see the last tune."

Afterwards, outside, I sold my yellow music note lighter case and a bunch of postcards to the guy pictured in the skirt, on the left side of the Mardi Gras Postcards. I gave him wholesale prices.

JGB is here for three days. Tomorrow, Van Morrison is at the Greek. Maybe we'll do that instead. I'm so tired of being shut out of Jerry shows.

April 14 1990
Late night – Willard North.

Took Elwood to Baker Beach while Corvette went to try to buy tix. Rumours said some were going on sale at 2PM. – Didn't happen.

Tix were really hard, as usual at the Warfield. Kevin and Roz had two whole tix from the night before. I wooshed right in on mine, but they stopped Corvette. At the same time KindBoy, Silas and Larby were attempting a 3 for 2 scam. Theirs worked, and they slipped Corvette a stub. In the confusion, Corvette was able to convince them they had already ripped her ticket. 4 for 2!

Inside there was a big, mean guard near our door. He caught sight of a fatty while Nori was hittin' on it. I managed to grab it out of her hand and throw it to Silas. The guard knew I did something with it, and yelled at me in a cool sort of way. It was a smooth save.

Did I write about another smooth save between me and Hackmen? I don't remember which town. Maybe Albany. Hackmen was in front of me, huffin' heavy on a fatty, and was seen. He passed it to me, and there was a guard. I tried to convince the guard it was a cigarette. He didn't believe me. "Hand it over."

I was like, "Dude, it was a roach. I dropped it when I saw you."

"Oh yeah? Well, if you dropped it, let me see it." And he shined his light by my feet. I still actually had it in my hand, but while the guy wasn't paying attention, I passed it off to Nina, who was dancing behind me. I picked a tiny roach off the floor. He shook his head, I shrugged. Not much he could do.

I have a stiff neck. Got a bunch o' massages, but it still hurts. Fritz grabbed my head to pull me to him. I told him how much that hurt and he's like, "I didn't know. I'm sorry. I've been drunk for a month and a half. Give me a hug."

April 15 1990

A crowd of us went to Easter brunch at Judy's down in the Marina. Great breakfasts! What a party. They loved us too. So nice to be treated like real people. We had Mimosas with fresh squeezed OJ. Judy gave us an Easter Basket full of candy and Easter balloons! As we drove back in Andy's work van, we had a balloon fight and got high going through the Presidio. Good ole Easter type fun. Corvette and I have balloons braided into our hair. We wrote on them, "I need a ticket," and, "I need one too."

April 20 1990
Forestville

We both got in for JGB at the Warfield on Easter.

Came home that night. Wow, home. We've been fucking around the house – hanging posters, sweeping up dustballs, doing laundry etc.

Garrett was housesitting at Freddy's. I went over Monday. I liked relaxing on the couch with him. I spent the night. Tuesday, he made dinner for me and Corvette. But he was not happy when we both left. Sorry babe. The sex is fun, but I can't handle how you mess with my head.

April 21st

Last night, someone gave Hackmen two free Rads tix. We were on the guest list so he gave them to Santa and GM Joe. Then he got bummed, saying, Joe would never have done the same for him. We had to remind him about ticket Karma – almost better to do it with someone who'd never do it for you.

Rosario was there, and Munch, and Hawkeye and Janelle. Hawkeye had fornicating skeletons all over his shirt. So cool! Fritz and Dean were hanging on each other – falling and stumbling in a comic buddy-buddy act. Fritz said he wanted to go somewhere.

Munch – "Where?"

"To heaven, where there's green buds, and keef, and big purple incandescent couches to kick back in."

Gunner was there. Raging loud as usual. And the Dead asked Beau to be a driver to LA, the Carson Shows. He's in with BGP!

I'm feeling directionless. Maybe more like bogged down. Can't seem to get anything done. Can't write, too stoned. Can't bead – not stoned enough.

Lots to think about, plenty to do, but just blah. Feeling a bit lonely too. I do okay for a long while, and then I let Garrett in, and it reminds me I'm alone.

May 2 1990

Stopped by Fritz's. Me and Fritz wrestled a lot. Dean kept instigating, "Yank his beard! Pull his hair!" He got into the fray once, and another time told Fritz, "Hey! Don't you hurt her." We didn't stay long. Never feel like staying too long at Fritz's.

Santa was headed back to the city to help Don take care of Indigo while Justine does some short time.

Today I heard they're charging Piper with 33 grams – the weight of the paper. That's fucked up. She goes to court in Ohio next week. She and Freddy are all moved out of Guerneville.

May 4

In Hackmen's car headed for the Carson shows. Hackmen says Silas got land in Colorado! Says he cut off his dreads and shaved his beard. WOW.

May 7 1990

Monday morning, waking at a beach campground. I slept in the car.

Selling postcards in Carson was tough – security, staff pro, and confiscation crews were everywhere. Schmitty lost all his *Loose Lucy* shirts to them. It was hot, and dusty, and rather uncomfortable, but then again, I just dislike LA.

I got a free ticket Saturday, Corvette had to pay $5. Then Hackmen found one on the ground as we were walking in. We gave it to a chick who'd just gotten turned away because she had a counterfeit. Guess what we missed again?

Yep. *Help on the Way*. I've heard mixed reviews as to how good it was.

Hilton John and Erika were there. They've been living in LA. Saw Remy for a second. Corvette heard a story that supposedly happened to a friend of Remy's. Selling doses, some locals pulled a gun and made him get in the car and leave with them. I wonder what happened beyond that?

Jumpin' Jack didn't know what he was doing after the shows. I hope he doesn't end up on Haight St., but I didn't give him our phone #. Even though (or perhaps because) he kept telling me how gorgeous I looked.

And I saw Tavi yesterday!! He could only come one day. He got out of doing jail time, but he's living in a rehab. I love Tavi. It was so nice to see him. I miss him not being on tour.

Fritz is being a dick again. He threw a large pincher bug on me. It went down my shirt and he didn't tell me until hours later that he had done it. (I found the bug, but didn't imagine someone threw it at me.)

Don was there with Indigo. Becky helped him a lot. Izzy too. Trinity is getting so big. So is Devon, with his mass of curly hair. Maureen and Domino welded a top to the back of their bus, – it's got a porch now. They had some shade, and had Lemonade and Tea for sale as usual.

I didn't find the Fatty Zone (partly because I wasn't looking), till 2nd set, on the 2nd day, – up by the wall – Phil's side. Dean was there. He's got such a calming presence. And when he hugs, his hugs are deep and true. I always feel like I'm gonna melt into him.

Garrett wasn't there. Neither was Freddy. Freddy's blond, biker-lookin' friend (I don't remember his name), kept asking me how to get in touch with Freddy. I kept saying I didn't know. I really don't. But even if I had, I wouldn't have told him. His vibe wasn't right.

Saw Dave Echo and Benny in the Fatty Zone. Saw Mavis too, lookin like ten miles of bad road (as my mother would say). Saw Lizette and Davy. He didn't look too bad. She looked fuckin horrible, with circles under her eyes that reached to her lips. It was sad. She's beautiful, like a China Doll. She shouldn't be lookin like that.

Everyone's starting to wake up – Mark Reese first, – he wandered off, and Corvette and Hackman just walked up from the beach.

There's showers here, I'm gonna partake.

Cool! Mark came back with coffee.

later

What a pleasant morning. I'm so glad to be headed north again. I hate LA, and I get such an attitude while there.

I was in a bad mood yesterday before the show, and Corvette made it worse. She's Aries – she doesn't always think before she talks. I told her to fuck off and go in without me. Maybe we've been together too much these past months. I just too often feel responsible for all that we have to do financially. She probably feels the exact same way. That's where all the problems stem from. But we did sell a bunch of Indican Shirts, and we got really close to affording everything.

Magoo just pulled out an intense crystal to show us. So many designs naturally etched into the planes of it. It's really something.

May 12 1990

Back in LA. for the Doors movie audition. We're early, without enough $ to go eat. We barely have enough gas $ to get home with. I've never been to an audition. What do you have to do to be an extra? Can't be much.

Briscoe told us he'd seen Jumpin' Jack on Haight St. So we stopped in the city with plans to kidnap him. Found him in one sweep down the street. Looking good even. He was with that wingnut chick, Deazy. Said he didn't need to be kidnapped, he was flying to Hawaii for the shows.

later

The Casting folk were psyched we came all the way from SF. The chick in charge told the group, "Val Kilmer plays Jim, and this is the scene where he'll be exposing himself on the Miami stage, so it should be a lot of fun."

We've been driving all day on 5 to get back to San Francisco for Bobby's show tonight. The car needs water every hour.

May 13 1990

Got to the Bobby show in time to get shut out. HA. But really, we weren't trying very hard. Hanging with Dave Echo, Benny, Camera Brandon, and Allie. We decided we weren't going in unless Bob came out onto Market St., greeted us each by name, and asked us politely to attend his show. It didn't happen.

May 14

Did lunch with Benny, then went to the panhandle for a fatty. Beautiful outdoor bud. Elvis, Dave Echo, and Malt were there playing basketball.

Not too many people at the Warfield for Toots and the Maytalls. Santa talked us into blowin' off the postcard-selling-thing and letting him buy us dinner in Chinatown. Honey-walnut Prawns. Yumm. Thanx so much Santa.

Back at the Warfield – standing along the fence, – jokin' with the door guys. "Are you sure you don't want to let us in?"

One of the door guys kept putting his finger up and dancing around. Another was chanting, "Just need one." Mocking us, but in a nice way. Then they came out and gave us Comps.

Afterwards with Santa, we went to Don's house, where Nicholas is housesitting while Don and Indigo are in Hawaii. Justine gets out of Jail tomorrow morning, – tomorrow night she flies to Hawaii. Sounds like the perfect thing.

May 17 1990

We're hurting without buds. Called Briscoe, not expecting much. JohnRay answered. "Comeon over!" Got there just as the fatty was being lit.

Everyone asks why we're so broke nowadays, – we tell them, because we don't 'do' anything. Some ask why. Some offer great prices. Two Toke Tom said, "That's our world. That's how we must support ourselves or how can we do what we do? And if we stop, if they make us stop, then they're winning."

May 18 1990

When Nicholas called, we headed for the city. Santa goes to court today. Good Energy that way please. We don't want to lose Santa.

I called Kenny to say we had buds, and he goes, "Cool, you're swingin' again?" Yikes. Don't put it like that. In my mind swingin' means selling shit in the Dead lot. (Like Singles.) No thanks... Supplying friends with buds isn't swinging.

May 24   LA

We worked on the Doors Movie yesterday. What a shit job. It took so long between shoots it was almost boring. And it's weird cheering on cue. Best part of the day was that we smoked buds all day even though it was strictly "No Smoking." As if that ever stops us. We were supposed to go back today but fuck that. We're gonna do Hollywood for breakfast then drive up the coast.

May 31 1990

Freddy came by to work on Corvette's car. Told us it was Garrett's b-day, – said we should meet them in Oakland. With nothing better to do, we headed to the East Bay.

We met outside Olly Oxen's house, then went to Triple Rock for Garrett's B-day dinner. Went to the hills I remember from my early Berkeley days. It was drizzly and wet. One hill was so muddy none of us had any traction. But we did have a bottle o' wine! Between the slipping and the sliding, and the laughing, it's surprising we got to the top.

Happy 25th Birthday Garrett!

While we were on the very top, the fog enveloped us, then passed. The moon came out, and we had a clear view of the whole Bay Area. This place was a total hippie hang till UCBerkeley sold it and some guy built his house right on the crest of the best hill. We snuck onto his land and sat drinking in his driveway. We walked back to Freddy's van before the next wave of fog reached us. Freddy and Corvette were arm in arm and it was assumed I'd sleep in the Hearse with Garrett, but me and Corvette said we were leaving.

Freddy wouldn't let Corvette out of the van and she had to pass me her keys, while Garrett tried to stop me from getting 'em, ie, a huge wrestling match. I got the keys, but the car was slow about its get-go. Garrett came out of the house with pillows and blankets in his arms, laughin', "Girl, You're not going anywhere." The car started and I grinned in triumph. But it only ran for about 17 seconds. They kept saying, "Open the hood, I'll fix it," while joking about the parts they could take out to make sure we didn't go. It became a fun battle to keep the hood shut and keep trying. I lost the keys to Freddy, but he had to give 'em back because the car-wench-voice wouldn't stop saying, "The key is in the ignition" even though it wasn't. We were in hysterics, and the street cleaner truck comes through, and all our vehicles are in the way. So loud, obscuring our laughter, making things even funnier. It was a grand old time. But I guess you could say they won. And the car hasn't started since.

It was nice with Garrett, but I feel like, afterwards, I'm always a bit bummed for one reason or another.

Freddy was already gone when I got up, and Garrett had to leave for work, so we gave him the car keys and said, "Please do what you can." We grabbed most of our shit and hitched home.

June 2nd 3AM

Just hitched home from a Dinosaurs show at the River Theater, in Guerneville. I Love to see Papa John Creach. He's so ragin'. Pinky was there from the city, – Told us she brought Jumpin' Jack back to her hot tub, and the next day, he was back with four women. That's Jack! She said, "Umm. No." But that means he's back from Hawaii.

June 2 1990

Santa stopped by on his way to the city. He told us some weird, hard to believe story about Munch and some other guy, stealing seven Harleys from Hawkeye. Youch. Not Munch. There's got to be more to the story.

June 6 1990

Sunday Skinny Jim called – headed for Berkeley, for Sunsplash, do we want a ride?

It was sunny and hot in the East Bay. I saw Garrett for a second. No luck with the car yet. They got a new starter – it started, but keeps engaging when it's already running. Fuck.

Saw Ditto with tix for Kennedy and Suzy and Suzy's sister, but the concert was two hours into it already. He gave the tix to us and Fritz. It was a good show. Marcia Griffiths rocked hard, but I thought last year's splash was better.

On Monday Fritz came over for his birthday dinner. I made manicotti, Corvette made a cake. Two Toke Tom and Kiersten were here, and we got a call from Hilton John and Erika. They were close by, could they come over? (John really just needed a place to fix his u-joint.) Mavis was in SF, – on the phone every few minutes raging at Fritz about who knows what. He left before cake to go to SF, but said he'd come by today, and bring us to the post office. This morning Fritz says he doesn't have time, so we're out of luck.

What a Dick!

29
June 1990
Cal Expo and Shoreline

June 9 1990   Sacramento

There was talk of getting a rent-a-van to take to Cal Expo with Two Toke Tom and Kiersten. But when I called Tom, he said Kiersten didn't know if she was "coming or going." I didn't catch his meaning till our next conversation, when he growled, "Kiersten's leaving. She can't hang."

We're back to our original plan of catching a ride with Aaron. I got cramps, and my period, on the ride, so I sat under a tree all day. Pixie and Newburgh sat too. Also Camera Brandon and his girlfriend. I know her trip was the same as mine. I think Pixie's was too. Corvette kept bringing folks to my tree to say hi. And who did she find, but Sid! Yeah!!!!!

Sid is back and mean as ever. He's trying to collect money for Dawn's lawyer, and ready to beat up anyone who owes him – especially Hawkeye, he said.

Saw Mavis – all mad at Mason. Said she forgot her tix but he grabbed 'em for her, and now, she couldn't find him. Later, I saw Mason, "Fuck her. She was all nodded out when she left. She shoulda remembered her own goddamn tix." Yeah. I didn't think she looked too good. Mavis you're blowin it.

Lots of people were fucked up on heroin yesterday. There must have been an abundance.

Speaking of... I saw Josh from Xmas. He looked all shiny, and happy. Sat and talked with me awhile. Thanked me for talking to him so much at Xmas. Said he didn't last through those shows. Got busted for something stupid, ended up in Jail for three months. He's been out three months and he's still off heroin. Says he won't go back to it. He looked so bright eyed, it was a pleasure to see.

Janice, pointing to little Timothy, told Sid, "Look what I made while you were gone."

Crafty Adam sat with me awhile. When Bill Graham parked his bike near us, and took a walk, Adam put a 'We Love You' note on his bike seat.

We saw Dave Echo getting ready for the Fritz birthday bash. As in – bash in the face with a chocolate pie. Fritz was expecting something, waiting for it all day. But Dave missed. He missed! I wouldn't have missed!

When I saw Fritz he gave me a half-hug. I mentioned the cake he never came to eat. He apologized and gave me a real hug. I said, "It's cool. We drank your beer."

Saw Garrett for a split second. He introduced us to the chick he was walking with. He barely looked at me, didn't even give me a hug. Whatever.

Tix were really hard. And of course the No Vending rule holds strong at Cal Expo. I didn't see any stuff taken away, but lots of warnings. We eventually got one ticket, but because we couldn't find another, we sold it to Dread Todd for what we paid.

Saw Hackmen's friend Joanne. She wanted to go in, but had Hackmen's ticket. She gave it to me and said I could have it if I didn't see him. I did see him though, just long enough to give it to him.

Jumpin' Jack didn't get in either. Hung out with him most of showtime. He gave me a nice massage on the grassy hill. After the show, there weren't many options of stuff to do. Jack wanted me to hang with him in the camping lot, but I wanted a real bathroom in the morning. I saw Alex Schmalex heading back to Willard North. That sounded good to me, but not to Corvette. I wasn't having the greatest time, and was makin' no money, but I knew I didn't want to be in Forestville today with no ride to the show. When we found Skinny Jim, she went home.

Earth First is putting out a call for Redwood Summer. Please come help save the trees! I'd love to.

June 11 1990   Forestville

Saturday night counterfeits were everywhere. Everyone getting bunked. When I first got there, I went to the camping lot, with a bracelet Maureen groundscored. It was nice to see a lot like it all used to be. Tarps and chairs and tents and barbecues and sleeping people at all hours, and dogs and tunes and small time vending and trunk couches and kid swimming pools and bunches of bicycles. It felt good in there, but not everyone could get there. I hung awhile by Domino's bus, Murph's bus, and Kevin's RV. Hilton

John's bus was across the way, and the hearses just down the row. Sold a few postcards, but I started to hear, "I bought one for 50 cents yesterday." Aaron is out there undercutting us. He drops his lot price if they don't sell immediately.

I didn't get in. Again.

So many people were getting bad tickets. I didn't try real hard to get in. Isaac got bunked, but Hackmen's was real. I walked with Isaac as he was trying to trade buds for a real ticket. When he admitted defeat, we went in search of beer.

Everyone had Budweiser. Yuk. Finally I saw a Becks bottle, between feet, from a row away. It turned out to be Jumpin' Jack and some other guy, really high on X, and I can't remember where I've met him before, but I have.

We bought beers, and smoked a fatty and a few bowls. Me and Isaac went back to his car, smoked more, and drank, and talked – ticket karma, shows, Eugene. We could hear the second set. Phil sounded great.

Earlier, Garrett, had actually talked to me. Thanked me for the b-day sex. Ha. After the show, I went into the camping lot to visit him, but he was asleep, and not wakin' up, so I went back out to the non-camping lot, and hooked up with Chloe and Parker. We took a cab to Dandy Andy's Residence room, which was packed. We all chipped in and smoked a huge fatty. I rolled it, while watched by Alec, who didn't think it was possible to fit all that pot in one paper. It was a chubby indeed, but I'm a professional.

It put everyone to sleep.

I slept sort of under the sink, and left pretty soon after having a morning butt with Parker. I went right to the camping lot. Saw King, and paid him $132 towards the Indican shirts. Sat in the shade with Justine. Wasn't as hot as the other days.

Bob Snodgrass gave me two fatty smokers and a Skeleton Marble to try to sell. Nothing sold, and I ended up losing the marble when I got up from sitting with Rockafucker, Mindy, and Della.

I went by the hearses. Sitting with Garrett and Freddy, doing bongs, me and Garrett had our legs entwined. One of his little girlfriends who stopped by for a second got visibly mad about me. Ha. I brought Jillian down by the buses to go see Trinity. Got high with Dean and Izzy while the children raged.

Eventually I made it out to the tourist parking lot to sell postcards. Didn't make much money, but I got a ticket from Joanne – Hackmen's friend who had had me hold Hackmen's ticket 1st day. She felt bad I didn't get in that night.

I hung out, drinking and people watching with Jack, or Flash as we've started to call him. (Garrett rolled his eyes when he saw me with Jack.)

Jack had a ticket, and so did I, so we weren't looking for any, till Gene Gene the Dancing Machine told me Corvette was here, needing a ticket. Suzy told me too. Found a ticket, – Jumpin' Jack bought it for $15, – found Corvette, and went in in time for the *Bertha* opener. Yeah!

It was a weird show, the kind where I feel so high, I wonder if I got a little bit dosed. I was very glad to be inside.

Rumours lately, said Phil is leaving the band, after Eugene. On stage Phil said he's heard these rumours, and he wanted us to know, "It's a bullshit LIE!"

2nd set, getting high with Mark Reese, Johnja and Jumpin' Jack came skipping along through the hallway, arm in arm. They stopped only a moment. Jack gave me a hug, and Johnja sucked on my ear lobe, then off they went, twirling and frolicking down the hall.

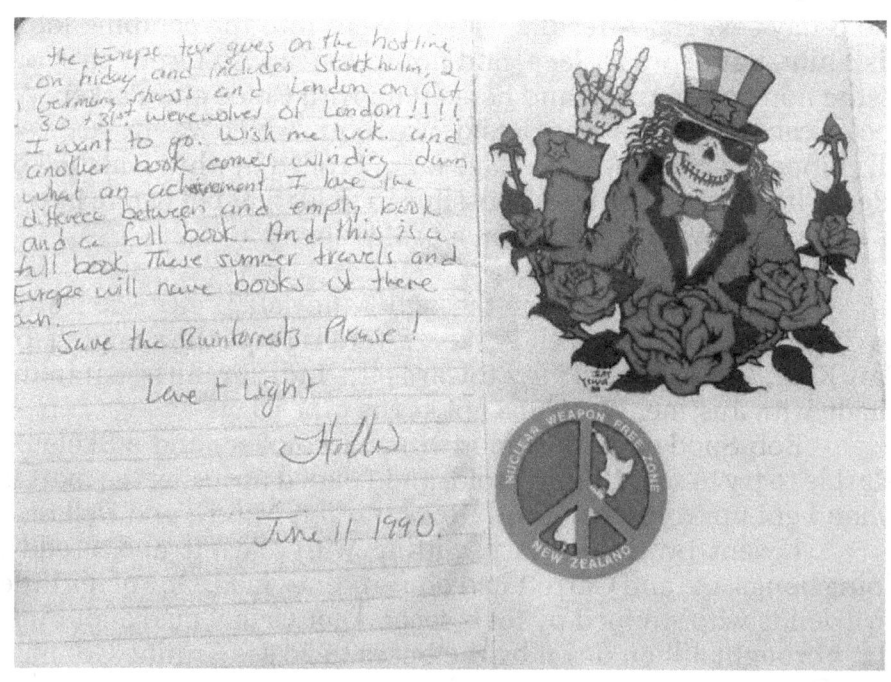

After the show, I scammed into the camping lot to wait for Garrett so I could get Corvette's car keys. When he appeared, he was irritable and downright nasty. See? I can't deal with this Gemini shit. Gee, which Garrett is this? – the Garrett who adores me and won't leave me alone? Or the Garrett who ignores me like I don't matter to him at all? It's infuriating. Went back out to the selling world of post-concert crowds and found Corvette.

Skinny Jim was our ride home. We went to his car. Way off, across the street, a block or two down a road. He wasn't there yet, so we waited and sold postcards to the high tourists stumbling by. Made $10. Not bad considering what a shitty selling weekend it was.

Oh! We heard, from Arthur and Jasmine, that the Europe tour goes on the hotline on Friday and includes Stockholm, two Germany shows, and London on Oct 30 and 31st. Werewolves of London!!!!

I want to go.

June 15 1990
Forestville

JGB played the Warfield Tuesday and Wednesday. We went down Wednesday to sell postcards, and meet up with GM Joe. Found him swinging balloons. It was pretty cool to be out on Market St. not even caring about a ticket. There were too many people to even bother trying.

Jack wanted to come home with us, and I was even considering it. But Garrett said the car was working, and he was gonna drive it up here Thursday. Since Garrett was gonna bring us the car, I didn't want Jack there too, so we told Jack he could come home with us after Shoreline. Garrett was trippin though. None of the above happened. He didn't even call.

Roz called. Says she has her own place, that she's cleaning out her body and being pure. We talked a lot about Jack and Sid. Everyone but me seems to think Sid has mellowed.

First Shoreline show is tonight. We don't know how we're getting there yet. But it's only 10AM.

June 16
Beau and Amanda's

We hitched to Shoreline. We got one ride to the highway, where we stood by the on ramp. An older blue truck swerved from the fast lane to get us. It was Aggie. We had to put his 2½ year-old boy Kato in our laps. Aggie was headed to the city and didn't realize Shoreline was today. At one point, we pulled over on the side of the highway, so he could teach Kato how to pee out the truck door so no one could see him.

We got to the lot and made a little money on postcards but not nearly enough. This one cop-like guy kept telling us we didn't have a permit to sell. One time Garrett was there. "She's not selling them. She's trying to trade for a ticket. We've all learned the only way to do anything out here, is to trade. Trade for tickets. Trade for drugs. Don't sell. Never sell."

So we were keeping our eye on him, and selling. I looked to where he was, and he wasn't anymore. Exactly then Corvette goes, "The cop's not there anymore." And he was in front of us.

"Move along."

How'd he do that? As a student of such moves, I was impressed.

Saw McNeel only for a second. He's got a golf cart these days. Tickets were incredibly easy. I got one for $5, Corvette got a freebee. I had to walk in with the people I got mine from, because they wanted the stub. After a quick stop by Matt Ackerman's booth, I went up the hill with Jack and I finally caught *Help on the Way*. And a damn good one. Oh man those first power cords — Barw-narw. Barw-Naaarw. Dancing and twirling on the mostly empty hill. Beautiful. I love that song. It was a raging 1st set. Even played a *Stagger Lee*. 2nd set was played well, but stayed on the slow side. I felt really high at this show too. The whole show, like I was just getting off on something.

We had a silly crowd. Jack, Pele, Lyndelle, Corvette, Ditto, Santa, and Dave Echo. It was a fun dancing crew. Santa smoked a fat one with us and gave us bites of his chicken sandwich. Dave Echo had on ripped shorts, and we ripped 'em more every chance we got.

Saw Crafty Adam. He always seems to have such problems. He asked if he could come to our house till Eugene. We told him yes.

Beau invited us home with them, said we have no excuses — because Elwood wasn't with us. Jack wanted me to go with him, but I'm spoiled, and not happy not knowing what I'm doing, or ending up with a bunch of wingnuts. Jack said he was going with us, 'like it or not', but he disappeared. Garrett wanted me to go with him in the hearse, but I blew that off too. When we went to get our stuff from John's Hilton, we heard that we were expected to go with them. Then we saw Neil and Winnie, "Oh you're staying with us at Hackmen's tonight, right?" When it rains it pours.

We didn't sell shit after the show — when there's vending inside, people spend their money there. We piled into Tabitha's bronco, and fought major traffic back to the city. Got here, and watched part of *The Meaning of Life*, and then little Chaya started projectile puking, just like the end of the movie.

We didn't get up today 'til 1ish. Rebel's coming over, and we'll head to Shoreline around 4:00. I hope we do better on postcards today. We need to pay them off, and pay the phone bill at least.

Later

We're finally on the road. I'm in a pissed off mood. Amanda was being as slow as she possibly could. It's like 5:30. Fuck.

June 17 1990

I got in a better mood once we picked up Rebel and he said he'd help us get in. He got us vendor bracelets. Freddy and Two Toke Tom got in on 'em too. Freddy smoked a fatty with us at Matt Ackerman's booth. We sat there a good part of 1st set.

Jack's bummed with me because I never hang with him at night. I don't like not knowing where I'm crashing. He wanders till there are no choices left, then sleeps in a horrible sounding place. Not my style.

Inside, walking with him, we passed Murph rolling a joint. I wanted to stay. Jack wanted to go get a soda. Murph is like, "What? Do you need her to hold your hand?" We got a soda and chicken sandwich, and made it back in time for the fatty, only because Sid, Della, and Mindy were in the front of the food line.

Last night we seemingly had no options of where to stay. Quite the contrast to the night before. When we were running around trying to find something to do, we saw Fritz and I yelled, "Fritz! Take me home with you."

"No way Babe."

We took Santa's invite to go to Atlanta Mary's room. When we met, by Santa's car, Fritz was there. I told everyone, "Fritz won't take me home with him."

"I'll just have to dream about it tonight Babe."

"Same old, same old."

Everyone laughed.

Inside

Break time. They're playing something weird that sounds like Humpback whales.

We got here early enough today for Santa to get in the bottom lot. Sold a good amount of postcards. Needed that.

I heard undercovers went on Murph's bus and took Dreadless Manny. No-one knows why, but it's probably got something to do with the tri-pod cameras on the hill.

30
Summer 1990
Eugene – DeadFeat

June 20 1990

I thought Jumpin' Jack would be coming home with us after Shoreline. He's been wanting to, I promised he could, and I thought there'd be no stopping him. But after the last show there was no sign of him. Domino said he went to the top lot, to go spare dollaring for bus gas money, and didn't come back.

We left Shoreline with Hilton John and Erika. The Hilton Bus got us happily home, and John even got into our driveway at 2AM. And John fixed the Van. A silly thing – just needed its connections cleaned. Wooohooo! And, Dead Feat stickers were here when we got home! A funny line from the past few days. "The weirdest thing about Erika, is John."

June 21, 1990

Illinois River State Park, OR

Summer Solstice and I'm drinkin' a beer in the shade, appreciating the breeze. When we pulled in, John's Hilton, Murph's bus, and Domino's, were here. Dragon Dave and his pregnant dog Noel, are with Murph. And Murph's new girlfriend, Sahana. They got harassed at their last gas stop by loggers who called Murph a 'fuckin Earth Firster.'

I've seen way too many log trucks, and I heard on the news that loggers are participating in demonstrations in hopes of slowing the cutting. Corporations don't give a shit about the loggers any more than they do the trees.

<u>GRATEFUL DEAD - LITTLE FEAT</u>
<u>June 23-24, 1990</u>
<u>Campground Rules & Regulations</u>

Camping facilities will be available in the parking lot of Autzen Stadium beginning at 12noon on Friday, June 22, 1990. Camping closes at 10am on Monday, June 25. The cost will be $20.00 per vehicle. The driver and all passengers must have tickets for both Saturday's & Sunday's concerts. If you are planning on attending only one concert, please arrive in Eugene on the day of the show and plan on leaving after the concert is over.

1. For safety's sake NO OPEN FIRES!
   Cooking will be allowed only on campstoves and in approved fireproof metal containers, ie. Hibachis.
2. Because of excessive noise and fire danger, no generators allowed.
3. No loud noise (radios, tape players, ect.) from 10pm to 8am.
4. Camping allowed in designated areas only. No camping allowed in the adjacent area of Alton Baker Park.
5. WARNING: THE NEARBY WILLAMETTE RIVER IS A DANGEROUS PLACE TO SWIM!
6. Please use the trash bags provided for your refuse. When full, place them along the edge of the fire lane and our staff will pick them up. Be aware that a recycling effort is afoot this weekend. Your cooperation with this is greatly appreciated.
7. There is no vending allowed in the campground or anywhere on the U of O Campus. There will be food stands available in the campground for those of you not prepared to feed yourselves.
8. The sale of alcohol & drugs is against the law & will not be tolerated. ANYONE CAUGHT SELLING ALCOHOL OR DRUGS WILL BE EJECTED FROM THE CAMPGROUND & WILL BE SUBJECT TO ARREST!
9. For the safety & comfort of all, no dogs allowed.
10. Before entering campground, be sure you have all the provisions you need for the weekend. There will be no in's and out's for vehicles.

Water, toilet, garbage & shower facilities will be provided. Please help make the concert experience enjoyable for all by keeping the camp area clean! For locations of the facilities, please refer to the map on the back of this flyer.

Thank you!

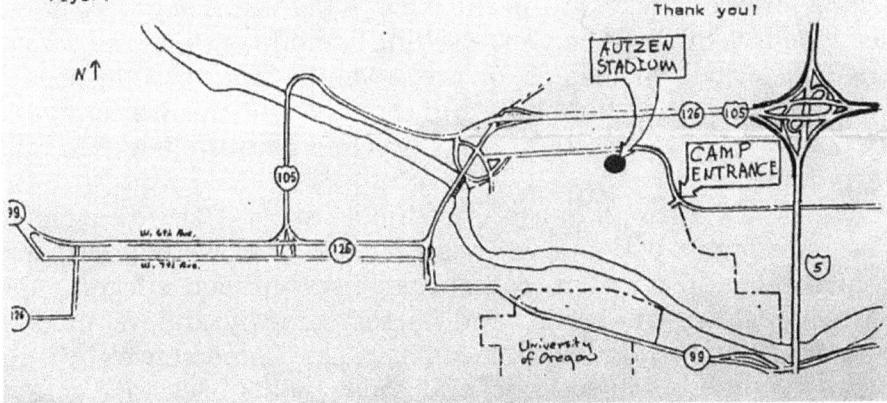

June 27 1990

This was the most fun Dead weekend I've had in ages!!! The first 'real' lot in a long time. Camping – $20 per car. No fucking bracelets needed.

After our stop at the Illinois River, we drove northward with an electric sunset. Passed Domino instantaneously (he's slow), and Murph in about 20 minutes, but it took hours to catch up to Hilton John. Reminds me of Ozzy with how fast he goes.

We spent the night at the last Rest Area before Eugene. A total party. In the morning we cruised hotels until we found a place to bum a shower.

The lot opened at noon. At 11:45, we scammed up near the front with Domino, but there was no sign of Murph, or Hilton John. When the line started movin', we saw the Hilton was already inside – parked near the Hog Farm buses. One of which is Ozzy's old Dead Ringer bus, and the other has a sign on the front reminiscent of Lucy in the Peanuts, "Advice 5¢."

When we got to the gate, Jake, a BGP guy who parties often on John's Hilton, and Lloyd, Janey's boss, were there. Told them we're supposed to work for Rebel, – so Jake slapped a camping pass on our windshield. We parked next to Hilton John, and found Janey back at the gate. The three of us handed out maps of the place, flyers with messages from the band, and garbage bags. Once the line of cars diminished, we only needed one of us so we switched off all day and into the night. It was even kinda fun. Seeing folks you know as they come in. Checkin out the gorgeous guys, and telling folks how to scam, if they couldn't figure it out themselves – like, only the driver needed tix.

We went back to the van and drank beer with Janey. (Something we'd talked about all day.) I spent most of the evening selling bumper stickers from the back of the van. They were going fast – so much fun when you're selling something everyone wants. They track ya down. "There you are! I want a sticker!" Beau cruised up crazily on one of those little golf carts. His job this weekend was to 'take care' of golf carts. He was psyched because he got to take Jerry for a ride.

Next morning, morning of the 1st show, Corvette went to find out about work, but my head felt like a basketball so I was gonna blow it off. I'm content selling bumper stickers and postcards at the van. Freddy and Garrett came by, and we're doing a morning fatty when Corvette comes back. "Comeon, we gotta go. We're supposed to meet Rebel and Janey by the backstage gate in 10 minutes."

I really didn't want to 'work' and debated not going. But what the fuck? "Haven't I been waiting for the chance to suck up to BGP and start getting in free?" We can't blow it now that it's happening. Everyone agreed. So I got ready, and jumped out of the van, "Let's go Kiss Ass!"

Freddy loved it. "A woman after my own heart."

We got over to the backstage gate, and waited, and waited, and waited, and waited. A few BGP people bought bumper stickers.

Rebel appeared and said, Little Feat wanted stickers. Sam Clayton came out to meet us. He said they'd seen the stickers in Maine, but didn't know where they were coming from. Did we have any Maine ones left? No. We told him we were in N'Awlins for their comeback show in '88, and talked about that a bit. He was super nice. Rebel told us, "No work today – here's your passes – go have a good time." Janey had to walk us in, – volunteers have to be walked in by a laminate. Missed a few Little Feat tunes by losing track of Janey, but it was no biggie.

Heading for the back of the floor – Phil's side, of course. There was no one around except Janice and Timothy so we started the Fatty Zone between two concession stands. Eventually the crew showed up. Don, Justine and Indigo, Kerry, Izzy, and Trinity, Dean, Santa, King, Lyndelle, Danni, Rockafucker, Newburgh, Pixie, Kestrel Jim and Mirabeth, Tricky, Fritz, Jumpin' Jack, Domino, Maureen, Kennedy, Shane, Benny and Dave Echo. Mutz, John and Erika, Katarina and DigDoug. And Macy! The Fatty Zone is such a fun place, full of activity, conversation, and occasional mayhem.

Me and Corvette walked around the whole place with Jack. Bumped into Nanette. She was delighted to see Jack. He bought a bunch of cheap necklaces from her, and gave them to me, Corvette, Marla, Poco, and some chick walking by.

The first Dead set was good. Started with a rippin *Help Slip Frank*. Ragin tune selection all around. *They Love Each Other*. *Cassidy*. 2nd set had a sweet *Morning Dew*.

I bumped into Janey playing in the windy hallway with Alandra Moon. Some guy said to Janey, "Hey. I met you <u>somewhere, sometime,</u> with your blond friend, with the chipped tooth."

"Yeah – that was my brother, and this is his daughter."

The next tune was *He's Gone*.

Ah Damien. We all miss you always.

People inside were dropping like flies. One chick fell right in the Fatty Zone. We weren't far from Rock Med, so we saw many of the casualties go by. There must have been some bad something out there.

After the show, we raged hard on bumper stickers. Sold all but 100, which we saved for the 2nd day. Sold beers to select few people. Good beers weren't easy to come by. Dean was a big customer, as was Rosario. (Rosario got busted with 200lbs of pot in Arizona. He'll probably have to do some time.)

Bus row was amazing. More than half the buses there were parked in one long line. Saw Bob Snodgrass selling pipes. Ginny and Marie came with us when we checked out the punk band that was playing in the lot.

Next morning, Rebel pulled up to the Van in a golf cart, in official BGP capacity, and said, "The Band wants stickers."

We laughed, "What Band?" But seriously, we were pleased. They wanted them for their equipment etc. We also sent a High Council Indican Shirt for Phil.

It was Erika's b-day show. Santa made mushroom tea to celebrate, then got so high he asked me to wear his fanny pack for safety.

Met up with Rebel, "No work, here's your passes. Meet me in 20 minutes to get walked in."

We saw all of Little Feat that night, but none of the family was inside until just before the Dead came on.

Saw Hackmen, Isaac, and KindBoy. KindBoy had a great embroidered skeleton shirt that Dante brought back for him from Indonesia. It was strange not to see Eden or Riley here in Oregon. We heard at Hawkeye's, that they've split, and Riley is Jonesin on the East Coast. I hope that's not true. Also heard that Sid beat up Nurka for turning Claudia on to dope.

It had been cloudy most of the day, but by break it'd been sunny a while. I was worried about Elwood in the hot van. One of the guys at White Bird lent me a worker's pass to go out and check on him. I aired out the van (it wasn't too bad), and gave him some ice water.

After the show Corvette sold the last of our stickers except for what we held for ourselves, and for Rebel, – he kept giving his away.

The guy who bought Ozzy's bus told me I should give him a sticker for his really cool bus. I asked him to buy one. Told him I was doing this so I could afford Redwood Summer. He said I could certainly afford to give him one. I told him he could certainly afford to buy one. He didn't, and as far as I know the Hog Farm didn't get any.

The Hog Farmers were on a mission of 'talking to people' – telling 'em to slow down, or stop LSD sales. Bad publicity and cops are their reasons. It's a controversial matter. Everyone has an opinion. "LSD dealers are not helping anything." "The scene needs us." "There's too much, it's all too much." "Only continuing tradition." "It was never this big before. We're actually in danger now." "This entire world was built on easy access to such things." "The whole thing could fall apart." "No one tells anyone what to do – not even Jerry." "It's too important to give up." "Humanity needs this."

First show, Ken Kesey drove here in his bus; old, but not the original. It was crazy-psychedelic, screaming day-glow, with a porch on top, full of bean bag chairs. His bus was out of hand, and impractical for 1990. He couldn't get across country in that thing without being stopped 100 times. To look out into the lot from the stadium's top, and see one outrageous bus that sits around Eugene, and 36 mellow-looking, low-key buses that actually travel this country's highways, was quite interesting. I felt like Kesey was being unrealistic by having a bus like that. But has Kesey ever been realistic? Thankfully no, so why should he start now?

After 2nd show I was drinking with Dave Echo. He's cynical and fuckin hilarious. He bought me a pack of cigarettes. Because bumming 'em was becoming a drag, he said.

Domino and Murph were 'getting ready to leave' all night. It was always 'any minute now.' When they finally left, Jack left with them – headed for the Rainbow Gathering in Minnesota. Lots of people were going there. John put up a sign, "This bus is not going to Minnesota," to stop the continuous flow of folks asking for a ride.

Real late night – in John's bus with Tricky, Corvette, and Benny, I went to my van to get something and found Freddy behind my van listening to two acoustic guitarists who weren't bad at all. I brought him back to the bus, not thinking about his dislike of the Hog Farm message and methods, and John's closeness with them.

Freddy and John clashed on many ideas about what the Hog Farm was doing. I was like "great," as they argued. But they were both psyched, and thought that with these two opposing attitudes, if they talked and worked on it long enough, they'd probably come up with some solutions. I hope they do. The whole thing is like a battle for the integrity of our scene, but everyone has a different view of what integrity means here.

Corvette and Benny slept in Mutz's tent, and in the morning, us three were dying to find a shower. We went to Hawkeye's house. There'd been a scene there, the night before, with Janelle and Jersey Marie, – Janelle was still raging about it. After delicious showers and a fatty, we hit the road.

When we got gas, our gas pumper started talkin about the spotted owl and how it sucks they made it an endangered species, because now lots of mills have to close, and kids will starve. I kept shakin my head at Corvette hoping she wouldn't give her opinion. I didn't want her to get the guy going. But she's right (as she ranted when we got back in the van), – why is an owl less important? It's not. It has as much right to live as any child. That's a big issue in Oregon right now. So is hemp for paper. There's some Pro-hemp guy running for governor. He had a truck in the camping lot with a big fatty on the flat bed, reminiscent of logging trucks with one big ole tree on the back.

31
Summer Tour 1990
Indy, Chicago, Losing Brent

July 4 1990

Today is a holiday. We're free because we tromp all over others! Whoopee! Us Americans – we're too much. I love this country and I wouldn't want to be anything other than American, but damn, we're kind of awful to others.

Tour starts today in Kansas City. Corvette's Uncle bought us tickets and he's bummed we didn't show up. It was 104° there. It's gonna be a hot hot hot tour.

Friday we went to Jokeland to see Nicholas. Stopped at Arthur and Jasmine's on the way home, they were psyched. Heard from both Abe and Freddy. Everyone is dry but Nicholas, so we headed to the Bay again, on Sunday. At Abe's we drank wine Freddy brought, and Jackie put out a plate of cheese, bread, and cherries. How yuppieish, and tasty.

We sat around in a beading frenzy Monday and Tuesday. Cranking out the beadwork in anticipation of the European tour. Doesn't look like we'll make it to Redwood Summer before the Oregon Country Fair. The Redwoods are so important. I can't believe I might not have time for them.

We're off to get buds today (again), and do fireworks in the city.

July 9 1990

On the 4th we went to Beau and Amanda's and walked up to Buena Vista park to watch the fireworks. Elwood came with us, he enjoys fireworks.

Friday we went to Berkeley to get Corvette's car. 150 bucks, and it's still doing funky stuff. Ugh. Visited Nicholas again, then home to bead more.

We were ready to head north Sunday, but Hilton John called from Hawkeye's. They're completely dry, so... One more trip to the Bay Area to get more smokeables to bring north with us, and no one's home.

So we sit, waiting and waiting and waiting.

July 13

At the Oregon Country Fair – we went right to the Dog Pound – Yeah! Bruce and Olivia from last year had a pass for me. I was gonna trade buds for it, but Olivia chose earrings, and some working shifts instead. Their friend had a pass for Corvette if she'd work some of his shifts. So we're both working the Dog Pound this year. We joke that Elwood is our 'dog bait.'

July 16th 1990
Hawkeye's house

My van parked, and covered with a tarp. Sitting on John's Hilton – packed and ready to roll. What a crew heading east; a white cat called Elwood, a black dog named Hoover, me, Corvette, Santa, John, and Erika.

July 17 1990

At a Rest Area west of Billings, Montana. It's a hot day, no clouds.

Elwood caught a bird in mid-air. I wouldn't have believed it if I didn't see it. He was zeroed in on it and stretched to the end of his leash, making his bird face. John said, "Aw, let him go. It's not like he's gonna catch it." He shot towards the bird. The bird took off, and Elwood jumped like six or seven feet, and got it! I had to run over there and make him let it go. Dumb bird. There's nothing sneaky about a deaf cat wearing a bell.

The first Indy show is tomorrow. We're only about ½ way. I can't wait to get there. I don't even know what they've been playing, or how tour's been. It'll be so great to see everyone. I wonder if I'll see my Hitchhiker again? And how's Fritz, and Jack, and Don, and Dean? I hope everyone's having a fun and safe tour.

For a second, just now, it was absolutely quiet. No passing vehicles, and no idling engines in this Rest Area, or the one across the highway. All you could hear was the wind, and the lighter inside the bus.

A couple hours later:

We're in Billings – that's as far as we got. What we thought was vapor locks – isn't. Now we're outside the biggest NAPA any of us has ever seen. Santa is taking off the fuel pump, and we're hoping that's the problem.

July 18 1990

After we got the fuel pump fixed, I learned to drive the bus. Fun, but it is work. My limbs were tense after one tank of gas, so Santa took over. I took it again, about an hour before sunrise, and drove another 200 miles. We stopped at a KOA so we could shower. We're in South Dakota with too many miles to go between us and Deer Creek. None of us has any idea what time the show starts tonight.

Evening

Middle America, bad roads, and hours too late. We're gonna miss the first Indy show.

July 19 1990

We're here! Set up behind the bus selling Indican Shirts, postcards, Hemp bumper stickers, Jewelry, and a book called *The Emperor Wears No Clothes*. People say there is a vendor's row, but it's too hot to bother moving.

King's motorhome is falling apart – the A/C has waterlogged the roof. He says he hasn't shut it off since Kansas City.

Justine is bumming big time. Someone used her "Beagalize it" T-shirt idea. Again. Saw Garrett and his new whatever, Windy. Saw Aaron, – he was psyched about the green we brought, – that debt can be considered paid.

The people next to us have a huge Elvis head on top of their car.

Inside   Deer Creek.

Jack Straw, Now – *They Love Each Other*.

I got my ticket from Louziana Steve. He's always got an extra, and he always only wants face, and I almost always don't have it. I guess I either owe him, or it was free.

We had a bit of excitement on the way in to the show. Me, Corvette, Erika, John, Hackmen, and Isaac, all headed in different gates, and suddenly, Isaac was on the ground surrounded by cops. Fuck. Hackmen hands me his bud bag, and follows as they're leading Isaac away in cuffs. Danni and a few others are freaking out. Nobody has any idea what happened. Next thing I know, Hackmen is trotting by, smiling, and waving Isaac's bud bag.

Desolation Row and Isaac's in. After they searched him, and found nothing, they tossed him out. He got right back in. Adrenaline to start the show.

John shared a great getaway story. In Pittsburg a few years ago, cops were fucking with Domino's bus. John asked what they were doing. They told him, 'shut the fuck up.'

'Why should I shut up?'

They tossed him in a Paddy Wagon. As the wagon backed up to leave, they almost backed into Kerry. Kerry saw John's wide eyes in the back window, so he opened the door. They both ran off and got away!

Break

Ended the set with *Promised Land*. Then we hear there was a big bust last night. Mutz's bus is impounded, and Mutz, Pixie, Grant, and Kovack are in the County jail. Nobody knows exactly what happened.

I saw Mavis, dressed in green velvet, but not looking too good.

And did I write about the rumour we heard in Oregon? That Elijah, with the Spinners, got busted for contributing to the delinquency of minors. We laughed. But now we hear the truth of the rumour. The Spinners rolled their van, and one girl died, one is in a coma, and they got Elijah for transporting minors across state lines. Bummer. Not so much to laugh about there.

Oh and more news – Europe tix went on sale two days ago – mail order. Two days ago! We don't have the cake right now. Figures, doesn't it?

Cute Allen is sitting with me. I haven't seen him in a while.

After the show

We've left the lot, and we're in a long line, on a bumpy road toward the highway.

2nd set was fun dancin', and I gave Allen a long massage during drums/space. After the show he and I sat talking on the hill for too long I guess, because someone had stolen his shoes by the time we went to get them. We talked about the idea of being free, and how it scares people. They get jealous, and hostile, because they choose not to live like us.

When he left, I went to sell postcards and some biker-looking guy confiscated my Dead photo postcards, but left me with the tye-dyes. I was bumming. I made no $ after the show. Met up with Allen again out in the lot. Hackmen scored some bud for us. Allen was Jonesin', so I got some for him too.

Me and Corvette stopped to talk with Dean and Danni. Danni did pretty well collecting bail money for Mutz and them. I heard they only had buds – just head stash. So that's something. We somehow got to talkin' about Dean being Chinese year of the

Fire Horse (1966) and being a Cancer. I said, "Wow. With all that fire and water you must be a pretty steamy guy." He blushed when we, all three, called him Steamy Dean. (Which quickly morphed into Dreamy Dean.)

Saw Riley tonight. He said Eden left him. Said she needed her space, but, next day, he found her in bed with some guy. When we were at Hawkeye's, we heard Riley was Jonesin and left her. He didn't look like he was Jonesin, but sometimes I'm oblivious to that because I don't want to see such things.

King's Fatty Wagon was a ragin dance party after the show.

Late night

Almost out of Indiana. I'm copiloting for John. We're both exhausted, but if we keep talking, we can stay awake. We're both certainly qualified to keep talking.

July 21 1990   Chicago

During the show, but I'm not inside. I wanted to go in, but it's Saturday, and tix are impossible. I haven't seen any, at any price.

Sitting outside the bus. It's sprinkling and looks like it wants to rain more. I'd rather be inside. But I can hear fine from here. So it's cool.

So far – *Touch O, Greatest Story, Jack-a-Roe*. And now, *Walkin Blooze*.

Vending was a free-for-all today, but we didn't sell shit. Erika was set up right next to us, and she did great on clothes and stickers.

July 22 1990

Morning. John had the idea to drive south and crash at a rest area. There's some heads here, but not many. In the bathroom a little girl said, "I like your skirt."

"Thank you."

"I bet it keeps you warm when it's cold."

"It does."

"I hope I can have a skirt like that someday."

"I hope you can too."

(I swear we were talking about way more than my skirt.)

Last night Corvette scored a ticket for face and came back to the bus to convince me to come look for another. We went walking. No luck. And we could hear pretty well, so we sold the one she got to a friend of Fritz's.

We almost got in on a random lucky gate pop, but they shut it in our face, with adrenaline high, and nowhere to run. Or dance.

The show sounded ok. The *Scarlet Fire* that opened 2nd set sounded fun. No biggie though, not being inside. Lots of Indicans were outside with us too.

We talked awhile with Fairy Mary about the split among tourheads. Heroin vs. No Heroin. She says there has been a lot on this tour. Said she hasn't done it in two years. Good for her.

It was Kerry's B-day. He might ride back across country with us because Santa has to fly back to California for court.

Mutz and his crew are out! None of them have any clothes, and they'll probably keep Mutz's bus. I don't know what charges they got.

Last night, on John's bus, we met Jack Herer. He wrote *The Emperor Wears No Clothes*. It's about how the government systematically got rid of hemp. In the 1600s, and 1700s, Farmers were required to grow hemp. In fact, they were arrested and fined if they didn't. He was psyched about the newspaper clipping I found in Oregon. Said he'd use it in the next book. It's actually the juxtaposition of two articles that makes it worth the book. In the top one, a man who killed his four-month-old son got 10 years, and a $100,000 fine. Below this, an article about a man who was growing pot. They chased him from Oregon, to Arizona, to Alaska, where they finally got him. They slapped him with 20 years and a 4 million dollar fine.

Later

Stopped at a grocery store. Deja Dan was there. He came on the bus for a quick bowl. A bit of bad news he shared. Garrett got busted. Dan isn't sure for what, or how much, but it wasn't buds. Who's gonna help Garrett?

Showtime   Breaktime

I didn't get in. I guess Corvette did, since she's not around. I was walkin with Jack, Icarus, Newburgh, and some others. We were tryin', unsuccessfully, to bribe guards to let us in.

Outside Domino's bus, Maureen's rolling fatties for a wedding. There's a huge crowd. I don't know the couple, and I'm too far back to hear. All I can hear is the band opening 2nd set with *Sam and Dee*. They opened the first set with *Box O' Rain*.

Late Night

I got drunk tonight, hanging with Jack and Dave Echo. Dave bought Rose posters from Jack, who had just bought 'em from some guy. I helped Dave sell them to tourists. Dave's in love with some chick who's got a boyfriend, and he's bummed about it.

When I went back to the bus, it was a ragin scene. The Fatty Wagon crankin Disco, and the fatty crew dancin up a storm. What a sight! John gets so uptight though. He invited the Fatty Wagon into his space, even moved to help them fit, then he's upset about the dance party.

When we left, Matt Ackerman came with us, and we're at some Holiday Inn somewhere. Me and Corvette are in the room with Matt. John and Erika are out in the bus.

I called Freddy, about Garrett, because I didn't know what else I could do. I asked Drippy Danny, Gimlet, and Downstairs Dave if anyone was doing anything for him, and they all shrugged.

June's boyfriend Tig got popped in Indy too. He's being held without bail. Uncool. It all sucks and I don't know what I can do about it.

7-23-90

Tour is over, it's the night for goodbyes. – Even though we haven't been on the whole tour, goodbyes are just as sad.

Had all kinds of fun hanging with Dave Echo off and on. He wore a skirt in the show. Malt wanted to pull his skirt down, particularly in front of Little Jeffy for some reason, so there was lots of wrestling. Mutz was chasing Dave, in his skirt, around the Fatty Zone. Everyone got involved in the fun. When Dave ran by me for the third or fourth time, I went to trip him. He leaped over my foot, and while he was in mid-air, Fritz body-checked him. He went down hard, and Mutz and Malt both landed on him!

King's Fatty Wagon, with the James Brown crankin' – It's the King-Fatty-Monster-Jägermeister-party. What a scene that mobile is! It's probably been like that all tour. Every time the cops came by, we all dispersed a bit, then, of course, we came right back. Can't keep it going forever though. They kept comin' back.

I'm sitting outside the Hilton bus. Can't move yet, too many cars around us. Speaking of can't move. This morning, at the hotel, a couple of Chicano guys were parked in the way of the bus. John asked them to move, and they pretty much told him to "fuck off hippie."

This went on a while and was feelin' pretty ugly. We couldn't do a thing with their car there. Then John says, "If you don't move your fucking car right now I'm going to take out a vial of LSD and douse you in it." Of course he didn't even have such a thing, but those guys got wide-eyed, and left pretty fucking quick then. Ha!

Yes, I got in tonight. Corvette too. Tix were easy, and Louziana Steve had tix for us both. The show was good, but not spectacular. They closed 1st set with *Truckin' Smokestack,* and encored with *The Weight.* I spent most of my time, inside, with

Jagger. I told him how I felt about Mavis' ways these days, and asked him to keep himself free from such burdens. He's so kind-hearted, and has such a fresh mind when viewing the Dead Scene, doesn't see the bad stuff. It uplifts me to get his happy vibes.

Right now, Hoover is eating corn-on-the-cob and a passerby just called him a corndog. Ha!

Ah! So the shows are over, with no sign of James the Beautiful Hitchhiker. I wonder what happened? His card said he'd be here.

Even though I only got in one night in Indy, and tonight, I'm glad I came. It was a good time, and we completely paid off Aaron for the postcards.

July 26 1990

We left Chicago last night. I drove the bus all night. Iowa to Cheyenne, Wyoming. I have some of my best ideas/thoughts while I'm driving, but now I can't remember any of them. That's my downfall. (Or maybe my saving grace.)

We're at a KOA. It's been hot today, but it's breezy now, and the guy here said, "expect it to go down to 38° tonight." Yikes.

later

Erika made spaghetti, and we're settling in for the night. 800 or 900 miles from Eugene.

Thinking about what's coming up. Reggae on the River is next weekend, the very next day, is JGB at the Greeks. I wonder if it's even worth it to go all the way down there. I got shut out of JGB Greek last year.

On the 11th Ma and Ed arrive. I've got to plan a good week for them. Plus, we have to figure out the Europe thing, and the rent thing. I've gotta get a passport. And try to do something about some European show tix. I'd like to have some before we go. And contacts. I need new contacts.

July 27 1990 Wyoming.

It was frigid last night, but now that the sun's up, it's ok. There's low-flying planes spraying some nasty chemical shit. Smells gross whenever one goes over.

Everyone's still half asleep. I'm ready to move, I wish everyone else was. We're so close, but yet so far, and we're all almost out of buds. I want to get home. See if there's a letter that says why my hitchhiker didn't make it.

Come on you guys – Wake up. Wake up. Wake up. Let's eat and hit the road. Less than 1000 miles left. We could do it today!

July 28

Before we left that KOA we had to rescue Elwood. He'd run off with his leash on and gotten tangled in a tree. It took all of us to find him. He was so close to the water on the other side of the stream, we couldn't hear him cry out. As we all saw him, Hoover went bounding through the stream, excited and proud. "Here he is you guys! I found him!"

John drove till midnight, then I drove till the headlight went out. It's nearing noon now, and we're about 100 miles from Hawkeye's. I can't wait to get out of this bus. Don't get me wrong, it's the kind ride, but I want my own space back.

Later

20 miles from Hawkeye's. We just made our last gas stop.

Fuckin' bad news.

The guy pumpin' our gas says, "Bummer about Brent huh?"

We're all like, "What'd'ya mean?"

"Found dead in his house. Thursday."

We wanted not to believe him, but he went and got today's paper to show us.

It's true.

Fuck.

What a total bummer.

I can't quite comprehend yet. Brent is dead?

No shit.

You tried to party too hard didn't you Brent? How could you do this to yourself? What will this do to our world?

Oh man.

Chicago 1990, Brent's last Shows.

I hope this hits the junkies hard.

What a Fuckin' Bummer.

No one has said a word since we read the article.

What is there to say?

Just silence.

32
Summer 1990
Reggae on the River,
Jerry, Mom & Ed, Movin' Out

August 3 1990   Eel River

On Wednesday, Atlanta Mary and Tammy called and wanted to come by. Sure, No Problem. Later, Bob and Marie Snodgrass called, and they, and Ginny, came by too. Bob set up and worked on the porch. I love watching him blow glass. He does a funny stoned monologue as he works. Fritz and Two Toke Tom came by, so did JohnRay and Paige.

Everyone left yesterday, and I got my contacts, and my passport pictures.

Beading last night, and Fritz called, asking for a ride North. So this morning we got up early. Made brownies (we made the greatest, greenest butter!), and got moving by 9AM. Fritz said, for my b-day, he'd be nice to me all day. I said, "Elwood too."

He sighed, "Okay."

We got here around 1^{ish}. First stop – this little collection of cabins (just past Richardson's Grove), – all occupied by people we know. Quite a crowd. Murph, Jeremy, Atlanta Mary, Don and Justine, Kerry, Izzy, Trinity, Katarina, DigDoug, Shane, Dragon Dave, and his dog Noel, with four puppies. Soon after us, John and Erika, and Santa, pulled in.

Lots of gossip. Skye is out of prison and in a halfway house in SF – not far from the Warfield. She can have visitors! Other news; Sid beat up Hawkeye? And King Henry got busted in a Chicago hotel after the shows?!?

August 4 1990   Morning

We followed Hilton John in to French's Camp as they opened because he has Hog Farm friends. Bob and Marie Snodgrass followed us and we all got great spots overlooking the river's edge, and totally in the shade. This place is a party!

Kevin was just checking out Bob's elaborate dragon pipe and might order one.

It's true about Sid and Hawkeye. I'm not pleased to hear it. Kevin said Sid tried to get a council to sit and talk it all out. Hawkeye said ok, but never arranged it. Sid asked him for some buds, and they met at a rest area, where they fought. Sid broke Hawkeye's glasses? What a mess. Sid's here but it seems Hawkeye's not. Kevin's view was pretty Sid-sided. Ike was there, as we talked, and he was like, "No. Hawkeye does not have five brand new Harleys."

Bob had a bunch of gorgeous guys watching him blow glass, and buying pipes as fast as he could make them. The view was nice, and I kept getting called to the bus for birthday fatties and I got a great foot massage from Kerry.

When I crashed, Bob was still working (right behind the van), but his clientele wasn't so cute anymore. Kennedy woke me early, with a quick hello, and word of buds. I went back to sleep till Jack showed up with coffee and cigarettes, and gave me a nice massage.

On the bus now, for a fatty. Erika's doing the cookin' thing. She wants me to write that she made her first omelet ever, and it came out good.

Inside.

Freddy had a great bumper sticker idea:

"SAVE LOGGERS AND THEIR FAMILYS – LEAGALIZE MARAJUANA."

There is a huge issue here. The US Army has invaded Humboldt, marching through the mountains, looking for pot, and scaring the shit out of people. They harass innocent people in their own homes. It's an invasion, costing the government thousands of dollars every day. Locals are pissed. Demonstrations everywhere, with mad cops, mad men, and camouflaged 18-year-olds. What is wrong with America that we won't wake up and see that hemp can save the world? For paper – four times more yield per year than wood. It's useable as oil, fuel, fabric, rope, and if it wasn't illegal, doctors would list it as a cure for many minor things. I see this so easily, I have trouble understanding why others don't.

Well yes, I understand their closed-mindedness. But Freddy's right, someone should tell the loggers that pot is their savior. They live in the best pot country in America. There could be the hemp farms for industry, and the bud farms – they'd be like wineries. Its bad points aren't as bad as alcohol's bad points – zero addiction, and less impairment = fewer ruined lives, and fewer accidents due to the use of.

The army thing is sick. This is America folks. Is this to be allowed to happen?

August 5 1990   10 AM^{ish}

Sitting in the sun, overlooking the parking lot across the river. Lots of people are getting stuck in the gravel as the cars trail away. JGB at the Greek today led a bunch o' folks out of here last night, or hurrying now. There's also a hemp rally somewhere. I'd like to go, but I don't want to take my van there. Domino (when he heard me say that), said, "Oh? So you're committed, but not that committed?" Maybe so. Instinct tells me I don't want my van at a big hemp rally. My person yes, my transport, NO.

Below me some guy is skinny dipping, and washing his hair. Two passing chicks said, "Dude, I hope that's biodegradable shampoo."

And he said, "Every day I shit, piss, shower, and live in these rivers. Thank you for being here, now go home."

August 6 1990

We went to the cabins when we left the Eel.

We were gonna go to the rally in the Hilton bus, and Domino and them were gonna go in his bus, but Kerry came back from Shelter Cove and said they were stopping obvious vehicles, and planting pot in the vehicle, even if you didn't bring any. So none of us went. Apparently, even Domino is not committed enough to lose his vehicle. We're all too scared to stand up for what we believe in. This is ridiculous. America. HA!

Maureen and Domino are splitting up, but she won't leave 'till he gets her a car or somethin'. Jack's sort of Domino's travel partner now. Says he's been spending a lot of $ on the bus – tires etc. Jack's a good guy. I sat in the shade with him all afternoon. Sometimes he gets bummed at me because I don't go along with all his crazy, spur-of-the-moment ideas, and I'm not into surrounding myself with people who aren't always so pleasant to be around – like wingnuts, and slimy old men. (I think Jack knows every slimy old guy in the lot.)

August 8

Fuckin Jack. We didn't go to last night's Jerry show at the Warfield, and the van got stuck in the driveway at our house. It's been stuck all day, so we couldn't go to tonight's JGB Show either. I just got off the phone with Rosemary, and she just got off the phone with Spaz, who just saw Jack get busted on Market St.

Damn it Jack, you just won't learn will you?

August 9

Morning, and my van is still stuck in the fuckin driveway. I'm at an angle where the tires just spin and I can't move because of the trees.

Night

In SF, at the Warfield. Inside even. And I would prefer to be home.

We hitched here. First a crazy-driver, dyke-woman, then two hippie chicks brought us to Berkeley, and we BARTed over here. Got my period on the way, and I have no drugs to stop the pain. Market St. was as ugly as ever.

We had tix already. We'd traded buds to some of Aaron's friends.

So. The story with Jack was that he was selling stickers and narcs thought it was pages, so they searched him, and found pages. Skye said Domino was trying to bail him out, but lots of people won't kick to bail Jack out again. There's no sign of Domino tonight. Skye looks good. Strong, and more solid than she used to. She says seeing me in the hall, writing was one of the things she missed when she was in prison.

I hate feeling so weak and woozy. I just want to lay down and go to sleep.

Dave Echo is with that chick Ann. She must have finally dumped her boyfriend or something. Benny's rolling a joint next to me. I'm not even into getting stoned.

Miranda is gonna run to Rock-Med and get me some Motrin. I didn't even know Rock-Med came to JGB shows.

Thanx Miranda.

later

Jerry is rippin' *Second That Emotion,* and I can't dance. Cramps have subsided, but I still feel weak.

I can't believe Jack's busted again. Most folks seem to be mad at him about it. I'm mad too. I told him this is what I was afraid of. Afraid for him, but I guess it didn't matter. Skye said her and Jack were talking just yesterday, about freedom, and how to hold onto it.

August 10 1990

While I was staring into space with my book open, Corvette appeared, "Jumpin' Jack's downstairs, he wants to see you." Amazing. Out on his own OR, and an address Domino gave them. I'm glad he got out, but it seems to me that Jack isn't taking the whole thing seriously enough. He was pretty drunk by the end of the night. I made him call Rosemary so she could stop worrying. He doesn't understand why people like me, Rosemary, and Roz worry so much. I bitched at him for even having shit in his pocket. About taking it all so lightly. But he talked of magic and rainbows, with a sparkle in his eye, and I don't think he heard me at all.

August 12 1990

Abe gave us a ride to the airport, and greeted Ma and Ed with us. He was busting my ass about being excited. Of course I'm excited. Ma's in California! They rented a car, and I drove us through Chinatown, then to Coit Tower.

They didn't want to go out today, so they're kickin back at the house cooking steak, and we're about to go to Accidental Mary's party.

August 13 1990

About a mile before the party, "Is that Domino's bus?"
"Yep, and there's Jack."

We stopped, but I was impatient waiting for Maureen and Domino. I don't like loitering on the road that leads to Bohemian Grove. I suspect Domino thinks I'm a bitch. He rolls his eyes and looks at Jack like, 'what do you see in her?'

It wasn't a bad party. We missed Crazy Fingers, but saw Nick Gravenitis. He didn't rage. It was just background music. Jack was bummed by the lack of rainbow décor. We drank our own beer all night. There was lots of food, but all I ate was some fruit pie that Poco brought. Sid was there, and Washington George sold us expensive B-grade buds.

Jeremy and his mom were gonna crash at our house, but his mom picked up some guy and left with him, so instead, they made plans to meet in Santa Rosa, next day. Jack made plans to meet Domino there too, and Jack and Jeremy came home with us.

Me and Jack only cuddled. Funny, the one time I actually bring Jumpin' Jack home, is when Ma and Ed are here. Jack took my rainbow pouch with the blue phantom crystal, and said he wasn't giving it back, so I put on his most recent rainbow necklace, and told him I was gonna keep that. He nodded.

Jeremy came back alone tonight, after dropping his mom at the airport, – told us Jack has court in the morning. He didn't even tell me that! Please let there be no reason to put Jack back in jail.

August 17 1990

Ma and Ed left early this morning, then we went to drop off Corvette's car with the mechanic in Berkeley and her car caught fire right there at the garage!!

We BARTed across the Bay and did the Haight St shuffle for two or three hours, till we found Ryan from Atlanta, and his girlfriend Lila. They're giving us a ride home. We found Jack and told him we're kidnapping him. Saw Don, but he couldn't help our green jones. Ryan had an idea for that, so Corvette took a ride with them, while I stayed with Jack. Domino came down the street with the bus. We jumped on for a second so Jack could grab his stuff. Domino did not look happy about Jack leaving with me.

August 20

It was fun to do the flea market with Jack. We always knew it would be. As the day wound down he and Ryan were digging through everybody's leavings, bringing back anything at all, with Jack yelling, "anything for a dollar," then, "anything for 50¢," then, "anything for 25¢." Jack even got Lila yelling. Lila is not at all the type to yell. She's got such a sweet southern attitude, and a heavy accent.

We had no buds so I called Two Toke Tom. "Tom, I need a shower. Can you shower with me?" It was a yes. Me, Jack, and Ryan went over. Even-Steven was there, and Tom tried to get us to take him with us. Jack wanted that too. No.

Back at our house Jack had Ryan reading aloud from, *What a Long Strange Trip it's Been – a hippie's history of the 60's and beyond*. We laughed a lot. Ryan kept trying to put the book down, and Jack would make him start reading again. And I kept saying, "I warned ya, I warned ya not to listen to Jack." It became the joke of the night.

We're thinking of moving in with Lila and Ryan somewhere up here.

I think I could live with them, we've been having a blast for days.

Last night Jack said coming here was the best thing to happen to him in a year.

August 22

Me and Jack had a really nice morning this morning. Finally. Sometimes a good old hippie man is just what a girl needs.

We got a message from Briscoe that Buddy Green had arrived. So we went over. When Fritz saw Jack, he goes, "Oh man, it's the shaded rainbow." Yeah, like his house isn't shady anyway. They use the Guerneville onion all the time, and they talk on the phone way too much for my liking.

I got a letter from Garrett, from Jail. It was a handwritten fucking chain letter. Be real Garrett. I wanted to hear about you. Fool.

August 27

A lazy morning. I enjoyed it. Maureen and Domino, and this chick Crystal came by to shower. Me and Corvette spent the afternoon looking at houses. Saw some okay ones, and some awful ones, and one that was perfect, till we found out the landlord lives across the street.

Stopped by Aaron's. That's where we found out about Stevie Ray Vaughn. He died last night in a helicopter crash on an Alpine Valley Ski Slope. He had just finished a show with Eric Clapton and Robert Cray. There was so much about it on CNN. Especially compared with when Brent died. There's more glory in dying in a helicopter crash than ODing. Goodbye Stevie Ray. You knew what it meant to Rock-n-Roll.

Hilton John dropped King Henry off at the market and I went to get him. He'd accidently pocketed some of John's head buds. I was not bummed, but John was when he called.

Jack and King talked a lot about what it meant to deal in this day and age. And why do it? It was interesting, and I wish I dared write it down.

August 29

King and Jack went to the city with Lila and Ryan and me and Corvette packed like crazy. It finally looks like we're moving.

Funny moment to remember – the other day when Hilton John dropped King off, and I picked him up, King goes, "Wait, should I get something to eat?"

"No. If you've only got $16, don't spend it on food. We've got tons of Burrito shit at the house."

"Burritos?! How far does this 'being poor' go? I had burritos last night."

Poor King.

~~~~~

The Dead has a new keyboardist. Vince Welnick from the Tubes. Sounds good to me. Bruce Hornsby will still play MSG with them. Two Keyboards, that'll be fun.

~~~~~

Jagger called. He's upset about Mavis. Says she's Jonesin bad, always nodding off, and Hot as shit there in Ohio. He's hurt by the way she's treating him.

Sept 2 1990

I talked to Ma the other day. Our Paris and Sweden Dead tix are there!!!

It's been a crazy time here. We keep looking for, and expecting to get a new house before we leave, but nothing's coming through, and we have no idea what we'll do with all our stuff.

We went to the city to look for buds. No luck. Jack was having fun, sitting on the Haight, drinking from a paper bag. Everyone loves to take Jack's picture. This one lady asked him, and he said, "Sure, for a buck," but he didn't take the dollar she offered. How many foreign visitors to the Haight have a picture of Jack as their 'American Hippie'?

Night before Jerry, King calls, "Can we come by?"

Ok! We packed with good motivation till 3AM, when they got here. Then we partied! The big bummer is that CAMP got Kerry's and Jeremy's buds. FUCK.

Yesterday morning, Corvette's room was a cloud of fog, while Kerry, Santa, King, and Jeremy worked. I love when a motherlode stops by us before going to the Show.

We headed to the JGB show at Shoreline about 1ish. Me, Corvette, Lila, and Ryan went in the van. It choked and sputtered going up the mountain towards GG Bridge. We stopped in the city to see what's up. Spraying gas everywhere. We got Lila and Ryan a ride with Chloe, and brought the van home before it could lose all its gas. We grabbed Lila's truck, and headed back South.

Got to Shoreline after Los Lobos' set, and there was no one outside. Well, no one we knew anyway. There were also no tix. The box office had a few, but we had no cake.

Rebel walked us in as Jer broke into *Dear Prudence*. We went to the good seats and got nice and stoned. Then up to the top. So uncrowded! Lots of hilarity, much rowdiness, and a ragin Jerry show. One of the best!!! We swiped Dave Echo's hat and he was tackling Jack, and Danni, and Tricky, trying to find it. And Fritz with the ultimately timed body checks. Fun fun.

Sept 4 1990

Jack suggested getting a Storage Shed while we had enough vehicles – Lila and Ryan's truck, Domino and Maureen in her mail truck, and Skinny Jim with his truck. Jack directed the packing into vehicles, and into the shed. He was good at it, and he kept us laughing as we worked. We got a place called SpaceMart. Forget getting a house.

Garrett called from jail – he's hating life. His girlfriend, Windy, won't testify that she saw him selling tye-dyes, and he's bummed because she's been sleeping with Sid (or so he's heard). He sounded totally hopeless, and I couldn't get into it, because the landlord was standing there, waiting for me to get off the phone, and wondering exactly when we'd be out of the house. Garrett hung up on me.

Fuck.

Sept 5

The van is parked at Aaron's till we get back, and we're going east with Ryan and Lila. We are so packed into Lila's truck, it's comical. Elwood is not gonna be Lovin it like he was on the bus. We got 2000 postcards from Aaron, then went to Parker's. He wasn't home and we had to wait 45 minutes for him. It was totally worth it, except we're spending someone else's money. But we had to. Can't go across country budless.

In Reno now, waiting for the $4.50 breakfast buffet to open in 15 minutes.

33
Fall Tour 1990
Ohio and Philly

Sept 7   Richfield, Ohio

Went right to the Holiday Inn to see James the beautiful hitchhiker. No one home. Aw man! The hotel looked killah! Huge hangout room with ping pong, a pool, and sauna! I left a note and I guess we'll go back after the show. That's what I wrote in the note anyway.

Rumours of a ticket check in the lot were strong, but untrue. None of our buses, or RVs, are here. And not many recognizable vans either.

Inside, me and Corvette got stoned with Riley as they opened with *Cold Rain and Snow*. He shaved, and has red and blue hair. It took me a second to recognize him. Saw Hana and Marshal, with their new baby – Franklin Jerome. Marshal looks so fuckin happy.

Jack had sky-box tix. We found our way up here to look for him. Lots of space, a bar, carpets, and better sound than in the hallway. Been hanging with Kara. She's so fun. Jack bought us drinks. He was talking with these biker folks, and we smoked a fatty with them. The biker chick's name is Suki. I would have thought she was on drugs, except she told me she does no drugs, – only 'smokes the sacred herbs.' She kept telling me I was beautiful. She asked, why someone as beautiful as me, is here alone. Then called Jack over to introduce him to me. Ha!

It's been an interesting show. All day we wondered how Vince was doing. Was he nervous? – We were. The crowd was so hyped. The first time he jumped on the notes the crowd went wild, and he seemed a bit surprised. He'll work out. He's holding back some. He'll learn not to. All the song intros are long, while he gets into it. It feels different and it's mellow. It's missing Brent, and it's noticeable. Vince has big shoes to fill. Bobby introduced him in the middle of the 1st set.

First night of tour feels unusual. It's the same hallway, but it's not the same hallway at all. I kept seeing totally familiar faces, but it wasn't a face I knew.

Sept 8 1990

After the show we sold postcards, then drove to Brecksville, to eat. What a disaster. The waitresses were horribly slow, and they fired the dishwasher. Eventually a long hair went back there and did the dishes, another bused tables, and someone else started seating people and delivering food, because it was just sitting there. Everyone helped themselves to whatever they needed and the waitresses didn't care. We left money on the table for the bus-hippie and left just as the cook quit, and stormed out.

Got back to the Holiday Inn late, and woke James up. It was just him and his brother Ricky in the room. We smoked a fatty, and talked and laughed, till sunrise.

Inside   Ohio

In the sky-box bar again. We were smoking a big fatty a bit ago, and just now this cop (Where did he come from?) leaned over the railing to these kids near us, and asked, "Do you need help with that?" (The kid was rollin' a joint.) He grinned, "Light it, and you're going to jail." Corvette told me that her and Nina were smoking a joint and that same cop flashed the light on the fatty, and it was gone – disintegrated. She said, even she didn't know where it went.

There's more people up here tonight. It's a good vibe. Izzy and Trinity, Two Toke Tom and Kiersten, Erik the Rude, Nonnie and some Spinoffs. Kara says Jack's still outside.

Tix were hard. Me, Kara, and Corvette resorted to asking Jake (from BGP) if he could help us get in. He hooked us up with Brokham. We had to pass out GDP merchandising pamphlets. No Problem, we can do that. Yeah Jake! Thanks!

Today was fun outside. The lot raged, with only a few confiscators. Nitrous was way out in the open. Lila and Ryan had a friend with a tank, and Jack popped a balloon of theirs. Doesn't like N_2O I guess.

Later

Where's the fucking Fatty Family anyway? I remember Don saying (years ago) how it was our job to dance in the halls. He's not coming here, or going to Europe. No Benny or Dave Echo here. No King. No Kerry – he was supposed to fly in last night but no one has seen him. Izzy's worried. No Santa. No Dean. No Murph. No Kevin. No Tavi.

Throwing Stones is wailing! Vince is doing ok.

We were over on Jerry's side of the coliseum club with James and Ricky, and some friends of theirs. Ricky told their friends, "These guys came to our hotel room last night and smoked the fattest joint I've ever seen." James said I get him too stoned. He usually smokes 5 or 6 joints all summer – he's already smoked 4 with us.

NFA! Wooohooo!

Made in Canada

Sept 9

More who aren't here – Kennedy, Suzy, KindBoy, Silas, Sid. Sad that the Fatty Family is dispersed. Is it already history? Was it something that couldn't last? Aaahh. I don't want to think like that.

Overall, I liked Richfield, Ohio. No complaints.

Afterwards, I was walkin with Jack and Kara. Selling "Fuckin Eh" stickers, and postcards. Kara is great. I wish she was on tour. Instead, she's on Probation, and must live here in Ohio.

We bumped into Jack's Canadian friends. They had the BEST Stickers – "Who are the DEA? And why do they keep following me?" with a bear, smoking a fatty, in handcuffs. At first you read it as "Dead" because of the question mark. We smoked hash joints, and drank Canadian beer with them till the cops came swarming in.

We packed up the truck – it takes some doing, we're packed in there pretty tight – and hit the road caravanning towards Philly. I rode with James, while Ricky slept. We talked. – Real talk. Telling each other the stories of our hearts. We have such a great connection. It's so nice to see him again.

9-10
Inside/Philly/Spectrum

It's a Fatty Zone! Hoo-Ha! Jeremy, Dean, Benny, Blake, Poco, King, Kerry, Marla, Mojo, Riley, Atlanta Mary, Yes Ma'am Sam, Mutz, Tammy and Fritz.

And Janey is here!!! It's been a fun fun day and it's a Good Energy show.

Shakedown opener, and they closed the 1st set with *Promised Land*. I wondered how they'd handle that. It was all Brent before, but Jerry took most of it, and Vince raged. He can handle it! Yeah!

Feels much nicer here in Philly, – more family around.

I don't think Jack got in. Corvette said he looked pretty down out there. I only saw him for a second, – I had clothes I'd just bought as part of his B-day present, so I didn't stop.

We got our tix through Brokham again. They asked where Kara was, and we told 'em she didn't come, but we had another chick who would love to help. We got Lila.

They just did the biggest *Dark Star* tease – Like maybe they'd open 2nd set with it, but noooo it's a *Victim*. Maybe later guys?

Sept 11

They didn't do *Dark Star,* and most people didn't even hear the tease that me and Benny heard. It was a good show. A raging *Scarlet Fire*.

This cute young black guy asked what I was doing, then asked if I'd write about him. We talked awhile about Deadheads, vs what it's like when that many black people get together. We talked about growing up in different environments. He's a scalper. His tix cost $80. I tried to convince him to go inside tonight. He asked where my man was, and said if I didn't have one, he'd love to volunteer for the night. I told him I had one, but if he'd come inside tonight – we'd dance, he and I.

Inside

Janey helped us with the merchandise-catalogue-pass-out-thing tonight, and Lila felt bunked, so Jake let her do it too. And Kara's here so Jake let her do it too! She doesn't work till Friday, and Jack bought her a plane ticket.

Sounds great in here. *Jack Straw* and now *Bertha*.

I hope Jack got in for his Birthday. Johnja thought he did.

Oh! I want to write about the Spinners, and Icarus. Icarus was standing next to them with a "Life is for Everyone" Bumper Sticker, and screaming, "I don't like people, who only like people, who are exactly like themselves." And he told Elijah "Fuck You," right to his face.

Wailing – *Greatest Story*! Gotta dance this.

~~~~~~~

Candyman was great too, and now it's *Queen Jane*.

Ivan is here, and KJ and Mirabeth, Atlanta Mary. Where's Tricky? I haven't seen Fritz all day. Marla's here. She's bringing us to Connecticut tomorrow after the show. There's Dean, ah, and now I see Fritz.

What's the next tune gonna be?

Brown Eyed Women.

Alright.

There goes Fat Matt, rollin' and twistin' by.

Used to Love Her.

Janice is here. She lives in Pennsylvania with her Mom and little Timothy.

Tennessee Jed!

There's Yes Ma'am Sam. He makes me smile.

Kerry keeps bumming Clubs from me, and he just delivered me the joint.

Riley called this – *Hell in a Bucket*.

<div align="center">2nd set</div>

China Cat to open. *I Know You Rider.*

Looks Like Rain, and I'm headed for the bathroom.

~~~~~

I found Janey, as they broke into *He's Gone*. Of course, because *He's Gone* is always about Damien.

Late Night

This place is weird weird weird tonight. First time I came outside to smoke, Jack was highly upset, and lookin' for fruit to, "Keep the mutherfucker Alive, or he's gonna die like Damien did!"

"Who? Where?" He pointed to Church Mouse, across the parking lot.

The energy is jittery. Kara has to go back to Ohio tomorrow, somehow, and she's fighting with Tony. The wavery sounds of a faraway drum circle.

~~~~~

I went upstairs and smoked a joint with Izzy and Corvette.

I came outside again.

Jack is chasing Church Mouse, splashing water and laughing. Church Mouse is chasing Jack, and people are saying, "If he can run, he'll be ok." But Jack keeps splashing him, because he shuts his eyes. There's no security in sight.

I'm somehow proud of Jack, – Keeping Church Mouse awake, and Alive. He won't give up.

Damien is all over this night, and it makes me think of Janey, and how much I love her. She said tonight, to tell Jack, Happy Birthday. I said, "Tell him yourself," and she said she'd have a hard time doing that. She has a hard spot in her heart for him, but she could send the message through me. They used to be friends, when Damien was alive, but when Damien died, and someone moved his body, that someone didn't call 911. All kinds of people told her they'd partied with Damien that day, always apologizing for being part of what killed him. She knows it's no one's fault but his own that he OD'd, but no one ever owned up to moving him. And Jack has never talked to her.

Someone left Damien, and that's the thorn. If it was Jack, too scared to own up to it, I think it haunts him. There's no bringing Damien back, and there's no undoing any of it. So here's Jack? Trying to stop a new tragedy?

How strange that it's all happening on Jack's birthday.

Lots of people are helping keep Church Mouse moving now.

What am I doing here? Should I be helping too? Seems like it's not my world. Like I'm just uselessly watching with pen in hand.

Go for it Folks. He needs you, but he'll be ok.

Some stranger has been sitting here quietly with me, watching it all. He just gave me the hugest hug, and left. Johnja walked by, thanked me for wearing purple, and kissed the top of my head. Kara and Tony, quiet now, in concentrated discussion.

I think Church Mouse will be OK.

~~~~~

Time slips by. Jack's still splashing and cackling. Church Mouse is lucky to have these people. Maybe if all the people around him weren't so drugged, someone would have done something for Damien.

Sept 12 1990   Philly

Sitting outside the back door handing out the flyers. The lot seemed full of assholes today, so me, Corvette, and Janey hung out here.

Lila and Ryan left for Georgia. We moved our shit (and Elwood too), into Marla's Mustang Convertible.

Jack made it to our room sometime in the light hours of this morning. We began waking up about 11^{ish}, but didn't get out till 1:30. Everyone was beat, and it seemed no-one had had enough sleep. Too true. It was like 5:30 when I went back upstairs this morning, and everyone was still awake.

Tix are hard tonight, and all the Scalpers have counterfeits.

34
Fall Tour 1990
NYC

                    Sept 14 1990   Inside

WOW! Bobby is kicking *Black Throated* again!

We hunted up Jake when we got here, he said there was nothing to hand out.

Went by the Penta, to find somewhere to put our stuff. We asked these two cute guys if we could put our shit in their room. William and Dana, – from Rhode Island. We smoked a fatty with them, and they said we could stay for free, if we ended up with no money. They even made me take $5 for beer in case we didn't get in.

Tix were impossible. It's a Friday. Went looking for Jake again, as a last hope, and he was like, "Where ya been? – it's happening!" Tonight he introduced us to Jory.

We missed *Stranger* – came in on *Sugaree*.

Now it's *Cassidy*. I'm glad to be inside but I hate drunks singing in my ear, and I hate NY. Some guy outside heard me say that, and gave me and Corvette each the longest, long stem roses I've ever seen. One thing I do like about NY is King Kong, holding court over the marquee, looking majestic.

It's break time already. Crowded. Our seats are right along the rail, so we get to watch all the New Yorkers walk by, and spill beer.

2nd set

Scarlet Fire Truckin Terrapin. It's too crowded to go walking, and I don't like to dance in a packed place. But I'm havin fun watching Kerry dance.

Terrapin is sounding Sweet.

Drumz now, rolling into what sounds like the *Other One*, but they just did that last night Philly, didn't they? Yup, it's the *Other One*.

Kerry just delivered us a few hits off a fatty. Thanx Kerry.

Wharf Rat again.

Sugar Mag, and isn't this just like the last show we saw? The place is rockin', literally, but I don't feel like dancing. Sigh.

I have nothing to be unhappy about. Yet, I don't feel very happy. What's my problem? I feel like I'm missing something, as the floor shakes, and the building vibrates rainbows.

Why is it so hard to find Love?

SSDD.

Only the Dead can move this many people at once. No other band, I swear it. Whistles and lighters. What will the encore be? *Quinn* would be nice, or something rowdy like that.

Ok. I guess *Useless Blues* will do. Postcard time, then Lindy's...

5AM   William and Dana's room

The bar was packed so me and Corvette got some beer from the store around the corner, and drank in the lobby with Rosemary. She's extremely bummed 'cause Johnja's doing dope again.

King Henry was pretty high. He tried to follow us for a fatty and got lost. It's cool though, he made it back to the bar after a while. Once it clicked to midnight, it was Diggety's b-day. He was fuckin drunk, and ragin', and screamin' about havin' $9,000 in his pocket. I tried to tell him keep his mouth shut about that, but he wasn't listening to anyone.

Rosemary wanted to go crash, but she was waiting on Jack. The bar started to clear out, and I went back in. Jack had me roll two fatties. He's got some way kind. Riley joined us, and some young boy named Royce. He's maybe 17, very high, and cute as shit. – Here for the weekend from his boarding school in Virginia. Jack was switching everyone's hats around. Jack had a tam, Riley a Guatemalan fez-type-thing, Royce a cowboy hat, Corvette her velvet feathered beret, and me with my biker hat.

Sept 15 1990

William and Dana checked out, so we went to the only room I could think of – the room # Riley told me last night. So here we sit, smokin a fatty with Riley and his high school friends Bea and Rachel. We'll leave our stuff here today.

Mid-afternoon

In Lindy's drinking a Pina Colada with Cannoli Ron. Saturday night and tix are looking hard already. I hope we can work tonight.

We heard the bartender ask Even-Steven where Carp was, "Ya know, Jumpin' Jack's brother, where is he?"

later

Waiting for our tickets. Word is Jack brought some Joneser back to life last night. I didn't see it – it happened during the show.

There's quite a cop show of force here today. What are they trying to prove anyway? New York is so outta control. I hope it mellows a bit after this Friday/Saturday madness.

Inside/Break

We covered for Janey. Did all the shit ourselves and got all three tix from Jory. No sign of Janey. What to do with the extra? Miracle someone? Trade for two miracles we can give out on another night? Or keep looking for Janey? We couldn't decide. So we went to get Pizza.

Saw Mirabeth and KJ, without even one, or the extra would have been theirs. One last look for Janey by the backstage door. Nothing. Walking back towards the front, we see Fritz's head bobbing through the crowd. He's lookin' desperate, "Do you girls have a ticket for me?"

"Well... um... maybe..."

As Jake appears. "Did you find Janey? She's right over there."

Sorry Fritz.

We've got great seats on Phil's side. Perfect for the *Box O'* we just got. I can see Washington George in the 4th row. He once told me, if he can't be within 20 feet of the band he doesn't even want to go in.

Sept 16 1990

Outside the ramp waiting for Jake. Corvette is off selling postcards, 'cause we are too broke.

Last night *Throwing Stones,* a great *NFA,* and the encore was a wild *Saturday Night*!!! Woooo! Fun shit.

Afterwards, everyone went over to the Penta Bar. They are so cool to us there. It was ragin'. Riley, Benny, Meredith, and Gwen were going to the Village. We decided to go too. Me, Corvette, Jack, and Dean jumped into a cab to Ponchita's.

Great drinks. Big frosty things. Margaritas, Daiquiris, Pina Coladas, Toasted Almonds. After us, in came Marla, Poco, and more. And after that, Ethan in his dress, and Fat Matt, and some other Spinoff types. They were fuckin drunk. It was some guy's b-day, from that Spinner crowd, and they were drinkin like Spinners don't. Meredith, sarcastically, "I'm so disillusioned. I didn't think Spinners acted like this."

Everything was being added up on one bill. Benny and them left, leaving enough $ for their drinks. We left too, also paying – even over-paying – for our drinks. I knew what was coming. I grabbed Dean, "Comeon, you don't want to be the last one here."

We went to a store. As we walked away, I saw Fat Matt and the waitress counting $.

When we got back out into the street, some woman from the restaurant was ragin, and looking for the hippies who owed her. She recognized the clothes both me and Jack had on, and started telling us we owed her $120, and she was callin' the cops. There were guys with billy-clubs surrounding us. Corvette went into a bar to "look for the others," as me and Jack slipped away by ducking into a restaurant, and out their back door.

I was afraid they had Corvette, – she had buds in her pocket. Jack sat in a doorway and held my buds, I went back to look for Corvette. Dressed in that silk dress, I was worried about being 'caught' again, but I had to make sure she was ok. No sign of Corvette, but I saw Benny and Riley at the door of the place, arguing with the waitress.

Benny looked at me and said, "I'll pay your bill, and hers (meaning Corvette), but I'm not payin' everyone's."

"You don't have to pay for ours. We paid."

Riley said he saw Corvette get in a cab with some blond guy. (What? He didn't recognize Dean?!) I found Jack again, and we jumped into a cab back to the Penta.

Corvette was already upstairs. I couldn't bring Jack up there, so he and I hung outside. It was weird out there. People were fucked up, and beers kept hitting the ground and breaking. We were halfheartedly trying to find somewhere to go. I was tired.

Some young kid gave Jack $20, "Buy some beers, have some fun, take the lady to breakfast."

Finally I said, "Either get me outta here, now, or I'm gonna go pass out upstairs."

We got in a cab and went to the Carter. Checked on both of Jack's rooms. They were packed with stray hippies, as expected. Jack kicked people off a bed so we could sleep on it. Icarus was there. And five or six people I didn't know. I didn't care. I had a bed.

Got up around 11AM and called the Penta. Bea and Rachel were still in the room and I had to get my stuff. Jack came with me. I sold Bea the 1/8 I had so luckily gotten. Had to. Couldn't fuckin' afford to keep it.

And now we had nowhere to put our shit. Too much to carry. I swear, I'm gonna bring nothing to Europe. We bumped into Atlanta Angela and she let us put our shit in her truck, over at the park-n-lock.

I can't believe we almost got arrested in the Village last night. The further behind us that event gets the funnier it will be.

Inside

They're doin it again – Rockin the whole place to the rafters. This time with a ragin' *Deal*. Just smoked a fatty with Ozzy and Riley. Now it's Break, and the Fatty Zone is forming around us. Benny is jumping on the seats in a pretend tantrum. Haven't seen a good Fatty Zone in a while.

As Break neared its end, we raced to our good seats. Two guys were bumming. "But Hey, we let you have all 1st set." I was psyched for the *Sam and Dee* opener. I used to laugh that I never heard anyone say, 'I hope they play *Sampson and Delilah* tonight.' But I've thought it all three nights here in New York.

Aiko – that was raging, but too full of Bruce's accordion. Jerry seems to like that Los Lobos sound. It's a different world this close to the band. Seeing their expressions and stuff.

Just finished *Looks Like Rain* and going into *He's Gone*.

Late Night

In some Chinese food place called Wo-Hop with Isaac, Atlanta Mary, Hackmen, King, Merlin, Anjalee, and Martin. This restaurant is good. Open late, very friendly.

The end of the show was nice. They played *Standin on the Moon*. I Love that tune.

To Lindy's. Door Control.

Letting limited folks in, but 'limited' included all of 'us.' We all stood around and told them who could, and couldn't, come in – who was, and wasn't, one of us. They like us – we're the regulars. Though we almost got kicked out for rolling a joint, but the bouncer guy said, "Ah Fuck it, just spend money."

Sept 18 Inside

Kerry got busted selling pot. Izzy got to talk to him by saying she was his wife with no phone, and she wanted to be his one call. He's charged with possession and assaulting an officer. He's such a bliss-ninny, it's hard to imagine him assaulting anyone. At the end of break, Izzy was leaving the show to go see if she could do anything.

I thought the first set was kinda lifeless and I wasn't very into it.

2nd set we came down to our seats with Jack and Riley. *Eyes Estimated Foolish* – Space and a good Jam with Jerry, Bruce, and some guy on wild Drumz with Mickey. Who is that?

Would they do a *Dark Star* without Kerry? Sounds like it could be, but these guys are the biggest teases. I hear there's some special micro-dot around. I believe it, it's getting really weird in here.

Late Night

– outside the Penta. Oh Jah, am I really waiting for Jack?

After the show I went to where James hangs. I sold a few postcards, and he sold out of his Calvin and Hobbes shirts. He came to the Penta with me. Jack told him, "Beware of hippie girls like her." James wanted me to drive home with him, but I thought that would be weird. He's married, and I don't know his wife.

Corvette went with the majority of Indicans to see the Spin Doctors, at the Limelight. Jack is waiting for Murph to come down from upstairs, then who knows. We'll probably go crash at the Carter.

Ivan, Gene Gene, and Doughboy (lookin' like a shady crew), got in a car to take off, and it wouldn't start, so now it's stuck here in front of the Penta, and they jumped in a cab.

Tonight's energy is all too weird for me.

Sept 19   The Dumont.

Everyone's asleep, but Little Jamie let me in. I took a shower. It seems weird in here. I have no idea what's going on. Jamie says it was fucked up here last night, says people were losin' it. King coming out from the other room, looks tweaked. Says, "Just another night of not enough sleep in NY, except this night was full of fucked up shit." They're discussing moving to the Eastgate and getting out of this room. Is it shady?

Possible word is that they're gonna hold Kerry for 72 hours. Benny's up now.

Holy Shit!!!

I just heard what happened... No way.

Rosario died.

Heroin – not an OD. He choked on his vomit. He died like Hendrix. Alcohol, dope and food. I guess it happened just after the show.

No way.

Fuck.   FUCK.

Oh Jah.

Damnit.

Fuckin Heroin.

Fuckin New York.

No wonder it feels weird in here.

Oh Rosario...

I can't believe Ivan, Gene Gene, and Doughboy didn't know when they were outside the Penta. Or were they running from that?

No way.

This sucks.

It's also Benny's b-day today, and a year since Pony died.

What a Bummer this all is.

HEROIN SUCKS!

Another beautiful brother lost to the dark forces. Shit.

Why, Rosario? Why does the world work like it does?

Everything feels tilted and wrong.

2nd set

It's a *Playin* Jam.

Fatty Zone was full during break. They closed 1st set with a Raging *Help Slip Franklin's*.

Kerry's here!!!!

Meredith has a b-day card going around for Benny, and there's a party for him after the show, – in the downstairs private room at Lindy's.

Ship o' Fools. I don't usually like this tune all that much, but the notes and melody seem to fit my mood. Back into *Playin* Jam, and *Uncle John's*. Bruce, please put the accordion away. It sounds odd.

Let it Grow.

"Listen to the thunder shout I AM! I AM! IIIiiiii AMmm!"

They are definitely Hot tonight! Sweet. And a jam with Bob, Jer, and Bruce on his Grand Piano. I wonder what sort of band politics is going on with the Dead as this tour rolls towards the end.

Goin Down the Road.

"Going where the guac buds taste like kind."

5:15AM

I'm in a strange diner with Riley. I don't even know where we are. Everything about these shows is off kilter. The energy is unstable.

At Benny's Penta b-day party, the ceiling fell, due to a flood upstairs. It landed smack on DigDoug's head. Hilarious. We got caught smoking a fatty. The bouncer guy – made us toss it in a ½ empty glass. I tried to get it back – telling him how expensive it was – No go – he threw it down the sink. Oh well, they didn't kick us out. We left at last call. Corvette went back to the room. I went lookin for Jack. Everyone headed to King Tut's WaWa Hut. Benny, Meredith, King, Jeremy, Dragon Dave, Marla, Ethan, Fat Matt (doing quite the party circuit this tour), Dean, Fritz, and some dreadhead who followed us from the Penta.

King Tut's was a hardcore punk club. Jack passed out, and got yelled at. "No nodding off in here!" Also, "no smoking pot!" I made last call there too. Jack was outside, sitting against the wall when I stumbled out with Riley. We were supposedly headed for some afterhours club. Our crew got split up when Benny, Meredith, and company went on ahead, and me, Riley, Jack, King, and Fritz stayed to smoke a joint with some hilarious skinheads. We walked with them to the afterhours club that didn't exist when we finally got to it. Benny and them were milling outside, ready to head for another afterhours address. We let them go. That left King, some chick who followed us, the skinheads, me, Jack, Riley, Dean, Fritz, and the dreadhead. No one knew where they were headed.

Cabs started pulling up. King and that chick jumped in one, Dean and company in another, and me and Riley headed for a third cab. Jack wouldn't get in the cab with us. What the fuck?

Jack and me had some weird conversations tonight – about him not wanting an old lady, and me not wanting to be anyone's old lady. For as much as we agreed, it sounded and felt like we were having a major disagreement. Just this weird NY shit energy I think.

So anyway, me and Riley left and here we are.
Wherever the fuck here is.

Sept 20

It's packed in here. The only ones missing are Jack and Danni. Hundreds of heads got in free. Jack I can see not even trying for a door pop, but Danni shoulda been on that.

"The sun's gonna shine in my back door some day!!"

Bruce Hornsby is kickin ass on the Grand, and ya don't even hear Vince. Bruce plays it up big. Vince doesn't.

Wimmen R Smarter.

Oh man – me and Corvette went to Roy Rogers today and jokingly asked, "Whatever happened to Dollarbill Towerhouse?"

The guy said, "You remember him? From two years ago? Wow. He in jail man. Armed Robbery. 10 counts. Two of em here."

Hackmen, Atlanta Mary, and Isaac all got in on a door pop, so Hackmen went out to sell their tix. Merlin is standing on the stairs watching me write. He looks pretty high, and I don't think he even knows he's staring at me.

When we saw Jack outside, we barely recognized him, – dressed in denim instead of rainbows. He bought us beer, and we went for a walk. He'd just gotten a new Rainbow Warriors T-shirt, and we made him put it on. He also had just bought me and Corvette each a skirt, so he made us put them on. We all changed our clothes in front of a church, while bullshitting with the church security guard. Jack asked me if I wanted to blow off the bar tonight and go to a nice dinner after the show. Definitely.

DARK STAR !!!!!

Sept 21st 1990
Connecticut

At Mom's, listening to Jesse's tape of last night's *Dark Star*. It was out of this world. Enchanting. Wild. Free.

Last night everyone decided to head for Sophie's on 5th and A. I found Jack and was like, "What up? Last I knew, we were gonna blow off the bars and do dinner." He said we still would, but first, he had to go get his stuff. And he ran off. He came back tweaked about losing his backpack in a van that was headed for Canada. He was totally bummed and pretty well drunk. He wanted to stay in front of the Penta because he lost his stuff. As if that would help to get his pack back from a van that had left already. I finally talked him into a cab, with Beatnik Bill, and we headed to Sophie's.

Jack was in a rotten mood. He'd gotten a message, from Rosemary, – his mom was in the hospital, and not doing well. He was pissed off about the attitude he says people give him these days, and didn't want to go where "they" all were. And he kept mumbling about me leaving him on a NY street corner last night. He and I were arguing about everything. He made the cabbie change directions two times, but we ended up at Sophie's nonetheless. Half the crew was already moving on to King Tut's.

We called it a night. Me, Jack, and Beatnik Bill went to the Carter. Jack didn't want to deal with those already packed rooms, so he bought another room. Him and Bill both passed right out. I was pretty drunk too, but I wrote Jack a note. I left it, and the bud he had me holding on to, and his necklace on the table next to the bed and I left.

Walking out the door at 7AM, don't know when I'll see him again. Don't know why it got so weird. People staring at me, totally bug-eyed. Everyone I saw seemed to be wearing grey. I enjoyed being colorful, and looked at like I was from another planet, bouncing down 43rd Ave in my tye-dye, on a NY morning. I got coffee and went to the Eastgate. Woke Corvette up quietly and we left. Went to Grand Central Station and took a train to New Haven.

Met a guy on the train. In NY to see the Spanish consulate because he's moving to Madrid. They were closed so he figured he'd try to get in to the Dead show. He'd never seen them before. He found a $25 ticket. (I didn't know they existed last night.) It was for a sky box, and all the free beer you could drink. Then some woman showed up in the sky box and handed out floor seats that turned out to be right in front of Phil. This guy was glowin', and lovin it, and couldn't stop talking about how wonderful it all was. That kind of interaction always sets me straight about my own priorities.

35
Europe Tour 1990
Amsterdam, Stockholm, and Essen

Oct 9   Amsterdam

Freddy's plane landed about the same time as ours. When he came bouncing through the gate we took the train to Central Station. We met Cecilia in the Square, recruiting guests for a hostel. We've got a private room – 35 guilders per person, per night – huge room, but disappointing. This place is a fleabag. Smells like bug spray or somethin' gross. Corvette's quote of the moment, "I hope all the rich men on tour didn't bring girls with them."

Gotta go trade some greenbacks for psychedelic gilders and check out the city.

Evening

We walked down some street I can't even remember how to say, let alone spell. Bus-like trains, cars, bikes, and pedestrians all share the roads. No sidewalk. Streets of zigzag inlaid bricks. Bright green phone booths. Incredible architecture.

Freddy and Corvette went out. I'm lounging in our room. I feel – iiihhh. Jet-lag I guess. I just want to lay around and get stoned.

I'd be a liar if I said I wasn't a bit intimidated here. I hate not being able to read signs, understand announcements, or distinguish street names.

Oct 10

I went out last night and met this guy Gerry at a pub. Gerry went AWOL from the Navy. After three years he turned himself in saying, "I've been here in SF high on acid for three years and the other day someone told me I was supposed to be in the Navy still. That can't be true, can it?" Ha.

We smoked (what else do ya do in Amsterdam?), and when the place closed, I found Freddy, Corvette, and Original Bob out in the Square. We ended up in the Hard Rock. This is an Indican's dream town.

Back at the hotel, we set up our crystal table and crashed.

I woke in the middle of the night to Freddy, "I want to go to Murder Point." He was squinting at a framed map on the wall in our room and lighting a fatty. I was back asleep by the time it was a roach.

Me and Corvette talked to Cecilia for a while today. She's from Australia. She bought Corvette's black skull necklace, and the Morning Wand, for 200 guilders. Cheap prices, but at least it gave us some more money.

We walked to 'Homegrown Fantasies.' They have a great menu, with sample baggies, and pictures of the buds before they're picked. Such a selection!

We don't yet know how we'll get to Stockholm.

~~~~~

Streets are boisterous, and somewhat dangerous. Today we saw two bicycles collide in front of a Tram. They sort of bounced off each other, out of the way, and after the Tram went by, they puffed each other up like pillows and went their separate ways. Polite.

And that's how Police is spelled. "Oh look, there's the Polite."

Lots of folks took the Eurorail to Copenhagen tonight. I hear the trains are booked solid already. We considered the car rental thing with a bunch of other sisters, but it's too expensive. I guess our plan is to hitch. We'll leave tomorrow morning. Two days oughta be enough time to hitch to Stockholm.

~~~~~

Went down a side street following a sign for the Easy Times Rasta Café. It was a Reggae place with Bob Marley posters on every wall. Everything was red, green, or yellow. There was no kind bud on their Menu so we had hot chocolate, and smoked a fatty of skunk B with the bartender. He was like, "Wow, no tobacco."

Oct 11 1990   night

We're still in Amsterdam. And that was not the plan.

Me and Corvette got out of the hotel at a reasonable hour today. Walked to Homegrown Fantasies. It wasn't open yet, so we sat outside eating yogurt and granola. Who comes walkin' up but Anton and Gitch. Yeah! Few minutes more, and here's Freddy. Stylin! When they opened, we had a big ole Fatty Circle. It was fun, but me and Corvette left so we could hitch to Stockholm.

At Central Station, we got our maps and got the subway to the A-1 highway. We sat on the exit ramp for three hours with our "Stockholm and/or Copenhagen" sign. It was fuckin cold and windy. No luck at all. Unbelievable. Three different guys yelled angry things at us, but we've no idea what they said. That's fuckin frustrating. Two people pulled over, then drove off before we got to the car. And some folks swerved at us. What the fuck? After getting way disheartened, we took the tram back to Central Station. Decided to look for rent-a-car heads, and found Pino. He's one of those 'together' heads like Aaron or Spencer. Surprised he didn't have a Eurorail. We got a decent rate, – 169 guilders a day – unlimited miles – but ya need a credit card. Pino had plenty of cash to cover a deposit, but no. Credit cards only. Too bad we lost track of Anton and Gitch.

We made our way back to the hostel only to find it was full. Oh no. What to do? Just then Matteo and Katarina walked into the lobby. They had the private room we had last night. It was cool with them, so the night desk guy let us crash in there.

Saved by Indicans.

Went out for fettuccini that wasn't good (no food has impressed me in this town – where's King Henry to tell us where to eat?) and bumped into Shane out on the street.

We're at the Easy Times Rasta Café. We're all tired, listening to the rasta tunes, smokin' and drinkin. Aaah how we torture ourselves. Shane looks like he's gonna fall in his beer. He's got his head propped up on his arm, yet he's totally asleep. Jet-lagged, and stoned. Corvette thinks we should take a picture of him right now, and blow it up to give out for Christmas. We'll label it "Fatty-igue."

We have got to get to Stockholm. It would cost us as much to live, and stay in Amsterdam, as it would to go to Sweden. Maybe we'll hafta get Eurorail passes. – I don't know. I'm grabbing at strings. One will pull me through to Sweden. I'm sure of it.

Oct 12

On a train, headed for Germany. To make it in time at this point, we have to change trains five times, but we're gonna make it!

We got Eurorail passes in Utrecht this morning, where they are supposedly cheaper than elsewhere. Seven days travel, in a month, for 200^{ish}.

Late Night:

A brokedown train left 30 or 40 of us stranded at the Hamburg Train Station for four hours. Everyone lounged out on their luggage, tunes blaring, thanks to Shane's boombox, with

Germans staring at us and our stuff. What looks we got! Some brave ones sat down to talk, others hurried by like we were contagious. A couple people asked, "What are you, some sort of tour group?" We said yes, but it's not likely we had the same sort of tour in mind. A traveling couple from Canada had no idea there was a Dead Tour going on. They dropped their packs, sat down, and joined us. Some hippie walked up, loud and animated, "I bet no one can beat this. I flew into Switzerland and thought it was Sweden. Anyone want some Swiss chocolate?" We gave him a round of applause.

Oct 13

Woke in the middle of the night; our train was parked. It was surreal, stepping out of the train car into a warehouse full of train cars. We were on a huge Ferry. I found stairs. Bank, Post Office, Cafeteria, Water Closets, and Lounges. Went up another level, to the deck. What a view! And there was Orion. Hadn't seen Orion in a long time.

Now we're in Sweden, with five or six hours till Stockholm. We're in one of those little six-seat compartments with Gitch and Anton. Katarina is in the compartment next door. Turns out she's a local. She grew up in Sweden.

                        Inside Stockholm
                        land of gorgeous blonds.

About to start.

A whole trainful of Heads exploded out of the train station following Katarina, and her sister, who met her there. The sister kept looking over her shoulder, and, I bet, asking something like, "Are all these people WITH you?"

Not sure we'd have found the place without locals to guide us. We got here just in time to get our tickets and come inside. We met Robert Hunter's mom, waiting for her pass at the backstage door.

Some guy proposed to Corvette as soon as we walked in the door.

Sounds like *Hey Pocky Way* but, it couldn't be… – nope, it's *Cold Rain and Snow*. No Bruce on stage. This place is so unpacked.

Bad story about Tricky. He got thrown off the train somewhere in Germany for having a fake Eurorail pass. Shit. I hope he's okay. Saw Benny. Marla. Neil and Winnie. Schmitty. And Gypsy Linda!!!!

Feel Like a Stranger. Perhaps this one is for Benny – he's melting down pretty heavily right now.

Candyman.

Found Yes Ma'am Sam, Kevin, Seth, and Accidental Mary. Cooool.

The sound is weird – maybe because it's not full in here.
~~Minglewood~~ nope *Walkin Blooze*
Loser
Queen Jane
Bird Song
Promised Land – What a Blowout.
Swedish is such a weird language.
This is such a goof! Look where we are!
Wow and Wow again! Kevin has a joint. Yah Mon!
Freddy is having fun freakin' with the locals in the hall.
~~~~~

We had to work through break because we were late. It was a short break, but it was a bummer to work and not just hang out.
Touch O'
Estimated
There's more beautiful blue-eyed guys here than I've ever seen in one place, but I've never seen a show with so few people dancin'. They watch, more than participate, and most Swedes look like they'd never be able to dance freely.
Crazy Fingers
We're gonna blast right after the show with Gitch and Anton. Only a Deadhead could travel 24 hours for a show, and turn around to go 24 hours back. I've had my dose of Swedish blue eyes, and Swedish high prices. I'd better go, before my heart, and my pocket, are broke. Oh, and these Swedes! They bum cigarettes like fiends. Even if they speak no other English, they can say, "got a cigarette?"
Playin', and Phil is soundin' great. We saw him drive in tonight. I "peaced" him, and he gave the thumbs up.
This is a really fun Drumz, and the Swedes are Lovin' it. The smell of hash is abundant.
An article appeared in the Stockholm paper about us this morning. Can't read it myself, but the word is it was a bad one. Said wherever the Dead goes, there's LSD in the elementary schools for months afterwards. That's so much Bullshit. They don't even know.
Space, and I'm gonna.

Oct 15

Left the show right after it ended and jumped on a local train back to the station where our stuff was in a locker. We booked a train to Goteburg, Copenhagen, then Cologne, – Taking the long way back to Amsterdam, because the cars going direct were full, and we were able to get reservations on these. Between the local train station and the other one, we got lost by a couple blocks – we're laughin about confused hippies swarming through the streets of Stockholm. We were ten minutes late, and thought we missed it. Some heads said, "If you wanna get on the train you'd better hurry!"

"What train?"

They pointed. "That one."

We jumped on it, having no idea what train it was. Of course it was the right one. Had to buy sleepers, but it was cheaper than a Swedish hotel would have been. We managed to snag showers in the Goteburg station between trains.

Got to Kobenhavn about 3 yesterday, or maybe it was noon. I don't know. But we had to wait till 9:05PM for our next train. Also at 9:05 was the train straight to Amsterdam – same train even – cars split at different stops, and go to different cities. With so much time to wait in Copenhagen, the four of us went bar-hoppin'. We were drinking 7.8 beers, and shots of Jägermeister. The cheapest place we found to drink was a porn bar. Got pretty drunk, and had a lot of laughs. Talking about the Swedes, and how some seemed bored by the show. Anton says, "They were born bored."

"Born Bored? Isn't that a tennis player?"

When we stumbled back to the Station, our train was packed full. We shared our little room with two Japanese Heads who came from Japan for tour. We sprawled all over each other and passed out.

There was a chick sleeping in the luggage rack outside our car. I suspect that's what Anton was thinking when he got up and said, "I'm going to find somewhere to stretch out." Come morning, we go looking for him, to make sure he gets off at the right place, and he's nowhere to be found. There's only so many places you can be on a train. We have his backpack, his fanny pack, his sweater, his shoes, even his passport. Youch. I hope he's laughing too. It <u>is</u> kinda funny.

I am so tired. It's so much work to get around.

Later – Homegrown Café

Found Anton here. Socks blackened. He'd gone to sleep on a luggage rack in a car that came straight to Amsterdam. Gitch was funny as he shouldered both their backpacks. "I told him not to pack so much! I knew I'd end up carrying all his stuff!"

Saw Tricky outside Central Station, so we can stop worrying about him. Said he spent almost all his money to get from where he got thrown off the train to here, and he wasn't sure what he's gonna do next. Freddy heard about some guy that got busted with a small bit of pot by the German border guards – he got a $50 fine and got put back on the train. A better outcome than having a fake Eurorail.

Corvette bought the last of the skunk-B. We smoked it with Anton, Gitch, Atlanta Mary, Freddy, Gypsy Linda, Cliff, and Shane.

It was a rough trip to Sweden but we made it. Feel like I accomplished something, like we all did.

Inside – Bruce Hornsby Show
Paradisio.

Wild little place. It's sold out, and hot in here. Anton and Gitch gave us their extras, and Benny paid our membership charge. – $3 to buy a membership card – can't come into the Paradiso without one. Bruce is ok. He did *Masterpiece* pretty badly, but some of his own shit is pleasant.

There was a wingnut chick in the Homegrown today. Didn't say much except, "are you writing a book?" real enthusiastically. We think she was tripping. Sometimes she'd smoke with us, and sometimes not, and when she did, she'd hold the joint a long time staring into space. When her boyfriend went to sit, she pulled his chair away and he fell on the floor. She laughed hysterically.

We ate at the Egg Cream – a recommended semi-veggie restaurant. It wasn't bad, I had an omelet. At the Rasta bar next door they were funny. Regulars it seemed, but they said they'd only been open three days. They were pushy at first. Like scamming, "Buy this, or this," or "Hey, hey, look at this – I got a special price just for you." After a few minutes the commotion of us being there died down, and they settled back into their chairs. It was like a TV show. Jamaican Cheers. A gorgeous Rasta Man, with long dreads, came in and put up a poster of his band – playing on Halloween. We laughed, "It's like a preview to a future episode."

Becky is here with Devon. They flew into Frankfurt the other day.

I don't think Jerry will show up here tonight, like everyone hoped.

Oct 17 1990

On the train to Essen, with Mojo playing his mandolin. It's wet and rainy. Yes Ma'am Sam and Fritz, are in the box next door. Fritz flew in yesterday. We first saw him just now. He mushed me against the window as a greeting. We burned a fatty out in the hall.

Lots of folks did the museum thing yesterday, or the Heineken brewery thing, but we just smoked our pot, and did some beading during the day.

At night we went to the Melkweg to try to get in free for U-Roy. It wasn't lookin too good. Most people out there said it wasn't possible, but we stood around anyway. Cliff and Gypsy Linda were there, and Anton and Gitch. Eventually two overtired heads sold us two tix, including memberships for 10 guilders.

Tiny place. I can't quite imagine the Dead playing there. Some Moroccan guy tried to pick us up. He bought us beers. Linda had one, me and Corvette had two. Linda could talk to him a bit in French. Some Canadian guy talked to him in Spanish. Canadian guy joked about how he could change the interpretations and we wouldn't even know. We got the Moroccan guy to take a hit off a joint. After a while though, he got to be a problem. He kept trying to get me to leave with him. I told him, "Look, I understand what you are asking, and no thank you." Shaking my head and trying to say it with my eyes.

Still he followed us till Corvette, hands flying, eyes flashing mad, "No. No. No. Go away – Fini!"

Linda joked later that she was ready to tell him, "Look, I may be a pacifist, but I WILL kill you."

This morning we went to Chocolate Bakery. Yes Ma'am Sam was there. He fed us Space Cakes and Hash Truffles.

Inside

Essen is great! This place isn't sold out, but it's got a good bunch in here.

It was a twenty minute ride to the Grugehalle and the place was right up the stairs from the metro stop. Everyone was burning on the trains and there's plenty of smokables here! But no one has any Club papers!

Nice show so far.

Postcards sold well, and we got tix from Jory. Gonna work during break, but I think it'll be fun. Germans are into the Dead.

The scene outside was cool. A few locals, some German hippie vans, and some rent-a-vans, acting as hippie vans. Everyone set up, selling stuff – a friendly atmosphere.

And we found Helena! Yeah! She's so psyched to see us here. She's been traveling Germany in an old VW mail truck, selling tye-dyes. She lives in it, just like we do in America. It looked like a stylin mobile. We stashed our shit in her van.

We found Ryan and Lila, then we found my beautiful hitchhiker James and his wife Megan looking for riders so us four will ride to Berlin with them in their rent-a-station-wagon.

WOOO *Maggie's Farm*!

~~~~~

Had to dance for *Maggie's Farm*. They all did a verse in this order – Bob, Jerry, Bruce, Vinnie, and Phil. After, I said to Corvette, "That's the first kick of the Europe tour."

A German near us, dancin', and obviously lovin' it, asked, "This is the first kick? Did they not kick in Berlin already?"

"No. No Berlin yet. They played Stockholm last weekend, and they'll be kickin' in Berlin in two days."

Phil keeps waving to his kid. (I heard he broke his leg in Sweden.)

2nd Set

Fatty Zone is by the stage. Phil's side of course.

~~~~~

Marla and Dean have backstage passes because they sold buds to the band! Hoo-ha! Jerry wanted it, but didn't dare bring it.

Absolutely Wailing *Miracle* Jam into *Black Peter*.

Oct 18

Germany looks so neat and tidy. Yes, tidy is the perfect word.

Stoned again, ridin' down the Autobahn with James and Megan. We just passed a hippie bus!!!! I'm psyched we get to do some vehicle cruisin' through Europe. The Autobahn is wild. Lots of construction and the workers wave tiny little flags when someone steps out into the road. No speed limit.

After the show was a typical late night lot scene, on a much smaller scale. A drum circle, and people wondering what they're doing. We had to wait for James and Megan – they had shit to do – and we had to get Lila and Ryan's stuff from some random train station. We never left the scene till late.

What a joke trying to find a hotel. Anything that'll speak to us in English at 4AM is expensive. We ended up at a Rasthof (Rest Area). Lila and Ryan set up their tent behind a tree. We four slept in the car.

36
Europe Tour 1990
Berlin, Frankfurt, Amsterdam Again

Oct 19

Morning in a hotel in West Berlin. Scammed the American way – six people in a two person room. What a time we had finding this place.

We crossed the border, into East Germany, like it wasn't even there. I guess it wasn't actually, just lots of closed-down, dark, stark buildings. East Germany looked less tidy than the west. We wanted to find a room before Berlin, so we got off the Autobahn in Magdeburg. No rooms there. In the tiny town of Zeisar, a small hotel with a family eating. The guy was ready to make room for me and Megan, but when he heard us say "six", he grabbed his head, wild-eyed, "nein, nein."

When we got to Berlin, because we were on back roads, we entered the city from the East German side. We kept passing the 'East Side Gallery' – a mile or more of beautiful murals about freedom and world peace, painted on the Berlin Wall, but we couldn't find the way over, or through, the Wall. Asked some locals, and those who spoke English didn't have the right words to tell us what we needed to know. So they'd tell us in German, and James would say, 'yes yes,' as if he knew what they said. We'd drive off laughing, because we still had no idea how to get anywhere. We had a map even locals couldn't make any sense of. They'd squint at it, and spin it, and squint smaller, and shake their heads. We eventually threw it out the car window in a fit of laughter. As we drove in circles, truly unable to find our way to West Berlin, we saw the Polize, so we pulled up behind them to ask directions. During that split-second, when they jumped out of their car headed for ours, all stiff-walking, with trenchcoats and clomping boots, they looked like the SS coming at us. My heart stopped, as if they would search us, looking for something we didn't have. (Except I did have a small bud hidden in my boot.) It was a moment drenched in all the panic, fear and helplessness of history, as if our entire futures revolved around this moment. What a feeling. Yikes.

When we asked how to get to West Berlin, they pointed at us and laughed, saying, over and over to each other, "Americans! Ahahaha!"

A relief at first, but it went on long enough to become annoying. They finally showed us how to get to the crossover bridge – the entrance of which was a couple blocks away from the Wall. We'd have never found it ourselves.

The hotel search was a bitch. Just like it happens in the US, but not in a familiar language. All very hilarious, except we wanted sleep. We finally saw a huge hotel so we tried it – awfully expensive. Hotels charge by the person here. As we turned to leave, a businessman caught our attention, "Are you going to the show?" He's from Denver – here for some home-building convention. Mr. Businessman told us we'd have no problem buying a room for two, and all of us sleeping in it. He bought postcards from us, and a shirt from James.

Berlin   Inside.

Wonderful outside scene again. Really mellow. We did great selling postcards, and we've got orchestra seats tonight – the lights just went out.

~~~~~

I can see Jerry's Hula Skeleton up close. Some big, red-headed kid, who goes to school in Austria, just smoked some kind buds with me.

This place is shaped weird – it's gotta be pretty new. It's small inside, and our seats are like school desks with little attached tables.

The floor is rocking, literally. It's kinda weird with the sound sort of behind me.

Phil has his eyes closed most of the time.

<center>2nd set</center>

Break was fun – even working, handing out flyers for Brokham.

Fire now, and I'm leaning on the stage to write. Seth was about to smoke a joint with me when some goon showed up and stood right between us. There's quite a few Indicans in this up-front Phil corner. It's packed up here. They have no control, but it's ok – we have it all under control.

That *Scarlet/Fire* was hot!

I guess we'll go to East Berlin tonight with Benny, Fritz, Shane, Marla, and a few more. They got a weird, but cool-sounding, situation. See, there's all these empty tenement housing projects in East Berlin, because when the Wall opened up, most folks this close to the border left. Now they're functioning like hotels.

The goon left. Seth just handed me the joint. It's *Terrapin* now and it sounds perfectly sweet.

late night

Fritz and Benny's room sounded too full, so we tagged along with Kevin, Freddy, and Little Jamie, to the Hotel President. Seth and Accidental Mary are in the room next door.

Helena came here with us. She has Seth melting, because she can communicate with people. "Talk German to me." Seth says, every few minutes, with dreamy eyes.

Little Jamie has her teaching him phrases like, "Do you want to go have a beer?" I'm glad she came with us. We haven't partied with her in too long. I love Helena.

Today, before the show, some guy was scalping tix for 100 marcs. Cost was 52 marcs. Shane grabbed the guy's briefcase and ran. When the guy almost caught up to him, Shane tossed it into this opening in the square that looks down on the taxi stand and parking lot. That briefcase hit the ground and exploded – poof – there were Dead tix everywhere – lots of em – for every show – floating in little wind tornados all over the ground. Then they were gone.

Now the ½ way bad part of this story – This is one of the guys who arranged Tour packages and managed to get bulk tickets. He had the tickets, for the rest of tour, belonging to his tour group – plus a bunch of extras for every show. He was scalping the extras. I'd probably sue him for being such a dumb fuck and taking chances with my already-paid-for tix, that he, as a business, is responsible for.

It's 3AM and this room is still ragin'. Little Jamie is headed out the door to use his new German phrases.

Oct 20 Berlin – Inside

German hotels have never seen the likes of Deadheads, – the concept of more people per room than the amount of beds, just doesn't enter their minds.

Kevin bought us lunch. Nice restaurant. Put us in the corner, just like they do in the US. I had broccoli soup, which I had to skim the veal pieces off. Yuk.

Just finishing the best *Jack Straw* I've seen in years. This bouncing floor is outta hand. We're in the 4th row – Jerry's side. Getting high with Gypsy Linda and Cliff.

All over this town Deadheads have spread. As tourists, as vendors, as bringers of good vibes. The locals are friendly. Last night Little Jamie met some local guy who drove a bunch of them all over East Berlin. And locals also made sure there was plenty of hash here today.

Anton and Gitch got us high with a soda can as a bowl – no one carries a pipe in Germany.

Berlin is an interesting city. There's sculpture everywhere. One of my favorites is the huge golden Angel in the middle of a Rotary. Buildings have gargoyles, and faces, and men dying in angel's arms. There's a church, bombed in WWII, – it's the only bombed building they left standing – to remember what happened to Berlin. It's stark and important.

Walkin Blooze – usually my cue to take a walk, but I'm not leaving this seat.

~~~~~

Somebody yelled, "*Black Throated* Bobbeeeee" a mere second before they broke into it.

Break

After *Let it Grow* was a magical Jam. Quiet throughout the place, and just the soft sound of tinkling keys and/or guitars, it was spell-binding. Bruce looked to be in another world. Then I saw Bob look at Phil – "What do ya think?" and they broke into *Box o' Rain*.

How long has it been since I've seen folks sitting on the stage during break?

Oct 22   Inside Frankfurt

Lots of Military Police here. We just had to put the fatty out.

Me and Corvette rode here with Helena. Jah what bad traffic! Helena says since the wall opened, everyone goes to Berlin to party on the weekends and we were

~~~~~~~~~~~ !!!!!!!!!!!!!!!

I was gonna say stuck in the stau – Jam. A word Helena made me learn. But someone majorly bumped my arm, "Excuse me."

I said, "No problem," and looked up. It was Hackmen!!!!!!! He and Silas flew in today!!!!!!! I loved the way Hackmen got my attention!

The Fatty Zone is to my right. The place is a huge General Admission floor, and reserved balcony that we can't get to.

I got to do some German driving through a nice sunset yesterday. Too bad VWs don't go much faster than 100 kph so we couldn't take full advantage of the autobahn's limitlessness!

Got to Frankfurt last night. Parked across from the Hall, and slept in Helena's van. This morning we walked to the train station for the bathroom. Some chick was shaving her face and shooting up, while talking to the matron. Then the matron lady yelled at <u>ME</u> for scamming into a Water Closet without paying my 50¢!

Outside it was cold and windy. We asked Jory if we could work before the show and just walk in with him. He said sure, but the goon at the gate spoke no English and wouldn't let anyone by, even though Jory kept saying, "They're with me." Then he said, "What if they have these?" and pulled out backstage passes. It worked, but we had to put them on. Jory asked us please not to go back there. Said it's too small, and besides, "ya need someone with a laminate to walk ya in, even with a pass." We could find a laminate if we wanted to, but I suppose we shouldn't. It's like giving a kid an ice cream cone to hold, and telling him he's gotta let it melt on his hand and can't eat it.

Oct 23

Frankfurt show was good and fun. Afterwards we got our stuff from Helena's van and went to the train station with Ryan and Lila. We spaced around for a few hours, smoking with Cannoli Ron, and a tourhead named Dondi, that I've never partied with before. I still sometimes get a bit skitzed at the idea of sitting around a public place, in Germany, getting stoned. I mean sure we do it in America but...

There were as many weird people outside Frankfurt train station as there is outside Grand Central in the middle of the night. Even worse when we took the escalator down towards what looked like it'd be a good place to smoke. The lower station was full of Aqualung-looking people – dirty faces, ripped trenchcoats, and dragging legs. They started coming at us like zombies and we barely got on the up escalator fast enough to escape them.

As it started getting light, we headed for the hell-train to Amsterdam. And hell-train it was. For a while we were in an empty hallway, but after two hours, we got kicked back into a packed car. Later they packed it even more by dropping cars that were full of Deadheads and making everyone move into already over-packed cars. It was pretty bad. Worst I've seen yet.

Got to Amsterdam and had fatties and coffee with Benny and Shane as they went to crash at their hostel. We went to crash too, but we crashed in Vondel park in the sun for a few hours.

Went to the Homegrown when we woke up. Bought some pot and when deciding where to sit, we nodded to each other, "The kid with the hair."

His name is Nadav. He's 17 and homeless. He sleeps regularly in Vondel park. He asked us about our world. The more we said, the more light came into his eyes. So... After a series of minor trials not worth mentioning, we are on the train to Hamburg.

Nadav is with us.

37
Europe Tour 1990
Hamburg, Paris, London

Oct 24

Sportshalle, Hamburg. 10AM.

Almost no-one here. Maybe 20 people? It's like the old Dead days must have been. Nadav went to check out Hamburg, Lila is beading. Corvette is asleep on the sidewalk. I might do that too. It's nice and sunny, with hardly any breeze, so it's warmish.

late night

This place was a small, brick building, reminiscent of a large High School Auditorium. The Fatty Zone was behind the rafters on Phil's side. I hung there most of the night, though I went down on the floor, with Silas and Hackmen, for *Help on the Way*. Nadav dosed. He wanted to make the best of it. We brought him to the right people. He smiled all night. I brought him up close to see drums, since he plays drums. Afterwards, we fattied in the train station. Proud feeling – fattying in a German train Station.

We tried to get Nadav a ride back to Amsterdam with Gene Gene the Dancing Machine and his crew, because they had a car. Nadav has no money and had to get back for work, but they didn't want to feel responsible. We took a chance and put him on the 3 o'clock to Amsterdam, – the hell-train – with Hackmen, Anton, Gitch, and Silas. It was too packed for us to consider, though we don't know what we'll do tonight. This café is closing.

As they headed off toward the train, Nadav looked back, grinning, "Thank You."

Oct 25

Me and Corvette took a train to Köln. It was empty, – we slept! Got to Köln at 9AM. Seven minutes till the Amsterdam train!

We made it. Another empty train and we slept more. Got to Amsterdam at 1:30. "Last stop – get off."

Found Nadav at the Homegrown. He told us a confusing story. "One minute I was with the police. And then I was with your friends again. I do not know what happened." He also didn't know where any of them were.

We hung out with him and his friend, Gypsy. Every time we've ever been in the Homegrown, Gypsy's been there in his snake skin pants, black vest, greased back hair. He'd laughed that Nadav was going with us. Today he asked, "Was good? This concert?"

The Paris concerts came up in conversation. We joked to Nadav about going with us, and he said slowly, "I am thinking about it."

Gypsy scowled, "What you do to make my friend follow you?"

He pulled Nadav away for a walk. Nadav was like, "I will see you later, yes?"

We said, "Yes, of course."

Gypsy growled at us, "My friend take walk with me. You no need follow. He follow me now."

Oct 26

Morning – Paris. Slept on the train. Never found Silas and them in Amsterdam. Didn't see Nadav again either.

Kevin, Seth, and Accidental Mary smoked a joint with us by the truck exit. I needed that. Seth is in line for hotel reservations and they're gonna let us tag along.

Ah Paris! Francs now. No more Guilders or Marcs.

Oct 27   Inside Paris

1st night. On Phil's side. As close as possible. What a smoker! Wailing hard. Buzzed. Been drinking with Henrik and Stuart all day. Henrik is a guy we met at Jazz Fest a couple years ago.

Masterpiece even!

Bird Song, and I made it to the hall where I can see the page. Kona Paul just got in on a miracle. He's lovin it. I guess tonight is a hard ticket.

Henrik and Stuart met us at the Bastille. We had coffee, then got beer and cruised Pari! We went to Jim Morrison's grave at Pére Lachaise Cemetery. (I saw Oscar Wilde's grave too!) There was a small party gathered around Jim's grave. Just a rectangular rock at the end of a patch of dirt. We cruised the Eiffel tower. Henrik and Stuart are fun. Stuart won't let us pay for anything. We got our tix from Jory and gave Henrik and Stuart the ones we had gotten via mail order. (Stuart tried to pay for them but we wouldn't let him.)

Saw Freddy as soon as we came in and hooked him with Henrik and Stuart – they're both smiling big.

Promised Land!

Break

Got the story from Hackmen and Silas of what happened with Nadav. The train got raided – looking for free-ride scammers. They got Nadav and took him, along with all the Spinners and such, and marched them off through the train station for punishment/processing/something. We'd left Nadav in their care so they knew they had to do something. As the line of freeloaders passed a stairwell, Hackmen pushed Nadav out of the line and towards a short flight of stairs, where Silas and company were waiting to catch him. Hackmen took his place in line, and when they got to processing he said simply, "I have no idea why I'm in this group, here's my Eurorail pass right here."

Oct 28

Going to Silas and Hackmen's hostel last night, we lost track of time. Then. Oh No! The hostel has a 1AM curfew! We got there a few minutes after 1:00, but the nice family that runs the place let us in. They loved their job, and life. You could tell.

Not like the place next door. They also had a 1AM curfew, but would let no-one in, just minutes past one. He wouldn't even let people get their stuff, and he started throwing water out the window at them. He maced Katarina, and others, who were in the street trying to get someone to throw down their backpacks. Our people made us stop looking out the window – said that only makes it worse. It was nasty, wet, and cold, and late into the night we heard heads screaming about needing their fucking shoes. Atlanta Mary and Ethan made it through the night inside, but they were awakened with guns, and screaming, "Get your shit and get out!" There was a fight. They punched Mary. And Ethan was kicking them. Yikes.

As we left our happy little place (after a pleasant breakfast of coffee and baguettes) there were heads outside talking about going to the consulate. Their stuff was still inside and no-one would answer the door.

Inside Paris

Henrik and Stuart came to the show again. They found us inside, and Dante did em up. Henrik says he is not high at all. Stuart looks too high. That kind of thing can happen when you're eating pieces of a $5 bill. Should have waited till we found Freddy again.

This place is like a little bowl. It's very small and very cool. And the Dead has been playing so sweet. Freddy likens the crowd to a haystack waiting for a match. The hallway has chain link walls, and everyone's stuff is hung to dry.

Hackmen is calling the Bruce moves already. "Accordion. Does that mean *Uncle John's*?" Yes. But Yikes. I am not always into the accordion. I thought his little solo there just sounded 'off.'

My clothes are still wet. I always knew Paris would be wet.

Oct 29

On a packed train towards Bologne.

What a night!

Heading for Yes Ma'am Sam's hotel room with Benny and Fritz after the show, we bumped into this wild playground-park-thing. Neon designs on the ground and weird Pan-Flute sounds coming out of pipes. Then we found a dragon. A huge thing with climbable back and a tongue that was a slide. Deadheads were lovin it, climbing and playing on everything. A huge mirrored ball was a clock, playing music to count off the minutes, seconds, and hours. Cool shit. Corvette, Fritz and Benny disappeared around a corner to check out a submarine. I took a few steps to see where they went.

Splash!

I didn't even see the water. What a joke. Fritz was absolutely rolling on the ground laughing. I told him I did it just for him. I'd gone in up to my chest. Everything soaked. My coat. Boots. Everything.

At the hotel bar, because all my stuff was in a train station locker, everyone gave me different bits of their clothes so I could get out of the wet shit.

later

We had to wait two hours in a little coastal French town. I was glad for the time to find a laundromat. Ha! My boots and coat clunking around in a French dryer, while small town French folks looked at us sideways. I just smiled and shrugged.

Now we're on the Hovercraft. What a machine! Amazing to see it crawl right out of the water and onto the land.

We're nearing Dover. Ahhh the white cliffs.

Nightime – London

Queen of England Pub. Had no problems through customs. No one even looked at us. We had no idea what we were gonna do, then this woman appeared, "'Commodations?" in a thick British accent.

Edie was taking people to her house for 8 pounds a night. We decided to go with her when we saw Palmer was going too. We always see Palmer by the backstage doors, he's friends with Bill Kruetzmann. Palmer smoked his last skinny with us, and we came here to the Queen's Pub. He's buying us beers and says we're funny.

Oct 30   Wembley 1st set.

Londoners are so fuckin' rude. Fuck. I don't like it here. This place sucks. There's a huge hallway on the floor, but they keep clearing out the dancers. Sorry folks, no dancing? Get real.

No one wanted the flyers we have to hand out and they were rude as shit. It doesn't help not being stoned all day. But that's being taken care of now. While handing out flyers, security tried to arrest me. Like, actually arrest me. Said I didn't have permission. I told him I work for Brokham. He said the Dead doesn't have permission. Apparently it costs to hand shit out because of the garbage it creates. Makes sense to me. But I'm not getting' in trouble over that shit.

Oh well. I feel a little bit better now that I'm stoned.

~~~~~

The floor is sticky, and there's huge bolts that suck to dance on.

Bruce is doing a Grand Piano solo now at the end of *Let it Grow*. Bruce is great on the Grand.

Nov 1st

At the Hilton last night, we went with Dean to his room to get stoned. In the elevator was a bus boy, and the conversation went like this:

Dean: "Sold out tonight, eh?"

Busboy: "Yes. We have."

Dean, "We usually sell out all the hotels wherever we go."

Me, "We're great for a local economy."

Busboy, "We don't need you."

Dean, "What? The Grateful Dead?"

Busboy, "Every year the Dead comes here and people run out on their bills."

All three of us – "Dude, the Grateful Dead hasn't come to Europe since 1981."

Busboy, "Well, Americans... It's happening already."

Later, in the bar, some frat boy threw a glass as hard as he could at the wall. Guess who they'll blame that on? The staff didn't make any effort to clean it up, so finally a bunch of heads cleaned it.

Yesterday Edie heard some of us say that we had no Halloween costumes and brought us to an old Ambulance stocked full of used clothes, – like our 'for sale' stuff. She had bags and bags of it. We couldn't pull it out on the streets though, so we had to get in on top of those bags. We had fun digging through it. She had so much funky stuff, we convinced her to go to the show and sell some of it for Halloween costumes.

We all headed down there in her old Ambulance – including two chicks who were staying at Edie's illegal boarding house. They're Israeli – named Sheee-a and Oh-lee (who knows how those names are spelled).

We helped Edie sell clothes. Katarina made some great scores. Even Freddy got his costume from us. Edie made like 20 pounds and she got a free ticket from a friend of Kevin's.

We found Jory and because flyers aren't happening (The Dead didn't pay for that privilege), he tried to pretend he didn't have tix for us, but laughed and said he couldn't do it. Whew.

Headed in, we saw Edie, "Come on!"

She pointed to Sheee-a and Oh-lee, "They don't have tickets." So me and Corvette started running around, 'I need a free one.' You know, the usual rap. Got one for 5 pounds, and one for 4 pounds. They were so excited that we were able to do that.

Inside Sheee-a said, "I enjoy the Grateful Dead, but I am ashamed to dance."

"Close your eyes... Just listen to the music... Let your body move." Soon she was dancing away.

Night before, Fritz had said, "Tomorrow is Halloween and everyone's dosin whether they want to or not – even you Hollie."

I told him, "If you dose me in this horrible place I will never forgive you."

I had such a good time last night though. Hung most of the night with Arthur, Jasmine, Silas, Hackmen, Marla, and Dante. I was drinking and having fun. Dean smoked a joint with us. Perfect timing for *Good Lovin,* then an encore of *Werewolves of London*!

Milling around, after the show last night, we kept hearing about a party at Columbia Hotel. We decided to go. They closed the bar to restock it just as we got there. Then said they wouldn't open the bar again until everyone without a key left the hotel. Yes Ma'am Sam told them, "Ya know, we had a party in Chicago and spent 23,000 dollars. It was a $6,000 last call." They huffed. Couldn't handle so many hippies in their nice hotel. Uptight British.

Corvette is off looking for tix. – But the way Jory said, last night, that he couldn't bunk us after we'd worked all tour... Maybe with that attitude he'll hook us again tonight. Either way I expect it to be an easy ticket.

Inside 1st set.

Tix were lookin scarce but Jory came through!

Bummer though, the bowl is fuckin spent every time it gets to me.

1st night inside I had this flash thought. 'Where's Tricky?" I hadn't seen him since Hamburg that I could think of. I asked Corvette, and she said, yeah, she saw him in Paris, but she hadn't seen him here yet. No biggie, I hadn't seen a lot of folks yet. But yesterday it became obvious – he's not here. And yes, there is reason to worry. Shit. Please Tricky, be ok, and not in any weird trouble in a foreign country.

Yeah! – gotta tell Maggie, here in Britain, that we ain't gonna work on her farm no more. Let's hear it Phil!!!!!

Nov 2nd   London

Checked out of Edie's place this morning. We're broke and headed to some dorm – Gypsy Linda's friend Rhonda says we can stay till we leave.

Looking back through this book it seems like a boring trip. We didn't do most of what people come to Europe to do. What we did do was make some new friends and spread a few smiles and maybe we helped take a step or two closer to world peace.

38
Fall 1990
No House, No Buds, No Nothin'

        Nov 7   Connecticut

  I got us a drive-away car – Mom's lending us gas money. We have eight days to get to San Jose. I'm thrilled to be headed home so soon. Connecticut's getting wintery and cold.

        Nov 13 1990

  We're here!
  California!
  Outside Mojo's place in Tahoe, Elwood had a long walk, and I saw Orion – crisp and bright, in the only sky space visible between the trees.
  I'm so fucking glad to be back in California. Now I want a place to go – my own space – something a bit bigger than the van – something with its own bathroom.
  At the same time somehow, I gotta get the van fixed.

        Nov 16   Oakland

  Most of our usual places have reasons for not wanting us there right now. It sucks not having anywhere to go. Thankfully when I called Parker and Angie, I got a different story. They're moving to a huge new place, and invited us to stay as long as we need.

        Nov 20 1990

  I kinda wanted to hang with Jack tonight. I've been anticipating seeing him today at the Jerry show. I got a hello just as I would have wished it. A big hug, a kiss or two, more hugs, and a vague reference to him having a hotel. It was Domino's b-day, he and Jack got in. We didn't. Warfield's always hard.

Jake couldn't help. It was good to see him, even so. We tried to get him to come smoke with us, but he said his job was on the line. He had to go talk to Bill Graham and he didn't want to be too high. He said they're starting to wonder why everyone asks for Jake. – It's because he gets personal with the folks in the lot, and he has a heart. I joked, "They're wondering whose side you're on." He said something about how he's ready to be just a Deadhead. Said he'd be a good part of our team, knowing what he knows.

We're like, "Jake. You already are part of our team."

Got all the gossip. Lots of it bad. Sid's been arrested again on a drug deal gone bad. And Tricky. Fuckin Tricky got caught coming back into America on old warrants – including the Fed one from Boulder Creek when some guy turned state's on him.

It was excellent to see Dave Echo. I got the biggest hug, and he said he's been thinking of us – so he didn't wear any ripped clothes. Ha!

Corvette says I have three infatuations: Jack, Garrett, and Dave Echo.

Maybe. But Dave Echo not really. I mean, he's always lusting after the super pretty chicks, and doesn't even see me, so I don't really consider him.

Garrett I saw for a quick moment. He laughed, "Oh, so you don't like Chain letters?" He gave me a hug with massaging fingers.

And Jack.

Well... yeah. I really like Jack, but ah... I... I don't know.

Thanksgiving 1990
Parker and Angie's – Oakland

Last night Corvette got in with Rebel. Jack bought me a ticket, then traded his ticket to a puppy-eyed chick for a gorgeous peyote stitch that she was supposed to give to Fritz. At the end of the night Fritz walked off with it anyway. I asked if Jack wanted this ticket back, he said no. He didn't get in.

Dave Echo bought me beers all night, and Garrett told me I'd lost weight.

Izzy, Trinity, and Kerry were there. Don and Justine. Word is Dante and Marla are traveling Spain. Dimitri is here! He was in jail, none of us even knew. They deported him – but he got off the plane before it left!

Nov 27 1990

Considering the circumstances, everything has been ok. We're not doing too bad being homeless, vehicleless, budless, and broke. Hanging at Angie and Parker's – Four other hippies have been here too, since JGB at the Kaisers. They are Mark (who tries to call himself Serenity) and Marigold, a cute young dreaded couple, and Janine and BamaJohn. They're all beginning beaders, and have been doing small hair stitches for days. These kids are bus hippies with The Drifter, and Wandering buses. Buses I don't know, except from the outside. The younger generation.

later
    I feel like I'm accomplishing nothing – living in someone else's space, with no particular place to go, and no direction. Just existing. And not badly, so I should have no complaints... but... I don't know. I'm bored. I want beads. I want the van fixed. I'd like a home. And buds. I want buds. It's getting unseasonably dry.
    On the Haight we saw King Henry. Yeah! We went to Benny's for bongs then back to the street. – We went by Distractions, – it's full of Matt Ackerman's stuff, and soon, he'll have his own store in the back room. The owner-guy bought four pair of Corvette's earrings, so that was helpful. We cruised through the park for a few beers and a fatty with Jack and Johnja before coming back to the East Bay.

Dec 5

Two Oakland Coliseum shows. 1st was a mellow scene – free tix everywhere. 2nd night tix were hard. We saw Rebel. He said, "Walk with me, talk with me." And walked us right in.

Second day we went to the show early with Markness. (I refuse to call him Serenity.) Parked by the hotels and did the neighborhood walk. No real scene – not crowded all over with us Deadheads. Found a fatty football game behind the Holiday Inn. Jeremy, Mason, KJ, King, Kerry, Schmitty, DigDoug, Rockafucker, and Little Jamie – watching on the side was Katarina, Jumpin' Jack, and Hawkeye.

Oh! And John and Erika were there! They offered to let us ride with them to Arizona, shame we can't afford that.

I snagged a ride to Cotati with Freddy. Now I'm sitting in my van. Still broke-down in Aaron's parking spot. Seems to be too much going on with it for an easy fix. Aaron's mechanic has gone off to get ether.

Freddy told me some bad news – King and Santa got busted for buds in the Holiday Inn last night. It's a total bummer. They both have pending pot cases already. Whoa – not even – Santa's just got dealt with two or three days ago – he has to do 120 days, starting in January. I wonder how this affects that?

My mind is frazzled. I can't think straight. I need to sell buds. I need to pay December's rent on the storage shed. I need the van going – today!

Dec 7   Oakland

He got the van running and I got it down here to Parker's. Didn't manage to sell any buds up there – everyone says it's too expensive.

We almost had Skinny Jim talked into driving to Arizona, but he decided no. Oh well. I wasn't all that into it somehow anyway. Sounds excellent though – day shows – in the warm desert sun. But some cosmic decision was made somewhere, and we're not going.

Dec 16

Last night we crashed at the Broderick house – it was Danni's b-day.

Word was 1st Arizona show sucked, 2nd raged. Denver got a *Wang Dang Doodle* and a two part *Dark Star* on two different days.

Everyone's looking for buds. I can't believe how dry it's been. And what little can be found is fucking expensive. I also can't believe we've spent a month just sitting and beading at Parker's. It's cool by them for us to be here, but it's a lazy place, it's always trashed, and we're always cleaning it, and I'd love to get out of their way.

Dec 24

Merry Christmas from Oakland. Angie told Jack he could stay here. He and I argue so often it makes life not worth writing about. I've about had enough of this whole deal – me and him. One of my favorite things about him was how special he always made me feel. These days it's, "call this # for me," "drive me (and however many hippies) here," do this for me, do that for me. Jack's unappreciative of his regular hang crowd. I'm not enjoying that.

New Year's Eve 1990

Not inside. We fucked ourselves trying to get walked in. Someone had been selling fake laminates, and when caught, said, "Jake let me copy his." Which can't be true, but it had the place all up in arms. Jake was unable to walk anyone in, and Rebel and Beau couldn't either.

FUCK they're playin *Promised Land*. I love to dance to this, but it's kinda hard to do sittin in the van. It's soo cold out. We waited so long by the back doors, we missed all the tix that appeared. Calico came out to Murph's bus and sold everyone in our circle tix for face.

Damn this isn't fair. I don't want to be out here! I want to be inside with the people I Love. Yes Love. And I love them no matter what Two Toke Tom says. That's a whole nother weirdness.

We've been in a hotel room at the Days, with Jack. Two Toke Tom came over, morning of the 2nd show, and it became intense, in a funny-scary sort of way. He was saying how no one really loves all the people they say they do, and the only people he loves, are the women he's sleeping with. Domino telling him there are many forms of Love. Icarus spouting hippie dippy stuff about Love.

I told him, "We who love you, are here to prove you wrong."

He kept bitching about Kiersten, – how she left because he was running out of money. – Because his good friend, Even-Steven, who says he Loves Tom, – ripped him off for $5,000. Tom kept sayin' he needed to make money, so he could make a home for Kiersten, so maybe she'd come back. But to make money, he had to sell mushrooms, and she didn't like that. Every time Markness opened his mouth Tom screamed about his manners. Tom kept telling us we didn't understand. I said I now understood his beliefs, and mine were different, and he howled – "I'm not talking about beliefs! I'm talking about truth!"

The whole conversation lingers with me. He was telling us none of us were real. – Corvette because she goes under a fake name, Markness because of his dreads and skirt, and the way he went off on Jack for being illiterate was uncalled for. Mark offered Tom a hug as he left. Tom was disgusted. We saw Kiersten later in the day, talking about needing to get away from him. I don't blame her. There was something too dark in Tom's eyes.

Beau just stopped by. Him and Amanda stayed outside to Dance under the Blue Moon tonight. It's almost midnight so I guess I'll roll a fatty, grab one of Jack's bottles of champagne, and we'll go over to the hearse.

later

So that's the deal. We were supposed to hear *Dark Star* while dancing under a Blue Moon. At Midnight, Crafty Adam sprayed champagne all over everyone.

Cute Allen was outside too. His friend had a Ram Wand. What an amazing thing. Made of a ram's horn, it wrapped around your arm. It had been up for trade for two tix, yet they got shut out. When Allen introduced us to his friends, one guy was like, "So you're Hollie... Allen came home from Deer Creek singing your praises for the kind buds and the kind back rubs."

39
Winter 1991
House Magic and some Oakland Shows

Jan 2 1991

On the morning of New Year's Day I tried to talk to Jack about what he was doing or where he was going, because me and Corvette were headed for Janey's B-day party. (And I certainly wasn't going to bring him there.) He was mad I wasn't falling into line with his lack of a plan. I left the hotel room and went downstairs.

Domino walked up, and I said, "Alright! You can take Jack's stuff so I can get going."

As I piled Jack's stuff on the sidewalk, he laughed, "Is this what Jack wants?"

"Well, he wants to get his stuff out of the van, but he doesn't know where he's going yet. It's probably not what he wants, but I can't do anything right anyway, so..." Domino was amused, but his bus was pretty far away actually, so we threw the shit back in my van.

When Jack came down from the room, he barked at me, "You have to wait till I find somewhere to put my belongings."

If he had asked politely I probably would not have had the reaction I did. If he had said 'Please,' I probably wouldn't have said, "No Jack. I don't <u>have</u> to wait for you to find a ride. I have somewhere to go. I have my own life to lead."

He glared at me, "Fine... just fine." He stormed to the van and threw his stuff out onto the pavement. I wanted to tell him, nicely, why I didn't think, at this point, that we should go in the same direction, but every time I went near him he stalked away. So now he's pissed at me, and he wouldn't even look at me as I drove off.

Bummer it got like that.

We went to Janey's brunch in Berkeley. The company was fun and the food was delicious, – the first real food we'd eaten since the shows began.

Jan 5 1991

We spent the past two days driving Sonoma county looking for a house. Markness came with us. His parents are sending him money and he wants to live with us. Lila and Ryan called from Georgia. They have money, and want us to find a house that'll fit them too. So that's our plan.

Before we left the Bay, I went to Haight St. to try to find Jack. Wanted to see what he was up to. Is he looking for a house, or just blowing his $? While I was looking for him, he called Parker's. Markness took the call and told Jack we'd been looking at houses.

"With whose money?" Mark said he sounded sad.

The place we looked at yesterday was perfect for us. It was in Cloverdale. The woman – Francesca – told me on the phone that the place was trashed by some people who weren't paying rent. It's listed in the paper as a, "HUGE Funky 3 br." We got to the end of the long driveway, and collectively said, "Holy shit."

It's three stories tall. The top two floors have porches all around, – hung with mobiles and stained glass panels. A tree in the yard appears to grow bowling pins, and there's plenty of room to park buses or whatever.

WOW!

Thrashed for sure though.

Inside – dust, and broken junk everywhere – books, books, and more books, and pieces of Amethysts everywhere. Beds, tables, and chairs, all broken. Bits of hippie art through the years, are visible everywhere. Stairs are rickety, doors don't shut right.

Jan 9   Oakland

When we gave King a ride to Humboldt, we heard Santa turned himself in, and is now in jail. Too many charges racked up against him. Poor Santa.

After we dropped King off, we went to Cloverdale again.

Francesca is an older hippie-type woman. We hung out for hours. Talking about the house – poking through stuff, and helping clean. We told her how much we wanted the place, and she told us her troubles. Her husband is an alcoholic – she left him, and the house. He went into a recovery program, and abandoned the house to his buddies. She kicked them out, got screwed on all the bills, and she's broke, trying to pay the mortgage.

She told us, "I'm afraid. I've only known you an hour, – I like you, but you look like people who can't afford to pay your bills, and you look like you have friends who would put railroad spikes in the walls to hang their guitars from."

"Don't worry, we don't know any guitarists who'd come visit, just a bass player."

"Oh no, cute bass players are the worst!"

"We didn't tell you he was cute. How did you know?"

"All bass players are cute."

Her helpers are Taco and Jordan – known to her this week as, "Brute Force and Ignorance." Francesca went to town and we were entertained by Jordan and Taco as they shoveled nasty food garbage, six feet deep – tossed right off the balcony – for months and months. Taco, singing to and about the garbage. "It's just a can o' pork – I don't know who put it there – Wonder why they didn't eat it – still could, if you'd care," and offering it to us. Chasing mice, screaming, "Lunch!" loud enough to echo across the valley.

When she got back, Francesca was visibly distraught. "On the one hand, I have the Sheffields, who've lived in the same house for 11 years, and have always paid their rent on time. Now, they want a house in the country, so the kids can play outside. And on the other hand I have you."

I asked, "Would you like us to leave till you make your decision, or should we just hang out here till you rent it to us?"

When it got dark, and we'd been discussing how it would be if we were to move in, I pulled out, and handed Francesca $1000 in cash. She squealed. Taco jumped up, put both hands on her shoulders, and said, "Now Francesca, look her in the eyes, hand back the money, and tell her 'NO'."

Francesca backed off, "I can't."

Taco winked at us, and said, "You're in there."

WE'VE GOT A HOUSE!!!!!

Our official move in day is January 15th. We have to come up with another $1000 by then, but we can start staying there now. Perhaps this is why we couldn't find a place before Europe.

We came back to Parker and Angie's to discuss who we want to move in with us. There's Markness, Ryan and Lila, but there's room for more. Ditto wants to get out of the Bay Area. Maybe he'll be interested? I'd like to find John and Erika, see if they want to move in with us.

Then there's Jack. That's a problem I'm not sure what to do about. I don't want to live in a house full of Jack's entourage, and fight about it all the time.

Jan 13 1991   Cloverdale

Sitting on the top porch, enjoying our new house. We have a fantastic view of the fog-filled mountains, and we can see the highway way off.

Francesca, while cooking dinner for us, was boppin around the house, singing, "I'm so glad I didn't rent to straight people." She told us she was at the very first Grateful Dead New Year's Eve. – Country Joe and the Fish, Quicksilver, and The Dead. After Midnight they jammed till 4AM as "Dead Silverfish."

The word from Ditto is that Kennedy got a 30 day extension before he has to go in for 2½ years. I hope him and Suzy come up here for a few.

Feb 1, 1991

Been workin' our asses off on the house. Lila and Ryan got here, with their VW van, and their two ultra-cute puppies (Sunshine and Daydream), a day or two before JGB. They love the house. Of course they do. It's an ideal hippie house. Ya gotta Love it.

We went down to the JGB Warfield shows. Got tix the first day – traded postcards for one, to the guy pictured in the Ape suit on the Mardi Gras postcard, and Steamy Dean bought us one. Inside was a crazy night. Everyone was beating on Fritz. He said to the usher at one point, "Come-on, aren't you gonna stop all this violence?"

And the usher said, "Who me?" as Don slammed into Fritz again.

Kennedy is still here! That's a wonderful thing. Hawkeye paid Johnja $10 to kiss Kennedy on the lips. Kennedy freaked. "What the HELL are you doing?!?!?" Me and Corvette were laughing so hard, he came over and knocked our heads together and we couldn't do anything about it except laugh harder. When he found out the deal, he jumped on Hawkeye. Hawkeye grabbed ahold of his legs and ran, with Kennedy at first trying just to hold on, then getting a grip, and whooping and swinging one arm like a cowboy. It was that kind of wild night all through the hallways.

After the first show we went to Schmitty's hotel. We were gonna crash there, but Shady Nathan the Narc appeared. I don't care what Briscoe says, I still feel like the guy is a narc. We left, and went to Jack's place. He's rented a boarding room on Masonic, between Haight and Paige.

Next day we didn't have tix, but we stood at the bus stop till the bouncer at the door waved us over, "Go in, Go in." Okay, hey, I always listen to guys in those coats. Thanks! Apparently Jack always gives this guy buds, and on his way in, he pointed us out, and told the guy, "They're my family, they have to be inside."

Jack got really drunk, and told me what he and I had was nice, but what he needed was a best friend, because he's lonely, and no one really gives a shit about him. He kept saying I didn't understand lonely, because I have Corvette.

At the next show I learned he didn't remember our talk, too drunk.

Whatever. It's not like I actually want to be a couple with Jack anyway, right? I mean, I really don't, so why is it still sort of a bummer?

3rd night we got in free with one ticket, and a postcard trade with Original Bob – he said it was because we kicked him a ticket in Essen – cool.

Feb 2nd 1991

Really really bad news from Rosemary. She's scared. A friend got busted. She has no ability to pay me. We think she'll be okay, that the guy will keep his mouth shut, but losing that much right now hurts. Hurts is an understatement. We're fucked.

Feb 8th 1991

Sunday at the Warfield tix were hard, and word was, most folks didn't get in on Saturday. I gave Jack back all his shit – shoes and clothes – his jewelry. Everything.

Jack and Domino got in with Cindy/April. We gave up trying and just came home. We did manage to bum some buds before we left. Kevin kicked me a pre-roll. Hackmen kicked bonghits. Fletcher and Banjo each kicked us a bud too.

I started beading a stick to give to Kevin for all he's done for us.

Markness brought folks home from the show and fed them with our food. We bitched. He said he'd replace it – he did. Then they ate it all again. Money is a very serious problem since Rosemary's news – we can't afford anything.

Oh, and Kenny got busted. His bail is $5,000. Jack's hoping they'll lower the bail. He was being stupid on Haight. I always warn people about that. And did I mention that Tavi is back in jail? I'm not even sure why.

Feb 14 1991

Ditto showed up with bad news. Kennedy got busted at the airport. They'd been following him, and off the DEA went to the Walnut Creek house. They found two unrinsed bottles, and lots of blanks. Fuck! Ditto claimed he was just passing through and they believed him and let him go.

Damn it. It's not fair. Kennedy's on such thin fucking ice – and that's only because he's got a great Lawyer. They also took last month's $600 phone bill off the table. That's major bad news for everyone.

This is the worst scene I can imagine.

It was pure luck, or karma, that got Ditto out of that house. They took Suzy, because everything at the house is in her name. They'll have to let her go though, they'll find nothing on her. Oh! I love you both. Be strong.

Ditto went north to make himself scarce.

Feb 16

Crafty Adam got here last night. He says Jack's hanging with Deazy. Deazy is weird. She dresses like an office worker, but looks more like a hooker. Adam also said Deazy looks like she's on dope these days. He said Jack's out on Haight, swinging hard. I think that's crazy, and it's better for me to have nothing to do with it at all.

Feb 23 1991

Went to the shows in Oakland. 1st day I didn't get in till last song of 1st set. Ohio Dave gave me a ticket as he was headed inside. That last song was *New Speedway Boogie.* Haven't played that in 20 years.

It was an ok show, but I was worried. A couple days before, I'd gotten a nasty call from Freddy because I hadn't paid yet. "This isn't like you."

I wanted to deal with that, and get it over with, but every time I found him, he waved me off, "Later." The third night we finally talked. When Freddy heard about Rosemary's friend he understood why I hadn't paid. Of course he's happy to hear that everyone's safe, and I'm glad we talked, but nothing makes this situation any better.

Anyway.

2nd night, didn't get in.

3rd night, Jack gave me a ticket, and Hilton John bought Corvette one. Yeah! Got in early. Was with Abe and Jackie for the opening *Help Slip Franklins*. First one in the Bay area in six years. It was a good Chinese New Years – Year of the Ram now. The Dragon parade was fun. Trinity couldn't stop talking about it.

John and Erika like the idea of moving in with us, but they're gearing up for tour, and invested in jewelry makings, which they left in LA. They're gonna go get all that before they come check out the house.

Skye has a new bus. So cute, – a small bus, red-pink color, – the inside, with couches, a bed, tapestries. Its name is the Scarlet Bee. Skye looked like Queen of the lot. Everybody was hanging at her bus. Dean, Don, Fritz, Izzy, Trinity, Kerry, King. Even Hawkeye. I thought him being there was pretty stupid, but that's probably because I've been listening to Freddy and all the ways he's down on Skye, and the crazy things he believes about her.

Today we went to General Bead, and to Golden Gate park for a Ceasefire concert. It's sad how few people were there. Half the cool folk on Haight didn't even know it was happening.

After that show, Jack came home to Cloverdale with us. We're home to the news that there's no water. Again. The well ran dry the day we left. I don't think Francesca has the cake to do anything about it.

Now for some of the truly bad news.

1st night, on the way to the show, Memphis Mike and Wyler were pulled over, and somehow that led to a search of Wyler's house!?!

Armand has been living in one of Hawkeye's houses in Oregon. He got pulled over, supposedly on something routine, but the DEA showed up to search his car, asking questions like, "Who pays your electric bill?" Armand said it was weird and scary. A couple days later, random unknown people went to Armand's house and asked for Hawkeye. Yikes.

And supposedly Atlanta Angela got busted through an express mail receipt in the garbage – Not from the phone bill like we'd heard.

Accidental Mary was working security at the park today. She told us Hawkeye got busted on the last night of the shows. She only knew because Baldwin (the lawyer), called and asked if she'd put up her house for his bail. She couldn't.

Hawkeye.

Oh man.

They are all over that circle. It's bunk. And we can't help but wonder where's Ditto? Is he ok?

Feb 26 1991

Yeah! Ditto called! Hawkeye's with him. It was just a traffic violation, and everyone, – even Baldwin, jumped to conclusions.

Sunday because of lack of water, we hiked up the mountain, and we all washed our hair under the runoff from this spring up there.

Me and Jack ended up really having it out. He said something about me being bitchy, and I said, "Maybe it's the company." He got all mopey and walked off. I followed.

I certainly don't want any sort of relationship with him, and he doesn't want that with me, but I definitely want to stay friends. I told him I was afraid it was headed to a point where we'd walk off from each other and, "What are we gonna do, walk past each other in the lot like we don't know each other, because we couldn't get over this?"

We talked a lot throughout the day, and I got a massage before we crashed. I think we have made it back to the good friends point I prefer. We actually seemed able to truly smile at each other next morning.

In the middle of the night Mark came home announcing, "Fatty!" at the top of his lungs. The whole house gathered on the porch. We smoked four fattys and went back to bed as it was getting light.

This morning, Lila, Ryan, and Jack headed for the city. They found John and Erika in the Hilton bus, camped in town. They'd been in Cloverdale since yesterday, but didn't know where to go, and couldn't get in touch with anybody who could tell them. We had the best news, – Because Francesca can't rent a house with no running water, she told us, "Don't worry about rent again till we get some water hooked up, and even if we started drilling tomorrow it'll be 6-8 weeks."

Yeeeeeeehaaa!! A free house!!!!!!

What incredible magic! We're lovin' it!

Already Hilton John hooked up a PVC pipe to the run off from the spring up on the hill, so we've got water from a hose. Stylin. We're gonna build a shower. Not so pleasant is the shitter we had to make in the woods. It works though.

Mark came home from the shows with all his rent $ and since it was unneeded, he spent it on food, and beads for everyone. What wonderful colors we now have. And he definitely redeemed himself in the food department.

40
Spring 1991
When Shit Hits Fans

March 2 or 3

  I don't know – it's Sunday. It's been raining since the day after we hooked up the PVC pipe. Raining nice and slow, so the ground is soaking it up. The river below us is almost full. Jah, I haven't seen a full riverbed in what seems like years. The land needs this so bad.

  There were three JGB shows at the Warfield. Corvette didn't bother with any of them, and says she's not gonna do tour either. I only went the first night. Markness went with me. He made a killah necklace for Jumpin' Jack – Rainbow of course, with a globe and a peace sign on one side, and the other side says, "Peace is the only way out."

  Not too many people at the Warfield, at least not from our used-to-be circles. Tix were on sale but I had no cake for that. Eventually, I got comped by a door guy.

  Told King Henry that if he bought me dinner this night, he'd be getting off easy because there's only one of me. He thought that sounded smart. After dinner we went by Broderick house. Danni was tweaking. The house is still full of stuff, and they were supposed to be out by midnight. She and Gwen will be riding East with me this tour.

  I slept at Jack's and left after a morning fatty with him and Crystal. (She's got a room there at the boarding house too.) Went by Kevin's to give him the beaded stick I made for him. He was like, "This is horrible. This is just awful. What did I do to deserve this?" He was grinning so big.

  There were lots of folks at his house, but the only one I knew was Cindy/April. She's got such weird vibes. Kevin smoked a fatty with me – fattest one I've seen in a while, and I sat in the massage chair listening to the Hamburg tape, getting the ultimate mechanical massage, and thinking of Nadav.

They were going to see the Doors movie – this is its first week in theaters. I came home though. Psyched to bead with the bit of keef Kevin gave me.

I'm pretty broke these days and this rain hurts my finances – we may even have to pay March rent – I need money to get across country with, and I have zero income, but I will not wish the rain away. My finances aren't as important as Mama Earth at all.

Sunday March 10
Cloverdale

Earlier this week – Crafty Adam, who's been at our house since the Warfield shows, went out with Lila and Ryan. When they came home, Lila wanted a house discussion while John and Erika were gone. Adam says, "Hollie you're such a bitch, – no matter what anyone does, or says, you bitch."

I turned to him, "Adam, this is a house discussion. You pay no rent here, you have no say in a house discussion."

"I don't even want to be in this house. I don't want to be a part of it. I'm leaving. Tonight. You're such a bitch."

"That's good, because you've been here too long anyway." (Corvette told me, earlier that day, she wished Adam would go away.)

He'd been drinking and he flipped out. He started going through his shit, tossing everything he had taken from our 'for sale' stuff. He was throwing his own beadwork around and it was breaking. There were bead needles, and crystal shards, sticking out of the rug. Muttering about me being a lazy bitch, and that my money problems are becoming everyone's problems. At one point he screamed, "Fuck you, Fuck this whole scene, Fuck Jack too."

Jack wasn't even around. But, later, Corvette told me, Jack had called, and told Adam the last Rainbow piece he beaded wasn't good enough; he wanted something with real rainbow colors.

"Adam, we welcomed you into our home, because you needed a place to be, but if you can't control yourself, and act like an adult, then please… do leave."

Lila and Ryan had retreated to the kitchen, trying to avoid it all. That's about the moment the propane stove chose to explode. Just like in the cartoons. I saw it pop – its sides all went out about a foot, and yellow was everywhere. The air in the whole house went "Whoooof." The doors bulged open, the burners popped off, – the heavy griddle popped up a foot too. It blew Lila against the wall, but she was ok. Ryan ran and shut off the propane in the cellar. What a personification of the explosion in the living room.

Adam gathered his shit (leaving everything we'd given him in a pile) and went out into the yard to wait for Ryan to give him a ride to the highway. I smoked a cigarette and watched him from the porch.

He looked sad. I felt sad. It was so much worse of a fight than I've even written.

I felt like I could see the shattered remains of our friendship scattered along the porch, and in the living room, and out in the driveway. And it was because of alcohol.

My head hurts. I have so many upsetting things to write to finish this story.

On Friday, Murph and company stopped by, headed for tour. They're in a new bus. Looks comfy. Bunks and cedar paneling.

They didn't have any buds either. Buds are so scarce, I keep saying, "I can't remember why I have memory loss," and I've been singing, "Everywhere I go, Everyone I know, Everybody's smoking that Shwag."

Saturday, me and Corvette went to Jack's in the city. Lots of people there, and bad news. Jack's mom died.

Rosemary did the double phone thing, so Carp and Jack could talk, and we all got to talk to Carp. Johnja, Spaz, and Rosemary in New York, Carp in jail in LA, and in SF, the phone being passed from me, Corvette, Domino, and Jack. Everyone is trying to find some law that will get Carp home for this ordeal. He's not a murderer, rapist, or child molester, he should be allowed to go home for his mom's funeral.

Me and Corvette had to try to make some $, so we ducked out and went to Buffalo Exchange, then to another of those free concerts in the park.

There was an oddly intelligent wingnut guy there. Said he used to be an English Teacher in Berkeley. Till he got arrested and fired.

"For what?"

"Acid." He said.

"Doing it?"

"No. Selling it."

"To the kids?"

"No, in the mail. They came and got me in the library at the school. Walked right up and handed me an indictment. Cuffed me, and took me away. The kids at school always used to ask me, ya know, always trying to please the teacher, they'd ask me 'what should I write about?' Usually, I'd tell them 'write about something that concerns you, or excites you. Something you care about.' But that day, I was able to yell, as they were taking me away – 'Write about the day they took your English Teacher away!!!'"

Back at Jack's. Knock Knock.

"Who is it?"

"Your mama." Crafty Adam. I looked him in the eye. He looked away, stayed only about 45 seconds, or a minute, and said, "I'm going back out to the street."

Jack convinced us all to go to dinner before he left. (He got a flight at 11:15PM.) We went to the East African place on Haight. Everyone had fun, but I felt un-fun. They were drinking wine, and tossing around the Frisbee bread. I couldn't eat. Seeing Adam made me feel ill.

In the middle of dinner, King came into the restaurant, and we all applauded. He blushed, and was like, "Don't do that." He sat a bit and kicked to Crystal. Ha. He was trying to be low key, and we applaud.

We took Domino's bus to the airport, Domino parked in the bus lane. I waited in line with Jack. I wished I could do something to make him feel better. But there was nothing, except help him check-in, and help him spell words for a letter he wanted to write.

After he checked in, we all stood around outside, talking, and playing, and jumping on the luggage scale, till cops pulled up outside Domino's bus, with the lights flashing, and a bullhorn, asking, "Is there anyone in the vehicle?"

We all gave Jack hugs goodbye and went towards the bus. As we walked off, the airport speakers blared, "Security Alert. Security Alert. All passengers who have finished the check-in process must report to their departure gates immediately." I guess that was for Jack. How can they be so scared by a bunch of hippies?

We drove quietly back to the city.

Went by the Warfield. Saw Sadie. Just sitting there. I heard Banjo got busted with 20 pages, while getting stoned in the park the other day. I asked how she was doing. She said she was ok, except all the liquor stores in this area were closed, and she didn't want to walk to whatever street it was, where one was still open.

We decided to sleep in Jack's room, and decided we didn't need blankets, or to check on Elwood. Plan was to wake up by 7:30 and head for the flea market to work.

Got outta there by 7:45 – to the van – Raped.

Violated. Broken into, gone through, left in a pile.

Elwood still there, thank Jah.

I cried.

Jack had just given me the video camera to take east – gone. My backpack – gone – emptied of clothes, and thank Jah, this book was thrown out of it too.

They went through everything. They took food I was supposed to eat and drink going across country. They took my lock box. They'll be bumming when they open it to find just van receipts and bumper stickers (lots of em, from all through the years! Just gone!)

Fuckers.

I cried each time I discovered something else. Like all the beadwork I'd done for tour. Gone.

Elwood was tweaked. He jumped every time the van shifted. Our own clothes and flea market stuff was thrown all over. Absolutely nothing of Corvette's was gone. Was it Adam? Would he do this to me? He'd bitched about Jack and knew the camera was Jack's. Jack's stuff and my stuff is all that's gone.

I fully want to believe it wasn't Adam. But I just don't know. To have this happen when a drunk ex-friend has such a vendetta against me.

I called Danni and cried to her. I don't know how the hell I'm supposed to do this. They took my food, and I've got 20 bucks. How am I gonna get to the east coast with $20?

I called Rosemary's and cried to Jack too.

The video camera! Gone.

I feel ill.

March 12 1991

Angie heard on Haight today that the feds got Jumpin' Jack. I tried to hope it was just a rumour, but I got through to Rosemary, and it's true. They have Jack. She doesn't know what they've got him for. The only thing I can think of is the blown off court date here in SF, but then, why pick him up in NY? Rosemary said they followed him around his hometown for two days before they came and got him this morning.

I can't believe you're in jail again Jack. FUCK. Damn it. What's the fucking point? Jack's no criminal. Not really. The Original American Hippie. What harm is he doing to them? Aw damn it Jack.

3-15-91

45 miles till Memphis. We're making incredible time. Danni's driving now. The van stalled on her first gas stop. 4AM. Some creepy guy jumped it for us. He was big, and breathy, with a

few grey teeth. Kept asking stuff like, "So it's just you girls travelin around huh?"

I drove all night. There was some serious hail in the Tehachapi mountains and in Flagstaff, snow, with ice underneath. Everyone had chains on but us.

Sunrise near Williams, Arizona with snow and fog was otherworldly and magical. Everything was white on white on white – road, land, sky, air... everything. Just white. Danni and Gwen were both asleep so I didn't get to share it with anyone. One of the most beautiful things I've ever seen.

The snow followed us across New Mexico, and all through Texas the snow was still chasing us. I finally let Danni take the wheel in Oklahoma. That was a drivin stretch of 28 hours. Maybe 29.

I saw a shooting star as I drove in the middle of the night. I made a wish for Jack.

41
Spring Tour 1991
Landover, Albany, Nassau

March 16 1991
Landover, Maryland

60 hours and we're in the same hotel me and Corvette stayed in last year, but it's the Capitol Budget now. This is the place we first saw Jack when he got out of jail last time. Knocked on the door, Don said, "who's there?" "It's a gas gas gas," and the room exploded into a hello scene. I wish I knew what was going on with him.

– Got through to Rosemary. Here's the deal – it is the SF thing and SF has ten days to come get Jack there in NY, if they want him. Ten days is up on the 22nd.

3-17-1991

At the Sheraton with Danni, Gwen, Ivan, and others. Don't actually know whose room this is. I miss my tour crew – Silas, Hackmen, Nicholas, and of course, especially, Corvette. I miss Jack too. I even miss Fritz.

Real poor showing of the Fatty Family so far. But Garrett's here. He's part of Jake's cleanup crew and was waiting by the back door. He wanted to take me to dinner and massages. I do need the massages, but I don't need to deal with Garrett right now.

Jake said Jory needed help, but Jory said, "No sorry – Nothing to do – Nothing coming all tour." Tonight I was ok, because Original Bob gave me his ticket as he walked in with Owsley. Tickets were hard – lots of counterfeits. People selling 'em for 5 bucks. It was bad.

I thought a lot in the show. Not too many people really give a shit about Jack being in Jail. Some people asked me, some told me, but not too many cared.

I thought of things like letters I could write to the band to let them know what it's like out here. And a poem that formed in my head. It started, "I Love you Grateful Dead – That's why I've got to leave you." Wished I had my notebook. I need a bigger fanny pack.

But what a show! The Dead did *Ruben and Cherise*!! Incredible. And another *New Speedway Boogie* that was ragin'. But nonetheless, I just sat there, staring off into space, thinking of all the things I want to do in life.

3-18-91

We called Fritz last night, "AhHah! *Ruben and Cherise!*"

He called back this morning, "Is that true? Did they really play *Ruben and Cherise*?" He'll be here by Albany.

Seems there's perhaps reason to be worried about Riley. I don't know anything about it, but Gwen says he hasn't called when he was supposed to.

Perhaps I'll do Jazz Fest before I go back to California. I mean what the fuck. I'm really getting a bit sick of all this shit. Yes, I'd be bumming if I had missed *Ruben and Cherise*, but it wouldn't have killed me.

later

Showtime and I'm sittin' outside. Got 400 postcards confiscated. They'd give me a receipt if I showed them my ID. Yeah right. Slimeballs. Roses are copyright infringements; so are skeletons, rainbows, and lightning bolts. Bastards. All I'm doing is trying to get by.

Murph had a ticket for sale – 11th row. Wanted $25. I didn't have it. I'm still gonna have to pay for the 400 postcards they took. Jake keeps cruising by but he hasn't seen me. He just got mobbed by hippies. "Jake we need tix!"

"All of you?" I heard him tell them, "Stay out of trouble. I'll be back."

It didn't sound promising to me, but... well... they're all over by the ramp. I guess I'll sit here and at least see what happens when he gets back.

I saw Johnja. He said Spaz got popped with too much in his pockets. Spaz, what a bummer dude. I warned him this is the DEA's backyard.

Maybe it's a blessing in disguise – Jack not being here.

The yellowjackets just kicked the Jake crew outta there.

Why am I still around this hell scene when it doesn't even make me happy these days?

There are soooo many cops out here. It's really unnecessary. This whole scene has lost so much, and the band doesn't give a flying fuck about the counter-culture it created. They don't even seem like they're on our side.

The Jake crew hasn't gone far.

I'd love to get in. I bet they'll kick out something ultra-cool again tonight.

What's with all these cops anyway? Do they make the Dead pay for this overtime? What a bunk scene. How did we ever let it come to this?

What is the point of all this? The analogy in *Box o' Rain* – how a moth is drawn to a flame – is so true. People just want to be near this magical light that is the Grateful Dead. But it's like the train's gone off the track or something. Or maybe it's just the way of things, like everything eventually goes into a downward spiral. The center cannot hold – what's that poem?

Why does the band sacrifice all that we are, for their shows? Do they really want us to stop coming? We made them, we are a part of them, and they don't care about us. It can only be a bad omen to shun us and take away our only means of existing. Don't sell drugs, and don't sell legal shit either – well, what are we supposed to do? Don't say go away – it's unrealistic. We belong here. I guess I have to give them the benefit of the doubt – perhaps it's beyond their control – but if so, they should be trying to change that. But they aren't helping at all. They just go on with their happy little lives and, "who gives a fuck about the people who love us." It depresses me. It seems so hopeless sometimes. But how can it be? It's too important to let it slide.

I can hear the place vibrating from here.

I tell myself I don't care.

Cops, Cops, and more cops – this is so lame. I should just go back to the hotel.

...

Jake just pulled up and gave me a ticket! Just as the yellowjackets came to tell me go away. Thank you Jake!

Inside

Note to myself as I'm being chased around the floor and shooed off from everywhere I stop to stand, or dance – Make a running commentary someday of *Uncle John's Band* and how it relates to life on tour.

later

Murph and Sahana stubbed me down to the 11th row. The music is sweet and nice and I hadn't <u>seen</u> the guys since Europe.

But they don't mean what they sing about, or at least don't show it to be so by their actions. Hence the *Uncle John's* note above.

A security guard just came over and asked, "How can you see?" I told her I can't, but I write anyway, in hopes I can read it later.

Later

I'm back in our usual Phil corner. Writing in a press box. Security is harsh – must have tickets to exist, and they're on the lookout for folks getting stoned.

What a Space note! –– rattle my ears! Rattle my soul!

– *Miracle* – Danni called it.

Lovelight was good, but so what... I miss Silas – leaning against him at the end of the shows. I'd like to go right back to the hotel and not even deal with the parking lot. Will this be my last tour, or is this just a bad week?

Maybe I've grown up. Maybe that's my problem.

March 19 1991

We had a women's fatty with Marla and Katarina. Seems like it's mostly women here in Landover. It's sad that our guys in the family are afraid to be here, or can't be.

Danni had big plans for today but didn't do any of it. I had no plans and carried them all through.

Went for coffee and hooked up with Don and Justine – smoking and bullshitting. It was nice, but I was bummed when everyone went out to dinner. No way could I afford it. I remember King's declaration – everyone owes everyone, so do what you want anyway. But when ya don't even have the money to borrow from yourself...

March 20

Can't wait for the Maryland shows to just end. Afraid to chance losing more postcards, but have to today because I'm broke. The shows are one thing, but what makes tour life fun is the shit you do around it. The things to do or see in whatever city you happen to be in. Fuck this broke hippie shit. It sucks.

Spring Tour is for change. I feel like I must change. My mind is constantly flipping through alternatives to this shit that doesn't make me happy. None of what I can think of compares.

Inside

Got in for *Althea* and now *Black Throated Wind*.

Couldn't get a ticket for a long time. Lookin hopeless. Cruised by the backstage door. Jake said Jory needed me – they sent stuff. This chick who'd been waiting for some lighting guy to come get her, was all, "Oh Please sister. Please let me help." Jory gave me two tickets and I gave her one. She promised to come help me after the show.

I miss Trinity. I wish so many people were here – and they – just aren't. And I hope there's no reason to worry about Rockafucker and Kay. Last anyone knew they went to Tennessee – Kay's hometown. But they should be here, it's not that far.

Tennessee Jed. Music Never Stopped. Might as Well. And the kids are dancin'. Been a long time since we heard a *Might as Well*. I remember how "we" used to dance. Fritz once said it was our job to dance. As I thought that, Don walked by. Maybe it was Don who said it. I can't remember.

Maybe some people have too much on their minds to dance.

Like me, – I'm sitting on a closed-up concession stand watching the crowd.

Late night

I had a great time tonight. Sat in that spot all night, there on a counter where I could see over the heads of the dancers. The hall was horribly crowded so it was nice sitting above it. What a sea of people. The *Might as Well* was rockin' – a balm to my tattered soul.

Met this puppy (20 years old). Watched him dancing 1st set – in a skirt. Come 2nd set, puppy didn't dance either. He sat with me. The stand we sat on was labeled Novelties. All night people asked, "Are you Novelties?"

Affirmative.

We Bullshat. He's from Jersey. He was perfect for me to talk to in the mood I'd been in. He sells Guatemalan clothes. I hadn't found much reason to smile these past few days, but I found many things to smile at tonight, while people watching, and sharing comments with Jay. I didn't find out his name till the *Weight* encore as we were walking towards the door.

We made plans to meet there tomorrow.

The chick I gave the ticket to bunked me. Garrett helped me hand stuff out. Psyched it's on recyclable paper now – not that nasty shiny paper.

I even had fun handing out that shit. Got majorly fucked with by security out in the lot – but I told him I was working and kept doing so. He saw that I was giving shit away so he switched tactics and said, "You're blocking traffic."

He had jumped out of his car to deal with me – parked it all cock-eyed – cars couldn't get by and were lining up in both directions. I said, "No, sir. It looks like you're blocking traffic." Truth hurts.

Our room is full – too many people I barely know. Some chick Darlene just said, "We all could have lice." What? Nasty. Gross. Everyone freaked. Then she said she was kidding.

Ugh.

March 22 1991

The lot set up in Landover was better on the last day. People were right on top of it. A good system of warning calls when "they" approached, and everything on tarps – set for quick rolling up all the sellable shit, just ahead of the confiscation crews, and easy to roll it back out once they passed. Gotta be tight to fight the system. But man, they sure have taken the fun out of selling. No more can you just toss some shit outside your vehicle and make a couple bucks. No more can you get <u>your own</u> artwork out into a very appreciative scene. People love this stuff. All this art and commerce is a part of it all. And what right do they have – they – ha! Jory! – Brokham! – the people I work for for free tickets! – what right do they have to take people's original artwork? They took the Batik wizards from me and said it was Jerry's face. It's not! It's just an old wizard. Not every old man with a beard is Jerry.

Saw Jory and worked before the show. That probably makes me a hypocrite.

I handed all the flyers out myself and got two tickets.

Had the hardest time trying to decide what to do with the extra. A gorgeous guy in purple fringe almost got it, but Markness hasn't gotten in at all here in Maryland, so I gave it to him. He's unhappy with the Dead, and thinking about doing Hemp Tour with Jack Herer instead.

Found Jay there on our Novelties stand. Ah-hah. These puppy boys are good for my soul. Both Jay and Markness turn 20 next week.

Afterwards, I brought Markness to his parent's house by Philly. Dropped him off, and I've got his parent's old computer in the van – Yeah!

I pushed on to Rosemary's. First thing she says, – "I don't think Jack's getting out today." SF's 10-days has been extended. She's also worried about Johnja. He hasn't called. Poor Rosemary. What heartache Johnja gives her.

I let Elwood out to run – he's psyched. It's all wet, and I'm sure it smells great – if you're a cat. I'm an over-exhausted, under-nourished, vegetable right now. Rosemary's mom is cooking. I'm looking forward to a mom meal, then I'm gonna crash hard.

March 23 1991

Van would not start. I practically begged it. No go. So I piled into Jean Claude's car with Johnja (he showed up), Rosemary, and Elwood. Off we go.

Cop. Pulls us over, – now I know why the van wouldn't start – Because it runs on magic, and it didn't want to deal with the upstate NY cop scene again. They gave Jean Claude the exact same rap they used on me last year.

"Why was I pulled over?"

"I'll tell you after I see your license and registration." Came back and said, "In NY state you can't have anything hanging on your mirror." So Jean Claude took it all down. "Mind if I search?"

"No reason to."

"Well if you've got nothing to hide…" Slimeball. It's the exact same script. "Where are you headed?"

"Albany."

"What for?"

That's none of his business. We could be going there to pick our noses. He doesn't need to know where we are going or why. It should have no consequence here.

"For a concert."

"What concert?"

It's not your business! It doesn't matter! It's hippie harassment. They fuck with our rights because of what we look like, and do. It's NOT FAIR. It makes me so mad.

"Grateful Dead."

"Got any weapons? Drugs?"

"No Sir. I don't do drugs." The pig laughed – That's humiliating and unfair.

"You don't mind if I search then, do you?"

"I don't think you have any right to search."

"Get out of the car sir." He searched Jean Claude in the street. In the rain. There was no need for that. He went through all our bags in the trunk. I saw him get excited when he found my vial of jewelry. And he tried to open the cat food can as if it were some stash can. Dude, see the cat? I wanted to offer him the can opener. It was ridiculous. It makes me hate the world, especially so-called authority figures.

We had nothing, they let us go, and I consider us lucky they didn't plant drugs on us.

later

I'm with the homescum – Amy, Jesse, and Deek – in their hotel. None of them have tickets. And everyone on tour needs bail $ and wants me to help collect.

March 25 1991   Albany

Jesse and Deek brought me to Jack's sister's to pick up his stuff there. Per Jack's request I got his backpacks, and a good bunch of his rainbow magic.

Last night, who should be sitting on the stairway as soon as I step inside? Novelty Jay. I was so psyched to see him. He and I have a good effect on each other. We called the show correctly to each other all night. Wailing show. Totally smoking.

Help Slip Frank – Wang Dang Doodle – Jack-a-Roe – Beat it on Down the Line – Brown-Eyed Women – Desolation Row – Deal.

2nd set – *Sam + Dee – China Rider – Looks Rainy – He's Gone – D-S – Wheel – Standin on the Moon – Good Lovin – US Blues.*

I miss so many people when I hear *Standin on the Moon*.

Been trying to collect lawyer money for Jack. The better the lawyer we can get, the less time he'll do. Suki gave me a $50, but it's a slow process. Nobody has much $ to help. I'm getting more promises for $ than actual money. Supposedly Cindy/April collected $75, but I heard she spent it. And his sister only had $100 of $260 Jack left her with. So much for blood family.

Inside

What a great feeling – getting hooked with two tickets per night!

Being near the music is almost enough to make all the shit worth it. Each extra here in Albany goes to one of the homescum. They're all helping to do the work. Jesse came in with me the first night, and Amy last night. Tonight it's Deek.

Right now they're playing *High Time*. I think I do that often – tell people goodbye when I mean Don't Let Me Go...

Ever since I've been spending shows with Jay I'm back to Lovin the shows and being happy just being stoned, and happy just to dance and rejoice to good music.

Used to Love Her... Not bad Bob –

The place is rockin' – they had it movin' last night too. Vince is havin' a great night. He had his longest solo yet during *Red Rooster*. He's really loosening up and kickin' it out.

Shakedown – (Yeeha) *Red Rooster, Stagger Lee* (Vince had to pull out a song book) *– Queen Jane – High Time – All Over Now – Tennessee Jed.*

Speaking of Tennessee, still no sign of Rockafucker and Kay. *Promised Land, Touch o'*. Break. 2ⁿᵈ set – *Greatest Story, Crazy Fingers, Truckin', Spoonful* – Russian Lullaby Jerry Jam – (wild – wonderful – sweet) – D-S – *Other One* – Black *Peter, Throwing Stones, Playin' Reprise, Lovelight* – what a good encore.

Late night

Skye's here on tour. During break her and Danni did the Jumpin' Jack lawyer collect. Got 300ish. Thanks ladies. I needed some help. I was beginning to feel like nobody was gonna actually kick down.

March 26 1991
Connecticut

Got AAA to jump the Van and left Albany early. (Ziggy's gonna work on the Van this weekend.) Mom made a dentist appointment for me for Thursday because I told her I wasn't going to Nassau. But now, I'm itchin' to go. Just itchin' to go. That old time feeling of knowing how close it is and just wanting to be there no matter what.

Maybe I could go and get home for the Dentist in between. Amy offered to take her car, if I drive, and if she can work with me to get in. I told Jory I wouldn't be there, but maybe I could still work if I got there early enough.

Or should I blow off the 1st one, and just go Thursday and Friday? Same old Dead shit.

One of mine and Jay's big jokes is, 'We should sue the Dead for mental anguish."

March 27 1991
Connecticut

10:30PM. I'm not at Nassau.

I called the lawyer Jeffery Scovino today. He's gonna take Jack's case. I told him what I know. He said, "Work on bail money." And when I tried to talk about $ for him, he said, "Don't worry my little flower, we'll work it out." He's gotta be a hippie.

March 28 1991   Nassau

After the dentist Amy picked me up and we headed to Long Island. Worked flyers to get in. Some grey-haired guy from Brokham was calling us the 'flyer babes'. After the show, he almost caught me selling postcards – that would not have been good.

The show was unbelievably short. With a *Terrapin* encore. I never saw that before. I thought they'd make it a long *Terrapin* to stretch the show, but no – it was short too.

Afterwards we went to the Marriott bar. Ragin, but not 'the scene' I was remembering. I had Kenny carrying around the bail jug I made. Got the returns tonight at the bar $61. This is too slow for $5,000. What the fuck? I know no-one has any money, but I'm so tired of hearing it. Sebby had kicked me $100 in Albany, and tonight I find out they popped him with marked money.

Found Cindy/April – she spent the money she had for Jack.

Me and Amy were on the look-out for floor space. Marriott rooms were all so full. Crystal had a room I was afraid of. I worry about her. Something's too shady there. She was tweaked tonight and ready to go home to SF. In the lot tonight Garrett got picked up. He was standing with her when they took him away. Crystal convinced the cops to give her the keys to Garrett's car, and she drove it over to the Marriott. I hope she takes heed of her own instincts.

Skye bought me a drink and when some guy kicked it over, I was totally ready to leave. Suddenly there was KJ and Mirabeth needing a ride to the Best Western.

So here we are.

I'm exhausted. No reason to be. Just brain activity – wearing me down. And wearing me out. Thinking the same things in circles. Without yet coming up with any helpful solutions, or inspirational ideas.

April 1 1991   Connecticut

Friday night I found Jay out in the lot while handing out "Free shit." We had a few beers and went in together. Went to where he'd been hanging – top row, Jerry's side. A row of chairs had been ripped out. It was a great place to dance.

During break we swung by the Fatty Zone, got a few tokes, and collected another 350^{ish} for Jack. Skye, Murph, and company were busting my ass, bowing and kowtowing when I sat near them. "Oh here she comes. Too good for us these days."

I tell them it's nothing personal. "I just don't have the cake to do the things you do." I miss hanging with my usual tour people – the ones that are here, Fritz, Don and Justine, Dean, King – but I can't be this broke around them.

My plan is to leave tonight for Atlanta. No way am I doing Greensboro this tour.

Van's doing well. Got a new battery, and Zig did all the big and little fix-its.

The lawyer said to bail Jack out. Angie found a bail bondsman who'll do it for $500, but whoever signs for him will have to pay $5,000, and all court costs, if Jack should decide to blow off any court date in this case. His brother in Concord won't do it. Jack insisted I call and ask. "No. Sorry. I did that for Carp, and when he fucked up, it almost ruined my marriage, and my whole life. I can't put it all on the line like that again for my fucked up brothers. If I did, and if Jack blew it, my wife would leave me." I can't say I blame him, but Jack was pretty upset.

42
Spring Tour 1991
Atlanta, Orlando

April 4 1991

Inside 2nd night. Atlanta. Opener – *Good Times Roll*. *Stranger* is rockin!

I'm not in a good head space today. I Love Atlanta, but somehow it's not right these days. (What is?) I'm on Jerry's side – stage level – with Jay. Got cramps bad, and I'm hatin' it. Glad I've got Jay to hang with. Keep that smile on my face. Today the lot was bunk. Get caught vending? – if ya got an ID, you get a ticket, NO ID – arrested. Caught 2nd time – arrested. Scary.

They Love Each Other!!!! So far it looks to be a hot show. Good, I need it.

This song is so beautiful. There's nothing like a fine connection. I miss Silas. Spring tour isn't the same without him. And without Corvette it's a whole different world.

Bruce is on stage. Didn't even notice if he was here last night or not. Now it's ~~Minglewood~~ nope, *Walkin Blooze*.

So... the escapades of late: Left Ma's and went to Jay's mom's place, slept, and left around 10:30AM, instead of 5AM like we had planned. Jay had this chick Cheryl with him. Can't help laughin about us caravanning, in two overly-stickered vehicles, through bum-fuck Jersey.

We had a good ride – 17 hours.

I don't think Jay had ever driven so long in one stretch. At one gas station he was dancing in manic circles 'cause he'd been eating No-Doz. Next time we stopped, he was lookin' green. Said the No-Doz and Dr Pepper hit his stomach hard. I bet. At 3:30AM just outside of Atlanta, we're trying to call Danni at the hotel she's supposed to be at, and she's not there. Fuck.

So I call Shawna – disconnected – and Carlos – answering machine. We don't know what we're gonna do. Jay's ready to sleep right there in the gas station. Then I find a slip o' paper which says, "King Henry in Atlanta." It looks pretty old, but I decide to call anyway. I figure I'll say, "I'm sorry it's 4AM, but I'm a friend of Henry's, and so are you. Do you know where I can find him?"

And who answers the phone but – King!

Ramblin Rose.

Jay and Cheryl went right to sleep. We sat up smoking with King till just before sun-up. I was overtired and it took me forever to fall asleep. I was awake by 10:30. We relaxed all day and wished it was a break day. But it wasn't.

Memphis Blooze.

That first day we didn't get to the lot till 4:30. Jay was bummed it was too late to set up. So last night him and Cheryl went to a hotel room with a friend of hers. They set up early today and made no money anyway. Bummer.

I hooked up with Jethro last night. Psyched. Went back to his new place. We drank a six and bullshat till 4AM, then I actually slept till 1PM!!!

High Time. This is probably my tune these days. "Nothing's for certain, it can always go wrong."

Promised Land.

2nd set – Why do we keep coming back? – Me and Jay ponder.

Help Slip Franklin's

I say, "We keep coming back because no matter how bad things get here, it's better than the rest of the world."

Vince wails, as Jay says, "Some come to laugh the past away, some come to make it just one more day."

Accidental Mary is in front of us – she gave me a bud for my cramps. It did the trick for a buzz, but I still can't dance. Sometimes dancing is the buzz. Just letting go.

Tonight is King Henry's famous warehouse party. I want Jay to come, I've been telling him about it since Albany.

I told Jay I probably would have given up this tour long ago if I hadn't met him. He said the same. "So why did we meet each other? To keep ourselves in a hell hole?"

It's like Meredith says – Deadheads are like lobsters – every time a lobster tries to crawl up the side of a tank to get free, some other lobster pulls it back down into the mire.

Last night Jay and Cheryl disappeared while I walked with Jethro. Jay said he'd wanted to stay, but the guy they were going with had to leave right away so more people wouldn't come to get their $ back for the bunk doses he'd sold. Yikes! Jay! Stop hanging with people who sell bunk doses. You're coming with me tonight. No ifs, ands, or buts. King's Warehouse party is the social event of the tour season.

He's Gone.

The security guard near here is pretty cool. She's good at catching amateur scammers – only the best get by her. Some people get mad, and she says, "Hey man, my boss is right there." So they say "ok" and leave. She winks at us and says, "Works every time."

Reminds me of outside Maryland, earlier this tour – a guard with a funky checkered hat says, "Time ta go. Get in the van."

And we say, "Can't. Person with the keys isn't here yet."

"That's what everybody says. I know it ain't true for half of you, but it works... it works."

We smile and say, "Every time."

late night

At the party. Yikes. Just Yikes. It's all kinds of tweaked here. The energy is all wrong.

Jay left the show after *Standin on the Moon* to go vend and I started heading out after *US Blooze* – hit the hallway and fuckin Cindy/April is the first to say, "Did ya hear? The Feds got Fritz."

NO!

I walked off. I didn't want to believe her. I didn't want her talking to me. As if that could change what I'd heard.

I saw Skye and she told me too. They came and got him there in the show. Men in suits walked up to him, sitting in the hall, "Are you Fritz?"

"Yes." And they took him away.

Oh! Not Fritz. Oh god! Oh goddess! NO!

I saw Jay outside. "They just took a good friend away," and my eyes water.

Poor Jay. I feel like I'm making him hate the whole scene. A lot has happened to make him hate it all by himself, but my attitude and input probably only makes it worse. He didn't want to come to the party and I didn't force it. He went to that same hotel room with the bunk doses guy.

I was gonna go by Fritz's van to see if there was any news, but I bumped into Sahana who shook her head, and said, "Don't. There's undercovers hiding behind it – peeking around every once in a while."

She went and tambourine-danced all around them till they left.

Tammy finally 'did the nasty', as she put it. Someone had to. She went and got his van and drove it here. It's here – at the party – parked under a bunch of lights, right next to a skateboard ramp Fritz would have loved.

The scene was so tweaked and weird outside. Crystal, reeling drunk and making a scene. "Why is Fritz's van here?!?"

I came inside but found it no better. Everyone is sketched. Weird vibes and a hard-to-swallow-tonight motto of 'We Will Survive' (like the flyers said).

Smoked a fat one in a corner with Yes Ma'am Sam and Ethan. Sat with Benny a few. He had a relatively mellow space as he waited for the music. He was pretty high and psyched to dance to the funk of Habernero.

So many things here make me miss Fritz. It's not the same without him – however much of a dick he is, I love him, and I wish he was here. I keep working on getting drunk, and I just keep hearing more and more bad news. Or skitched rumours.

Fritz had a hotel room key on him, and as soon as it happened, Kovack raced off to the hotel. He didn't return to the show, and hasn't shown up here yet. Everyone's sure there were cops in the room. I keep trying to tell folks there's another possibility – Kovack could have done ok and just be avoiding the party.

Sitting with Louziana Steve. Thinking of some good news. Jethro has Corvette's deposit from Josephine. There's our rent and phone for this month.

Danni came by and dropped off a small pile of money for me to count. Glad to learn it's not the Fritz fund (which I thought it was when she dumped it on me). It's the band fund. $85. I'd have been bummed if that's all there was in the Fritz fund.

FUCK.

My second possibility about Kovack is not holding up too well. Rockafucker – (Yes, they finally got here – they were just kicking back and avoiding tour.) Anyway, he called the hotel room. Unknowns answered. He said, "Is Kovack there?"

"No, he stepped out for a few, but come on over. Who's this?"

"Who is this?!?" They wouldn't say, so he screamed, "Fuck you pig." And hung up.

My pen is Dead.

Fritz I love you.

April 5

Tricky's situation is bad. It's simply a matter of money, or no money. We get $6,000 soon – and he gets 22 months (6 already served). We don't get $6,000, and he gets 5 years, straight up.

This, and Fritz, are the first things on my mind this morning. Morning. Ha. It's 4PM.

I don't like this world I'm living in. Even though I still believe it's better than the rest of the world.

What should I do?

later

I keep experiencing waves of despair. Hopelessness overwhelms me and I don't want to move or go anywhere. I'm so sad, and I don't know what to do with my life. Even going home to Cloverdale doesn't sound all that good.

Inside

Shakedown opener – Shakedown... that's for sure.

Everyone is so tweaked, the Fatty Zone is in a totally new place tonight, and I'm hibernating in my Killah seats.

When I saw Jake, we both frowned about the Fritz thing. He said they won't tell anyone why they picked him up. That makes things even scarier.

After Break –

Aiko Aiko. I bumped into Kirby from Alabama – cool beans. And while we're talking – who should appear – eyes popped wide and mouth too – but Cash Hamlin. Both he and Kirby were like, "What happened to y'all? It's been over a year!?" They've had no way to get in touch with us. We got too tweaked to keep in touch with them. Kirby said he owed Corvette $200. And Cash threw me a $50, saying he was sure he owed us something.

Up in the Fatty Zone – Kovack is here! They <u>were</u> in Fritz's hotel room. Kovack got $135 fine for possession of marijuana. Since they already know he's a friend, tomorrow he's gonna try to find out exactly what's up with Fritz.

King wants to ride to Orlando with me. Says everyone else is too sketchy right now.

Saint of Circumstance.

"Well I'm still walkin, so I'm sure that I can dance."

(Is that true? Is that how it works?)

Sure don't know what I'm going for... but – you know how it goes.

The Dead is like a fucked up relationship where the only thing good is the sex – the music, the concerts. So good, sometimes you want to believe the rest can be fixed. But some relationships can't be saved. Sometimes it's too painful to try. Sometimes, no matter how good the sex is, you're better off to just go.

"Terrapin, I can't figure out. Terrapin, if it's the end or beginning."

April 7   Orlando

Jory spaced me out and I got in really late. I caught *Uncle John's*, Drumz – Space –and then... *Box o' Rain*. Some guy behind me called it, and I thought, 'no way, not outta Space.'

King got me high during *Going Down the Road Feeling Bad*. It was wailin', I was lovin it. I so know the feeling. Jay wants me to do summer tour with him. Yeah right. I have been going down the road feeling bad. Something's gotta change. Am I even gonna keep doing tour? I really didn't care when I was stuck outside tonight, yet I was very happy to be inside and hear those few songs, and *Lovelight*.

Saw Mavis. WOW what an intense trip that was. She was talkin' a mile a minute, and I think she was really high. Seems the Fritz thing is an Ohio thing having to do with Mavis' friends. Yikes. She was way too tweaked for me. I just wanted to get away.

Afterwards me and King stressed each other out ridiculously. He made me feel bad about staying in his room and having no $. I think he was just mad because I didn't want to drive all over Orlando while having no idea of exact directions and although I did it, I bitched, because that's me, I guess. By the time I dropped them off (at what turned out to be the wrong Marriott because he couldn't get it straight), I was this close to crying.

It sucks. Being this broke – what am I gonna do?!?

Tour is almost over and I have no idea.

April 9 1991   Orlando

Hung by Jay all day. Worked alone and sold my extra. (I need the money.) The show was really good. Got a *Dew*. And a *Johnny B. Goode* encore that was excellent. Dancing was just what I needed.

Jay says, about the sex/music/relationship thing, – "Seems to me, when all that's good is the sex, it's a matter of how long is it worth putting up with it?" And that's the truth of it here, isn't it?

Last night Yes Ma'am Sam invited me to his room. I waited all night in my van at the wrong hotel. There's two Days Inns within two blocks.

late night

In Yes Ma'am Sam's room.

Tour is over.

What a wonderful day today was. And so much fun tonight! Jay even had me out there dancing barefoot in the hall. Wow, that'd been a while. Of course – last day of tour – make me love it like the old days. I had such a good time. Even though the music was much more "on" the first two nights. I loved *Saint o'*. And they closed with *Brokedown* – predictable, but very nice.

I got another $160 for Jack during my collecting. Schmitty even did some collecting during break. Right on.

Things are lookin bad for Tricky, though. I wish I could help somehow. There's more big busts, and need for money, than we Tourheads can keep up with. Most of us barely have the cake to keep going, let alone help everyone. Danni says if we don't cover Tricky's $, she's going to the court for his sentencing. Oh Jah, the thought of them sentencing Tricky to five years hurts me.

In the Fatty Zone tonight was a serious collection for some guy I've never heard of. And what has happened to/with Spaz? And Garrett? And most awfully, there's no word yet about anything we might do for Fritz. They've got him pretty tightly.

Hung with Jake tonight. He's the greatest. He does what he can for us, but still, some people fuck up no matter how good they got it. He tested his garbage crew tonight. – Told them, "No tix tonight, but clean up anyway and I'll be watchin'." He had tix for them, but none of them did any cleaning. He kept the tix in his pocket all night.

After the show he told me it was bad outside. Some guy drowned in the pond, and a van was driving through the lot, grabbing chicks, and molesting them. Yikes. What happened? Where was the someone to stop these things? No one went in to the pond to save this guy? Well, I heard eventually one guy did, and couldn't find him. Just one guy.

Everything seems fractured. (It's only fractured.)

I hope we're not doomed.

It's getting nigh on 4AM. I guess I should crash.

Oh, tour's over... For all I've hated it, I know I'm gonna be wishing for it before long.

43
Spring/Summer 1991
N'Awlins, Cal Expo, Cloverdale, and East Coast DeadFeat

April 13 1991 New Orleans
Here in N'Awlins I found Ohio Dave and Ethan. I'm on their hotel balcony in the warm New Orleans' breeze with no fucking clue what I'm doing. No idea what could be ahead in my life. I used to love the fact that it could all be different two weeks from now. But right now... it makes me uneasy. Perhaps it has to do with getting older. I mean, I'm 26, and what's my life about? What am I headed for? The Jazz Fest? Summer tour?!?!? Oregon Country Fair? Those are just destinations, but even so, – then what? And to what purpose? Is any of this life real? Or is it some elusive dream? Some fantasy that doesn't even exist?

April 14   New Orleans
Dave got a call this morning telling him that Mavis is in jail too. Dave says she's never been arrested for anything before.

April 16
I'm at Mirro's. Every day he swears there's a job for me here, or there – tomorrow. Always tomorrow. Living off breakfast bars and pretzels.
I feel alone. Thinking always about my tour people. My Family.
Thinking about Yes Ma'am Sam, and how he described the family as, "in one of its exploding times." And said, "It always does this, and when it comes back together, some people are gone, and some new ones are there. You and me are old hippies Hollie, we've seen it happen before." Ah but Sam, never to this level. We're being squeezed from every direction. The Dead wants us gone, the cops

want us all in jail, and we're even getting on each other's nerves. "It's all good." He said. "The Family will be fine, you'll see."

April 23 1991 New Orleans

I came to Brady and Joy's because I was sick of thinking Mirro's ever gonna come through with a job. When I got here Joy goes, "I know you. You're Schmitty's friend." Yep, that's me. What a change of atmosphere. Tye-dyes and Dead tunes. This house is breezy and cool. The living room has a high ceiling, chandeliers, and a balcony with two bedrooms off it. It's relaxing here. Joy goes to school at Tulane. Brady is Schmitty's t-shirt partner. He had some brown buds. We did bonghits wondering whether Schmitty will show up for Jazz Fest, or do Las Vegas and Cal Expo shows? If he comes here, we both hope he'll bring green buds.

I really just wanna go home. Not even sure how I can afford to get home. Brady offered to let me help sell shirts. I hear that selling outside the Jazz Fest is a hassle, but it can't be as bad as Deadland.

My problems are so small compared to some people's.

I'm thinkin of Fritz... and Mavis. I worry for them constantly, and no one seems to have any real news. Thinkin of Jack, and Carp, and Garrett. And Tricky... Oh Tricky. I wish we could do something for you. It sucks that $6,000 can make a 3½ year difference in his life. What kind of justice is that? Freedom for the rich enough? Kevin said Sid was sentenced to 9 months, plus time served. Said it cost a lot of cake for that. Sigh. What will Fritz and Mavis cost? And is there any amount of money that can save Kennedy?

Kevin believes someone is telling them the truth.

I hate this.

So much injustice and nothing I can do about it.

late –

I just got off the phone with Jumpin' Jack. I was blown away when Crystal accepted the collect call and said, "Yeah, hold on." In court today he talked his way out on OR. It's the best news I've heard in weeks.

Jack's going to Las Vegas, of course.

April 24 1991

It's a beautiful day in N'Awlins. Hanging with Brady and Joy has done me a lot of good. And the fact that Jack's outta jail is good too. Now I need to hear that Tricky's $ appeared.

April 26 1991

It's pouring, and no Jazz Fest for us today, but we're going to the Meters at Tipitina's tonight. Jack says he has enough money for the lawyer. He wants me to spend what lawyer money I have to get home.

May 3rd   California!

1st night Sacramento.

Dean got me high as soon as I landed on the lot. Then so did Shane, then Seth. So appreciated! Found Parker and Angie and Alex Schmalex. They all said I looked skinny and tan. Wolfboy Taylor said the same thing. He looked good too – clear-headed, and cute as he does at his best. I'm glad. I hate seeing people look like they've been indulging in the nasty drugs. Markness told me Corvette says she's gotten over the Dead. She's not here.

Jack bought me a ticket and we came in with Johnja. It's been so good to see Jack, but I can't keep up with him tonight. I came to Jerry's side to sit and write. I'm exhausted. Until I started writing I was about ready to close my eyes. Jack was bummed I didn't stay with him. He thinks I don't want to go with him tonight. I do, kinda, but I don't want to wander for two hours while he decides what we can do, and hopefully comes up with something that's ok by me, when I could jump in my van, head for Dandy Andy's Residence room, and be crashed within ½ an hour.

China Cat and now *Rider*.

Estimated.

It's dusty in here but the *Estimated* is hot. At least it sounds good to me. California!

Skye tells me things are rough for Fritz and Mavis. Word was spread around the jails that they're narcs, so they're really having a hard time in there. Telling people that is a real asshole move. People in prison don't like narcs. Poor Mavis, Poor Fritz.

Skye also told me what her and Calico discussed – About how the Dead can't help any of our friends in jail because the DEA would love to "get" them as a part of it all. What a joke. Like me, they're too scared to be a part of it – but dammit... this isn't about save-your-own-ass and pretend-you-don't-know-the-drug-dealers. You don't know the drug dealers! This is about our whole scene, our way of life, all the things we believe in. True, they have so much to lose. But can't they stand up for the injustice without looking like kingpins? Do we matter at all? I still think they could help somehow, if they really cared, anonymously if they had to.

Obviously they don't. And if that's true it makes the heart of this whole scene suddenly seem very hollow.

May 4

Outside. In the van. Didn't even try to get in.

Last night I went to the beer garden and got accosted by screaming happy California folk. The welcome was nice. Saw Yes Ma'am Sam. He always makes me smile. I also saw Freddy. He was psyched I gave him as much money as I could.

Things aren't too good with Jack and me. I wanted it to be better. But it just isn't.

May 6 1991   HOME

Already this morning Aaron has called to see if I have $ for the postcards. And John gave me a lowdown about his 6AM fights with Ryan over the puppies, and how he wants to buy this place from Francesca. It looks great around here. The neatly manicured garden – damn, John even scrubbed the old kitchen sink in the tree.

May 8

House meeting last night – Lila and Ryan are moving out. Santa is moving in.

May 10   Shoreline

Me and Markness came early and got in the good lot. I'm on the grass outside Domino's bus. Markness keeps coming by with his friends to smoke me out. Danni and Dave Echo stopped by and gave me a beer – a serious no-no. They're busting people for beers. It's getting close to ticket time. This sucks. I am so sick of being broke, needing a free ticket, having no buds. It's the lamest.

I miss Fritz. I miss being able to smoke pot whenever and wherever I choose. I hate the guys on the hill with their binoculars.

Kennedy got sentenced to 15 years. Fifteen fucking years. Oh Poor Kennedy, and Suzy too. Tricky got 22 months county time – Nasty but short. It's all so sad. I can't deal with it very well when I think about it.

4:44AM   Cloverdale

Hung most of the evening with Jack. NO one we knew up along the top. It was weird. Elsewhere we saw Justine, but no Don. Saw Shane, Dean, Benny, and Camera Brandon. And DigDoug and Katarina are around, but... well – it's not like it used to be.

I wasn't into the hotel scene. I'd been following Jack around all night, and I was tired and displeased with everything. I bummed $10 off Kenny for gas money and headed home.

May 18

Jay called, "Oh my god! I had to call you right away! I just heard a commercial for the Dead at Giant's 'with special guests Little Feat.' That means you can do summer tour! You said you might, if you had a way to make some money."

It's great news – without a doubt. Mostly it means we'll be able to make it to Abe and Jackie's wedding in NY. The timing couldn't be better – DEAD FEAT!

I'm gonna call the printer on Monday.

May 23rd

Yay! Corvette wants to go too. $318 per plane ticket and we're ordering 4,000 stickers for $880. That's more than double what we ordered last time, but it's New Jersey.

Kerry stopped by on his way to the JGB shows tonight. He had green cookies!

Corvette got a letter from Kennedy. I was pleased to find out Kennedy is intelligent! He writes neatly, and can express himself well. Yeah Kennedy.

I wrote a couple times, but haven't heard back from Fritz, or from Mavis yet. Izzy, Trinity, Becky, and Tammy have gone out to Ohio to visit them. I heard the Irvine thing caught up with Fritz too. Nonetheless, I can't help but hope they give him no time, I hope they end up with absolutely nothing on him, and I hope he's free soon.

May 24

Me and Corvette came to SF last night and halfheartedly tried to get in for Jerry at the Warfield. Everyone needed a ticket, so instead we went to Matt Ackerman's place, and drank strawberry margaritas.

Danni says Kennedy's lawyer was told "they" have phone conversations of Kennedy and someone in Maryland. Riley is in Maryland, and like Kevin said, it seems pretty obvious that someone is narcing. I don't want to believe it could be Riley, but his absence is jarring.

May 28   Cloverdale

Things are getting annoying around here with John. Yesterday he didn't agree with something and he went off. I told him to drop it. He wouldn't, and he kept getting louder. I do not like people screaming at me. Finally I let loose, "You're screaming at me! SHUT UP!" Corvette said he jumped, and she almost laughed. Later, in private, he apologized for losing his temper, then tried to re-enact the whole argument. He needs to learn to drop it. Pretty hard I guess, when you are John Principle Pemberton.

June 4 1991

Woke this morning to Santa wailing. "John says no one can plant on this side of the hill – we all have to go over the top because he's got this side." John apologized for all this yelling waking me, then tried to blame it on Santa.

June 5
Summer tour starts tomorrow.
Jack went to court today – postponed. Again.
I'm going to the city this weekend. Freddy wants me to help him shop for Abe's bachelor party.
Why me Freddy? "Because you owe me."

June 8 1991   SF
Freddy thinks Skye and the Hog Farm are CIA. I think he's overly paranoid. Yes, it's pretty sure someone is talking, but I don't think it's Skye, or Murph, or the Hog Farm.

June 13   DC
Washington Metro 7AM. Everyone is dressed in stodgy, business suits. The corners on everyone's mouths curve down. No smiles here folks. What do they think as they ride off to work? Seems the older the face, the deeper set the frown. And as the faces change with each stop, my observations hold true. So many frowns. God this is horrible. May all these people feel something today to make them smile. I've always heard it takes more muscles to frown than to smile. Typical America, wasting energy.

June 14 1991 –
Inside RFK. 2nd set. *Help Slip Frank,* now *Estimated.*
Jerry's hair is getting long, but he doesn't look so good.
DARKSTAR!
Drumz.
What a good show. Very glad we added DC to the trip.
The video screens are intense. Computer graphics are amazing these days, flying Yin-Yang hearts leaving trails. Dancing bears with spinning tye-dyes behind em. Dillon thinks there's subliminals coming through the video screens.
Lovelight has got the rafters rockin.

June 15 1991
Ozzy's apartment in NYC
Yesterday was the kind of day, and show, that makes the Dead almost like what it used to be. Thank you DC.
We saw Ozzy. He had no riders and we had no plan, so off we went with him and drove all night – well, Ozzy did. Corvette and I both slept. Woke up near Meadowlands and made our way to Deek's hotel. Deek picked up the Dead Feat stickers in Connecticut for us.

June 18 '91
Ozzy's apartment

I love Ozzy – he helped us so much this weekend, selling stickers, playing chauffeur, and he's gonna bring us to Connecticut today. Although I had fun, I'm glad I'm not going to Pine Knob. I think perhaps it was more fun for that reason.

What a weekend it's been!

Me, Corvette, and Ozzy got a room, then drove around selling Dead Feat stickers in hotel parking lots to get enough money to pay for it.

Saw James the beautiful hitchhiker and his wife Megan – they said they might come to California soon. Dimitri said he looked for us in Ohio so we could go to that Restaurant where we met. He bought stickers – we wholesaled to lots of people.

Some guy offered me an un-bloomed pinecone, "I'll trade you a Pine Knob for a Dead Feat" Good one! I had to give him one.

It's hot and humid here on the east coast, but 2nd day, about showtime, it finally rained and cooled off a bit. That day we had to rage on stickers. We had too many. Sell sell sell, and I have dead feet from so much walking. I'd say we have 1,400 stickers left. Yikes huh? Oh well, at least we're out of debt for postcards, and we made it for the wedding.

We gave Jake handfuls of stickers for both bands. Little Feat's manager sent Backstage passes for us, and Jake gave us two extra tix. We gave one ticket to Ozzy and the other to Armand.

We had to deal with some tripped out tweaking chick. Where did she even get drugs? There's nothing psychedelic around. Well. Maybe that's why she was tweaking – there's nothing GOOD around. Just about everyone with the good stuff is shut down.

After the show I hooked some Connecticut acquaintances up with Shane. Jah Love. They were psyched. They got the best, the beautiful, the family stash.

Speaking of best and beautiful, Dimitri had the winning line for selling stickers. "I got the Big Sticky Purple."

June 24 1991

Abe and Jackie's wedding was beautiful. Freddy was best man, and Jillian was the flower girl. After the receiving line, we found our way to the groom-room for fatties.

Freddy kept coming up with bottles of champagne, and we chowed on appetizers, "Where's the shrimp lady?" Once Abe told them not to ignore the hippies, – we were honored guests, they brought whole trays of the good stuff.

They played *Scarlet Fire* and, as per request of the newlyweds, all us dressed-up Deadheads got out on the dance floor and made a scene.

44
Summer/Fall 1991
John You're Such an Asshole – Reggae – Avoiding Shows

July 1

I hate living with John. He's wound too tight. This morning him and Erika were cleaning. I could feel the attitude in the air. They think we should be cleaning too, or that we should have done it already.

Me, Santa, and Corvette agree that living with John is not working out, but we don't know what we'll do about it.

Santa left this morning without a word to anyone.

July 7 1991

Don and Justine had a party. Me, Corvette, and Markness went. Up past Garberville and out along dirt roads. What a crew up there. Santa (that's where he's been), KJ and Mirabeth, Dean, Kerry and Izzy, June, Katarina, DigDoug, Becky, JohnRay and Paige. There were lots of Farmer folks I didn't know, and some nice fattys. I hadn't seen a crowd like that – sittin smoking fatties – in a long time.

Trinity is so talkative. She could say too much. Probably no public schools for you Trinity. We can see it now – showing pictures to kids like they do these days, "Do your parents have one of these?" And she'd say, "No, my Mom's bong is a Graphics."

We caught some good fireworks. I kept joking – "How would we know we're free, if we didn't see stuff exploding in the sky once a year?" Kind of ironic that we spent so much of the day writing cards to friends in jail, on a day when we're supposedly celebrating freedom.

JGB at the Eel was cancelled. Rumours say Jerry is in the Hospital or rehab. With the Eel cancelled, it's gonna mean lots more Deadheads at the Oregon Country Fair, I hope not too many though. Too many Deadheads can ruin almost anything – sad but true.

Got a letter from my beautiful Hitchhiker James. He and Megan are packing it up there in Jersey and moving somewhere. They're not sure where yet, maybe North Carolina, but he promises to keep in touch.

Today's Sunday. We're working the Sebastopol flea. It's slow. Kinda cold, and hazy. Yesterday we did great, – Mark came with us. He walked around swinging buds. Afterwards we went to Lila and Ryan's new place. None of us wanted to go home to Cloverdale. Santa stopped by too, so we ended up with a little exile party.

I don't enjoy my own house with John living in it too.

None of us do.

July 25 (26th?)
Cloverdale

Life with John continues. It's such a double edged sword. I often dread what the house would become without John's ingenuity and willingness (need, even) to do the dirty work – ie – get the dead cat out of the well. Mark tried to tell us he can do all that John does. We told him, "that may be true, but... you don't."

We've gotten into doing the 420 thing. It's a fun concept with two possible backgrounds. #1 – there are 420 psychoactive chemicals in marijuana, or #2 "4-20 in progress" means marijuana smoking in cop language. It probably cosmically came from both of those two factors. Anyway the thing to do is get stoned at 4:20 and put energy towards pot being legalized – it can't hurt.

July 30th 1991   Jokeland

Last night John and Erika went out to dinner. While they were gone, the other four of us poured over the phone bill. Fretting over the unclaimed calls – like every month.

When they came home – a fight at the top of everyone's lungs. I told them we'd all decided that we'd like them out by November 12th. (We picked that date so his ladies will have time to mature and be harvested.)

John threw a fit. Saying it was bullshit to say we liked him, but didn't want to live with him. Mark reminded him that he'd said exactly that about KJ and Mirabeth. John lives such a double standard, and you're in for it if you say so. He'd point out things about me he didn't like, and I'd point out that he was the same in that respect, – that's why we clash.

All that yelling. I felt like I was gonna puke.

FUCK, what a mess.

John couldn't accept that we tried. We invited them to live in OUR house. The one WE found, but we just don't live well together. He could only see that we were attempting to take something away.

This morning the feeling of nausea remained. I wanted out.

I went to Lila and Ryan's. They were fighting about the phone bill. Ugh. I left, and came to Parker's.

August 5th

Did some good talking and maneuvered the van to the right lot at Reggae on the River; where the schoolbuses were. I wedged my van in between two rows, just across from the 'old crew' scene.

Kevin had his RV there. Seth was parked next to the RV, and Santa and Corvette behind it. Both of Murph's buses were there, and Skye's Scarlet Bee bus, and Kerry's new bus, which was empty, except for four schoolbus seats, and some futons in the far back. There were lots of fattys on that bus.

At midnight I got a birthday surprise. Markness had brought Kahlua, vodka, and milk – Yeah! Loving the white Russians on my b-day.

Next morning a skinny with Schmitty. Then Jumpin' Jack came by and gave me a pair of pants and a lighter case. Maureen gave me a necklace of a Dragon Claw holding a tiny crystal ball. Told me she groundscored it at a biker fest and hadn't even worn it until she left for here, and when she heard it was my b-day, she knew it was for me. Corvette gave me a blank book with a blue gemstone cover.

At night, Jack made himself comfortable with his head in my lap. He said he'd give me a massage. We went to my van and just sat there, not even talking. Eventually he asked, "Are you kicking me out of the van tonight?"

"Sort of. Probably."

"Don't worry, I know the way," he said, and jumped out. Slept in Kevin's tent I guess. Kevin had two huge tents set up for whomever. That's where Santa and Corvette slept.

Actually Jack took it rather well.

Next morning I was walking over there as he got up. We bullshat, got stoned, and went for coffee.

Overall the Eel kind of sucked with how many fences and hassles there were. So militant. Not like the old days at all. Used to be you could wander from campground to campground in the middle of the quiet Humboldt night.

Now you need the right bracelet for each different campground, and there are all-night road cops, and huge spotlights over the place lighting it up like mid-day.

I don't think I'll go to Jerry this weekend. Beau reminds me that Jerry's getting out of rehab, and everyone agrees, Jerry plays best when he's just out of re-hab.

But, I just don't think I care.

August 6th

As I draw up my calendar for the rest of the year, I write in the Tour dates and such. Yet I'm not sure I want to be there anymore. I don't care what they play. And I think upon the Joseph Campbell article where he says of the Dead, – They tap into the song of being, and allow 8,000 souls to be at one with the song of life and each other.

I've been there. I've done that. I even got addicted to it. The energy that surges through the concert hall – twisted and swirled and becoming the music/myself. What an unbelievable feeling, – To Dance freely while the music plays the band. But it's more than that. It's the mind, the heart, the soul. The conversation between these notes and deep deep wells of Knowledge. Stirrings of ancient feelings, and to be at one with such an awesome thing.

Lewis Sanders' book has a foreword saying – the heads who follow the Dead are spiritual seekers, looking for a way to hold on to the divine knowledge conjured by the Dead, and by the Deadheads themselves when the spirit is right. Something about finding nothing to believe in, spiritually, in the "real" world. And it's true. It's all true. I've always been searching. Still am.

I wonder how it is that the life dance no longer hits the chords in me? I mean, what have I lost? Is it perhaps only possible for one to attain such absolute bliss and Love of life by being somewhat naïve? Not letting things get to you? Only caring about the music and the spirit of freedom, – Government, and Authority figures, and all the bad things in the world be damned! And is this carefree dance-filled world no longer attainable once one is no longer immune to seeing horrible things for what they are?

I know that others still dance blissfully, eyes closed, heart and mind full of music, souls communicating with souls on another level where we know we are the eyes of the world.

It goes on, yet it seems I too have gone on. For I have been faced with injustices that link me to the real world. I'm not sure what I'm trying to say. Except that I have been a part of the most wonderful, magical singing of the human song. I have been "it" with 1,000's of others. It has been me. It is still in me, but now, it seems low and distant, as it seems in so many other souls I've seen, in so many many places. Lucky are we who have basked in its full orchestral strength. Lucky to get a feel for what it really means to be alive. Too many are the people who live their entire lives without a hint of the peace and magic we worked towards creating and becoming each night of a show.

Perhaps it is merely time for me to move on to the next lesson in what it means to be alive.

So what is next? What goes beyond the fat man and his magical musical cohorts? After Donna Godchaux left the band, she was spotted as a Christian born-again gospel singer. Theo, who left us for the Spinners, then left the Spinners, lives in his hometown in Indiana going door to door as a Jehovah's Witness. That is not the answer for me. I'll not go from the Dead, and a celebration of many individuals made one, to a worship of one outside source. Oh no.

Somewhere inside me I know why it rains. I know how to make an H-bomb if anyone else knows it. I get tripped up on things I think I know, or think I need to know.

And here I am – composed of, and composing, the most magnificent forces imaginable. Being myself, a part of all that is – yet such a tiny part – so un-fucking-believably small, it's hard to fathom that I matter at all. Yet I'm sure that I do.

If I leave, where will I experience the life song again? When will I find that I'm in the perfect position to be it, and to be happy in and with myself, and everything around me? For that can be the only goal – to experience the joy of being all that we are.

And I write and I write and I write, for all these years, not having any idea what I'm aiming for. And each step I take, each thought I think, each word I write, leads me to something.

Something.

Something about where I'll understand, maybe, that there is no better or different than here, when you know the things we all know in our hearts...

I got all philosophical and cryptic with myself there. It's confusing, so I'll just go back to my calendar and try to figure out what I'm gonna do about rent, and what I'm gonna do about MSG and Boston Gardens shows. And the house? – what do I want to do about that?

8-9-91   Cloverdale

Not at the Eel River. JGB plays there tomorrow. Me and Corvette don't have tix and it was too militant at Reggae. Also, Rent is due Monday. We don't have it yet. Everyone we mention it to says, "something will happen." I hope so. I hope money appears for Corvette's rent (because she wants to stay), and maybe I'll sublet my room to Skinny Jim. He appeared yesterday, – been in Alaska.

8-11-91

Lots of folks coming through – back from the Eel and headed to Sacramento. Most notably, Santa showed up with Tavi! I was so psyched to see him. He was all tan and had a broken arm. He's been out of jail since June.

Cal Expo starts tomorrow. I don't care. I'm not going.

8-12-91   Cloverdale

First night of Cal Expo was tonight. I never could understand why people wouldn't go to a show that was so close. But, yet, here I am.

8-17-91   Cloverdale

I heard they did a 1st Set *Dark Star* at Shoreline, and a *Scarlet Victim Fire*. Markness said he didn't like the new unusual transition. I'd love to hear a tape. I can see the place so clearly in my mind. The dusty ridge along the top. We used to joke that from there, we'd never know if it was actually the band playing, or if they merely put on a tape and were bluffing us. Dancing is the only thing I'm missing about these shows this week.

8-21-91

Today I wrote jail letters – To Garrett (he gets out on Sept 23), to Fritz, to Carp, to Kennedy, to Tricky, and to Bradley. No wonder I'm so down on this world huh?

I have a buzz. We had a choice tonight – food or beer. We chose Red Tail Ales. And I am, as such, feeling the effects. Nothing like sitting around drinking Reggae, smoking Red Tails, and listening to kind buds.

Also, copying out my old high school notebooks onto Mark's computer is affecting me – giving me an overview. Life goes up to great moments, and back down, and inevitably, back up. A see-saw. That's all life is.

Maybe the point is not to get thrown when going up too fast, or jarred too badly when it slams into the ground.

August 27 91

John's Hilton, filled with people, got home from JGB at Squaw Valley yesterday with Dean, Becky and Devon, Jeremy, Kerry, Izzy and Trinity, Zingo Zango (King's latest nickname), June, and Dillon.

Instantaneously the house was alive, with music blaring, and two little kids workin a four hour bus ride outta their little legs at top speed around the porches. Izzy and Becky made Lasagna, and beer flowed. Trinity was amazed with the bed with water in it. This morning she and I watched videos in my room. The entire house was awake and ragin' by 8AM. It's 1^{ish} now and all have left.

The weekend sounded like good fun. I knew it would be, but it also sounded like the same old same old. Jeremy broke a hotel mirror skateboarding in a room. Ah-ha! The cops came into Tammy's van and found six ounces of kind bud. Izzy claimed it and it cost $5,000 in bail. Then another $1,000 for an old warrant of stealing in Redding. It was Kerry's pot this weekend, and in Redding, it was Lou who stole the wine. In both cases Izzy claimed it because the actual persons had warrants. It sucks that she'll go through this and neither time was it hers. Oh and it seems they've confiscated Tammy's van with no intention of returning it. Tammy must be hatin' it. She moved in with Don and Justine recently, and the DEA called her there, to ask questions about Fritz.

Scary!

Sept 2

Went to Accidental Mary's annual party. It was smaller than last year. My crew was there, but... something's different in me. I even manage to feel a bit out of place stepping up for a fatty. Feel like a stranger! And I have an Inner Circle gold card! That used to be our joke – 'cause when Fatty Circles in the hall were the rage, it would gather a crowd of wanna-bes, and wanna-get-high-folk. The inner circle was doing the rolling and kicking down, so fattys would circulate the inner circle two or three times before going out to the rest of the crowd. With an Inner Circle gold card one could come late, move through the outer crowds, and find room to sit (in the middle) where there was formerly no room. At those times I felt at one with the friends around me. Sharing what, to us, was comparable to a religious communion. – "Come, let us break buds together."

Complete Peace and Freedom in a heaven we had created for ourselves. What more could a soul really want? Isn't that what people aim for spiritually? Peace? And contentment?

9-10-91

Tonight is the 3rd night of the MSG shows. I wish I was there. At Lindy's, the Penta Bar, NYC. Last year the bartenders asked where Carp was. Do they wonder this year where me, Corvette, or Fritz, is? Do they ask? I know Benny and Don are there, and I'm sure there's plenty enough other Deadheads to fill the bar... but... I mean, – it's probably not like it used to be for us, probably not enough of one crowd of friends to fill the place. I wonder if they notice, at Lindy's, that most of us aren't there?

9-23-91

Today is the day Garrett gets out of jail in Nassau. Today is also the first plant cutting here at the house. And tonight I'm leaving for Olivia and Bruce's in Oregon – I'm gonna house sit for a month while they go to Amsterdam.

9-26-91   Oregon

Left Cloverdale Monday night. The picking of the early stuff at our house smelled wonderful. I got to Hawkeye's at 6:30AM. Still dark. The wolves howling to the moon as I went to sleep. Janelle woke me before she left for work and let me in the house. I spent the afternoon dozing and watching TV. When Hawkeye got home from work we Bullshat.

Work. Yep. Both of them. Work.

We talked about how 'they' successfully ruined 'us'. Talked about how we'll never have what we had before. Even when everyone eventually gets out of jail, it's not like it'll go back to what it used to be. It won't. It's sad. Everything we had is frayed and unraveling. With as fractured as it all seems, I find it hard to remember how Yes Ma'am Sam said it'll come back together.

Left Hawkeye's in the evening (after a buzz from his early cuttings) and came to visit Bob and Marie Snodgrass'.

~~~~~

And so I'm in Oregon. While The Dead is in Boston.

10-16-91   Oregon

Corvette called – Danni got busted.

Danni! No! My heart sank.

She had always said, "If anything ever happens to me, I want you to handle it." And I can't do anything from here.

"But she's out," said Corvette.

Oh man.

I called Danni. She went to the last two MSG, and five Boston shows. Her friend Addison got busted in NYC, and the cops broke his ankle in two places. On her way home something happened in Nevada. She didn't say what, but it doesn't sound good. They got her phonebook. My # is in it. The old Paranoia kicks in.

45
Fall 1991
Fare You Well Bill Graham

10-26-91
Home – Cloverdale

Just heard that Bill Graham Died in a helicopter crash.

No! We're trying to find news.

Oh man. I've always liked Bill, – no matter what people say about him. At this point I refuse to believe it.

later

It's true – Bill Graham is Dead.

This is horrible. He died last night in a plane crash in Sonoma county.

Nothing is cancelled – not even tomorrow's show. They plan to follow through with all his plans. They say, that's what he'd want.

Oct 28 1991

Yesterday we all rode down to the Oakland Coliseum for the show in the Hilton. I hadn't seen the Dead since June and I felt like I had to go – to say goodbye, or pay my respects. Something.

I hung a lot with Janey, working pack-check. Saw Meredith excitedly telling everyone, "I'm pregnant with Benny's baby." She was glowing. We hoped Benny felt the same way. When we saw him, we said our congrats, and asked if he was as happy as she seemed. He said, "I will be."

We saw quite pregnant Della – due in December. She said she was "trying to get on General Assistance, and get a place before the baby comes." She sounded as if the other half wasn't around, whomever he might be. I wish her and especially the child lots of luck and good things. Also saw Bianca – she was way pregnant too.

Didn't talk to her at all, but it was nice to see her smile from across the way.

Vance and Denise were there! Clarity's cute little pudgy cheeks have thinned as she's grown. She was bouncing around, "I'm from Canada and I haven't seen the Dead in two years. I need a ticket!"

Tickets were hard to come by, but Beau and Rebel took care of us.

I dressed nice – in mourning for Bill. He did more for Rock-n-Roll than any other one person, ever. I heard on the radio that he did an average of 500 shows a year – that's 1½ shows per day. After the first set, Bill's son David came out to make announcements. He was teary-eyed and having a hard time. "My Dad fucking loved you all." People did a lighter tribute – the whole place filled with tiny flames – like bits of Bill's soul that resides in each of us.

It was a great show. *Cassidy* in the first set was especially nice. Second set Erika rolled a ladies-only joint, and they broke into *Women are Smarter* but it became *Aiko* instead. And then – what? – what's this? – it sounds like *Hand Jive* – no – it's – it's *Mona*! Oh yeah! And there, on the stage, is Santana, and someone else, – wailing. I don't think the Dead ever did *Mona* before.

During *Miracle,* we laughed, wondering when Bobby will admit reality and sing, "I need a woman 'bout half my age."

Oct 30 '91

The 28th I had a great day, and a super fun show. Haven't had so much fun in a while. Even Jerry was having a grand time on stage. It's nice to see him enjoying himself.

When I saw Rebel, he told me how hard I'd worked and he walked me in and gave me a backstage pass too. He showed me where to eat (chocolate covered strawberries), and drink, and play free video games. And where the band might be on break, if I wanted to try to see them. (I didn't have enough pot to bother any of them.)

Rebel got two Bill Graham memorial armbands from some guy and we brought one to Beau, who was announcing the volleyball game. I didn't know they still did that. I remember it from my first New Year's show. We got stoned – me and Rebel – up in the stands, before he went back to work.

Bertha opener. Ooooo! Such a good one! *Wang Dang* was great too. I danced around by the side of the stage. I bopped through the halls a bit first set, and spent some time with Arthur and Jasmine, but I enjoyed the available space in the backstage areas better. During break, they had free Ben and Jerry's ice cream! Janey was back there – we schmoozed around together.

2nd set they opened with *Saint o' Circumstance*. It was long and spacey with loud catastrophic chaos, spinning and crashing, taking me. I danced like mad. I had so much room, and the sound was soooo good.

When I ventured out into the hall, I came upon a scene of a small fatty crowd being hassled by a cop as he looked for the fatty he was sure he'd seen. He didn't find it. He moved on to the next group, got some young guy rolling a joint, and took him away. All people I vaguely know. Not what I wanted to see or experience. I retreated to the uncrowded spaces in the special seating, got stoned, and watched the rest of the show in my own little world.

Went backstage again afterwards and watched the boys leave.

Nov 1, 91

We went to pack-check when we hit the lot. Corvette gave presents to Beau and Rebel – lady presents from the hill. They were quite pleased.

Rebel brought us inside early, we decided to save some good seats. Phil's side of course. We found a good to see, old time crew – Anton, Gitch, Silas, Jeanie, Hackmen, and an assorted few more. Corvette got to show them some ladies to be proud of. Rebel even made it by for a fatty after drumz.

Nov 3 '91
Golden Gate Park SF

Got up in the dark and left Cloverdale as the sun rose.

We're here. It's 9AMish. It's packed already. And it's a beautiful day.

Matt Ackerman's Dyes hang proudly from atop the stage!

And banners on the stage say, "Fare you well, Fare you well, We love you more than words can tell." As Skye said – Maybe this'll be enough to send Bill off right.

later

Janey came by with awful news. – Beau was just run over by a forklift – his ankle is fucked and he's on his way to the hospital. Oh Beau! Be okay.

later

Skip and Anna are here!
And Cute Allen's here! I love Cute Allen!

Robin Williams on stage, "The sunsets over the next few weeks are Bill's lightshows."

What a day! Bill We Love You!!!!!!!!!!!!

[Mark's handwriting]

> TODAY IS THE SHIT!
> WHAT AN INCREDIBLE SHOW.
> So many here to celebrate Bill moving on.
> It's amazing the effect his death is having on people – no sad faces, just joy and reverence for a man who was a sort of a Johnny Appleseed in the music biz. The bands are giving nothing short of their best – the high energy has been sustained from minute one.
> Praise Jah –
> The world stops for a day and ponders Bill Graham.
> A lone butterfly floats high above the festivities – could it be Bill Graham checking things out? I'd like to think so.
> Crosby!   Stills!   Nash!   and...   Young!!!!
> Wavy Gravy
> THE DEAD (NO HORNSBY)
>   BOB IN A BUCKET

[me]

> A plane flies overhead – Drops roses over the crowd.
> China -> Rider

[Mark]

> WANG DANG with John Popper
> "crack equipment crew, this may take a moment"
> with JOHN FOGERTY WEARING PLAID – do Dead men wear plaid?
> SMOKING!!

*Phil's bass and JF's voice
– Born on a Bayou ★★★
Smiling faces and dancing people everywhere –
What a rager!*
GREEN RIVER

[me]

This is the best Dead show I've seen in who knows how long. Thanx again and forever Bill

[Mark]

The shit eating grins tell the story – what a blast!
BAD MOON RISING
PROUD MARY (JF exits)
TRUCKIN – Steal it, Bobby!
-> Jerry Jam, Phil Other One-ish, but slow ->
THE OTHER ONE –   God I love this song –
Phil is Still Pounding
-> WHARF RAT
-> SUNSHINE DAYDREAM (I was wondering when they'd finish Sugar Mags from Sunday)
(E) with Neil Young
"Letter from Bob" FOREVER YOUNG
(E2) TOUCH OF GREY
JOAN BAEZ – Amazing Grace
GRAHAM NASH and KRIS KRISTOFERSON

[me]

Bye Bill. We love you more than words can tell!

46
Winter 1991/1992
Holidaze, Hitchhikers, Oakland Shows, and A Job (Shudder)

11-24   Cloverdale

Danni came to visit. Then Skye, Dawn, and Meredith showed up too.

Meredith is showing, and I hear Benny has abandoned her. I don't know whether to hope that's true or not, him being such a junkie these days.

Skye's also pregnant. And Danni told me (quietly) that she's pregnant too. Oh Danni! I hope you make the right choices for your particular life. I love you so much.

Me, Corvette, and Markness have begun to visualize our next perfect house. Now that this year's work on the hill is done, they both say they want to get away from John's energy.

November 29 91

Weird Thanxgiving. Hypocritical Holiday. We made no plans and ended up here with John and Erika which really darkened what one should feel on Thanxgiving.

But what am I talking about? What should one feel? – Thankful that we were strong enough to take the entire land from the Natives who shared our meal that first year? (Isn't that what John's doing to us?)

Nov 30

Saw Zero tonight at the Cotati Cabaret. Got a ride with Jeremy and his friend Ross. Zero wailed! I knew we'd bump into Saint Randy. Went by his house with the crew we had and smoked them out. Perry was there and so was Preston. They like to laugh about the days I lived under their dining room table.

Dec 1   Oakland

At Parker and Angie's. Glad to be away from our house. One minute Corvette wants to move, next minute she wants to stay and deal with it. I'm not wishy-washy at all. – I don't want to be anywhere near Cloverdale. (I just need to figure out where I do want to be.)

Dec 2 91

I took a bus to Telegraph to see Garrett. He doesn't look like he's doing too badly. Selling jewelry and getting by. Living on a bus that Freddy gave him. He had a good little crew. He told me so, many times. One deadbeat chick to get rid of, and two swingers that had to go. (Banjo and some other guy.) Same old same old.

I sat with him at his stand for a few hours. This chick Celeste bought buds from me, and Garrett left her to watch the stand, while we went to his bus and got stoned. We walked the long way around People's Park. He had lots of chicks to talk with and hug. He was Lovin life in a classic Garrett way. I'm glad for him.

I got some good massages. He was amazed I'd come to see him. Kept asking where I was sleeping tonight and I kept saying, "Not with you."

I'm definitely drawn to something in him, and I wanted to see him, but I didn't want to sleep with him.

Dec 8 91   SF

Inside the Warfield, way up in the top back corner. Last night I didn't bother trying to get in – being Saturday night. I didn't want to fight all the ticket-needers. It took me a while to get in tonight. I stood around by the bus stop long enough, and when Seth left early and I went to say Hi, the guards gave me a ticket.

I was talkin' with a kid who'd picked up tour in Boston. He was trying to decide between going to college back home in Rhode Island, or traveling like this for a while. He was young, and sweet and innocent. I wish him the best in his tour career. There was also some wingnut Junkie bitch throwing bottles at the Warfield from across the street, but she was slow, and loud, and easy to dodge. It was like everyone out on the sidewalk was playing a surreal game of dodgeball as they walked around pretending it wasn't happening.

Jerry's little quartet is wailing.

Ah Jah, thanx for the flowers. Buds and the Warfield go so nicely together.

Dec 9

Just home after a hard day of hitchhiking. Speaking of hitchhiking, Corvette says James and Megan are in Santa Rosa and coming to spend the night.

James is coming! My beautiful hitchhiker!

Dec 10 1991

James and Megan are frantically looking for a house. They packed up their lives in Jersey. They have a rent-a-truck full of all their shit, that has to be returned on Friday. Megan starts work in Sonoma Monday morning.

Dec 14   Cloverdale

It's fucking cold. I hate the fact that my fingers are freezing in my own bedroom. Next place of residence, I want it to be warm when I'm inside in the winter.

James and Megan moved into a place in Sonoma. More expensive than they expected, but they didn't leave themselves enough time to find a good house.

12-17-91

Got up Sunday morning to head to the Bay. Ice on the van. Actual ice and somehow the defroster no longer works. Went by Danni's. She was lookin through a baby name book. Best of luck to you mama.

Next I went to the Telegraph Xmas Street Faire. Road closed, vendors in the streets. Worked Garrett's stand while he swung my buds. He bought a bunch of our earrings for $35, says he can double that, and it'll be a good addition to his stand. Of course Garrett wanted me to stay. Of course I didn't. I love Garrett, and sometimes I wish he could be what I need. But he isn't.

Dec 18 1991

James and Megan want me to move in with them. The master bedroom is separate, with a den, and a bathroom. Megan was worried about the fact that I sell pot, because James wants to grow pot, and she doesn't like the idea of both going on. James' main worry was about how sometimes, living with people, you come to dislike them. (Ha! Tell me about it!) He didn't want that to happen to us. Jah, I wouldn't want that either.

Could I live with Megan and James? Can I live with John much longer?

Corvette read a quote out of a book tonight (as we finished writing Xmas cards), it said something like, "Go ahead jump in – either you'll learn to swim, or you'll drown, and if you drown – better luck next lifetime."

Dec 21 '91   Sonoma

Ross came down to surprise kidnap Corvette. (They've been seeing each other ever since they met.) She'll stay up north with him through Xmas. I'm waiting to hear back about a plane ticket I saw in the paper. RT to Boston.

I'm at James and Megan's house.

If I want the major change I say I want – here it is. I'm sitting in what could be my room. It's huge – with a bathroom attached. Pure luxury. It'd cost $200 a month – straight up, includes everything. There's central heat! Especially nice – considering the wood pile Santa brought to Cloverdale for us all (and he hasn't been there since), – the wood that I was using to keep my room warm so I could write and work, has been moved. Yes, John moved the fucking wood pile and won't tell me where it is. So no Fire = no heat in my room. I don't want to live with someone who'd hide a woodpile, but it feels like I might be taking a giant step away from my whole world if I make this move. Do I want out badly enough to move from a mountain paradise to suburbia?

Dec 22   Cloverdale

The plane ticket was sold already. I'm stuck in California for Xmas. I'm hatin my whole situation. No idea which way to turn.

Freddy visited last night. He brought Jillian. She's "4½ almost 5." At first she was quiet and shy. Then, when Freddy went out of the room, I asked, "Jillian, how are you doing?"

"Fine," looking at the floor.

"Really?" I said. "You look a little sad to me."

She pouted, "My mom doesn't live with us anymore."

I frowned with her, "Yeah. I know. That makes you sad huh?" She nodded. "And you miss her?"

"Yeah... and my Dad.... he misses her too... he's sad too."

"I'm sure she isn't happy to be away from you."

"She was only my step-mom."

"Yes, but she loves you. And you know what?"
"What?"
"Your Daddy will never leave you."
"I know." She smiled as we heard him coming up the stairs. And when he got back in the room she was her talkative, active, little Jillian self. She had two Xmas cookies, and we watched her bounce on the bed with sugar energy, singing Frosty and Rudolph for us.

later

I did the I-Ching.
I got RETREAT.
I can't win. Retreat is the best possible course. Retreat isn't a loss, but a regrouping, away from destructive forces. The others were UNITY – with a changing/ruling line which said – I was being brought to the right people for the necessary connection. And the last one was PROGRESS.

I seem to have gotten my answer right there.

Dec 23

I gave James the definite yes on that bedroom. Corvette will probably move in with Ross, grow buds, and live happily ever after. She's there all the time anyway, and not at all interested in looking for another house.

It's all such a disappointment – the potential this house held for us when we first found it. Like a nasty tomcat, John pissed all over everything till nobody else can stand the smell. I hope he's happy with his fucking dream house. I hafta believe karma will take care of him for me. Slimeball. (Apparently I'm bitter.)

Dec 24   Cloverdale

Helena came for dinner! (She's headed to Izzy's.)
Some of the talk tonight got me thinking about the family we all pretended to back when. How it almost happened for us hippies and the crew we called family. Pure belief in it by so many, for so long, almost made it a reality. But something went wrong for the Fatty Family. Was it the DEA? Was it Karma? Was it something we did wrong?

There's still family, but it's obvious to us all that it's coming apart. Where will we all be in 30 years?

Dec 26 1991

Beau's foot is fucked. That forklift really did a job on him. They replaced the bone with a rod. He jokes about how he beeps at airports now.

Dec 27 1991   Oakland

Just got off the phone with Danni. Dillon got busted in Ohio (Fuckin Ohio), and needs $1,000 by tomorrow morning. She's not going to the show tonight because it's raining and yucky, she doesn't feel well, and she has no tix. I have no tix either. But I can probably get in. She tried to make me feel like, – if I don't get 1,000 bucks for Dillon, he's fucked. Don't put this on me Danni. Let Gwen collect Dillon's money. I'm so out of that world, I want nothing to do with bail collects.

Seems suddenly to me like my own actions are part of family not being what it used to be. I think this family that I used to believe was so strong, has been coming apart at the seams for a while. Somehow I contribute to that. I don't wanna be surrounded by jail/paranoia vibes. I don't have anything to do with dealing drugs for a damn good reason. The money is no longer a good enough tradeoff for all the stress. I'm not even very supportive of that lifestyle lately. That's probably hypocritical, but hey I'm American. Hypocrisy is our thing.

late night

Went to the show and didn't think about Dillon at all. I wanted to forget and I did. I'm sorry Danni. Forgive me.

I got there way late. The rain had let up. Pack-check was closed already. No way to get walked in. I finally got a free ticket – last song before break, but I don't even know what song it was.

Saw Yes Ma'am Sam, Freddy, Janey, and Garrett as soon as I got in. We smoked a fatty, then I went inside and sat on the stairs with Garrett. He had a mega-headache but still gave me a back rub.

Dec 29 91   Break Day

Rebel walked me in last night. Hung out with Markness and his new girlfriend Simone. Her brother was there for his first Dead show ever. He had the usual "lovin-it-at-my-first-show-smile." Kept saying, "This is like nothing I've ever seen before."

I know.

I enjoyed the music quite a lot. Seeing the scene through the eyes of a first timer, is always pretty great. Still the Dead is the only band I know that can rock any place all the way to the rafters. They're beyond amazing.

late night SF

The Toronado was raging tonight. Don, Becky, King Henry, Elvis, Kestrel Jim, Danni, and Benny – who, when I remarked about his clean shaven face, said, "Yep. Face like an angel, and a heart like the devil."

"Can I quote you on that?"

"Yes, and I expect you will." He didn't look so haggard as he did the last few times I've seen him. I almost didn't recognize Dave Echo with his beard. Dave is one of the folks who can always make me smile.

Izzy looked drunkish and happyish clinging on a tall hippie boy.

I guess Kerry and King have a place together now. I don't know. I don't currently care much about the politics of Kerry or King's lives. I've had a sort of grudge against Kerry ever since I found out he's letting Izzy claim his buds and even do time for them. I just think it's too selfish on his part. Sure, Izzy offered, but he didn't have to let it go down like that. Izzy seemed distant tonight. Dean was there. He felt distant too. – So maybe it's me who's distant. Whatever.

Dec 31

Got walked in last night. (Thanx Rebel!)

I spent a few tunes 2nd set babysitting little Jillian. We had fun watching drumz together with some special guest (I didn't catch who).

No sign of Corvette. But I did see Jack. It was short and sweet. We hugged and squeezed each other a minute or two. He wanted to kidnap me. I said no and disappeared.

12-31-91

We've got the bong inside.

Bella Fleck and the Flecktones were wailing. The bass player was absolutely hot shit! Sitting with Corvette, Ross, Markness, Simone, Silas, Jeanie, Arthur, Jasmine, Schmalex, Skip and Anna, and Bob and Marie Snodgrass.

January 1 1992

During the break before midnight, they showed video clips of a bunch of Bill Graham New Years Eve trips. (Oh Bill, how we miss you.) They showed him putting on his Father time costume eyebrow by eyebrow. How bittersweet. Bill, on the spinning globe NYE 1983-1984 – my first. And the eagle costume that last Kaiser year. It was sad kinda, to see a lineup of spectacular Bill clips, then, really, nothing special at midnight. A few firework splashes, but no Bungee cords, no Golden Gate Bridge, no mushrooms, or huge cakes. No Bill.

Good setlists, but the songs seemed to get lost in the middle of themselves. I'd love to hear it again and see if that's accurate. Except the *Sugar Mag* – Bill's song – that was the most raging. The place was rockin so hard, we wouldn't have noticed an earthquake. Did ya like it Bill?

I spent most of the night inside watching the show. When I did go out in the hall I got a succession of gorgeous hugs – among them – Gene Gene the Dancing Machine, Matt Ackerman, and Cute Allen!

Today is Janey's b-day. There's a brunch somewhere or other that I'd like to find.

During the video clips, they showed the stuff from the year all kinds of Deadheads got videotaped saying Happy New Year, and there was Janey – so young! And Brent – alive!

It all seems so long ago.

Jan 7, 1992   Cloverdale

Janey's here. It's wonderful to have her visiting. Right now she's downstairs with John. I love her so much. She's been giving him shit the entire time.

As I say goodbye to this notebook, perhaps too I can say goodbye to my dealings and troubles with John. I hope to leave them behind and go on to do things that work towards my own goals, without worrying about what he took from me. May his energies and influences completely leave my realm of consciousness.

Jan 31, 1992   Sonoma

I started working at a small silk-screening shop. My first job was screening t-shirts – "Kiss French, Drink California." I like the woman who runs the place, but I'm feeling incredibly alone these days. Without my best friend, without my crowd of fatty friends. And though I think this situation with James and Megan is exactly what I needed, on so many levels, I feel like a casualty of the explosion of a family.

Maybe this spring I'll throw all my shit in storage and hit the road again – but where?

Dead tour doesn't hold much attraction for me.

What the hell do I want?

Feb 1

Went to LBC tonight, alone.

Ray Manzarek and Michael McClure (a beat poet), did some piano and poetry. Some of the images really struck me. "Here I lay listening to the shit drip from the fan."

After a short break came Robert Hunter solo. He did a 30-minute poem that I loved.

It was powerful. It was about what things are, because of how they're viewed, or whether something's worthy of being said, or how it was, compared to how it is – somewhat removed in time, and what it means to really hear something. It was epic, and it carried hints of all the things I feel these days.

Thank you Robert, I loved your poem.*

[*Parts of this poem are reprinted in the front matter of this book.]

47
Spring 1992
Kaiser, Oakland, Albany, New Jersey, Also – Beau's Bad Blood

Feb 7 1992
In Simone's car, headed for JGB. We're late and we're experiencing minor navigational difficulties, it's been a while since we've been to the Kaiser.

Inside

Run for the Roses, and Glenn knocked me for a loop with some P-bud! Feels like that old show feeling I miss, and don't even know how much I miss it, most days. It's a feeling of… a rush of… sweet, kind fog, high vibes, friends, Love.

"We can walk together little Children,
We don't ever have to worry
Through this world of trouble
We got to love one another
Take your fellow man by the hand
Try to help him to understand
We can all be together for ever and ever
When we make it to the promised land"

That's the rush of feeling. Jerry gave me the perfect tune at the perfect time.

Sometimes, when I'm here, I can almost still believe that we can make it to the Promised Land.

Saturday 8th
Parker and Angie's

Morning in my Van. Serene. I woke remembering once when Fritz said, "It's our job to dance." Oh how I danced last night.

Feb 22
Oakland Coliseum

Saw Tavi as soon as I got here. Huge smiles as he ran up to me, "Ya know. I really love you Hollie, it's good to see you." Yeah, Tavi's special. I love him too, and it's great to see him looking good and happy. Saw Jack for a few out on the sidewalk. A warm hug and move along. That was nice too.

It's a beautiful sunny day after weeks of rain. I'm working for Rebel. Got here when the lots opened (at 2 not 4). I haven't walked around yet. Just hanging, drinking and pretending to work.

Corvette's not coming down for the shows. She says she just doesn't care.

late night

Wailing show! – with a new Jerry tune – it'll take a while to know if it's a good one or a cheezy one. And a new Phil tune too.

Feb 23   Inside

Came in early with Rebel. There was a major OD happening in the lot – Rock Med folks kept running by. I hope the stupid fucker Lives. Of course heroin is involved.

Yesterday I saw Isaac! In December he fell off a cliff and was lucky only to break one leg, one arm and his jaw. Some guy named Toby swore he knew me. He dropped names and places but I still didn't remember. He invited me and Isaac onto their bus, and gave us a free balloon. When we got off there was a fightish-type thing going on. The cops appeared and I disappeared. Later I saw them searching the bus.

I can only shake my head at the whole scene.

It's all so out of hand.

Hell in a Bucket and both Bob and Jerry have music stands in front of them. Probably Bob will introduce his new something.

Tour starts in a week!

I almost want to go.

Peggy-O.

~~Minglewood~~ Nope, *Walkin Blooze.*

That's the signal to cruise.

Ramble on Rose.

Here's a new one – Vinnie's singing. It's got a good groove. – It's good to see the Dead once again with New Life Blood.

"It's a Long long way from home." It sounds ok. Great ending!!!

Black Throated Wind.

Another new one. Started with everyone, now it seems to be a Bobby song. Not bad.

I think all the new songs have potential.

Set 2

China Cat.

Stoned. I saw King and was thinking yet again about this family thing we all used to have. Now that it's officially bunk, and we know we're broken, I see everyone in small groups. No longer all of us in the whole of the hall. We're fragmented. I see reflections of what we were, everywhere, like looking at a shattered mirror.

Rider.

No matter how I personally feel about it, at least the Dead is still amazing. Still Rockin' 'em to the rafters and beyond.

"I know you rider gonna miss me when I'm gone!"

`*Playin.*

Terrapin. – with so many intricate subtle things going on. I flutter through them all.

The light shows seem to be testing out some pretty wild new spinning designs, color combos, and crowd lighting. At the same time that I'm thinking about how good tour might be, I'm thinking too of blowing off the whole Dead world.

Drumz – with Olatunji!

Space, *Miracle, Stella.*

Jerry missed a couple of verses this set.

Generally I think 1st sets have been better both nights.

Throwing Stones.

Perhaps I'll dance.

24th In the lot

About to go in. Worked the morning for Rebel, and the gate opening for Jory. Which meant I had an extra ticket for James right after Megan scored one. I'm headed in. Not bringing the book.

2-27

I have a feeling this'll be a great tour. It starts Sunday in Atlanta. Rebel says there'll be no BGP vending pressure, or cop problems. Only Brokham – so if it's not copyrighted, anything can sell. And Skinny Jim has a friend selling a one-way plane ticket.

3-1

Tour calls to me like a siren's song. Even though I know I don't really want to be there, if that plane ticket had come through, I'd be on the east coast right now.

3-3-92

Tonight is the last Atlanta show. I miss Fritz. I miss his "Livin large" sort of jerking acrobatics, his big grin, and even bigger hair. I've been thinking about him a lot. He's been gone a year. A whole year. Fritz – I hope you are well. I'm sending love and strength always.

I miss everything about tour as I loved it. I'm thinking of Suzy's willowy existence beneath her scarves in the hallways of times past, the guttural resonance to Carp's presence, as well as his voice, the supreme innocence in Tricky's smile.

3-20

I dreamed of Fritz last night. We were sleeping near each other and talking. The dream was filled with Love yet there was all the animosity between us that there ever was. I was afraid he would laugh at me if he knew I loved him, even though he loved me too. It was weird.

I've always loved Fritz in that inexplicable way it just is with some people, even though he's not very likeable. How odd that I should dream of him, – the love <u>and</u> the not likeable part. I never dream about others in jail, why Fritz? I haven't written to him in months, nor has he written me.

3-24-92   SF

Rebel says Beau might lose his leg! Oh no. Please no. Oh Beau! I want some miracle to occur to keep your leg healthy. May the infection go away! Oh, it makes me want to cry.

I called Corvette right away. She's coming down first thing tomorrow.

I'm upset by this news. I'm sending tidal waves of healing energy his way. Beau is the sweetest, most lovable, teddy bear of a man. I want the infection to leave his body. I can't see him losing his leg. Instead I see it healing, somehow. It must. It just must. So mote it be. (Please.)

later

I can't stop thinking about Beau.

The city seems especially cold tonight.

Or is it me?

Do I just feel cold at the thought of what life can do to someone like Beau?

March 25

When Corvette got here we walked the Haight. I bought a blank book for Kennedy. I offered, and he said he'd love one. I'm not allowed to mail him such a thing directly so the bookstore will mail it.

Beau goes to the doctor tomorrow to learn either that his leg is healing properly again, and so is the infection, or he checks into the hospital for more drastic measures in trying to stop the infection crawling through his body.

3-27

Beau needs another operation to fix the part of his leg that's not healing correctly, but the danger of him losing his leg has passed, Thank Jah.

April 4th 1992

I feel good today. There's a party in Honeydew for Jeremy and Trinity's b-days, – The prospect of being sociable with my old crew appeals to me.

4-8-92

We got to the party as the sun went down. A brand new crescent moon drifted along the tree line awhile before disappearing with Orion chasing it.

Saw Izzy! Hadn't seen her since she went to jail. She was with Kerry, still and as usual. Me and Corvette each brought a small present for Trinity. I gave her a necklace, and Corvette a coloring book. There was a trampoline and Trinity bounced on it in the dark – refusing to be tired, announcing in a breathless voice, "I'm 4, and I'm an Aries." I love Trinity. She's such a special, magical, little girl.

And the biggest news of all – I saw Rum Tom! It's been years and years. He's been in Canada. It was great to see him alive, when so many rumours through the years have suggested differently.

5-21-92

It's showtime. Third night Cal Expo, and I am nowhere near Sacramento.

1st night, everyone said the show was nothing special. "But those encores." – *Baba O'Riley* by the Who, into the Beatles, *Tomorrow Never Knows*! It's always so exhilarating when they do something off the wall like that. I can't believe I missed it.

They didn't do anything wildly spectacular last night. I went there with Ryan. We didn't get in. We tried, but obviously not hard enough. When the wind blew the sweet riffs of *Saint of Circumstance* towards us I wanted to dance. But I didn't. I'm not sure why. Maybe it's just not my job anymore.

Before the show Ryan and KJ were screaming face to face. I had to walk up and demand, "Shut up."

And KJ said, "But..."

"Shut up NOW!"

Thankfully he did. The cops walking by did not need to hear the details of that argument. They saw each other again after the show, talked, and shook hands. I was glad to see that. There's enough enemies.

Everywhere I went I experienced contradiction. Both in myself and in the larger scene. I saw most every side of Deadland and I found myself spending the day going, "I like seeing that." "I hate seeing that." The former, say, when a truck went down our aisle with a hippie boy bouncing on the back bumper, his long hair waving in the wind. And the latter when I saw two people screaming angrily, as Ryan and KJ would do an hour later.

Skye's not going into the shows in lieu of staying outside selling her Indian clothes. Didn't we all used to hate it when people came to the shows only to make money and didn't go in? She has long hair and is quite pregnant. The added weight to her face made her look so different.

I saw Dean. Got a nice hug and we talked a few minutes.

No Rebel. No Beau. And a Jake who was too busy to talk.

I saw Jumpin' Jack as the show let out. He was with Johnja and Wolfboy Taylor. It was great to see Taylor. They bought me a Red Tail. Jack gave me a two minute massage and asked me to come to his hotel for a hippie shower. As he massaged my shoulder, he kissed my neck, "How ya been doll, are you getting any lovin'?" I was almost tempted to go hang with him.

I didn't really want to go with Jumpin' Jack, but I was overcome with a feeling of wanting to stay hanging out in the lot. Thing is, where I wanted to stay doesn't exist anymore. I wanted a parking lot that lasted all night, where I could wander aimlessly and soak up some good energy. But even without the cops, it cleared out fast, because lots aren't like that anymore.

I came home with James and Megan. I slept till 3:30. They were leaving for the show as I got up. Am I sure I don't want to go?

I'm sure.

What will they do tonight while I'm not there? And does it matter anyway?

5-25-92
(26th really – it's 2:40AM.)

I blew off Shoreline but I had the feeling tonight was probably a good one. I was right. I was just crashing when James and Megan got home.

They did *Attics of My Life* – which I have never seen. They also did the *Baba O'Riley – Tomorrow Never Knows* encore again. James says it's incredibly psychedelic.

I'm sure there will come a time when I no longer care whether or not I see what they play. But, well – it's a bummer, deep inside me, to think I've missed two such amazing highs.

There's a height that Dead music attains which needs no drugs. Joseph Campbell said it was the closest thing he's seen to what it means to be truly alive. It is a place where my spirit can soar when they're playing something powerful. Ah, and so I missed it.

The pain is dull, background, almost nonexistent.

I question, these days, the reason I've done all I have. What has it gotten me? Have I made good choices as I went along, or bad ones? Where are all my wonderful friends – the family I used to share everything with? Few survive in my present day-to-day existence. Others are so far away – in jail, physically, or just far away from what I thought it all was.

5-28 – 10:30PM   SFO

Pretty cheap to fly east right now, so I'm doing it.

Janey-Baby visited me before I left. She had the tape of the incredible encores in Sacramento. Oh man. So nice. So sweeeeeeet.

Vinnie is no longer a mouse. He sings both the new tunes and he sounds great.

June 14, 1992   New Jersey

Me and Spencer went to Albany Friday night. We didn't get in. Hung out for a few hours, and as we walked to the car to leave, we got shot at, and hit, with paint guns.

For a split second I thought it was real.

We were standing at a crosswalk waiting for the light.

It happened so fast, if it was real, we'd have been two hurting units.

A car who saw it all, pulled over quick, "I'm a cop, are you okay?" Then sped off after the car that shot us. They aimed for my boobs (but hit my fanny pack), and Spencer's crotch – they got him in the thigh. That was extremely fucked up – I didn't see anything, but to hear the noise, and feel it, to look down and see a watery yellow splatter and think – what?

What IF it had been real?

A drive by shooting?

At a Dead concert?

Hell, it's completely fucked up even just being paint guns.

I almost blew off this Jersey trip. Right up until the last second, I hadn't made up my mind. But here I am, with the homescum, in the back of Spencer's truck. He's driving with his Rose-colored-glasses. This crowd refers to them as George Bush glasses. People take turns putting them on and commenting on the outlook of the world, America, the environment, etc. "Hey Spencer, how's the economic situation in America?"

"Not too good... Wait, wait... Let me get my George Bush glasses, – Hey now! Everything's rosy and things are lookin' up."

Maybe I need to borrow them.

later

I didn't get in. I haven't seen the Dead since February.

Hung with Jay mostly. Poor Jay. In Albany he got busted vending. They found a long forgotten dose in his fanny pack and took $3200 in cash. They gave him no receipt.

Since we're parked over the other side of the cattle walk I came back here way before the show ended. I hate the mooing of the crowd while being herded from one lot to the other. And folks always moo through the cattle walk. I'd rather write than moo.

They played *Baba O'Riley* and that whole bit tonight. I could hear it from across the highway.

I saw Remy. We laughed about how, even though no one we know is out here on tour, there are look-a-likes galore. The same hat, or walk, or stance, same beard, hair, demeanor. I swore I saw KJ and Dean, but it was only their look I saw.

One look that turned real was Rockafucker and Thorin. Says he's had enough of Tennessee – he's going back to California.

even later

After enjoying a lunar eclipse and a chicken barbeque in the back lots of the Meadowlands, we're back at the hotel. The eclipse wasn't total. The bottom smile stayed.

There is so much left unsaid. In my life, and in this book too.

This whole tour thing goes unsaid – my life, magic, east coasts, west coasts.

I'm just plain tired. And since I can't say all the unsaid right now, I guess I'll put out the light.

The lot scene rages outside – but my people aren't out there anymore.

48
Summer 1992
You Shouldn't Say
'Fuck You' to Your Friends

August 13, 1992

The big Dead news is that the Oregon shows have been cancelled. Jerry is exhausted and not healthy. James says an article in today's paper insinuates he may be headed for heart failure. I hope he gets better. But it absolutely sucks that Oregon shows aren't happening. They were sure to be the event of the year. Everyone was coming in from everywhere.

I was actually excited for Oregon shows.

August 26th

Not only were the Oregon Dead shows cancelled, so was everything through to '93. Jerry isn't doing well. He has an enlarged heart. They say he should be back by the beginning of next year. I wish him all the best vibes. Jerry's the brightest light I've ever seen.

And me? What kind of light am I?

August 27th

Listening again to a Jerry tape I listened to as I fell asleep last night. I remember feeling myself floating, spinning, and dancing as I drifted off to sleep.

Dancing communally, to feel and create the awesome power that is life... – I miss that.

August 30th, 1992

Fritz will be free soon because he talked about Memphis Mike. He talked!

I can't believe it. Mike is his friend! But this isn't just a rumour. All those things we heard about the Feds telling the other inmates that Fritz was a narc were true.

And there's going to be more than just Mike.

Yes, he's always had it in him to be an immature little fuckhead, but... this... I never expected he'd do this.

I'm heartbroken. And angry.

Fritz is really truly narcing.

How could he?

I always thought he was one of us. And dammit, I love him!

Fuck you Fritz.

I know you always hated when people said Fuck you to friends... ... – but really... –

Fuck you.

Afterword

***Some things get burned to ashes by fire,
and some things get forged.***
— The Grimm Generation

When I first took on the task of transcribing my chicken-scratch journals, I didn't know what would emerge. Those original books, written in dusty parking lots, overcrowded hotel rooms, busy stadium hallways, in dark seats of coliseums with questionable mindset and when I couldn't even see the page, came out at 850,000 words comprising my journey with the Grateful Dead. 850,000 words is far far far too many words for a book, and since I had no idea what story I had to tell, I began by editing out what was absolutely NOT the story.

How do you carve an elephant out of a block of marble? That's easy. You just take away everything that isn't the elephant, right? So that's how I approached these journals. I just kept reading them over and over and over, taking out everything that wasn't the elephant.

I shouldn't have been surprised to learn that Fritz was the elephant.

But I was. And every time I get to the end of this story, I get tears in my eyes.

Fritz broke the Deadhead outlaw code of silence and integrity. No matter how bad it ever got, there were certain things I believed about who we were and what we were, and he broke ALL of that.

You don't do the crime if you can't do the time. We all knew that. And while we'd mourn, and rail against the injustice of it all when our friends were taken away, never ever was singing or naming names an option.

It just wasn't done.
Until Fritz did it.
Until he sold his soul to save his body.

I've kept journals my entire life. I can't not write.

In my mind, my journal entries were just bare bones notes to myself that I'd use someday to craft a book. But the compulsion to write my life on paper has also led me to spend much time and attention reading and studying the writing of diarists and journal keepers, people who have been doing the same thing as me since the earliest days of written records. My fascination with this type of writing sits at the very core of my being. So, in heartfelt and grateful tribute to generations of life writers, rather than concoct a memoir using the journals as reference material, I knew I needed to find the story of my tribe in the journals themselves.

Now that I'm done, I know this: as a memoirist, I'd have cast all of us in a better light. I especially would have cast myself in a better light. We've all done stuff we're not proud of. We are all full of weakness and errors (Voltaire said that). Every single one of us, without exception, has demons and shadowy parts. Everyone everywhere every day is walking the line between the light and the dark. That's the human path. We are here to explore our dichotomies, the Yin-Yang of it all. There wouldn't be a shadow if there were no sunshine.

There are cringe-worthy human beings in this book who do wonderful and kind things. There are thoughtful and caring people in this book who do terrible, hurtful things. And there are honest, disingenuous beings who do a little of both.

And ain't that just like life?

This book was probably not a lot of the things you wanted it to be. Hell, it's not a lot of the things I wanted it to be.

When Corvette read my first draft, she sighed. "Kinda sucks that this is the story."

Certainly, I'd have been happier to find my journals filled with otherworldly descriptions of my beautiful friends, thoughtful musings on the transcendence of Morning Dew, sensuous descriptions of the bazaar that was the lot, and rich, layered essays contemplating the spectacle of the hallway, but I wasn't the sort of journal keeper who planned what to write. I rarely pulled out my pen knowing what I was about to say. Nor did I think overly much about what I *was* saying. My writing doesn't address as well as I wish, the shimmering gladness we embodied every day, because to my mind, it was a given that we lived in a joyous land of reverence and beauty. That's why we were there!

As one friend said to me when I expressed my displeasure with "not writing the bright shiny stuff"; "Hollie, why would a fish write about water?"

No. I didn't write about life-giving water.

I wrote the anomalies. I wrote about the things that weren't right. I was there, with my inner circle gold card, to see the shit hit the fan in the world of Tourheads.

I agree with Corvette, it kinda sucks that this is the story that's mine to tell. But I've come to believe that I was there, writing these events as they happened, because somebody had to document this shadow side of the scene. Somebody had to tell the story of the Grateful Dead Tourheads during the War on Drugs, and no one else was going to do it.

If there are people out there who think this story is better off not told, better off hidden in the back closet of our collective history, – well… to them I nod recognition. They might be right. But some of us find value and healing in exploring the shadows. To become conscious of the darker aspects is essential for true self-knowledge (said C.G. Jung). Those parts of ourselves which we hide from ourselves are where the demons and monsters that can undermine our growth reside. Any therapist will tell you that the things we repress are the very things that sow the seeds of our downfall.

This kind of existence, teetering between the seen and the unseen, between the surface and the depths, is eternal. It has always been here. Since the beginning of time humans have been exploring, adventuring, hallucinating, dreaming and dancing.

The Grateful Dead tapped into this wellspring of hope and joy and pain and found a way to make it relevant in the 20th Century. I think this scene, this movement, is here to stay. And that's probably an understatement.

I wish I could remember what author I read recently who mused that Grateful Dead music was so weirdly enduring that it was likely to turn into its own genre, like Jazz, or Blues. If that's true, I'd hate to have this unexplored darkness marring the bright future of Deadheads the world over. This stance in the world, that of being a Deadhead, seems pretty durable and solid as we work our way through the 21st Century.

That said, it's also true that there will always be complicated stories springing from this kind of scene that polite society might rather ignore. But you know what? Fuck polite society. I share this story because this is how it went down, and there's no reason to color it otherwise. It's the truth, even if it never happened (Ken Kesey, we love you).

This story is our history and we are stronger for it.

Soon after the closing pages of this story, I shut the door on this part of my life. I could not play the game any longer. What Fritz did shook me to my core. It sent me hurtling back to Connecticut where I got a job managing the office at a machine shop. It was disgusting. I made great money. Everything smelled like burning oil. And I plodded through the days.

Corvette retreated too. She moved to the coast of Oregon and did some indoor gardening at one of Hawkeye's houses while he went to prison (Cough-cough, Fuck you Fritz). I went to visit her out there and found something I'd been missing dearly in Connecticut. Here was the kind of indulgence in quality consumables that I'd gotten used to on Tour, – in the form of coffee! I couldn't be the only one in Connecticut who'd appreciate a cup of truly good coffee.

Let it be known that Grateful Dead Tour gave a lot of us superb entrepreneurial skills.

In 1994 I opened Klekolo World Coffee in Middletown, near Wesleyan University. Corvette came back to Connecticut to help me run it. "Klekolo" (pronounced Clay-ko-lo), is a word from Mali that means, "a system of rules to live by for peace and harmony in the world." Klekolo got popular, we had fun, we created community, and life was pretty good again.

Whenever I did an interview with the media, they'd ask me, "What did you do before this?"

I would respond that I had traveled and lived in my van; that one of my favorite claims to fame is that I've driven every interstate in this country. I would tell them about national parks and museums, or maybe about the whiteness of an early morning Flagstaff snowstorm. I would tell them about bayou boat rides and desert cliff houses, about getting a flat tire in the Everglades, about redwoods and Colorado wildflowers. Mostly, I let myself be a bit of a mystery woman. It suited me. And I really didn't want to talk about the Grateful Dead anyway.

As the years rolled on we got some visitors. Rebel stopped by every time a tour brought him close. Beau visited a bunch. Abe and Jackie showed up, as did James and Megan, and Justine and Don, and Janey, and Danni, and Ozzy, and Markness. Poet did a music gig at the coffeehouse. Kevin made a trip to come see us when he was in NYC. And one strange day, while racing around doing errands for Klekolo, I was literally running in the door to get the storage key when I stopped dead in my tracks.

Something.

Energy.

I cocked my head and looked to the first table there in the window. Hackmen! Nearly 10 years without missing a beat; just sitting there all nonchalant, smiling. He was always so good with surprise appearances.

Benny and Meredith had gotten married, and long about the turn of the century, Meredith OD'd and died. A chain of events that stopped Benny's downward trajectory, and kept him from ever doing heroin again, also, surprisingly, landed him in Middletown.

Now we had even more visits from tour folks. King Henry. Merlin. Elvis. Pele.

Santa came to us when he first got out of prison. Kennedy visited a couple times after he was released. And Hawkeye spent a lot of time around Middletown once he was freed. He got a job in the hospitality industry selling linens. It was kind of fun when someone asked what he was doing for a living. He'd grin big and say, "I sell sheets".

But I digress...

One day, well into the first decade of the new millennium, I was sitting around with Benny and a bunch of coffeehouse people. One of them asked me what I'd done before opening Klekolo. I gave my usual spiel; traveled in my van, blah blah blah, drove all the interstates, blah blah blah, state parks, museums, blah blah blah.

When I finished, Benny looked aghast. "Did you REALLY just leave the Grateful Dead out of your story?"

I'd been doing it so long, I hadn't even noticed. "Um. Yes. I guess I did."

"Why would you do that? They were a huge part of your life. They were everything! And you don't even mention them?!? I know how important they were to you! YOU know how important they were! They made you! They made this." As his hands gestured at all that was the coffeehouse.

"I... Well... they.... Um... it's just... it doesn't... I didn't...."

"That's crazy! I know who you were! Have YOU forgotten?!?!"

He wasn't wrong. I had forgotten.

On purpose.

And then came Facebook: a virtual hallway filled with my people, my history, my heart!

All the excitement! All the feels! All the love!

It was remarkable how quickly the web of interconnections reestablished itself. I spent hours with a cheek-aching grin and tears of happiness on my face, reminiscing with people I missed and loved wholeheartedly, people whose energy is woven into my DNA. Why had I ever let myself lose track of them?

I will never say that I hate Facebook. I don't care if the future plays out in such a way that by the time you read this Facebook is like some evil entity, horrible death star, ruling the universe (apparently I grant that's possible), I will always be grateful for the way it brought my people back to me.

Turns out I wasn't the only one who fled Tour Life when Fritz did what he did. A lot of us made ourselves scarce, be it out of fear, disappointment or just plain horror. (Plain horror – ha!) We scattered, shell-shocked, emotionally and psychically injured, dare I say traumatized?

Seriously! I didn't talk about the Dead for well over a decade. Other friends have told me they didn't listen to the music, or think about any of it for just as long. Some of the people in this book didn't see any incarnation of the Dead until well into the 2010s.

Through those many years, while I hadn't been paying attention, as each of us Tourheads went and lived our after-tour lives, what had been buried and left untended grew to be a garden much more lush and verdant than we could have dared hope for. Thirty-plus years later, we are elated to learn that those bonds we forged back then aren't fragile – they never were, and they'd been strengthening all this time while we paid them no mind. We built a sincere and sturdy mythology back then with the help of Jerry and the boys. Now, no matter how much distance and circumstance separates us, our shared love has proved to be something we can stand on solidly as we age.

When we lived on Dead Tour, bliss and delight were daily companions. Serendipity delivered constant bounty and we opened our arms and minds and hearts in jubilant Welcome! We were transported to realms some people still believe are unattainable. We knew no limits and accepted very few boundaries. Freedom bloomed in our minds and displayed itself with our bodies. We chased life. Laughing, giggling, stumbling over ourselves and each other; falling up, getting down and plunging onward. Ever onward.

Fogward through the On!

Our smiles were always enormous.

We knew that Family is whomever you say it is. And if you want to love life every damn day – then make as many of those days as possible into celebration. Woohoo! It's Tuesday! Yay! The sun came out! Fuck yeah! I got a hug from a cute hippie boy!

I have spent a lifetime so far trying to figure out how to live. Reading Joseph Campbell when my mother was dying, taught me to participate joyfully in the sorrows of the world. I really latched on to that. Life sucks much of the time and I'm pretty sure our job here on earth is to love it all anyway. Just like when we lived on Tour: a lot of shit sucked, but we loved every minute of it anyway.

We always joked that there were a lot more hippies in the 80s than there were in the 60s, we just weren't getting as much press. And now? There's exponentially more!

Much like myself in the 1980s when I first went on tour, there is a significant segment of the population displeased with the American social landscape. They are hungry for the experience of deeper realms that Grateful Dead music can provide, and for the camaraderie such a like-minded crowd offers. I am thrilled that it's still here for them.

This tribe is massive and still growing! I am wonderstruck to see how everything the Dead manifested into this world is vastly more popular now than it was on August 9th, 1995.

The cosmic sorcery the Grateful Dead set in motion is so much bigger than just the Dead themselves; so much bigger than my crowd, or your crowd, or those who are out there now being Heads. This whole dream experiment – the Dead, the Deadheads, the music, the touring lifestyle – it's beyond extraordinary. There's no question it has changed the landscape of America as well as the landscape of human cosmic consciousness. It's a juggernaut, and the importance of it all to humanity, I think, has yet to really play out.

There was magic there on tour. Real magic.

We grabbed hold of the chaos energy of really living in the moment, and we let all the other shit slide by with a nod or a tear or a big ole *Fuck You*. We accepted everything for exactly what it was, we didn't waste time trying to wish things were different. Maybe we tried to make them different, and maybe it worked or maybe it didn't, but none of it ever stopped us from loving life.

That's the miracle; participate joyfully in the sorrows of the world.

Our lives were charmed, simply because we said they were.

That magic is still here for us today. Whether we lived it at Dead shows or never even saw the Dead before, we always have the power to embrace that magic.

Life is always about choices. You can find a million reasons to hate everything and be angry at the world, but if you can reach back into the cobwebs of your mind and remember those days when your life was enchanted, there really isn't anything in life that can get you down – not for the long haul anyway.

We Deadheads have been so lucky. To come together as one all those many years ago gave us a life the majority of living beings on this planet have not had the luxury to experience. And to top off that luck – all these years later, along came a technology that gives us the virtual space to be in circles with each other again.

Wow!

Not only did we have it then – we've got it again!!!

If we want it.

All we have to do is notice it, embrace it, and believe it. (And P.S. You don't even have to be a Deadhead, or even to have ever seen a show to live this story.)

When you need it, I hope you'll remember: we are bits of a shattered fractal of all that ever was the Universe. We are made of clay and stardust. That's not woowoo hippie shit, that's science. Clay and stardust baby! – And look at us go!

I'm so impressed by all of us: the things we have overcome, the career paths we have traveled, the businesses we have started, the parts of the world we have healed, the way we have healed ourselves and others.

All that shit that seemed so awful at the time has proven itself to be transformative nonetheless. The people we loved and called family, have proven themselves mostly to still be family and loved. All the nastiness and sorrow and disappointment underscores the point; life is good not when it's perfect, but rather when you love every little bit of it. Life is good when you say it is. Life is good when you look at other humans and smile so heart-wrenchingly that normal people look at you like you're a little off.

If you want to make life enjoyable, simply enjoy it. Laughter and delight are some of the easiest and surest ways to access magic. We dealt with some real shit out there on tour; nonetheless, if you asked any of the characters in this book (and I have), they'd each tell you what a grand old time we had – because instinctively we knew then that that was the key to it all – Lovin' Life.

Life is short my friends, we might as well travel the elegant way…

Glossary

- **American Indicans** – a term Corvette and I invented to refer to our circle of Tourheads who were always deeply focused on smoking indica, not a universally known name in the scene
- **bake/baked** – stoned, high on cannabis; the act of getting high on cannabis, occasionally it might actually mean putting something in the oven
- **BFD** – Big Fucking Deal
- **BGP** – Bill Graham Presents
- **bitch handle** – gathering one's hair on top of the head, resulting in a pineapple top look
- **the boys** – a term of endearment for the collective band members of the Grateful Dead
- **Break** – the intermission between sets at a Grateful Dead Show or any other concert
- **buds** – cannabis for smoking, selling, trading, etc
- **bunk** – not legit, not real, bad quality, a bad deal, perceived as a bad deal, not acting in good faith, not treating someone well, a person who does these things
- **bunked** – getting screwed, ripped off, being treated poorly, not getting what you expected
- **busted** – arrested
- **cake** – often means money or cash, occasionally it means a baked treat – baked like in the oven, not baked like getting stoned
- **Clubs** – Club Cabaret ungummed rolling papers. The only rolling papers worth smoking. No taste. Leaves no ash when burned. Thin as a butterfly's wing
- **comp** – a concert ticket that has all zeros in the price area, a ticket not meant for resale
- **comped** – being given a ticket labeled "Complimentary"
- **coke** – most often in the text, cocaine
- **cop shop** – Police Station
- **counterfeit** – a fake ticket that looks real, a fake ticket that has been sold as real
- **cruised** – wandered a place in order to check out the scene
- **CSN** – Crosby, Stills, and Nash
- **DEA** – Drug Enforcement Administration

- **door pop/gate pop** – a guarded or unguarded door, or any other entrance, is opened from the inside of a concert venue, people outside, near the door, take this opportunity to gain entrance to the show (this is not the same as later years when gates were plowed down by concertgoers)
- **dose** – a hit of LSD, to ingest LSD, or the act of giving someone a hit of LSD
- **dosed** – high on psychedelics, took some LSD
- **face** – a ticket priced at face value, exactly what it says it costs on the ticket, a ticket sold with no markup in price
- **fattied** – smoked a fatty (see "fatty")
- **fatty** – an overlarge joint (marijuana cigarette). It is no exaggeration to say that fatties are at least the size of your thumb and often bigger than that. Really. I promise. That's not an exaggeration. The plural is often spelled fatties
- **Fatty Circle/Fatty Zone** – Any gathering of American Indicans for the main purpose of getting stoned
- **fatty smoker** – like a cigarette holder, but made of blown glass and sized for a Fatty
- **feds** – Federal Drug Agents or agencies
- **the fish** – this is a uncontrollable body movement sometimes experienced by persons ingesting N2O. Basically, they fall and flop around like a fish out of water. Not pleasant.
- **gate pop** – (see "door pop")
- **GDP** – Grateful Dead Productions
- **gopher** – a backstage worker – "go for this" "go for that"
- **The Grapes** – a Grateful Dead cover band in Atlanta, GA
- **Graphics** – a particular brand of glass bong
- **the Greeks/the Greek** – The Greek Theater in Berkeley, CA
- **groundscore(d)** – an item, likely dropped accidently, found on the ground, the act of finding such an item
- **groundscoring** – going for a walk specifically to see what might be found
- **hallway** – This most often refers to the scene in the venue's halls during a Show – The Hallway is a living entity. The Hallway is home
- **Hog Farm/Farmer** – a venerated intentional community of like-minded hippie-types who took their name from an actual hog farm in southern California where they lived in the 1960s – still (in 2024) active in many hip cultural activities, especially in northern California where the Farm is

currently located – the Hog Farm is the sort of entity that speaks – i.e. "The Hog Farm says…"
- **homescum** – this refers to my hometown friends. They gave themselves this name "Hey don't worry about us, we're just the homescum." It stuck
- **hot** – in regards to a person it would mean that the police are paying attention to their actions, in regards to a scene it means the exact opposite of a cool scene, in regards to a show, a performer, or a song, it would mean it was a damn good one, finally it might just mean temperature
- **hubbas** – the drug called crack
- **in/inside was/wasn't** – inside the venue during the show, "he was in", "she wasn't in"
- **Indica** – a type of cannabis with higher THC levels as compared to the generally available marijuana of the previous decades, Indica is common now, in the 21st Century, but it was special, unique, and still sort of new in the time period covered in this book
- **Indican** – see American Indican
- **JGB** – The Jerry Garcia Band
- **Jokeland** – Oakland, CA
- **jones** – the addictive need for a substance or activity – (not necessarily white powder) i.e. – basketball or a Grateful Dead Show
- **Jonser** – someone who pines for white powder drugs
- **Jonesin'** – someone looking/wishing for any particular thing, or the state of over-indulging in white powder drugs
- **Josephine** – the name of a house in Atlanta, GA
- **Junkie** – someone addicted to heroin
- **Keef** – as we used the term, is a high THC substance made up of the crystals that have been collected off kind buds, usually by shaking buds on a screen and collecting the dust that falls through
- **kidnapping** – kidnapping was always done with the full cooperation and interest of the kidnapee, "I'll kidnap you" meant "I will take you with me." "Kidnap me" meant "Take me with you"
- **kick/kick down** – "give it up", "give over the good stuff", "hand it over", "give it to me", "share it with all of us" – sometimes freely given, but often a demand
- **kicked** – gave

- **killah** – really really good
- **kind** – if used as a descriptor for anything – songs, clothes, food – it denotes the best of the best, otherwise: kind buds
- **kind bud(s)** – especially sticky, stinky, green marijuana
- **Ladies** – in this text, ladies are usually marijuana plants
- **laminate** – a more permanent type of backstage pass usually worn around the neck on a lanyard, reserved for workers and upper level guests
- **LBC** – Luther Burbank Center in Santa Rosa, CA
- **"losin it"/"lost it"** – freaking out via temper tantrum or via psychedelic and/or psychic meltdown, also the wavering of one's moral compass
- **"the lot"** – a parking lot, grassy field, or any area where cars park, or people congregate to create a happening scene before, during, and after Grateful Dead concerts – In the 21st Century this place is called "Shakedown" or "Shakedown Street"
- **LSD** – lysergic acid diethylamide, a hallucinogen
- **"the Mall Crawl"** – walking the downtown Mall in Santa Cruz, CA. The Mall was severely damaged in the 1989 Loma Prieta Earthquake
- **MSG** – Madison Square Garden in NYC
- **N_2O** – Nitrous oxide. Laughing gas. Nitrous is a dissociative anesthetic used by dentists for sedation and pain relief. Also used as a propellant for whipped cream and/or a cheap high for hippies
- **Narc/Narcing** – a person who rats out another person, anyone working in the capacity of a narcotics officer, or other officer of the law, an action of cooperating with law enforcement, or pointing fingers at someone for illegal activity which causes that someone to get in trouble with the law, often done by a person who hopes it will save their own ass from the law
- **NFA** – Song – Not Fade Away
- **onion** – Western Union money transfer services, or money transferred via said service, i.e. "Gotta get an onion"
- **OR** – (Capitalized) someone might be released after arrest on their Own Recognizance, no bail or bond is needed and they merely promise to appear in court
- **outta hand/outta control** – outrageous (see "raging")

- **Pack-Check** – a box truck provided by BGP for folks to stash their backpacks during the show
- **P-bud** – a particular strain of marijuana from Colorado at a time when buds with names were a rarity
- **pages** – LSD infused squares of paper perforated with smaller squares – in this text, interchangeable with "sheets"
- **"got picked up"** – got arrested/caught/busted by law enforcement
- **"got popped"** – got arrested/caught/busted/picked up by law enforcement
- **psyched** – pleased! thrilled! excited! looking forward to it!
- **puppy** – usually an actual baby canine, but sometimes a young male Deadhead
- **QP** – a quarter pound of kind buds
- **The Rads** – band, The Radiators
- **rage/raged/raging** – going overboard/crazy. It can be good or bad, and is indicative of wildness in dance, work, play, or a place – like the lot or a party. It could also mean – the hippest new thing, or doing/needing to do lots of fast business. Sometimes it means running a snarky monologue about a pet peeve, or screaming and having a tantrum
- **raking/raked** – making money, lots of it, or maybe cleaning up leaves
- **rippin' it up** – generally refers to smoking a fatty, also can be applied to Jerry's guitar playing
- **rolled over** – (see "narcing")
- **scam** – pull a fast one on anyone, in any place, in order to get what you desire – getting in to the lot, getting in to the show, getting onto the floor. We consider our scams to be mostly harmless
- **scammed in** – getting in to a concert, without a ticket, by any means that isn't quite legit
- **scamped** – camped where we weren't allowed to, or didn't pay to camp in a campground
- **score/scored** – acquired, found, managed to find what you seek for a very reasonable price, or against the odds. If used as an exclamation it conveys excited surprise and pleasure in finding what you seek
- **SEP/SEP field** – from the Hitchhikers Guide to the Galaxy by Douglas Adams, it means 'Somebody Else's Problem'. As in, when a cop sees the Van he thinks "that's somebody else's problem". Belief is 90% of making this tactic work

- **sheets** – LSD infused squares of paper perforated with smaller squares – in this text, interchangeable with "pages"
- **Shows** – the preferred term for Grateful Dead concerts
- **"the Shuffle"** – walking Haight Street in San Francisco to see what's going on
- **shwag** – low quality marijuana
- **singles** – individual tabs/hits/doses of LSD
- **sketchy/sketched/skitched/skitzed** – feeling jittery, freaked out, paranoid, or a scene or person that conveys such energy
- **skinny** – a small, or normal sized joint (marijuana cigarette)
- **slEasy8** – a play on the name of a hotel chain
- **snagged** – grabbed, took, got
- **space** – a portion of a Dead show filled with otherworldly sounds, sometimes means wandering – "I'm gonna space"
- **spaceshot** – a stoned, forgetful, person, not doing so well keeping a handle on details
- **Spinner/Spinners** – a group of religious-minded Deadheads who worship in the hallways of shows by spinning like Whirling Dervishes, often possessed of magic Show tickets when such things are hard to come by, seen by some as high holy hippies. I consider them American Indicans
- **Spinoffs** – Deadheads who hung pretty tightly with the Spinners but never quite converted to their lifestyle completely
- **stash** – a private stock of drugs or anything considered precious, a place to hide such things, or the act of hiding something away
- **state's/state's evidence** – most often "turn(ed) state's" – means a person is cooperating with authorities and will, or has, provided testimony against others. The benefit of turning state's might be reduced charges or less time in prison, a lesser charge for a crime, or even immunity from prosecution
- **stubbed down** – getting someone into a better/closer concert area/seat by using someone else's ticket stub, possibly multiple times
- **stylin** – living the good life! elevated in design or experience, doing things or enjoying things in/with style

- **swinging** – selling drugs
- **SSDD** – Song – Sunshine Daydream
- **Telegraph** – Telegraph Avenue in Berkeley, CA
- **tix** – tickets
- **tweak** – to have or feel a bad scene, bad energy, to have a meltdown induced by drugs, or to have a tantrum of sorts
- **undercovers** – law enforcement officers masquerading as Deadheads for entrapment purposes, often these people were very obvious to us
- **a vial** – sometimes a small, glass container filled with liquid LSD, sometimes a plastic film canister with beads, jewelry, or kind buds inside
- **walked in** – when an employee or friend of the venue, or of the band, takes people (singular or plural) through the front gates or back doors, telling door guards, "They're with me". No ticket required
- **went down** – got caught/arrested/taken into custody by law enforcement, might mean "something weird happened"
- **White Bird** – Volunteer medics staffing an area at Grateful Dead shows. Associated with White Bird Clinic operating out of Eugene Oregon since the 1960s.
- **wingnut** – crazy person, whack job, babbling fool, off-their-rocker-talking-to-themselves type, sometimes applied to those persons who might be "just a little off maybe", sometimes the term is used affectionately
- **wire/cake on the wire** – money coming via Western Union money transfer services (see "onion") (see "cake")
- **X/X-ing** – Ecstasy – the drug MDMA, now known as Molly, indulging in said drug
- **yellowjackets** – security at a venue. At no point in the text does this refer to insects, but, like the insects that share the name, yellowjackets have a reputation for being aggressive

Acknowledgements

I am Grateful to have been born in a place and time that allowed me to live this sort of life.
I am Grateful for all the people in this book. I love you all.
I am Grateful beyond words for the Grateful Dead themselves (and their entire extended family).
I am Grateful for Bill Graham.
I am especially Grateful for the people who keep show and song databases and provide all that info free on the internet.
I am Grateful for Jason Krug, who set this project in motion one springtime afternoon when he walked into my home and found me listening intently (and loudly) to Brent on YouTube.
I am Grateful for Scott, who dragged me to my first show and 31 years later provided me a loving home in which to start the work that made these sloppy journals into a book.
I'm forever Grateful for Yvette Elliott – that woman is a rock in my world.
I'm Grateful for my mother – Cecilia LaPlace Rose Fickett, and for the fact that of all the people in the world who might have adopted me, it was her specifically, who did. I simply cannot fathom what my life would have been without her.
Massive thanks go out to early readers, sort-of editors, and valued-opinion-givers; Barbara Saunders, Olivia Dresher, Gabe Barkin, Janna Barkin, Sarah Brooks, Andrea Adams, Lindsay Brink, Rick Roaman, Talia Rose, Hank Carver, Fred Ellis, Jim Lang, Cynthia Maddix, Robin Goldman,
Thank you to everyone who allowed me to use their photos.
And especially, I'm Grateful for you, the reader.
Thank you all. You make my world a better place.

Permissions

The Publishers wish to thank the following for permissions to quote lyrics.

MIGHT AS WELL
Words by ROBERT HUNTER
Music by JERRY GARCIA
© 1976 (Renewed) ICE NINE PUBLISHING CO., INC.
All Rights Reserved
Used by Permission of ALFRED MUSIC

ESTIMATED PROPHET
Words by JOHN BARLOW and BOB WEIR
Music by BOB WEIR
© 1977 (Renewed) ICE NINE PUBLISHING CO., INC.
All Rights Reserved
Used by Permission of ALFRED MUSIC

SHIP OF FOOLS
Words by ROBERT HUNTER
Music by JERRY GARCIA
© 1974 (Renewed) ICE NINE PUBLISHING CO., INC.
All Rights Reserved
Used by Permission of ALFRED MUSIC

DON'T EAST ME IN
Words and Music by BRENT MYDLAND, JERRY GARCIA, MICHAEL HART, PHIL LESH, BOB WEIR and WILLIAM KREUTZMANN
© 1980 (Renewed) ICE NINE PUBLISHING CO., INC.
All Rights Reserved
Used by Permission of ALFRED MUSIC

THE WHEEL
Words by ROBERT HUNTER
Music by JERRY GARCIA and WILLIAM KREUTZMANN
© 1971 (Renewed) ICE NINE PUBLISHING CO., INC.
All Rights Reserved
Used by Permission of ALFRED MUSIC

STANDING ON THE MOON
Words by ROBERT HUNTER
Music by JERRY GARCIA
© 1988 (Renewed) ICE NINE PUBLISHING CO., INC.
All Rights Reserved
Used by Permission of ALFRED MUSIC

LET IT GROW
Words by JOHN BARLOW and BOB WEIR
Music by BOB WEIR
© 1990 (Renewed) ICE NINE PUBLISHING CO., INC.
All Rights Reserved
Used by Permission of ALFRED MUSIC

I KNOW YOU RIDER
Words by ROBERT HUNTER
Music by JERRY GARCIA
© 1971 (Renewed) ICE NINE PUBLISHING CO., INC.
All Rights Reserved
Used by Permission of ALFRED MUSIC

HIGH TIME
Words by ROBERT HUNTER
Music by JERRY GARCIA
© 1970 (Renewed) ICE NINE PUBLISHING CO., INC.
All Rights Reserved
Used by Permission of ALFRED MUSIC

FRANKLIN'S TOWER
Words by ROBERT HUNTER
Music by JERRY GARCIA and BILL KREUTZMANN
© 1975 (Renewed) ICE NINE PUBLISHING CO., INC.
All Rights Reserved
Used by Permission of ALFRED MUSIC

SAINT OF CIRCUMSTANCE
Words and Music by ROBERT WEIR and JOHN BARLOW
© 1972 (Renewed) ICE NINE PUBLISHING CO., INC.
All Rights Reserved
Used by Permission of ALFRED MUSIC

TERRAPIN STATION
Words by ROBERT HUNTER
Music by JERRY GARCIA
© 1977 (Renewed) ICE NINE PUBLISHING CO., INC.
All Rights Reserved
Used by Permission of ALFRED MUSIC

AN AMERICAN ADVENTURE: CHAPTER ONE: Novus Ordo Seclorum
Words by ROBERT HUNTER
Copyright © 1993 ROBERT HUNTER
All Rights Reserved Robert Hunter Personal Archives

THE LAST TIME
Words and Music by Mick Jagger and Keith Richards
Copyright © 1965 Promopub B.V.
Copyright Renewed
All Rights Administered by BMG Rights Management (US) LLC
All Rights Reserved Used by Permission
Reprinted by Permission of Hal Leonard LLC

SMOKE TWO JOINTS
Words and Music by Chris Kay and Michael Kay
Copyright © 1983 Wishes & Dreams Music
All Rights Administered by BMG Rights Management (US) LLC
All Rights Reserved Used by Permission
Reprinted by Permission of Hal Leonard LLC

MY SISTERS AND BROTHERS (In Christ)
Words and Music by Charles Johnson
Copyright © 1991 DUCHESS MUSIC CORP.
All Rights Controlled and Administered by SONGS OF UNIVERSAL, INC.
All Rights Reserved Used by Permission
Reprinted by Permission of Hal Leonard LLC

www.ingramcontent.com/pod-product-compliance
Lightning Source LLC
Chambersburg PA
CBHW060448030426
42337CB00015B/1523